The Children of
Henry VIII

D0064536

The Children of
Henry VIII

Formerly entitled *Children of England*

Alison Weir

BALLANTINE BOOKS • NEW YORK

All rights reserved under International and Pan-American
Copyright Conventions. Published in the United States by
Ballantine Books, a division of Random House, Inc.,
New York.

Published as *Children of England* in Great Britain in 1996
by Jonathan Cape,
Random House, UK Ltd., London.

http://www.randomhouse.com

Library of Congress Cataloging in Publication Data

Weir, Allison.
[Children of England]
The children of Henry VIII / Alison Weir.
p. cm.
Originally published as: Children of England. London :
Jonathan Cape. 1996.
Includes bibliographical references and index.
ISBN 0-345-39118-7
1. Henry VIII, King of England, 1491-1547—Family.
2. Great Britain—History—Tudors, 1485-1603.   3. Edward
VI. King of England. 1537-1553.   4. Grey, Jane, Lady,
1537-1554.   5. Mary I, Queen of England. 1516-1558.
6. Elizabeth I, Queen of England. 1533-1603. 7. Great
Britain—Kings and rulers—Biography.   8. Queens—Great
Britain—Biography.   I. Title.
DA317.1.W45 1996
941.084'092'2—dc20
[B]   96-14849
CIP

Manufactured in the United States of America

First American Edition: July 1996

10 9 8 7 6 5 4 3 2 1

THE CHILDREN OF HENRY VIII

is dedicated to
all the children in my family:

At Carshalton,
John and Katherine Weir;

at Chesterfield,
David and Andrew Weir;

at Edinburgh,
Paul Masterton,
Stephen and Susan Scott;

at Kidderminster,
David and Peter Marston;

at Melbourne,
Gemma and Kevin Cullen;

at York,
Angus, Bruce and Douglas Weir.

Contents

Acknowledgments   xi
Preface   xiii
Introduction: The Loin's Cubs   1

Part One: Edward, Mary and Elizabeth

Prologue: 28 January 1547   23

1   The King's Uncles   27
2   Amorous Intrigues   41
3   A Royal Scandal   65
4   'The Most Unstable Man in England'   81
5   Keeping the Faith   102
6   Pining Away   130

Part Two: Jane and Mary

7   'Jane the Queen'   157
8   God's Miracle   170

Part Three: Mary and Elizabeth

9   'A Merciful Princess'   195
10   'The Marriages of Princes'   211
11   Heretics and Traitors   227
12   'Much Suspected of Me'   247
13   The Spanish Marriage   268
14   True Religion Restored   287
15   'A Miracle Will Come to Pass'   301

16   Bloody Mary   318
17   'Little Children Like Angels'   341

Epilogue: Elizabeth   362
Afterwards   364

Bibliography   367
Genealogical Table: The Heirs of Henry VIII   376
Index   377

Illustrations

1 Edward VI, portrait by Guillim Stretes. (The Royal Collection © Her Majesty the Queen)

2 Edward Seymour, Duke of Somerset, by an unknown artist. (By courtesy of the National Portrait Gallery, London)

3 John Cheke, by an unknown artist. (Private Collection)

4 Thomas Seymour, Lord Sudeley, by an unknown artist. (By courtesy of the National Portrait Gallery, London)

5 Portrait of Elizabeth I as princess. (The Royal Collection © Her Majesty the Queen)

6 Katherine Ashley. (Courtesy of Lord Hastings)

7 Sir Thomas Parry, by Hans Holbein. (The Royal Collection © Her Majesty the Queen)

8 Hatfield Palace. (By courtesy of The Marquess of Salisbury)

9 Allegory on the abdication of Charles V in Brussels by Frans Francken. (© Rijksmuseum–Stichting, Amsterdam)

10 John Dudley, Duke of Northumberland. (Reproduced by kind permission of Viscount De L'Isle, from his private collection)

11 Engraving of Lady Jane Grey by Willem and Madgalena van de Passe. (By courtesy of the National Portrait Gallery, London)

12 Portrait of Mary I by Hans Eworth. (By courtesy of the National Portrait Gallery, London)

13 Philip of Spain, portrait by an unknown artist after Titian. (By courtesy of the National Portrait Gallery, London)

14 Stephen Gardiner, Bishop of Winchester. (© National Trust Photographic Library/J. Whitaker)

15 Portrait of Edward Courtenay, Earl of Devon, by Sir A. More (From the Courtenay Collection at Powderham Castle, Devon)

16 The Bell Tower, Tower of London. (© Crown Copyright. Historic Royal Palaces)

17 The Remains of Woodstock (Palace) As They Appeared in 1714: from *The Progresses and Public Processions of Queen Elizabeth* by John Nichols, Volume I, 1823 (Shelfmark = A.5.287/1. Opposite page 9). (Courtesy of the Bodleian Library)

18 Elizabeth I, by an unknown artist *c.* 1558. (By kind permission of His Grace the Duke of Northumberland)

19 Reginald Pole, Archbishop of Canterbury. (Courtesy of the Archbishop of Canterbury and the Trustees of Lambeth Palace Library)

20 Portrait of Sir William Paget by the Master of Statthalteri. (By courtesy of the National Portrait Gallery, London)

21 William Paulet, Marquess of Winchester, by an unknown artist. (By courtesy of the National Portrait Gallery, London)

22 Sir William Petre, by an unknown artist. (By courtesy of the National Portrait Gallery, London)

Acknowledgments

I should like to express my gratittude to all those who have helped me with this book, and particularly to Mr Michael Cameron, formerly Senoir Consultant in Obstetrics and Gynaecology at St. Thomas's Hospital, London, for his kindness in reading the manuscript and for giving me his professional views in Mary Tudor's confinements; this invaluable assistance enabled me to arrive at a convincing solution to the mystery surrounding Mary's two supposed pregnancies.

My grateful thanks are, as ever, also due to my wonderfully supportive editor, Jill Black, who suggested this project; to my equally supportive agent, Julian Alexander, whose enthusiasm and encouragement never flags; to Pascal Cariss, for all his hard work on the manuscript; and to Sophie Martin for her painstaking efforts to track down the illustrations.

Lastly, but not least, I owe special thanks to my husband and children, who have patiently borne the absence of a wife and mother over so many evenings and weekends, so that this book could be completed on schedule. Without their unfailing support, it would not have been possible.

Preface

This book is not a history of England during the troubled reigns of Edward VI, Jane Grey, Mary I and Elizabeth I, but a chronicle of the personal lives of four English sovereigns, and the relationships between them, during the period 1547 to 1558. When Henry VIII died in 1547, he left three highly intelligent children to succeed him in turn – Edward, Mary and Elizabeth, to be followed, if their lines failed, by the descendants of his sister Mary Tudor, one of whom was the ill-fated nine-days queen, Lady Jane Grey.

The relationships between the royal siblings were never easy ones for several reasons: all had very dissimilar characters, and while they took after their father in many ways, they had each inherited diverse characteristics from their mothers, who had been the first three of Henry VIII's six wives. Each child had spent its formative years in vastly different circumstances, and had enjoyed – or suffered – varying relations with its formidable father. Mary's mother had been supplanted in King Henry's affections by Elizabeth's mother, who had, in her turn, been supplanted by Edward's mother. And while the King's daughters suffered several vicissitudes of fortune in Henry's lifetime, his son grew up secure in his august father's love and protection.

In the pages of this book, which begins at the point where my earlier book *The Six Wives of Henry VIII* came to an end, I have tried to portray the characters of these royal siblings and their cousin Jane Grey as realistically as possible, and to describe how their personal relationships with each other were affected by political and religious considerations. In order to achieve this, I have consulted a wealth of documentary evidence contemporary to the period, including numerous private and official letters, the great calendars of state and the masses of diplomatic papers, as well as memorials and chronicles by contemporary writers, including Edward VI's own journal, and more mundane records, such as lists of privy purse expenses, which can in fact yield fascinating information.

There have been many biographies of the later Tudor monarchs, but never a book in which their personal lives and relations with each other, and the effect of these factors upon the history of England, have been the central theme. One cannot of course write about kings and queens without touching on the political and social issues of their times, but what I have tried to bring into focus here is personal information that has until now been treated as generally subsidiary to the political ethos of other works. This book is not intended to replace such works, but to complement them.

In these pages, we go back in time to an age in which the personalities of monarchs and their familial connections had the power to influence governments, and it is vital to our knowledge of the period to understand what shaped the characters of these four monarchs, who were among the most charismatic and vivid personalities ever to have graced the throne of England. Naturally, our human condition makes us eager to learn about the private things, the everyday trivia, the scandals, and the sheer 'feel' of ages long gone. We want to bridge the gap, to discover that even these long-dead kings and queens felt as we do, and come to know them through the writings and mementoes they have left behind. We are fortunate, therefore, that the Tudor period is one rich in source material, in which fascinating – and sometimes astonishing – discoveries may be made. These, and one or two tantalising mysteries, are the things I have included in this book, the things that bring us closer to the past.

Set against a background of turbulent change and intrigue, the story that unfolds will, I hope, bring to life four Tudor sovereigns and those whose lives they touched, and will portray them not only as Renaissance princes, but as individuals, who, in the final analysis, were people not so very unlike ourselves.

Alison Weir
Carshalton, Surrey
May 1996

Introduction: The Lion's Cubs

The Tudors were not a prolific race; although King Henry VIII of England married six times, only his first three wives bore him children, and of a probable total of eleven pregnancies between them produced only three surviving children. The fact that these royal heirs were born to different mothers would have a direct bearing on the history of England for several decades, for old grudges and jealousies and disagreements over religion remained lively in the hearts of these siblings until death divided them.

Henry VIII, who ascended the throne in 1509, was a true prince of the Renaissance, a brilliant scholar and sportsman whose good looks, splendid physique and kingly bearing were the talk of Christendom. The magnificence of his court attracted many great and learned men, and in the first half of his reign no expense was spared on lavish ceremonial and display. The young King delighted in tournaments and in sumptuous pageants based on classical or allegorical themes, and spent vast sums on costumes and scenery, much of which was made from cloth of gold. Later in his reign the more dramatic masque, an Italian novelty, became popular. Besides these more superficial entertainments, Henry delighted in the company of scholars, artists and musicians, and his court became a renowned centre of culture. It seemed that England had embarked upon a new golden age of glory and prosperity, and that Henry would found a dynasty that would surpass even the splendour and fame of the Plantagenets, whose throne the King's father had usurped in 1485.

After his accession, Henry VIII wasted no time in marrying his sister-in-law, the Princess Katherine of Aragon, who had originally come from Spain in 1501 as the bride of his elder brother, Arthur, Prince of Wales. Arthur, however, had died six months after their wedding, and in 1509 Henry obtained a papal dispensation permitting him to marry his brother's widow, who possessed all the qualities and virtues required of a medieval queen. However, Katherine was unable to give Henry the one thing he wanted most: a male heir. Her three sons died at or soon after birth, as did one of her daughters; another daughter was stillborn. The only child of this marriage to survive was the Princess Mary, who was born on 18 February 1516 at Greenwich Palace.

When Katherine failed to bear him a living son, Henry VIII conveniently remembered that marriage with one's brother's wife was prohibited in Holy Scripture, and applied to the Pope for an annulment. Because of political pressure from Katherine's nephew, the Holy Roman Emperor, Charles V, who was also King of Spain and the Indies and ruler of the Low Countries, the Pope dithered for six years, having also heard that Henry's pangs of conscience over his marriage had been prompted by his falling in love with Katherine's maid-of-honour, Anne Boleyn. Tired of waiting for the Pope to pronounce sentence, Henry decreed that the Church of England be separated from that of Rome and made himself its Supreme Head and Governor, declaring that the Pope's authority no longer held sway in England. After this, he appointed a new Archbishop of Canterbury, Thomas Cranmer, who in 1533 declared that the King's marriage to Katherine of Aragon was null and void and that the marriage Henry had already entered into with Anne Boleyn was valid.

These events had a devastating effect on the young Princess Mary. Adored and cherished in childhood by both parents, she suddenly found herself at loggerheads with a father who had become a distant, frightening tyrant, and compelled to defend the cause of her beloved mother, whom she considered to have been shockingly treated. Katherine always maintained that she was the King's true wife and that she would never do or say anything to jeopardise her daughter's title or future succession; for this defiance she was banished from court in 1531 and thereafter kept in close confinement in one unhealthy house after another. Mary never saw her mother again. In 1533 she was declared a bastard and unfit to inherit the crown, and made to wait upon her new half-sister, the Princess Elizabeth, to whom Anne Boleyn had given birth at Greenwich on 7 September. Anne always treated Mary with calculated cruelty, heaping humiliations on her and urging the King to have her put to death. Despite her stepmother's threats to do away with her or marry her to a low-born husband, Mary would not capitulate or acknowledge Anne as queen.

In 1536 Katherine died of cancer; a few months later Anne herself went to the block, having been convicted of adultery and plotting the death of the King. Henry's new wife, Jane Seymour, begged him to bring Mary back to court and be reconciled with her, but Henry would not agree unless Mary signed a document acknowledging her mother's marriage to be incestuous and unlawful. Under tremendous pressure, not only from her father but also from her cousin Charles V, on whose self-interested advice she was to rely all her life, Mary signed, but she never forgave herself for betraying her mother's memory or her principles. That Christmas, she was welcomed back at court.

Thereafter, she lived as a royal princess, even if that title was no longer hers. After Queen Jane died in 1537 after bearing the King his longed-for son and heir, Edward, Mary was first lady in the land until the arrival of Henry's fourth wife, Anne of Cleves, who was not to his taste and whose marriage was annulled after six months, having remained unconsummated. Anne was replaced by the flighty young Katherine Howard, with whom Mary had little in common, and who went to the block for infidelity in 1542.

In 1543, Henry VIII married Katherine Parr, an intelligent, learned woman, the patroness of humanists and a secret Protestant. She was also gentle, dignified, kind and maternal, and she made an ideal stepmother for the King's children. She warmly befriended Mary, and it was thanks to her influence that both princesses were reinstated in the succession by an Act of Parliament passed in 1543, although neither were declared legitimate. Henry could think of no alternative heir if the son Jane Seymour had borne him were to die childless.

Renowned for her steadfastness and her piety, Mary – according to the Imperial ambassador, Eustache Chapuys – was 'universally adored' by her father's subjects, who saw in her the embodiment of the old order that was rapidly disappearing, and famed throughout Europe for her 'virtue and learning'.

Thanks to the good offices of her mother, Mary had been well-educated. Her first tutor was Thomas Linacre, who had taught Prince Arthur. He devised a formal curriculum for her and wrote a Latin textbook, *Rudimenta Grammatices*, which became very successful. Unfortunately he died soon afterwards, and in 1523 the Queen engaged a Spanish educationist, Juan Luis Vives, to teach her daughter. Vives had an excellent reputation as a scholar – Sir Thomas More called him the best teacher in Europe – and wrote a treatise entitled *The Education of a Christian Woman* for Mary's guidance. In it he advocated a rigorous programme of study of the Scriptures and the classics. If any pupil, male or female, did not work hard, they were to be whipped: 'The daughter especially shall be handled without cherishing. For cherishing marreth sons, but it utterly destroyeth daughters.'

Mary was subject to this severe régime for the next five years of her life, some of which were spent at Ludlow Castle on the Welsh border. After that time, Nicholas Udall, Provost of Eton, took over her education, since Vives had returned to Spain.

By now Mary was proficient in speaking and writing Latin and French, could read Spanish and Greek, and was well read in theology and history. When she was eleven, she was able to translate a prayer of St Thomas Aquinas from Latin into English; later on, under Katherine Parr's auspices, she translated Erasmus's *Paraphrases of the Gospel of St John* from the Latin. However, despite having had teachers who were all eminent humanists, Mary would have nothing to do with the new learning when she grew up, identifying it with Anne Boleyn's reformist opinions.

What Mary did excel at was music. She was an expert player on the lute and virginals, and had shown virtuosity on these instruments at a very early age. She practised and played regularly throughout her life, and her account books are full of payments for new strings for her lute. Even though her speaking voice was unusually deep and gruff for a woman, she could sing well, as her father did.

Mary had been a graceful child with glorious long red hair, 'as beautiful as ever seen on human head'. In 1531 the Venetian ambassador described her as having a 'pretty face, a very beautiful complexion [and a] well-proportioned physique'. Two years later, another Venetian wrote that she was 'of low stature with a red and white complexion, and very thin'. Her eyes were large and pale, 'so piercing that they inspire not only respect but fear'. However, her alarming stare was the result of her eyesight being so poor 'that to read she must hold the page close to her face'. She had a tightly-buttoned, thin-lipped mouth and a flat, retroussé nose; by the time she entered adulthood she had, like many of her contemporaries, lost most of her teeth.

The tragedies that marred Mary's life were reflected in her face; after the traumas of adolescence, no one ever again referred to her as pretty or beautiful. She had a delicate appearance, being small and spare with a thin body and arms. By the time she was twenty, she suffered chronic ill health. The onset of puberty had coincided with her parents' separation, and this in turn led to a succession of severe illnesses that were probably psychological in origin. From her teens to the end of her life she suffered from what now would be diagnosed as premenstrual tension; her periods were often infrequent or absent, and when they did arrive they were accompanied by pain, which she tried to counteract by taking long walks in the country. She suffered miseries from toothache, palpitations, depression, headaches, and the effects of what she called 'bad air', which were probably due to hypochondria. Every autumn during her adult life, she fell ill with a variety of symptoms – modern doctors might well conclude that she suffered from a seasonal affective disorder.

Mary displayed many great qualities, notably courage, steadfastness and compassion. She demonstrated staunch loyalty to her principles, her religion, and those she loved, in whom she in turn inspired a touching devotion. Many of her attendants spent the best part of their lives in her service, including Susan Clarencieux, later her Mistress of the Robes, who served Mary for twenty-five years. Her friends were constantly inviting her to be godmother to their children, a duty she performed punctiliously and with generosity. Her love of children was boundless, and she longed all her life to have her own.

Mary was virtuous, kind, truthful, affectionate, conscientious, dignified and gracious. Her abilities, however, were better suited to a married gentlewoman or nun than to a future queen. She was never happier than when she was in the domestic sphere, visiting the poor in their homes, attired simply, dispensing charity, discussing children with her ladies, or choosing the magnificent gowns and jewels she so delighted in wearing on public occasions. Despite her academic education, she was not really interested in books. She lacked the pragmatism of the other Tudor monarchs, being emotional, insecure, unable to compromise, and lacking in worldliness, foresight and political judgement. She could never understand an opposing point of view, being convinced that she alone was always right. Proud, stubborn and obstinate, as her mother had been, she stood on her regal dignity and, if sufficiently provoked, was capable of throwing temper tantrums. Even so, she was easily placated, and her outbursts never lasted long. She was not cruel, and her vices were few: her chief indulgence was gambling at cards or bowls, and sometimes losing large amounts of money.

Her innocence was the subject of many jokes at court. Jane Dormer, another of her ladies-in-waiting, recalled that she was 'so bred as she knew no foul or unclean speeches, which, when her lord father understood, he would not believe it'. He is alleged to have ordered a courtier to test Mary's virtue by using sexual swear-words during a court masque. Those within earshot smothered their laughter and the ladies blushed, but Mary was at a loss to know what the joke was. This innocence lasted throughout her adult life. Dormer tells how, when she was in her late thirties, and queen, her Lord Chamberlain, Lord William Howard, began flirting with Frances Neville, one of Mary's maids-of-honour, in the Queen's ante-chamber, little realising that Mary could overhear every word they were saying. Tickling Frances's chin, Lord William teased, 'My pretty whore, how dost thou?' Mary, listening, had no idea what a whore was.

A little later, when Frances was helping her mistress to dress, Mary exclaimed, 'God-a-mercy, my pretty whore!' The maid was shocked and begged the Queen not to use such words about her. Mary said she had heard the Lord Chamberlain use the term, whereupon Frances said, 'My Lord Chamberlain is an idle gentleman, and we respect not what he saith or doth. But Your Majesty, from whom I think never any heard such a word, doth amaze me to be called so by you. A whore is a wicked, misliving woman.' Mary replied that she had not intended any insult, as she had never heard the word before.

Throughout Henry VIII's reign there had been projects to marry Mary to various European princes, but all came to nothing, largely because Mary had been declared illegitimate. By the time she was twenty-five, she was trying to resign herself to spinsterhood, describing herself as 'the most unhappy lady in Christendom'. Not only had she been deprived of a husband, but as time went by her chances of motherhood became less and less, and the one thing Mary desired was children. Her frustrated maternal feelings found their outlet in illness, a vicarious interest in the marriages, children and christenings of those in her circle, and religion.

Her faith was the most important thing in Mary's life. She inherited her piety and love of religion from her mother, and made it her life's crusade to restore to England the faith to which her mother had been devoted. She could not tolerate the reformed faith and had no time for the genuine doubts of others. In the rites of the Roman Church she found the security of her early childhood; her first recorded word had been 'Priest!' The Protestant faith threatened the traditional concept of an ordered world, which was rapidly being overthrown, and Mary saw it as a very serious threat indeed. As far as she was concerned, such heresies must be ruthlessly stamped out and eradicated. That, she was convinced, was what God wanted, and she had absolute faith in her own convictions. The Venetian diplomat Francesco Soranzo says that she would often walk about murmuring to herself, '*Si Deus est pro nobis, quis contra nos?* – If God is for us, who is against us?'

The birth of Henry VIII's younger daughter, Elizabeth, in 1533 had been a disappointment to her parents, who had longed for a son, but before she was a year old the King had caused an Act of Succession to be passed in her favour, which made her his heir in place of Mary. At the time of her mother's execution in 1536, however, she too was declared a bastard and struck from the succession.

We do not know when Elizabeth first found out the terrible truth or who told her what had happened to her mother. In all her long life she made only two recorded references to Anne Boleyn. In 1553, when she was twenty, she intimated to the Spanish ambassador that her sister Mary was hostile towards her because of the injuries that Mary and her mother had been dealt by Anne Boleyn. On another occasion she firmly told the Venetian ambassador that her mother would never have cohabited with Henry VIII except in a marriage that had been declared legal by the Archbishop of Canterbury. In fact, Elizabeth had been conceived outside wedlock, but this was undoubtedly a highly sensitive point with her. Yet for all her silence on the subject of her mother, she showed remarkable loyalty towards her Boleyn relations – Careys, Howards, Norrises and Knollyses.

After her fall from favour, Elizabeth was brought up by governesses. The first was the warm-hearted Lady Margaret Bryan, who had to beg Mr Secretary Cromwell for such essentials as nightgowns and chemises when her young charge grew out of the lavish clothing ordered by Anne Boleyn. When Elizabeth was four, Lady Margaret transferred to the household of the newly-born Prince Edward, and the little girl passed into the care of Katherine Champernowne.

Katherine was the daughter of solidly respectable gentlefolk from Devonshire, and in 1545 became the wife of John Ashley, a cousin and senior gentleman attendant of Anne Boleyn's. Kat Ashley, as she was then known, came to exercise considerable influence over the growing Elizabeth, to whom she was utterly devoted. However, despite being kindly and very loyal, time would show that she was neither wise nor discreet, nor was she capable of properly controlling her charge. Elizabeth was blind to Kat's faults; she loved her almost as a mother, and later remarked that she had 'taken great labour and pain in bringing me up in learning and honesty'.

Kat Ashley, who had received an unusually advanced education for a woman at that time, took charge of Elizabeth's elementary education, teaching her mathematics, history, geography, astronomy, architecture, needlework, dancing, riding and deportment. She also imparted the rudiments of French, Italian, Spanish and Flemish. In fact, the education given by Kat was of such a high standard that Sir Thomas Wriothesley, who visited Elizabeth when she was six, was moved to comment that 'if she be no worse educated than she now appeareth to me, she will prove of no less honour to womanhood than shall beseem her father's daughter'. Kat Ashley herself had come to recognise the girl's remarkable intellectual qualities and took pride in her rapid progress.

Elizabeth spent most of her childhood in various royal houses situated north of London. Her household had first been established at Hatfield, a red brick palace built around a quadrangle by Cardinal John Morton between 1480 and 1497. Only the western range, including the great hall, survives today, because after her death the old house was demolished by Robert Cecil to make way for a splendid Jacobean mansion, Hatfield House, and what is left was much altered in 1830. In Elizabeth's time the palace was surrounded by pretty arbours, flower gardens, shaded paths and a deer park full of majestic trees, which stretched for several miles. The River Lea flowed through the park. Hatfield was granted to Elizabeth in 1550 and became her principal residence in 1555.

One of Elizabeth's favourite childhood homes was Ashridge House, originally a monastery founded by the order of Bonhommes in 1283. The house was attractively sited on the crest of the Chiltern Hills overlooking Berkhamsted, and was deemed to be a healthy place for the royal children. Henry VIII acquired the property after expelling the monks in 1539, and from then on Elizabeth and Edward stayed there often. In 1550 the house was granted to Elizabeth as sole owner, yet by 1564 it was reported to be in a poor state of repair. It was later demolished and rebuilt by James Wyatt in 1808 as a Gothic mansion, and is now a management college.

Another property given to Elizabeth in 1550, in which she had already stayed many times, was Enfield Palace. In the 1540s all three of Henry VIII's children had suites of rooms there. The palace is thought to have been built on the site of a medieval manor house. It was small, with only seventeen rooms and a great hall, but very luxurious and richly furnished, with gardens to one side and a hunting chase. It stood where Pearson's Department Store now stands. In the 1920s high Tudor chimney stacks could still be seen, but nothing now remains of the palace above ground, save a stone fireplace, wooden panelling and a plasterwork ceiling, all of which are now in Little Park, a private house in Gentleman's Row, Enfield.

Nearby was Elsynge Place, also at Enfield, a much larger palace, mainly fifteen-century in origin but much enlarged and refurbished by Henry VIII when he acquired it in 1540. Set in a great deer park in woodland, it occupied a site overlooking a wide lake and bordered by an avenue of trees and a stream called the Maiden's Brook. The house was constructed around two courtyards dominated by magnificent gatehouses. Entry was via a drawbridge over the moat. The royal apartments were approached through the King's Gate – Henry himself often stayed here, as did all his children. Nearby, for their recreation, were a bowling house, archery frames, orchards and gardens. Elsynge was demolished during the Civil War, and a Jacobean mansion, Forty Hall, now stands at the other side of the lake.

As a child, Elizabeth divided her time mainly between these four houses, remaining secluded from public life. Sometimes her brother or sister stayed with her. Her father the King could not, for a time, bring himself to see her, but the intercession of three stepmothers – Jane Seymour, Anne of Cleves and Katherine Howard – made him relent, with the result that Elizabeth received the occasional summons to come to court, albeit rarely. More often than not the King would send a messenger to enquire after her health and education. She knew little of his spasmodic plans to find a husband for her, all of which came to nothing because of the taint of bastardy and her mother's notorious reputation.

When Elizabeth was eight, Katherine Howard was executed for adultery. This event seems to have made a dramatic impression on her, resurrecting horrifying memories of Anne Boleyn's fate. Elizabeth had been fond of Katherine Howard, her mother's cousin, and in 1562, Robert Dudley, then Earl of Leicester, informed the French ambassador that he had known Elizabeth since she was eight and that from that time she had always said, 'I will never marry.' Perhaps marriage was irrevocably equated with death in her mind.

After 1543, Elizabeth benefited enormously from Katherine Parr's influence. The King allowed her to welcome his younger children into her household, and Elizabeth and Mary were chief among the Queen's ladies-in-waiting 'accustomed to be lodged within the King's Majesty's house'. Not only did Katherine now supervise Elizabeth's education, but she also acted as mediator when Elizabeth fell foul of her father for some unknown offence in 1546, which resulted in her being banished from his presence for a whole year. The Queen's quiet persistence led Henry at length to pardon his daughter, and Elizabeth's gratitude was boundless. To mark it, she presented her stepmother with her own translation 'out of French rhyme into English prose' of a poem entitled 'The Mirror or Glass of a Sinful Soul'.

Kat Ashley had ceased to be responsible for Elizabeth's education in 1542, when the child began sharing some lessons with her brother Edward under the auspices of Dr Richard Coxe. In 1544, Katherine Parr appointed her a tutor of her own, the Greek scholar William Grindal. Grindal had been associated with John Cheke and Roger Ascham in the education of Prince Edward, and Ascham in particular

took a great interest in Elizabeth's academic development, maintaining
a regular correspondence with her and Mrs Ashley from 1545, urging
his protégée to ever greater efforts. Ascham, a Yorkshireman who was
Senior Fellow at St John's College, Cambridge, later wrote, 'I have
dealt with many learned ladies, but among them all the brightest star is
my illustrious Lady Elizabeth.' He referred to Kat's 'diligent oversee-
ing' of her charge's private study, and exhorted the governess 'to favour
somewhat this rare intelligence, for the younger, the more tender, the
quicker, the easier to break'. Ascham also gave Grindal advice as to
which books to study and how to approach them.

Henry VIII never intended Elizabeth's education to be a preparation
for queenship. His purpose was that she should become an erudite
example of her sex and an ornament to the House of Tudor. From
Grindal, Elizabeth learned Greek (a recent addition to the traditional
curriculum thanks to the influence of Desiderius Erasmus, John Cheke
and others) and Latin, which she spoke, read and wrote fluently. This
study of the classics in time enabled Elizabeth to gain a sophisticated
understanding of history, philosophy and the art of oratory. In addition
she studied the Scriptures and the early Fathers of the Church. Battista
Castiglione taught her Italian; her earliest surviving letter, sent to
Katherine Parr in 1544, is in that language, and she later became
especially fluent in it, which gave her an advantage when it came to
conversing with foreign diplomats, since Italian was rapidly replacing
Latin as the language of diplomacy.

Elizabeth grew up to be an excellent linguist, although her French
accent, mimicked by a French ambassador, was marred by overlong 'A'
sounds, such as 'Paar Dieu, paar maa foi!' Blanche Parry, who had
served her in her chamber since her birth, is believed to have taught her
some Welsh, the language of her Tudor forbears. She even mastered
Spanish, but not until she was in her twenties. By the age of thirteen,
Elizabeth had presented Katharine Parr with several of her own
translations of devotional works: 'The Mirror of a Sinful Soul' (from
French to English), Katherine's own book, *Prayers and Meditations*
(from English into Latin, French and Italian) and *The Dialogue of Faith*
(from Latin into French).

Educated as she was by men who all held firm reformist views on
religion, Elizabeth could not have failed to be influenced by them, nor
could she have been unaware of Katherine Parr's own secret
convictions, for in 1547 she translated yet another work for her
stepmother, the *Institution de la Vie Chréstienne* by John Calvin, the
eminent French Protestant scholar and reformer. Yet already she had

learned to keep her own counsel in matters of religion, for while her father lived it was dangerous to hold Protestant views.

As a child, Elizabeth was taught to write in the 'secretary' script that had dominated European calligraphy since the time of Charlemagne. Castiglione then taught her to write a fine Italic script, which she later improved under Ascham's tutelage. As a result, she raised the skill of handwriting to an art form, signing her name with magnificent loops and flourishes. She also wrote a rapid, spidery hand when engaged upon private correspondence and notes.

Elizabeth's education was outstandingly successful and laid the foundations for habits of study that were to last all her life. Although the curriculum she followed was demanding and often strict, she was formidably intelligent and loved learning for its own sake. Her biographer, William Camden, observed later that never a day went past without her reading or writing something for recreation.

She was never beautiful, although she was striking to look at. She inherited her father's red hair and hooked nose and her mother's long, thin, pale face, pointed chin and witty dark eyes. Her eyebrows and lashes were so fair as to appear non-existent. There exists in the Royal Collection a portrait of Elizabeth at the age of about thirteen, which depicts a serious-looking adolescent in a crimson gown, holding a book. Her face is fuller than in later portraits and the eyes are dark and wary. Her air of gravity makes her appear older than her years. Yet already she was displaying her beautiful white hands with their long, tapering fingers to advantage, a habit that would endure into old age, for she was inordinately vain about them.

In 1552, a Venetian ambassador described Elizabeth as 'very handsome' and praised her regal dignity. Another Venetian, Giovanni Michieli, writing in 1557, wrote: 'Her face is comely rather than handsome, but she is tall and well-formed, with a good skin, though swarthy. She has fine eyes.' He described her as 'slender and straight'. One of the greatest compliments men could pay her was to comment on her likeness to her father, Henry VIII: given the rumours about her paternity, and her reverence for his memory, it is not hard to see why.

As a child, Elizabeth was usually composed, well-mannered and possessed of a certain gravity. William Thomas called her 'a very witty and gentle young lady'. Roger Ascham wrote in 1549: 'Her mind has no womanly weakness, her perseverence is equal to that of a man, and her memory long keeps what it quickly picks up.' Michieli was equally landatory, opining, in 1557, that 'her intellect and understanding are wonderful'.

On the other hand, Jane Dormer, who did not like her, remembered that at thirteen Elizabeth was so 'proud and disdainful' that it 'much blemished the handsomeness and beauty of her person'. And the Duke of Feria reported in 1558 that she was certainly clever but 'very vain'. She had inherited her inordinate vanity from Anne Boleyn, and, like her mother, she thrived on the attentions and compliments of courtiers. Both women were markedly flirtatious. Elizabeth was also very quick-tempered, easily provoked into violent outbursts of rage, which ceased almost as soon as they had begun. She could be sharp and caustic when irritated, and excessively temperamental: Anne Boleyn had exhibited immoderate, sometimes hysterical, behaviour, and her daughter displayed similar tendencies. Her childhood experiences had left her distrustful of others, cautious and emotionally unstable. Her neuroses expressed themselves in fainting fits, anxiety states and panic attacks during adolescence, in which she was filled with feelings of inexplicable dread, so terrifying that they almost paralysed her.

At other times, Elizabeth could display as much vitality and self-confidence as her father. Most people were impressed by her bearing, her shrewdness, her awesome intellect, her prudence, her pragmatic business sense, her tenacity and, later, above all, her consummate statecraft.

As far as religion was concerned, Elizabeth kept her own counsel. We know very little of what she was taught as a child, only that she came under the influence of the Cambridge reformers who tutored her and her brother, and of her Protestant stepmother, Katherine Parr. Although she herself came to embrace their views, circumstances often dictated that she had to be discreet, so she learned a certain pragmatism with regard to religion. As a result, she was never a bigot or a fanatic. She was not even very pious. As an adult, she commissioned a private prayer in which she gave thanks to God for having 'from my earliest days kept me back from the deep abysses of natural ignorance and damnable superstition, that I might enjoy the great sun of righteousness which brings with its rays life and salvation, while leaving so many kings, princes and princesses in ignorance under the power of Satan'. On another occasion she displayed an unusually enlightened view for her time when she declared: 'There is only one faith and one Jesus Christ; the rest is a dispute about trifles.'

Not surprisingly, Elizabeth's relationship with her sister Mary was rarely an easy one. Despite their mothers' rivalry and Mary's hatred of Anne Boleyn, she had in fact played a mother's part to Elizabeth after Anne's death, lavishing all her frustrated maternal feelings on her bereft little sister and showering her with gifts that included yellow satin for a gown, occasional pocket money, necklaces, brooches, a box embroidered with silver and a gold ball with a clock in it, made to contain perfume. Mary took great delight in Elizabeth's infant precocity, and on one occasion wrote to inform their father that 'My sister Elizabeth is in good health and, thanks be to Our Lord, such a child toward as I doubt not Your Highness shall have cause to rejoice of in time coming.'

But when that time came, Mary herself found that there was small cause for rejoicing. As Elizabeth grew more and more to resemble her mother, both in appearance and character, rivalry and distrust between the sisters became increasingly apparent. Mary's increasing antagonism and 'evil disposition' towards Elizabeth was attributed by foreign envoys to the simple fact that she was Anne Boleyn's daughter, but it went deeper than that. Mary did not believe that Henry VIII was Elizabeth's father, and would often remark in private to her friends and attendants that the girl 'had the face and countenance of Mark Smeaton' – a musician who was one of the men executed for alleged criminal intercourse with Anne Boleyn – 'who was a very handsome man'. Those who commented on the fact that Elizabeth resembled Henry VIII more than Mary did were doubtless nearer the truth, but this did nothing to allay Mary's resentment. Put simply, Elizabeth was a living reminder of all that she and her mother had suffered as a result of Anne Boleyn's bewitchment of her father. As far as Elizabeth was concerned, however, Mary's hostility stemmed from the fact that 'we differed on religion'. The devout Mary was appalled by her sister's leanings towards the reformed faith, and came to view her as a dangerous rival.

Henry VIII had waited twenty-eight long and frustrating years for God to answer his prayers for a healthy, living son, and from the time of his birth at Hampton Court on 12 October 1537, 'the high and mighty Prince Edward' had never wanted for anything. His father spared no pains to ensure his survival of the very real hazards of infancy. Stringent precautions were ordered to protect the Prince from any chance infection or disease. The walls and floors of his apartments were washed down thrice daily, his food was of the best quality and cleanly prepared and served, and an army of servants was appointed to administer to his every need. He was over-protected and almost suffocated by careful nurturing.

For all his much-vaunted love for his son, Henry VIII visited the child infrequently, and regular reports on the baby's progress were sent, not to the King, but to Master Secretary Cromwell. Until he was six, Edward was brought up, as he himself records in his journal, 'among the women', the chief of these being his nurse, Mother Jack. As he grew, he had impressed upon him the importance of his royal rank and the fact that his father was the greatest man in the world, whom he must try his best to emulate. When he was two, Hans Holbein painted his portrait as a New Year's gift for the King; the Prince is depicted in long robes and a feathered bonnet of cloth of gold, and holds a bejewelled rattle. The portrait bears the Latin inscription: 'Little boy, take after your father and also inherit his virtues. The world in its immensity contains nothing greater. You are to surpass the deeds of such a father!' Small wonder that the child quickly became a model of precocity.

What Edward lacked most was a mother's love. He had never known his own mother, and his first two stepmothers, Anne of Cleves and Katherine Howard, had little to do with him. It was not until the King married Katherine Parr in 1543 that Edward came to know something of normal family life, albeit on a grand scale. He quickly grew to love his stepmother, and in no time at all was referring to her as 'Mother'.

When he was six, the Prince was given over to the governance of men and his royal training and formal education began in earnest. His first tutor, or governor, was Richard Coxe, later Bishop of Ely, a progressive educationist selected by Henry VIII. Coxe held the then advanced view that learning should be enjoyed rather than instilled by constant beatings. He was also a closet Protestant, whose views were to influence Edward in years to come.

Coxe was soon joined by Dr John Cheke, a Fellow of St John's College, Cambridge, a renowned lecturer in Greek and a prominent humanist scholar. Katherine Parr is usually credited with having secured Cheke's services for her stepson; certainly she took a keen interest in Edward's education. William Grindal joined the Prince's household in 1545. By now, Edward was spending a great deal of time at his studies, devoting several hours a day to the study of the Roman and Greek classics, the Scriptures, history and geography. John Belmayne taught him French, a Master Randolph taught German, and Philip von Wilder lute. William Thomas, Clerk to the King's Council, gave the Prince regular lessons in politics and statecraft, while Roger Ascham was brought in to teach him Italianate handwriting. Edward was also taught manners, fencing, horsemanship and the rules of hunting.

So that his son should not be isolated from the company of boys of his own age, the King arranged for a privileged group of fourteen well-born children to share his education, and thus evolved an exclusive palace school. Edward's companions included his cousin, Henry

Brandon, Duke of Suffolk, Henry, Lord Hastings, Robert Dudley, son of John Dudley, Viscount Lisle, and possibly even another cousin of Edward's, Lady Jane Grey. The Prince's favourite companion seems to have been Barnaby FitzPatrick, a cousin of the Earl of Ormond; when Edward became king, Barnaby was appointed to the unenviable post of royal whipping boy, which meant he had to suffer the punishments that their governors would not dare to administer to the Lord's Anointed, their sovereign.

Although the régime imposed by his tutors was strict, Edward made rapid progress. He was a serious-minded, intelligent child who enjoyed learning for its own sake, and while his tutors may naturally have exaggerated his achievements, there is no doubt that he was of above average ability. In 1545, when he was seven, Richard Coxe reported that his charge had already 'conquered a great number of the captains of ignorance' and was proficient in conjugating Latin verbs. He 'hath made already forty or fifty pretty Latin verses, and is now ready to enter into Cato [and] some proper and profitable fables of Aesop. Every day he readeth a portion of Solomon's Proverbs, wherein he delighteth much, and learneth there to beware of strange and wanton women [and] to be thankful to him who telleth him of his faults.'

Unlike his father, the Prince displayed little interest in sports, preferring intellectual pastimes. This did not mean that he was of a sickly constitution, as has sometimes been stated. He was slight in build, with his mother's white skin and his father's red hair. His contemporaries thought him an attractive child, which was perhaps to be expected, but their opinions are borne out by surviving early portraits. His only defect was in having one shoulder slightly higher than the other. As a baby he had been healthy, and had taken his first steps before he was a year old. No concern was expressed about his health until he was four, when he suffered a severe fever, from which he made a complete recovery. He was an active child and was capable of holding his own in races against his peers, but he was not interested in taking part in tests of strength and tournaments although he enjoyed watching them.

From 1550 Edward kept a journal, though his writings in it betray little of his character. From infancy he had been taught to cultivate a regal reserve and not to show his feelings; hence he grew up to be so solemn that he is reported to have laughed out loud spontaneously only once in his life. As he grew older, he could be forbidding and cold in manner, and prim in his outlook, and was wary, alert and distrustful. Had he lived, he might well have become an autocrat like his father. Once, when his beloved Cheke was seriously ill, Edward informed everyone that the tutor would not die 'for this morning I begged his life from God in my prayers, and obtained it'. His priggishness displayed itself in letters to Barnaby FitzPatrick. When Barnaby was in France, the young King wrote:

> Shortly we will prove how ye have profited in the French tongue, for we will write to you in French. For women, as far as ye may, avoid their company. Yet, if the French King command you, you may sometimes dance. Else apply yourself to riding, shooting or tennis, with such honest games, not forgetting sometimes your learning, chiefly reading of the Scripture.

A disgruntled Barnaby replied, 'Ye make me think the care ye take for me is more fatherly than friendly.'

On another occasion, the eight-year-old Edward wrote to Katherine Parr, asking her to remind his sister Mary that 'the only real love is the love of God' and that she was ruining her good reputation by her famed love of dancing and other frivolous entertainments. Mary should, he warned, avoid 'foreign dances and merriments which do not become a most Christian princess'. Mary was then twenty-nine!

There is no evidence that any of Edward's tutors tried to impose their Protestant beliefs on him during the years prior to his accession; nevertheless, some of their ideas must have made an impression, for he was only too ready to embrace the reformed religion after he came to the throne. Indeed, he quickly showed that he had the makings of a religious fanatic, and became as fervent a Protestant as his sister Mary was a Roman Catholic.

Edward could also be cruel. Reginald Pole, later Archbishop of Canterbury in the reign of Mary, heard from 'people whose testimony should place it beyond doubt' that, in front of his tutors, the young King, in a fit of anger, seized a falcon that perched in his bedchamber and slowly plucked out its feathers, one by one; when the bird was bald he ripped it into four pieces, saying 'that he likened himself to the falcon, whom everybody plucked, but that he would pluck them too hereafter, and tear them in four parts'.

For all his precocious gravity, Edward could still be mischievous. Once, one of his young companions urged him to use 'thunderous oaths', as Henry VIII had done; their tutors, however, were not impressed. Edward was ticked off, and his friend whipped.

From his infancy, Edward had been doted on by his sisters. Mary, who loved children and looked on the prince as his father's legitimate heir – as she had never regarded Elizabeth – showered him with gifts, many of which she made herself, and took a warm interest in his education and progress. He grew fond of this much older sister, and in time responded with gifts of his own and letters composed in Latin, in which he told her he loved her more than anyone else. Mary's devoted maid-of-honour, Jane Dormer, remembered in her memoirs that the Prince 'took special content' in Mary's company, and promised not to betray any secrets she might wish to confide in him. It was only later, when he embraced the Protestant faith, that the gulf widened between Edward and the passionately Catholic Mary. For a long time they avoided the subject of religion on the rare occasions when they met, but he was well aware that she cherished the hope that he would one day see the error of his ways and return to the faith of his infancy. Such knowledge irked him, and would in time become a source of deep friction.

Because Elizabeth was only four years his senior, Edward was naturally closer to her than to Mary. His letters to her are warm and affectionate, and frequently bemoan the fact that they are rarely together, as in this example from 1546:

> Change of place did not vex me so much, dearest sister, as your going from me. Now there can be nothing pleasanter than a letter from you. It is some comfort in my grief that my chamberlain tells me I may hope to visit you soon if nothing happens to either of us in the meantime. Farewell, dearest sister.

What bound these two children so closely together was the fact that both had lost their mothers through cruel strokes of fate, and both shared the same awed respect for the distant, glittering father whose power over their lives was so absolute.

When she was only six, Elizabeth made Edward a cambric shirt for a New Year's gift. As they grew older, they corresponded frequently, often in Latin, encouraging each other to perform greater intellectual feats. Both were highly precocious and because of this there was a healthy rivalry between them. After Edward's accession their letters were more infrequent and marked by a new formality. On the rare occasions when they met, court etiquette prevented them from enjoying their former intimacy, yet the bonds of affection remained.

When Henry VIII died, he willed the Crown first to Edward, then to Mary, then to Elizabeth, and lastly to the heirs of his younger sister Mary Tudor, Duchess of Suffolk, leaving out the heirs of his elder sister, Margaret Tudor, Queen of Scotland; England was at that time at war with Scotland, and the English would not have tolerated a Scottish

monarch as heir apparent. There was also much ill-feeling against the
Scots because of their reluctance to allow their infant Queen Mary to
marry Prince Edward and so unite England and Scotland under Tudor
rule. Henry VIII had forced a betrothal after his armies had defeated the
Scots at Solway Moss in 1542, but the Scots had no intention of
succumbing to this 'rough wooing' and, after Henry's death, spirited
Mary away to France, where some years later she became the wife of
the heir of King Henry II.

In his will, Henry VIII left both his daughters well provided for, with
an annual income of £3000 each – the equivalent to that of an
important nobleman – to be paid until they married, when each would
receive a final payment of £10,000 in money, plate, jewels and
household goods. This payment was conditional upon the Council
approving each lady's choice of husband; if they married without
obtaining such approval, they were to be struck out of the succession as
though they were dead.

As unmarried females, both Mary and Elizabeth were at a social
disadvantage, especially Mary, since women were expected to marry at
an early age. There was really no place for them at the court of an
unmarried child king, and although they were the first and second
ladies in the land, neither was entitled to use the title of princess, for the
shadow of bastardy still hung over them. There was also the question of
whom they might marry. As heiresses to the throne they would almost
certainly be prey to ambitious fortune hunters; if they married foreign
princes, they might embroil England unnecessarily in European
politics or wars, or even bring about the accession of a foreign king,
which would be anathema to the insular English. Yet if they married
English noblemen this might instigate faction fights such as had led to
the Wars of the Roses in the previous century.

Mary, however, had the advantage. She was an adult, she had
powerful European connections, and the properties her father had left
her, four imposing houses in East Anglia, gave her a sphere of influence
as a great territorial magnate. As heir apparent, she was a personage of
importance in the kingdom, yet what must have been of even greater
importance to her was the fact that she would now enjoy a degree of
independence.

Of all her properties, Mary favoured Hunsdon and Newhall most.
Hunsdon House was in Hertfordshire, between the villages of
Hunsdon and Eastwick, near the border with Essex. Originally built in
the fifteenth century it was restructured by Henry VIII between 1525
and 1534. Faced with red-brick, it had a moat and a sumptuous range of
royal apartments off a great gallery. Edward VI granted it to Mary for

life in 1548, although she had often stayed there prior to that date. The house Mary knew no longer exists, having been rebuilt on a smaller scale in the nineteenth century; its successor may be seen from the road in the tiny village of Hunsdonbury.

Mary's most magnificent property was Newhall in Essex, or Beaulieu as it was known. Situated near Chelmsford, it had originally been owned by the Boleyn family, from whom Henry VIII purchased it in 1516. The King spent six years renovating the house to a high standard, at the enormous cost of £17,000. When it was finished it had been 'incomparably adorned and beautified' with superb Perpendicular oriel windows. It boasted eight courtyards, a five-hundred-foot entrance façade adorned with the royal coat of arms, a great hall, a grand staircase, a tennis court, a vast kitchen and a gallery. The royal apartments were in a wing three storeys high. Newhall was granted to Mary in 1548, when it was still in good repair. A north wing was added in the late sixteenth century, but the rest of the house was demolished in Victorian times, and the buildings that replaced them were badly damaged by bombing during the Second World War. All that remains of the house's Tudor splendour is the Elizabethan wing. Mary loved this place, and it was often her refuge in the trying times that were soon to come.

Part I
Edward, Mary and Elizabeth

Prologue: 28 January 1547

In his bedchamber in the Palace of Whitehall King Henry VIII lay dying. For nearly thirty-eight years he had ruled England as an autocrat, and already he was a legend. He had married six wives, had two beheaded, and founded the Church of England with himself as its Supreme Head and Governor. Now, prematurely aged with disease, he was preparing to meet his Maker and account for his sins.

Those sins would certainly include squandering his inheritance by mismanagement and extravagance, so that already by the 1530s he had been desperately in need of money and eager to profit from his religious Reformation. In his early years, ignoring the lessons to be learned from England's humiliation at the end of the Hundred Years War, he had sought glory and renown in France by attempting to emulate the example of Henry V, to little effect. During the last years of his reign, he again went to war with the French and also the Scots, but the cost was so crippling that the country was almost bankrupt when the King died. Even before these later wars, Henry had been forced to debase the currency. The vast spoils he had appropriated from the monasteries he dissolved in the Reformation of the 1530s had largely gone into his own pocket and been spent long since, or they had been used to win over a doubtful aristocracy to the cause of religious reform.

Yet Henry's Reformation had been essentially cautious. Although he renounced all links with the Roman Catholic Church and ordered that the Pope be addressed as the Bishop of Rome, he remained to the end of his life a devout Catholic, and expected his subjects to follow him. The changes he did introduce were welcome to a people who had long resented foreign interference in the English Church and had complained of abuses, but the King knew that the majority of his subjects were not ready to embrace the Protestant faith, and to the end of his reign he would burn those few who did.

Henry's religious policy did not please everybody and led in his later years to the appearance of both Catholic and radical reformist factions within the court and the government, each of which did their best to manipulate their ageing master for their own ends. When he died, these factions – taking advantage of the fact that his heir was a minor – would choose to interpret his intentions with regard to religious policy for their own ends, with disastrous consequences for England.

The closure of the monasteries had led to serious social problems. Prior to the Dissolution, monks and nuns had tended the sick, provided education, and offered shelter and food to the destitute. Now, thousands of monks and nuns had themselves been rendered homeless and unemployed, and were reduced to begging, thus creating a problem for the authorities. During the last years of Henry VIII's reign a few former monastic establishments were turned into hospitals and schools, a policy continued by his successor, but it was not until the end of the century that Poor Law Acts dealt efficiently with the social evils of poverty and destitution.

More social problems had arisen throughout Henry's reign from the enclosure of land formerly under cultivation and common land. This was used as pasture for sheep belonging to the greater landlords, and meant that small farmers who had grazed their animals on common land, or worked in the fields, could no longer earn a living and were reduced to penury. There was much ill-feeling on the part of these dispossessed farmers – of whom there were many – against this policy, yet it carried little weight with the landowners.

By 1547, therefore, the kingdom was in an unsettled state with manifest problems – religious, financial and social. For all his splendour and his formidable reputation, and his founding of the Church of England, Henry VIII's reign had been a catalogue of failures rather than achievements.

In the dark, cold early morning of 28 January 1547, Thomas Cranmer, Archbishop of Canterbury, was at the royal bedside, urging his master to show him by a sign, any sign, that he died in the faith of Jesus Christ.

Around the bed, waiting, stood the King's councillors and chief courtiers. Most prominent amongst them was Henry's brother-in-law, Edward Seymour, Earl of Hertford, whose sister, the dead Queen Jane, had been the only one of the King's wives to present him with a thriving son. The present Queen, Katherine Parr, was not present, having already said farewell to her awesome spouse some hours earlier.

With Hertford stood Sir Anthony Browne, Master of the Horse, and the Earl's faithful ally, Sir William Paget, Secretary of State. As the King's breathing grew more laboured, these three murmured their concern that the heir to such a monarch was a boy of only nine years. They were well aware that Henry VIII had appointed a council of regency, but knew too that a dead king's wishes held no force in law. They were agreed that Hertford, as the boy's uncle, should become Lord Protector of England during the coming minority, even though this was in direct contravention to the dying king's wishes.

Paget, fortunately, had been entrusted with the safe-keeping of King Henry's will, and had no intention of showing it to anyone else until Hertford had taken possession of the person of the new king and brought him to London. He was even prepared to suppress certain of the contents of the will and equally determined to override any objections that might be made by his fellow executors. In return for such signal service, Hertford had promised to make Paget his chief adviser, a position which carried with it many and great rewards.

The end was drawing near. At two a.m., the dying King convulsively squeezed the Archbishop's hand, which Cranmer announced was proof that Henry 'trusted in the Lord', and shortly afterwards 'yielded his spirit to Almighty God'.

The new king, Prince Edward, was staying at the manor of Ashridge in Hertfordshire. Because he was close to Elizabeth both in age and affection, Hertford and his friends decided that it would be better to take the Prince to Enfield so that he could be with his sister when the news of their father's death was broken to them.

Hertford wasted no time. Taking the key of the chest in which the late king's will reposed, he left Whitehall at once in the company of Sir Anthony Browne and galloped north to Hertfordshire. At the palace, foreign ambassadors enquiring about King Henry's health were informed that he was slightly indisposed but attending to business in private, and to lend veracity to this fiction his meals were borne into his apartments to the sound of trumpets.

Later that morning Hertford and his escort clattered into the courtyard at Ashridge. They bade the Prince prepare to visit his sister Elizabeth at Enfield, but did not tell him anything further. They then rode with Edward to Hertford Castle, where they spent the night. Hertford apparently could not sleep. He was regretting having brought with him the key to the chest containing Henry VIII's will. Surely, he reasoned, he could trust Paget. Between three and four in the morning he decided to return the key by messenger, with a brief, encouraging note.

He would be back in London with the young king within twenty-four hours; there would be no time for his opponents to unite against him.

When dawn rose the Earl took his nephew to Enfield. When he arrived he led the boy to the presence chamber and summoned the Lady Elizabeth to join them. He then announced to them the death of their royal father and made formal obeisance on his knees to Edward as king. Both children burst into uncontrollable sobs, which were so heart-rending that their servants were soon crying too. So long did their lamentations continue that the Earl and his attendants became concerned, but at length Edward and Elizabeth calmed themselves. Already a change was taking place, as both became conscious of their altered roles in life. Never again would they be so close.

There was little time anyway for grief, for soon afterwards Hertford left for London with the young king, now styled Edward VI, in order to seize control of the government of England.

Edward was soon writing to Elizabeth: 'There is very little need of my consoling you, most dear sister, because from your learning you know what you ought to do, and from your prudence and piety you perform what your learning causes you to know. I perceive you think of our father's death with a calm mind.'

Elizabeth had indeed quickly composed herself, exhibiting a self-control uncommon in a child of her age. Nevertheless, she would throughout her life revere the memory of Henry VIII, who – for all his faults and cruelties – embodied in her eyes all that a successful prince should be. When she was twenty-four, a Venetian ambassador would write, 'She prides herself on her father and glories in him.' Others might cast doubts on her parentage, but Elizabeth never forgot that she was her father's daughter.

Mary's reaction to her father's death is not recorded, although she was in Whitehall Palace at the time. What is known is that she was angry with Hertford for not coming to pay his respects to her for some days afterwards. Within a short while she had left court and taken up residence in one of her own houses. Thereafter, her visits to the capital were rare, and mainly through her own choice.

I

The King's Uncles

During the last months of Henry VIII's life he had come under the influence of a clique of lords with reformist or Protestant sympathies, who had effectively undermined the Catholic faction at court by engineering the downfall of the Howards, its leading members. When the King made his will on 26 December 1546, he left the government in the hands of a council of regency that comprised sixteen 'entirely beloved' executors, none of whom were accorded any precedence as Lord Protector or Regent. These men were to rule jointly in the young king's name until he came of age, and Edward was commanded by his father 'never to change, molest, trouble nor disquiet' them. These executors were all men who had only recently been raised to high office, and the most prominent amongst them were the Earl of Hertford and John Dudley, Viscount Lisle, both of whom had won renown through their military victories in Scotland, and Archbishop Cranmer. All except four were committed to the concept of royal supremacy over the Church in England and to the Protestant faith.

Henry VIII had been a great champion of the English Church against heresy, but even he discerned how the tide of opinion was turning. Already, by 1540, the English Bible had replaced the Latin one in many churches, the monasteries had all been closed, their wealth confiscated and their lands distributed amongst those lords who had supported Henry's reformation of the Church, and the King had chosen notable religious reformers to educate his younger children. Nevertheless, the religion of England was still officially Catholic, mass was celebrated in Latin, celibacy enforced among the clergy, and those who rejected the doctrine of transubstantiation were still burned as heretics. Yet while the provisions in Henry's will paved the way for England to turn

Protestant, his death removed the last brake on faction fights between the advocates of the opposing faiths, for only he had been strong enough to ensure that a certain cohesion was maintained despite the deep political and religious divisions within the Council.

Archbishop Cranmer for one believed that the late king had meant to establish a Protestant government, and he and his fellow councillors were committed to carrying out his wishes, if only through self-interest, for all of them had profited as a result of Henry's religious policy.

Hertford, of course, had no intention of sharing the government of the kingdom with his fellow executors. As the King's uncle, he felt he should enjoy no less a role than that of Lord Protector, and in this he was supported by Paget and others, not only through self-interest, but because it was felt that the Council was too large to wield power effectively without a leader. Hertford's connections, his military reputation and his commitment to the reformist cause made him a natural choice.

Henry VIII's death was kept secret for three days. As Hertford rode with Edward VI towards London, the Council met at the Tower, where on 31 January Paget persuaded his fellow executors to disregard the provisions of the late King's will and name Hertford Lord Protector of England and Governor of the King's Person. By unanimous consent they agreed. A public announcement of King Henry's death was then made, followed almost immediately by the proclamation of Edward VI as king. Edward rode into London with Hertford that same afternoon, and was greeted by a deafening salute by cannon as he entered the Tower, where his councillors, headed by Cranmer, were waiting to pay him homage. Later that day the boy signified his approval of Hertford's appointment by signing the commission authorising the Earl's appointment as Lord Protector.

Edward Seymour was at this time around forty years old, tall and dignified with fair hair and a full beard. He had first come to prominence after Henry VIII married his sister Jane in 1537, and thereafter his rise to power had been swift. Ambition drove him, and as well as being determined to succeed he was convinced that he alone was right. This made him insensitive to the opinions and feelings of others and high-handed in his manner of handling affairs. The Emperor Charles V's ambassador, van der Delft, described him as 'a dry, sour, opinionated man'. Nevertheless, he was also intelligent, hard-working, averse to cruelty, generous and well-intentioned, though his austere, stiff manner and his pomposity did not endear him to those around him. As a statesman and soldier he had undoubted ability, and he enjoyed considerable popularity with the common people, although his record of service was indelibly marred by his greed and his rapacious self-interest.

Hertford's best qualities were his religious tolerance and his genuine concern for the sufferings of the poor. These contrasted with his insufferable arrogance towards his fellow councillors, who resented the favour he showed to the lower orders of society. With the young King he was excessively strict, keeping the boy continually short of pocket money and banning any pursuits that might tempt him to be extravagant or frivolous.

Hertford had been twice married. His first wife, Katherine Fillol, had been caught in an incestuous affair with his father and banished to a convent. After her death Seymour married Anne Stanhope, who bore him nine children. Edward VI's biographer and contemporary, Sir John Hayward, described her as 'a mannish or rather a devilish woman, for any imperfectibilities intolerable, but for pride monstrous, exceeding subtle and violent'. She was haughty and volatile, and very conscious of her position as the Protector's wife. Mary Tudor was friendly towards her, and wrote frequent letters to her, addressing her as 'My good Nan' or 'My good Gossip'.

On 16 February 1547, Henry VIII was laid to rest in the choir of St George's Chapel, Windsor, in the presence of the new Protector and other members of the Council. Stephen Gardiner, the conservative Bishop of Winchester, celebrated the obsequies, as Katherine Parr watched unseen from Katherine of Aragon's closet in the chapel gallery. None of the King's children were present.

On the following day, Edward VI was knighted by Hertford, who was himself created Duke of Somerset, a title in keeping with his new dignity that brought with it sufficient emoluments to bring his income to a vast £7400 per annum. He was also made Earl Marshal, an office left vacant as a result of the Duke of Norfolk's imprisonment in the Tower by Henry VIII. At the same time, John Dudley was created Earl of Warwick and appointed Great Chamberlain of England. During the month that followed, several other supporters of the new régime were promoted. Somerset's younger brother, Thomas Seymour, was appointed Lord High Admiral in place of John Dudley, and created Baron Seymour of Sudeley. He was also made a councillor and a Knight of the Garter. Paget remained Chief Secretary, while Sir William Petre continued as Secretary and Sir Anthony Browne as Master of the Horse. Thomas Wriothesley was created Earl of

Southampton but deprived of his office of Lord Chancellor, which was bestowed the following October upon Sir Richard Rich, while Katherine Parr's brother William was created Marquess of Northampton.

Yet despite this distribution of the spoils of office, there were tensions on the Council. Warwick, hitherto Somerset's ally, now began nursing ambitions of depriving him of his authority as Lord Protector, and Thomas Seymour was already seething with resentment at having been ousted by his brother from the centre of affairs, for Somerset had been quick to make it clear that he had no intention of permitting Seymour to interfere with the government of the country or allowing him any position of responsibility within the Council.

There was concern also about the heiress to the throne, the Lady Mary. Her father had entrusted his executors with the supervision of her household, and it was soon arranged that a priest was to be always in attendance to say the offices of the Church, which might be attended by local people, who were to be summoned by a bell rung by Mary's clerk of the closet. Every member of the household was to attend these services unless they had a good excuse for not so doing. All persons joining the household had to swear an oath of allegiance to Mary, and undertake to give six months' notice if they left. Those senior attendants who were permitted servants of their own were to engage only 'cleanly young men' over eighteen, who were forbidden to brawl, bicker, swear or gamble at all times except during Yuletide. Mary was allowed to lay down any other rules for the guidance of her staff, and apart from imposing these few restrictions, which could only be to her benefit, the Council left her alone during the early months of Edward's reign.

It suited them very well to have her living quietly in the country, for they were aware of her popularity and her political importance, and feared that she might one day become the focus for opposition against the reformist policies that the Council was determined to introduce. Already there were rumours in France that Charles V was plotting to declare war on England in order to overthrow Edward and set Catholic Mary on the throne. The Pope was known to be working through his agents for the overthrow of what he regarded as the heretical régime in England. Should there be any rebellion in England on Mary's behalf, she could always look to Charles and Rome to support her, which made her a potentially dangerous rival to the new government. She should therefore be encouraged to stay away from court and remain on her estates. Paget wisely urged the Protector to adopt a conciliatory attitude towards Mary, which was not difficult because until now relations between the two had been friendly. Pressure could be brought to bear on her later to make her conform, if necessary.

Unaware of the Council's fears, Mary spent the early part of 1547 at Newhall, Framlingham Castle in Suffolk, or the royal manors of Wanstead and Havering-atte-Bower in Essex. Charles V's ambassador, van der Delft, found himself frustrated in his attempts to gain an audience with her, and wrongly concluded that the Council held her 'in very little account'.

On 19 February, Edward VI made his ceremonial entry into London prior to his coronation, wearing robes of cloth of silver embroidered with gold thread and a belt and cap which glittered with rubies, pearls and diamonds. His horse was caparisoned in crimson satin, and as he rode through the crowded streets his subjects hailed him as a 'young King Solomon' come to restore ancient truth and do away with 'heathen rites and detestable idolatory'. As was customary on such occasions, lavish pageants marked the various stages of the royal progress through the City of London. One portrayed a phoenix – representing Jane Seymour, whose badge had been this mythical bird – descending from Heaven to mate with the crowned lion, representing Henry VIII. Then a young lion stepped forth to be crowned by angels, as the phoenix and the old lion retired. One spectacle that particularly impressed Edward was the Aragonese tight-rope walker in St Paul's Churchyard, who 'ran on his breast from the battlements to the ground'. The King, we are told, 'laughed right heartily' and was reluctant to drag himself away and proceed on his way to Whitehall Palace, where he spent the night.

The next day he was crowned in Westminster Abbey, which had been hung with rich tapestries and strewn with sweet-smelling rushes for the occasion. The nine-year-old King was splendidly clad in a gown of cloth of silver embroidered with rubies and diamonds, girdled with white velvet and Venetian silk, on top of which was a white velvet cloak threaded with Venetian silver; his shoes were white velvet buskins. Once enthroned in St Edward's chair, he was presented with three swords, symbolising his three kingdoms, England, Ireland and France, but, records Sir John Hayward, his first biographer, he demanded a fourth sword, the Bible, 'the sword of the spirit', which he 'preferred before these swords'. Archbishop Cranmer conducted the ceremony, and trumpets sounded as three crowns were placed, one after the other, on the King's head, and a gold ring on his marriage finger. He endured the long hours of ceremony with remarkable patience and gravity, and after the *Te Deum* had been sung, he progressed with great dignity out of the Abbey to where his horse, 'with a caparison of crimson satin embroidered with pearls and damasked gold', was waiting, and greeted the cheering crowds solemnly. After the coronation came banquets and tournaments, in which Thomas Seymour excelled himself.

As king, Edward VI won golden opinions. His councillors hailed him as a new David or Samuel, or 'the young Josias', Josias having been a boy king of Israel who had stamped out idolatry and established the true worship of God. Edward's beauty and intelligence were lauded to the skies, and he was deemed to be so in advance of his years that 'it should seem he were already a father'. Perhaps consciously he took to emulating his own father, whose example he was expected to follow and even excel; in state portraits he adopted the same stance as Henry VIII, feet apart, hand on hip, staring piercingly from the canvas. He never forgot his royal dignity and remained remote and aloof from his councillors and attendants, never showing his emotions nor any affection towards those around him. In his journal, he recorded dispassionately sad or violent events in the lives of those close to him without ever betraying his innermost feelings.

Nicholas Udall spoke for many when he wrote: 'How happy are we Englishmen of such a king, in whose childhood appeareth as perfect grace, virtue, godly zeal, desire of literature, gravity, prudence, justice and magnanimity, as hath heretofore been found in kings of most mature age.' This was not mere flattery, for Edward was indeed remarkably intelligent and had benefited from a fine education. He had a precocious grasp of politics for his age; he knew what was going on in his realm, even if he did not yet fully comprehend all the issues involved.

One issue he very quickly came to understand, though, was religion. In the National Portrait Gallery in London there is a panel painting showing Henry VIII on his deathbed presenting the enthroned Edward VI to his subjects. Beside Edward sit the prominent reformists on the Council, and at the boy's feet lies an open book inscribed 'The word of the Lord endureth for ever'. Crushed beneath the throne are the figures of the Pope and two friars named Idolatry and Feigned Holiness. Here, for all Englishmen to see, was the Protestant champion, whom the Scottish reformer John Knox would describe as 'that most godly and virtuous King that has ever been known to have reigned in England'.

Edward rapidly became a passionate Protestant, bigoted and intolerant. He loathed the Roman Catholic Church and all it stood for, and wrote several tracts defending the royal supremacy and advocating the eradication of abuses within the Church. He loved long, complicated sermons, and would scribble notes in Greek as he listened. It is said that on one occasion he refused to stand on a bible in order to reach a high shelf. During his reign only a few people were burned as heretics, yet this boy did not shrink from signing death warrants when necessary, as in the case of Joan Boacher, executed in 1550 for denying that Jesus Christ had been a human being. As Edward's reputation spread, persecuted Protestants from all over Europe sought refuge in England.

Edward VI's court, however, was anything but godly; in fact, it dismayed the reformers who visited it. Unlike the King, most courtiers were bored by the long sermons favoured by Protestant preachers, preferring to absent themselves in order to indulge in more earthly pleasures such as gambling, drinking and fornicating. Many would have liked to see the King take part in tournaments and other sports, as his father had done, but he seems not to have been that way inclined, and even if he had been, the Council was too concerned for his safety to have allowed it. Indeed, his court was altogether less splendid than his father's had been, even though it inhabited the same sumptuous palaces – Hampton Court, Greenwich, Richmond, Whitehall and Windsor being the most magnificent.

Occasionally, water pageants were mounted, or acrobats and jugglers engaged for the King's amusement. He enjoyed masques and plays, especially if they portrayed the Pope as a villain, as at Shrovetide and Christmas in 1549. Edward was not musical like his father and kept only five musicians on his payroll, engaging others at holiday periods. Twenty-one other personal servants waited on him, ministering to his daily needs. As he grew, his literary interests came to influence the court, as did his piety. John Bale wrote that it was now fashionable for courtiers to pursue 'literature and the elegant arts', while many young noblemen, such as the sons of John Dudley, became sincere converts to Protestantism.

Many might have hoped that Katherine Parr would continue to exert a benevolent and godly influence over the court, but at the beginning of March 1547 the Imperial ambassador reported that she would shortly be taking up residence at Chelsea with 'Madam Elizabeth, daughter of the late King'. Henry VIII had left Katherine well provided for in his will, and the house and manor of Chelsea were her own property. She also owned the manors of Wimbledon and Hanworth. Although Henry had not allowed her any control over the regency or the young King, he had left her £3000 in plate, jewels, household goods and clothing, as well as £1000 in cash, above the jointure allocated by Parliament. He had also granted her precedence before every other lady in the kingdom, a privilege which caused the Protector's wife to seethe ineffectively with jealousy.

Chelsea Old Palace occupied the site of the present Cheyne Walk. Built by Henry VIII, it had been completed around 1540, and boasted many amenities including piped water from a spring in Kensington. The house itself was an attractive red brick building, with windows overlooking the River Thames. When Katherine Parr took up residence here she brought with her a staff of 200, including 120 yeomen who wore her own livery. Having been a loving and responsible stepmother to the Lady Elizabeth, it was natural that the girl should be entrusted to her care. Elizabeth, wrote van der Delft, 'will remain always in the Queen's company', and Katherine would continue to supervise her education. Elizabeth's household, headed by Mrs Ashley and William Grindal, came with her to Chelsea. The Queen also took charge of the late king's great-niece, nine-year-old Lady Jane Grey, whose affection for her may plainly be seen in surviving letters.

On 21 March 1547, Somerset was formally appointed 'Protector of all the realms and domains of the King's Majesty and Governor of his most royal person' and granted full power and authority to rule in the King's name 'until such time as we shall have accomplished the age of eighteen years'. Somerset, however, lacked the presence and authority of Henry VIII and many came to resent his liberal policies and his compassion. He established a court of pleas at his own London house in order that he might hear the cases of poor people, who soon began calling him 'the Good Duke'. Some of his fellow councillors thought him 'so moderate that all thought him their own'; others resented him taking 'the place of a king'. In his turn, Somerset failed to control the more headstrong among the councillors and was reluctant to address himself to the routine business of government. Paget complained on one occasion that the Protector had 'snapped' and 'nipped' so fiercely in Council that one colleague had been reduced to tears, appearing 'almost out of his wits'. At other times Somerset could be unusually tolerant, yet his refusal to allow anyone to be tortured or burned for their religious views was seen in his own age as a sign of weakness. Those who disagreed with him, notably Bishops Gardiner and Bonner, were confined in the Tower but then left unmolested with certain creature comforts; Henry VIII would never have been so lenient. Somerset, however, had no sense of political pragmatism – he was too much of an idealist, and the progressive social policy he favoured in Council, which included fixed rents and the abolition of enclosures, met with derision and suspicion among his own caste, who managed successfully to oppose it.

Although the Protector made a point of criticising wealthy, self-seeking men, his own greed and rapacity were notorious. By 1549 he had built for himself a sumptuous London residence, Somerset House, at the exorbitant cost of £10,000, significantly more than any subject had ever paid for a house. He also converted a former nunnery at Syon in Middlesex into a country house for himself, and had foundations laid for another mansion at Bedwyn Brail in Wiltshire, near Wolfhall, his ancestral home. He was even planning at one stage to demolish Westminster Abbey in order to build another town house. His accounts reveal that he spared no expense in emphasising his status and political pre-eminence.

Somerset was committed to establishing a Protestant state. Henry VIII might have broken with Rome and made himself head of the English Church, but it was still a largely Catholic church, and the King's will bears testimony to his continuing orthodoxy in forms of worship. Both Somerset and Cranmer were eager to carry the Reformation to its logical conclusion; many other lords had profited by it, having received church lands, and were greedy for more. London and some other cities and towns, as well as a core of intellectuals in the universities and gentry in the south-east, were already largely Protestant, though the rest of the country remained Catholic. Relying on religious sentiments in the capital, and ignoring the objections of conservatives on the Council, such as Gardiner and Wriothesley, the Protector and the Archbishop took steps very early in the reign to establish the Protestant faith as the official religion in England, and at Easter Compline was sung in English in the Chapel Royal to signify the King's endorsement of their policies.

The main thorn in the Protector's side during the first months of Edward's reign was his brother, Thomas Seymour, whose elevation to the peerage as Baron Sudeley had brought with it the acquisition of vast estates in Wiltshire and the Welsh Marches. But even this, and a seat on the Council, were not enough for the rampantly ambitious Seymour. His chief desire was to oust his brother from power and rule in his stead, or, if that failed, at least to share the protectorship.

Thomas Seymour was in his late thirties, dashingly handsome and charismatic, and a philanderer. He was tall and athletic, had a luxuriant red beard, and dressed like a peacock; he was boisterous and flamboyant, had a loud, penetrating voice, and a brilliant reputation in the tournament lists. He liked to present an affable and friendly image that was in direct contrast to his brother's Calvinistic gravity, and to reinforce this he displayed an ostentatious generosity that, on the surface, won him many friends. According to Sir Nicholas Throckmorton, a courtier, he was 'hardy, wise and liberal . . . fierce in courage, courtly in fashion, in personage stately, in voice magnificent, but somewhat empty of matter'.

He was, indeed, shallow, irresponsible and dangerously unstable. He thought only of himself and his overweening ambition, and could be unscrupulous and even violent in the pursuit of it. He had even less political judgement than Somerset, of whom he was obsessively jealous, claiming that Henry VIII had never intended that one man should rule both king and country, and through this malice, wrote Throckmorton, 'he went to pot'.

Seymour's festering resentment at being denied any real power led him to contemplate a number of extravagant schemes. First he attempted to suborn the young King, who was already resentful of the restrictions laid upon him by the Protector. Seymour decided to adopt the role of an indulgent and loving uncle, and bribed one of Edward's servants, John Fowler, secretly to take the boy gifts of money. Fowler was also to praise Seymour to the skies and put in a good word for him whenever the occasion arose, so that, when the time came, Edward would support his favourite uncle's bid for power. In the meantime, Seymour was poring over legal tomes and records in an attempt to find a precedent for a joint protectorship.

He was also planning to advance himself by way of a spectacular and advantageous marriage. It seems likely, although there is no direct evidence, that shortly after Henry VIII's death Seymour had asked the Council for permission to marry the Lady Elizabeth, and was refused. Mrs Ashley is said to have been disappointed to learn this, because she herself had encouraged him, saying that he and her charge were well matched. Gregorio Leti, an Italian who wrote a scurrilous biography of Elizabeth in the seventeenth century, reproduces a series of passionate love letters, purportedly written by her and the Admiral during February 1547, in which Seymour proposes marriage and she regretfully refuses, knowing that the Council would never allow it; these letters are almost certainly fictitious, as is much of the other material in Leti's biography.

Undaunted, for there were other fish in the sea, Seymour asked Fowler to sound out the King's opinion with regard to his uncle's marriage. Who would Edward recommend as a suitable wife?

Edward was in no doubt. His Uncle Thomas should marry either Anne of Cleves or 'my sister Mary, to change her opinions'. Bolstered

with royal approval, Seymour again approached the Council, proposing to marry Mary, but Somerset 'reproved him, saying that neither of
them was born to be king, nor to marry a king's daughter'. They should
both 'thank God and be satisfied' with what they had and not presume
to advance themselves any higher. Mary, he knew, would never
consent to such a marriage. Seymour replied angrily that all he sought
was conciliar approval for him to marry Mary, and he would win her in
his own fashion, but at this Somerset exploded with rage, and a violent
argument ensued, which ended with Seymour being warned not to
pursue the matter further. At this the brothers fell out, and the rift
between them grew wider.

Knowing it would be useless to pursue the matter further, Seymour's
matrimonial ambitions settled upon an earlier love, no less a person
than the Queen Dowager, Katherine Parr. Born in 1512, Katherine
had been twice widowed before she married Henry VIII. Around
1542–3, before the King had made his intentions clear, she had become
romantically involved with Thomas Seymour, but, as she later wrote,
although they planned to marry she was 'overruled by a higher power'.
Now, four years later, she was still only thirty-five, comely, and also
very rich. Moreover, by virtue of her rank, she was greatly respected
throughout the kingdom. Marriage with Katherine would confer upon
Seymour considerable status and, he hoped, influence, and so he began
to call secretly at Chelsea to pay court to her.

It seems that Katherine had never forgotten her earlier love for the
Admiral, for in no time at all she was responding passionately to his
addresses. Confronted by his charm and masculinity, all her piety and
learning, and her innate good sense, failed her. By May 1547, the lovers
had decided to marry and were engaged in an affectionate correspondence. In one letter Katherine wrote, 'I would not have you think that
this mine honest good will toward you proceed of any sudden motion
of passion. For as truly as God is God, my mind was fully bent before
the other time I was at liberty to marry you before any other man I
knew.' Now that they had been given a second chance of happiness,
she could only conclude that 'God is a marvellous man.'

With little conviction, she protested that they should wait two years
before they married, knowing full well that the Council would
disapprove of her marrying so soon after the late King's death, but
Seymour had little difficulty in overruling her scruples, and they were
married secretly, possibly in late April or early May. Afterwards, he
would visit her at Chelsea in the middle of the night, she having
arranged to leave a gate unlocked to facilitate his secret entry to the
grounds.

Queen Katherine had insisted that the marriage not be made public until she had had a chance to seek the King's blessing on it in person, but servants gossiped and rumours spread quickly. Early that summer Mrs Ashley met Seymour by chance in St James's Park and could not resist chiding him for failing to pursue his suit to the Lady Elizabeth.

'I have heard someone say that you should have my lady,' she told him archly.

'Nay,' he replied, in affable mood, 'I love not to lose my life for a wife. It has been spoken unto, but it cannot be. But I will promise to have the Queen.'

'It is past promise,' retorted Mrs Ashley, 'as I hear you are married already.' The Admiral said nothing, smiled and moved on.

Katherine Parr was anxious that the King should not think her disrespectful of his father's memory by remarrying so soon after his death, and fearful of the consequences of what she and Seymour had done. In May she paid a visit to the court and confessed all to her stepson, who seems to have taken the news well. On 30 May, he wrote to her, 'Since you love my father, I cannot but much esteem you; since you love me I cannot but love you in return; and since you love the Word of God, I do love and admire you with my whole heart. Wherefore if there be anything wherein I may do you a kindness, either in word or deed, I will do it willingly.'

He had agreed not to disclose Katherine's secret to the Protector until relations between Somerset and Seymour had grown less frosty; remembering his brother's reaction to his other marriage proposals, the Admiral had no wish to provoke further hostility. Nor did Katherine Parr wish to be a suitor for Somerset's favour. She told her husband, 'I would not wish you to importune for his goodwill. I would desire you might obtain the King's letters in your favour and also the aid and furtherance of the most notable of the Council.'

This was exactly what Seymour was now engaged upon doing, and he was also trying to obtain the support of the King's sisters. Early in June he wrote to the Lady Mary, telling her only that he had asked Queen Katherine to be his wife, and praying her to use her influence on his behalf and that of the Queen, whose close friend she had hitherto been. But Mary was horrified to learn that Katherine Parr had encouraged another man's advances so soon after the King's death. She replied,

> I have received your letter wherein I perceive strange news concerning a suit you have in hand to the Queen for marriage, for the sooner obtaining whereof you seem to think that my letters

might do you pleasure. My lord, in this case I trust your wisdom doth consider that if it were for my nearest kinsman and dearest friend alive, of all other creatures in the world it standeth least with my poor honour to be a meddler in this matter, considering whose wife Her Grace was of late; and besides, if she be minded to grant your suit, my letters shall do you but small pleasure. If the remembrance of the King's Majesty my father will not suffer her to grant your suit, I am nothing able to persuade her to forget the loss of him who is as yet very ripe in mine own remembrance. Wherefore I shall most earnestly require you to think none unkindness in me though I refuse to be a meddler in this matter, assuring you that (wooing matters set apart, wherein I being a maid, am nothing cunning) if otherwise it shall lie in my little power to do you pleasure, I shall be glad to do it.

For all the courteous tone of her letter, Mary was furious, both with Katherine Parr and the Admiral, and from henceforth her relations with her stepmother were cordial but reserved; the two women never recaptured the intimacy of former times. Mary was worried also that her sister Elizabeth might be in some moral danger through residing in the Queen's household, and wrote inviting the girl to come and live with her, stressing why such a move was of urgent necessity and expressing her sense of outrage at seeing 'the scarcely cold body of the King our father so shamelessly dishonoured'. His memory, she assured her sister, 'being so glorious in itself, cannot be subject to those stains which can only defile the persons who have wrought them'. But she did not want to offend the Queen, who had been kind to her, and Elizabeth 'must use much tact, for fear of appearing ungrateful'. Elizabeth, however, dissimulated; she was happy at Chelsea and did not wish to leave, so she replied that she would see how matters turned out. This did not satisfy Mary, who was already convinced that Elizabeth was becoming as light morally as her mother had been.

The Admiral, meanwhile, was still in regular contact with the King through the offices of John Fowler, who now slept in Edward's bedroom every night and therefore had the opportunity of private conversations with him. Edward was unhappy, and made no secret of it. His 'uncle of Somerset' was very severe with him and allowed him few treats. His tutors were strict and left him little time for leisure pursuits. He had no money with which to reward those who performed small services for him, and thus felt less than a king.

Edward had come to hate Somerset during the last few months and turned for comfort to his other uncle, who was only too willing to send him pocket money, often as much as £40, and who had begun to correspond with him in secret. Once, when, to cheer the boy up, the Admiral voiced the hope that Somerset was older and might not live long, Edward replied, 'It were better he should die.' If that happened, he told Seymour, he would himself seize the reins of government and rule under the guidance of his favourite uncle, which was music to Seymour's ears. Before long, the King was sending demands for money through Fowler, which his uncle was happy to satisfy, believing that the boy would use what influence he had when the time came, and would work to further the Admiral's ambitions.

Edward was true to his word. When news of the Admiral's marriage to the Queen leaked out at the end of June, he publicly gave them his blessing.

'I will provide for you both,' he wrote, 'that hereafter, if any grief befall, I shall be a sufficient succour in your godly or praisable enterprises.' In the face of such an open demonstration of royal favour, an enraged Somerset could do nothing, although he had been 'much offended and displeased' by the news. Nor had the lovers committed any crime; there was no chance now of Katherine being pregnant by the late King or disrupting the royal succession by the birth of a child whose paternity was doubtful. Yet the Protector's wife had her petty revenge. Furious at having to yield precedence to the wife of her husband's despised younger brother, she persuaded Somerset to confiscate the Queen's jewels, which were kept in safety in the treasury, on the grounds that they were state property and could not be willed to a queen dowager. These jewels had, in fact, been handed down from queen to queen through the ages, and some were of great antiquity, but Henry VIII had provided that Katherine Parr should enjoy them until such time as the young King married. Now Anne, Duchess of Somerset, was determined to wear them herself. The Admiral and his wife must not think that they could offend her and get away with it.

2

Amorous Intrigues

That summer, the swaggering, larger-than-life figure of the Admiral moved into the household at Chelsea and set himself to charm the inhabitants. 'His service was ever joyful,' recorded one man who served him at this time. He treated both his equals and social inferiors with calculated affability, and under his influence Queen Katherine's rather staid household grew lively and more relaxed. Each day was a new round of pleasure, and if Katherine was perturbed by her husband remembering urgent matters of business just as she was expecting him to accompany her to the reformed services in the family chapel, she did not complain.

The Lady Elizabeth, now approaching the impressionable age of fourteen, was especially vulnerable to the charm and handsome presence of her new stepfather, who was now her nominal guardian. At Chelsea, or the Queen's country house at Hanworth, or the Admiral's London home, Seymour Place, she became increasingly – and dangerously – aware of him as a man to whom she was, perhaps fearfully, attracted. Nor was he ignorant of her interest, for she was too young and inexperienced to conceal it from him. Katherine Parr might think her still a child, but Seymour was all too conscious that she was budding into womanhood and developing a talent for flirtation such as had made her mother notorious. For him, it was a piquant situation, made all the more alluring by the fact that Elizabeth was second-in-line to the throne. While, on the face of it, the Queen's household was an oasis of calm and happiness in a troubled world, it was in fact shortly to witness a drama that would end in tragedy for each of its chief inhabitants.

Unaware of her sister's peril, the Lady Mary was at this time touring her properties in East Anglia and appointing the chief officers of her household. Robert Rochester, a middle-aged man who had looked after her accounts for some years and hailed from Essex, was made Controller, while other local gentlemen, Henry Jerningham, Sir Francis Englefield and Edward Waldegrave, were also given positions of responsibility: Englefield was probably Chamberlain and Waldegrave Steward. Among the thirty-two male servants listed as being in Mary's household, only Richard Wilbraham and Randall Dodd had a record of long service. There were four chaplains, and a bevy of ladies-in-waiting, including Susan Clarencieux, Eleanor Kempe, Frideswide Strelley and perhaps at this time Jane Dormer, who, unlike the others, was very young and had not served Mary since the 1530s. Altogether the household numbered in excess of a hundred persons.

In East Anglia, Mary was warmly received wherever she went, giving the lie to van der Delft's claim that June that she was 'less and less regarded' and had been incarcerated in a house in 'the north'. However, in expressing his disapproval of the religious changes that were then taking place in England, he declared he was confident that Mary would remain firm in the ancient faith in which she had been raised; he had heard that she was hearing as many as four masses a day.

In July, the ambassador finally managed to obtain an audience with Mary, who explained that she had been living in some seclusion because she was in mourning for her father. She had not dined in public since his death, she said, but graciously invited van der Delft to share her table. 'She seemed to have entire confidence in me,' he wrote. He was scandalised to learn that the Council had not seen fit to disclose to her details of the dowry allocated her by Henry VIII, and expressed his opinion that her income was insufficient for a princess of her standing.

During the conversation Mary asked him what he thought about Queen Katherine's remarriage. He told her he quite approved of it, and divulged how rumour had had it that Seymour had first meant to marry Mary herself.

Mary laughed. 'I have never spoken to him in my life,' she said, 'and have only seen him once.'

During the next two years she would in fact be the subject of several marriage negotiations, but Charles V was probably correct in his opinion that the Council would not allow Mary to marry a foreign prince until King Edward was of an age to marry and father children, in case her husband led a rebellion on behalf of the Catholic heiress.

At Chelsea, John Ashley, husband of Kat, had noticed that, whenever the Admiral's name was mentioned, the Lady Elizabeth's ears pricked up, that when he was praised in conversation, she showed inordinate pleasure, and that she blushed when she spoke his name. The signs were ominous, and he said as much to his wife.

'Take heed,' he warned, 'for I fear that the Lady Elizabeth do bear some affection to my Lord Admiral.' But Mrs Ashley had a soft spot for Seymour and would hear no ill spoken of him. In fact Kat had encouraged her charge's infatuation by telling her it had been she whom he had wished to marry before all others. In vain did John Ashley point out the potential dangers in the situation; if there were any impropriety between Elizabeth and the Admiral both would be guilty of high treason, for which the penalty for Elizabeth would be death by decapitation or burning. Kat Ashley, however, naively believed the girl's interest in Seymour to be entirely innocent; she herself had fallen victim to his charisma, and could see no wrong in it. Had she been less irresponsible, she might have averted one of the most distressing episodes of Elizabeth's life.

We know about the events that followed from the signed depositions of Mrs Ashley, Thomas Parry, the princess's cofferer, and Elizabeth herself, given under cross examination early in 1549, and preserved in the State Papers of the period.

According to these statements, the Admiral had keys made for himself for all the rooms in Chelsea Old Palace, including one for Elizabeth's bedchamber, which was above Katherine Parr's. Then, although he had only been married for a few weeks,

> He would come many mornings into the Lady Elizabeth's chamber before she was ready, and sometimes before she did rise; and if she were up he would bid her good morrow and ask how she did, and strike her upon the back or on the buttocks familiarly, and so go forth to his lodgings; and sometimes go through to the maidens and play with them, and so forth. And if [Elizabeth] were in her bed he would put open the curtains and bid her good morrow, and make as though he would come at her, and she would go further into the bed so that he could not come at her.

This might have been – and indeed was – looked upon by Katherine Parr and Mrs Ashley as innocent fun, yet its effect on a young and infatuated girl was devastating. Seymour's arrival in Elizabeth's bedchamber, and his over-familiarity with her person, could not but have awakened her adolescent sexuality and aroused feelings she was powerless to control. In fact, it seemed as if he was deliberately doing his best to excite her. On the face of it the proprieties were being observed because Mrs Ashley was always present when these romps took place, but she seems not to have noticed that Elizabeth's response to her stepfather's teasing was not that of a child.

The Admiral then began to send Elizabeth and Kat suggestive notes, asking if Kat's 'great buttocks' had grown 'any less or not'. When the household moved to Seymour Place, he took to coming up 'every morning in his nightgown, barelegged in his slippers'. Elizabeth, becoming increasingly self-conscious, had in consequence made it her habit to get up early so that he found her dressed and 'at her book'; all he could do was look in at the gallery door and bid her good morrow as usual. Even Mrs Ashley could not ignore his behaviour, and told him furiously that it was an unseemly sight to come visiting a maiden's chamber so improperly dressed. Seymour was annoyed with her, 'but he left it' and did not present himself again in his nightgown.

Back at Chelsea he was up to his old antics. When Elizabeth heard him unlocking her door, she would jump out of bed and summon her maids-of-honour, who would hide with her behind the bed curtain; but Seymour waited until they came out. One morning he tried to kiss Elizabeth as she lay in bed. Again, Kat remonstrated, and 'bade him go away for shame', for already there was gossip. 'These things are complained of, and my lady is evil spoken of.'

'By God's precious soul,' he retorted hotly, 'I mean no evil, and I will not leave it! The Lady Elizabeth is like a daughter to me. I will tell my Lord Protector how I am slandered, and I will not leave off!'

Since 'she could not make him leave it', Mrs Ashley went to the Queen and voiced her concern about the Admiral's behaviour and the gossip and rumours that were spreading through the household. But Katherine Parr 'made a small matter of it', promising only to accompany her husband to Elizabeth's room in the mornings. She even joined in two of his frolics whilst staying at Hanworth, when both she and Seymour 'tickled my Lady Elizabeth in her bed'. And whilst in the gardens at Hanworth, the Queen was present when he romped with her stepdaughter and even held the girl when he cut her black gown into 'a hundred pieces' with a pair of scissors. 'When I came up,' recounted an outraged Mrs Ashley, Elizabeth 'assured me she could not strive withal' because of being pinioned by her stepmother. On this occasion, the governess felt, matters had gone too far, but the Queen did not seem to share in her disapproval.

Throughout these heady months, Elizabeth had continued to study under William Grindal, making brilliant progress. Roger Ascham was still taking a proprietorial interest in her education, hoping to secure an appointment as tutor to 'that noble imp'; in his letters to Mrs Ashley he was fulsome in his praises of her and her charge, and of Grindal, not knowing 'whether to admire more the wit of her who learnt, or the diligence of him who taught'. He sent Elizabeth a book in Italian, arranged for her pens to be mended, and constantly sent commendations to 'all the company of godly gentlewomen' at Chelsea.

One of those godly gentlewomen was Lady Jane Grey, Elizabeth's cousin. Born in October 1537, she was the eldest of the three daughters born to Henry Grey, Marquess of Dorset, and Frances Brandon, Henry VIII's niece, the daughter of his sister Mary Tudor by her second husband, Charles Brandon, Duke of Suffolk. Tiny in stature, with fair, freckled skin and sandy hair, Jane possessed a formidable intellect. She was almost the same age as King Edward, and since her infancy her ambitious parents had nursed dreams that she might one day be his wife and hence queen of England. They had structured her education accordingly, so as to make her a fit mate for a king, and appointed her first tutor, a young Cambridge scholar called John Aylmer, her father's chaplain, when she was only four. Aylmer began her education by carrying her around in his arms and teaching her good diction. The little girl was not used to such kindness, for throughout her short life her parents regarded her as a pawn to be moved at will, and ill-treated her in body and spirit.

Dorset was by nature self-indulgent and lazy, and thought of little but hunting. At the time of his marriage in 1533 he had been 'young, lusty and poor' with little or no experience of politics, and he owed his rise to prominence to his wife's royal connections and her aggressive ambition. He was impulsive, pleasure loving and 'a great dicer and swearer' who tended to dither when it came to making decisions, leaving them ultimately to his wife. Van der Delft thought him 'a senseless creature', who loved intrigue for its own sake but had little talent for it. Nor did he manage the family finances efficiently, and was frequently teetering on the verge of bankruptcy. Yet he could be generous when it suited him and affable to all except his hapless daughter Jane. Although he shared her love of learning, he regarded her as a poor substitute for the son who had died young before her birth.

Frances Brandon, on the other hand, was forceful, determined to have her own way, and greedy for power and riches. She ruled her husband and daughters tyrannically and, in the case of the latter, often cruelly, and was utterly insensitive to the feelings of others. Physically, she bore a marked resemblance to Henry VIII, and in later life she grew corpulent as he did. Yet she always enjoyed a robust constitution and was never happier than when she was on horseback, enjoying the outdoor sports that she shared with her husband. Although she was clever and well-educated, one friend, Sir Richard Moryson, spoke for many when he said, 'It is a great pity that so goodly a wit waiteth upon so froward a will.'

The Dorsets owned a London residence, Dorset House at Westminster, but their chief seat was the palatial, red brick Bradgate Manor in Leicestershire, where Jane had been born. Bradgate had been in the hands of the Grey family since the fifteenth century, but the house, which is now a ruin, had been built by Dorset's father and boasted turrets and a gatehouse, and was set in a deer park.

Lady Jane Grey had two sisters: Katherine, born in 1540, who appears to have been the beauty of the family, and Mary, born in 1545, who was a hunchbacked dwarf. To their credit, her parents did not hide her away but arranged for her to benefit from the same education as her sister Katherine, who was also being tutored by John Aylmer. Neither Katherine nor Mary showed the same intellectual ability as Jane. Katherine was a delicate little thing with red-gold hair, beautiful eyes and a straight nose, who spent most of her time in the country, devoting herself to her studies and girlish pleasures. She was placid and shy, and loved nothing better than to play with her pet birds, dogs and monkeys. At the same time she was imbibing the principles of the Protestant faith, to which she would remain devoted all her life.

When Jane Grey was six, another tutor, Dr Harding, was engaged to teach her French, Greek, Spanish and Italian. A visiting master taught her handwriting, and another dancing and deportment. She loved music, but her parents strictly limited the amount of time she was allowed to spend practising on her lute, harp and cithern.

The daily routine followed by Jane and her sisters was demanding. Up at six, they were served bread, meat and ale for breakfast before they visited their parents and asked for their daily blessing; one suspects this must have been something of an ordeal, for the Dorsets were not above administering beatings or delivering crushing criticisms for the slightest failing. In the morning, the girls were taught Latin and Greek, Jane receiving extra tuition in Hebrew. After they had dined they learned modern languages and music, or read the Bible and the classics. When supper was over they were expected to practise their dancing or needlework before going to bed at nine. This régime left them little time to themselves and Jane found it particularly irksome to be taken along on hunting or hawking expeditions with her parents; her obvious distaste for the sports they loved made them even more irritable with her, as did her frequent bouts of nervous exhaustion.

As a consequence of their ambitions for her, the Dorsets insisted that

Jane be treated as a princess of the blood, and dressed her in rich silks, damasks and velvets, although her mother constantly expressed the opinion that her daughter was unlikely to go far on looks alone. Jane, whose growing love for the reformed faith portended an adult fanaticism, hated this ostentation, preferring the sober black and white that she fancied became a Protestant maiden.

Two people brought some comfort to the troubled girl in her early years. One was her nurse, Mrs Ellen, and the other was John Aylmer. Aylmer was a vital, humorous little man, full of enthusiasm for the subjects he taught, and possessed of a great love for England. It was he who coined the phrase 'God is an Englishman'. He loved his precocious charge and the pains he took over her education bore fruit in its spectacular results, for it soon became apparent that, in intellect, Jane excelled even the Lady Elizabeth and the King. Yet Aylmer regarded his greatest achievement as being the instilling of strong Protestant beliefs and principles in his pupil.

Jane's life changed dramatically when, at the age of nine, she was sent to live with Katherine Parr to learn manners and social graces whilst continuing her education. The Dorsets felt that the Queen Dowager might be persuaded to use what influence she had to further their ambitions for their daughter, although in fact Katherine Parr had no say in political affairs and rarely saw the King. What she did do was welcome Jane warmly into her household and give her the motherly affection of which she was starved. At Chelsea, Jane was praised for her prowess and 'towardness', and soon the Queen's ladies were openly predicting that she would one day be queen, and told her so. This alone ensured that she was treated with deference and respect.

Soon after he moved in with the Queen, the Admiral saw in Lady Jane a means of furthering his own ambitions. Jane was fourth in line of succession, and in his opinion she would make an ideal mate for the King in every respect: they would be well-matched in birth, age and intellect. It did not matter that the Protector was planning to marry Edward to a Spanish princess, and Lady Jane to his own son, Lord Hertford, for the Admiral took a perverse pleasure in thwarting his brother's plans, relying on his influence with King Edward to bring about the desired end to his ambitions. Edward could not but favour the uncle who had arranged such a suitable marriage for him, and Seymour would have the satisfaction of seeing Somerset discountenanced.

Jane, Seymour knew, was 'most dear to the King, both in regard of religion and of her knowledge'. However, on the rare occasions when they met, court etiquette was so rigid as to prevent any familiarity or expression of feelings, and both were reserved children anyway. Jane would curtsey three times when she came before Edward and kneel while they conversed. They might play cards after he had graciously permitted her to sit on a cushion or low stool, and when she finally retired from his presence she would kiss his hand and walk backwards out of the room. They were never alone, as her two ladies-in-waiting attended her throughout the interview. Yet Bishop John Bale, the chronicler, who was close to Edward VI, was convinced that it was Jane whom the King wanted to marry.

What the Admiral and Bale did not know, however, was that Edward, as he confided to his journal, was determined to fulfil his father's wishes and marry Mary, Queen of Scots; if that were not possible, he hoped to make a marriage alliance with a European power that would secure for him 'a well-stuffed and jewelled bride'. Jane, who could bring him neither wealth nor political advantage, did not come into his schemes.

In blissful ignorance of this, Seymour sent John Harington, one of his gentlemen, to set Dorset's mind at rest with 'fair promises' that Jane 'shall be placed in marriage much to your comfort', according to the official account in the State Papers. Asked who the bridegroom would be, Harington replied, 'I doubt not but you shall see him marry her to the King. And fear you not, he will bring it to pass.'

Dorset agreed to let Jane remain at Chelsea for the time being, but when several weeks had passed without him receiving any further message from the Admiral, he went to Chelsea himself and spoke with him in the garden. Seymour explained that, if Dorset wanted to see Jane married to the King, he must appoint the Admiral her guardian. After some discussion, Dorset agreed to sell Jane's wardship and marriage for the sum of £2000, whereupon Seymour paid him £500 on account. But although he later expressed to Harington his opinion that King Edward, when he came of age, would want to marry Jane, he was in no position to take any steps to further negotiations for such an alliance – Somerset would have vetoed such a scheme with alacrity. Yet Dorset seemed content to wait, and Jane therefore remained in the Queen's household.

Using Fowler as a go-between, the Admiral suggested to King Edward that he console himself for the loss of the little Scottish Queen by considering marriage with Lady Jane, but Edward showed he was not interested. Moreover, his tutor, John Cheke, had become suspicious of Seymour's ambitions, having discovered that the King had far more money in his possession than he was supposed to have. Edward confessed to him that the Admiral had sent it, and also told him about the proposed marriage. Cheke was alarmed, and went straight to Somerset. The Protector, angry at his brother's meddling, summoned him to court and berated him soundly for his presumption. Then he calmed down and did his best to effect a reconciliation. Peace was restored, at least on the surface, but the Admiral's resentment and jealousy still simmered.

By the autumn of 1547, the government's programme of religious reform was advancing steadily. English was to be used instead of Latin in church services, the veneration of images and relics was to cease, restrictions on preaching and private reading of the Scriptures were to be eased, chantries were to be abolished and sold, and schools endowed with the proceeds – some King Edward VI grammar schools still exist today. A number of Henry VIII's treason statutes, heresy laws and his Act of the Six Articles were all abolished, heralding a period of greater religious tolerance. Most clergy accepted the changes without protest; a few Catholic bishops, such as Stephen Gardiner of Winchester and Edmund Bonner of London, publicly deplored the changes, but few supported them.

Not so the Lady Mary. When she heard that the sacrament of the mass was no longer celebrated in Somerset's household, she felt compelled to write to the Protector in protest. Her father, she pointed out, had left the realm 'in godly order and quietness', but the present government seemed to be doing its best to promote heresy and disorder by introducing new-fangled methods of worship. She was concerned that the King, who was still only a child and incapable of making mature judgements in religious matters, would be led astray.

Somerset replied courteously, expressing astonishment at her concerns and asserting that most subjects approved of the King's 'godly proceedings', pointing out that it was people like herself who were causing disruption. He did not wish to persecute her, and he would leave her alone to practise her religion in peace, but she must not challenge her brother's authority nor his lawful decrees. Edward was committed, he said, to doing away with 'popish doctrine'. Mary realised she was being offered an ultimatum, and forbore to argue further for the time being.

By November, the Admiral's jealousy of his brother had become obsessive. Having suborned the King by giving him money, he was urging Edward to sign a document to be laid before the newly-convened Parliament, in which he asked that the offices of Protector and Governor of the King's Person be divided between both uncles.

Edward was reluctant to sign it, and asked Cheke for advice. Cheke warned him against becoming involved in the Admiral's schemes, which could only compromise him, and consequently Edward refused to sign. Seymour, full of grievances, threatened to 'make this the blackest Parliament that ever was in England'. His friends tried to calm him down, but he cried that he could better live without the Protector than the Protector without him.

'If any one goes about to speak evil of the Queen,' he roared, 'I will take my fist to his ears, from the highest to the lowest.' He was then seen skulking in St James's Palace, where the King was in residence, and was heard to declare that he wished he had Edward at home with him in his house. He then went further, averring that it would not be difficult to steal the boy away from under the Protector's nose.

The Admiral's flirtation with the Lady Elizabeth was still going on, but the atmosphere in his household, now based at Hanworth, was becoming strained because Katherine Parr was growing suspicious. Evidently she had voiced her fears to her husband, who had immediately, it seems, made up some wild tale about Elizabeth having an affair with another man. The Queen went straight to Mrs Ashley and told her that 'my Lord Admiral looked in at the gallery window and saw my Lady Elizabeth cast her arms about a man's neck'. The governess questioned her charge carefully as to what had happened, but Elizabeth 'denied it weeping, and bade ask all her women'. Ashley was satisfied that the girl was innocent and that the Admiral's tale could not have been true, 'for there came no man [to the household] but Grindal, the Lady Elizabeth's schoolmaster'. Grindal was the last man to have attempted such familiarity; he died of plague in January 1548, which places this incident in the latter part of 1547. It was Mrs Ashley's belief that it was the Queen who had invented the story, so as to make the governess 'take more heed and be in watch betwixt [Elizabeth] and my Lord Admiral', though this seems uncharacteristic of Katherine Parr.

Fortunately, Elizabeth was invited to Hampton Court for Christmas, which afforded her some respite from a situation which was becoming increasingly fraught. Yet there was to be no intimacy with her brother, for the formality surrounding his every move was more daunting than ever. An Italian visitor to England, Petruccio Ubaldini, could not believe what he was seeing and condemned it as excessive. Elizabeth might 'neither sit under a canopy nor on a chair, but must sit on a mere bench which is provided with a cushion, and so far distant from the head of the table and the King that the canopy does not overhang her. The ceremonies observed before sitting down at table are truly laughable. I have seen, for example, the Princess [*sic*] Elizabeth drop on one knee five times before her brother, before she took her place.' Mary was also a guest at court, but remained in the background, although relations between her and the King were as friendly as ever.

Elizabeth returned home in January to find that Grindal had died. It was soon known that she was now without a tutor, and Roger Ascham prepared to seize his chance. On 12 February 1548 he wrote to John Cheke:

> The Lady Elizabeth is thinking of having me in the place of Grindal. I was with the most illustrious lady during these last days. She signified to me her pleasure and I did not try to make any bargain for my own advantage, but at once declared that I was ready to obey her orders.

The Queen and the Admiral, however, who were then in London, had chosen one Master Goldsmith to replace Grindal. Ascham, hiding his disappointment, told Elizabeth she must submit to her guardians' judgement, but Elizabeth had no intention of doing so. She herself travelled to London and persuaded her stepmother to change her mind. Ascham's appointment was confirmed and he obtained leave from the University of Cambridge to join the Queen's household.

Ascham hailed from Yorkshire. Still in his thirties, he was a brilliant teacher, and already enjoyed an international reputation as a scholar. He had travelled throughout western Europe and regularly corresponded with foreign intellectuals. In 1545, he had published *Toxophilus*, a popular treatise on archery, a sport of which he was extremely fond. He was also a master of calligraphy who did much to promote the use of Italic handwriting; Elizabeth's beautiful hand owed much to his influence. Ascham was also acclaimed as 'one of the politest Latin writers of that generation', Cicero being his favourite author. His chief vice was gambling; he usually lost.

In his book *The Schoolmaster* Ascham set forth his progressive ideas on education. He deplored the current practice of beating, by which 'children are driven to hate learning before they know what learning means'. Although, by today's standards, he set a vast amount of work, he believed, as he told Mrs Ashley, that 'if you pour much drink into a goblet, the most part will dash out and run over'. In Ascham's view, it was the carrot, and not the stick, that worked.

His curriculum centred upon the classics and the Scriptures. The study of classics relied upon a fine knowledge of Latin and Greek, in which Elizabeth was already becoming proficient; Ascham now introduced his technique of double-translation, by which his pupil translated texts from Cicero or Demosthenes into English and then back into either Latin or Greek. 'She readeth more Greek every day than some prebendaries of this Church do [in] a whole week,' commented her tutor with pride. Every morning, they read together the works of the ancient Greeks, such as the tragedies of Sophocles or the orations of Isocrates. Each day began with a reading from the Greek Testament. These works, thought Ascham, would allow Elizabeth to develop 'purity of style, and her mind derive instruction that would be of value to her to meet every contingency of life'.

The afternoons were given over to the study of Latin, which was based on the works of Cicero or Livy, or to the study of theology. For this, Ascham set the works of St Cyprian, or the German reformer Philip Melanchthon, which he considered best suited, 'after the Holy Scriptures, to teach [Elizabeth] the foundations of religion, together with elegant language and sound doctrine'.

But there was more to Ascham than this, for he inspired in his charge a life-long love of riding and hunting, pastimes they frequently enjoyed after lessons were over. 'Neither did she neglect music,' which Ascham also loved; she practised regularly on lute and virginals, and also learned to dance 'in the Italian manner'.

Under Ascham's guidance, Elizabeth made outstanding progress. Of all the learned young ladies he knew, she was, he wrote, 'the brightest star'. In his correspondence with European scholars, he would constantly refer to her accomplishments with justifiable pride. He had never, he wrote, seen a quicker apprehension or a more retentive memory. 'I teach her tongues to speak,' he told John Aylmer 'and her modest and maidenly looks teach me works to do. For I think she is the best disposed to any in all Europe.' He was entranced by her gracious manners and the simplicity of her clothes, a style expected of devout Protestant females. 'She greatly prefers a simple elegance to show and splendour, despising the outward adorning of plaiting the hair and wearing of gold.'

The result of all this tuition was a young woman with a great capacity for hard work who could converse knowledgeably on any intellectual subject, and whose love of learning was such that she kept up the habit of daily study throughout her long life, spending three hours a day reading history, which was her favourite subject. Moreover, her classical education and skill in linguistics was the best possible preparation for a Renaissance ruler.

The presence of Roger Ascham in her household could not, however, prevent Thomas Seymour from overshadowing Elizabeth's life. Early in 1548, she told her cofferer, Thomas Parry, 'that she feared the Admiral loved her but too well, and that the Queen was jealous of them both'. All the same, she was overwhelmed by her own feelings and desires.

Katherine Parr was indeed growing suspicious. In the early spring of 1548 she found herself, at the age of thirty-six, pregnant with her first child, and very sick as a result. No longer did she wish to join in her husband's early morning romps with Elizabeth; the imminence of motherhood had brought out the responsible side in her, and she was inclined to view the Admiral's pranks as tedious and even threatening.

Matters very soon came to a head as, according to Mrs Ashley, the Queen, 'suspecting the often access of the Admiral to my Lady Elizabeth's Grace', and finding one day that both had disappeared, went looking for them. To her horror, she 'came suddenly upon them, where they were all alone, he having her in his arms. Wherefore the Queen fell out, both with the Admiral and with Her Grace also.'

Shocked, Katherine Parr summoned Mrs Ashley 'and told her her fancy in that matter', showing, understandably, 'much displeasure' and some alarm, because Elizabeth was second in line to the throne and a minor under her protection. If the Queen made a public show of her anger, there would be a scandal which would probably ruin them all. For the present, therefore, she concentrated on venting her wrath upon the unfortunate governess. Elizabeth had behaved disgracefully, showing marked ingratitude for her stepmother's kindness; Ashley had failed in her duty towards Elizabeth and the Queen; and the Admiral's conduct was vile and inexcusable, for while Elizabeth was an innocent girl of fourteen, he was an experienced man of the world.

After this painful interview, feeling sick and exhausted, Queen Katherine decided that Elizabeth must be removed from this dangerous situation, right out of the Admiral's orbit. She therefore wrote to Sir Anthony and Lady Denny, asking them if the girl might come to stay with them at their house at Cheshunt in Hertfordshire. Joan Denny was Kat Ashley's sister, so it was an ideal arrangement. We do not know if the Queen told the Dennys the real reason for the visit, or if she made her pregnancy the excuse for it. They were only too happy to oblige, and when she received word of this the Queen sent for Elizabeth and told her that she was to leave her household. There was no argument or open breach. Katherine told her stepdaughter that a princess in her position had been foolish to court such a scandal and that she must be sent away for her own protection. Elizabeth, having been shocked into an awareness of how badly she had behaved, was now terrified of the consequences, and begged the Queen to let her know if there was any gossip about her. Katherine Parr did not think there would be because the matter had been handled so discreetly, but assured Elizabeth she would inform her if she heard anything detrimental.

Elizabeth left Chelsea with her household on the day after Whit Sunday. She was quiet and withdrawn, yet parted on good terms with her stepmother and the Admiral, who was sufficiently chastened to humour his wife, especially in view of the hoped-for male heir she was carrying. No one, except John and Kat Ashley, and perhaps the Dennys, knew the reason behind Elizabeth's departure, and it seemed that the danger of a scandal had been averted.

Sir Anthony Denny and his wife received Elizabeth warmly. Cheshunt was a large, moated house built around a courtyard and boasting a forty-foot-long great hall with an impressive timbered roof. Here, Elizabeth settled down to her studies with Roger Ascham, calmer now, although her conscience still troubled her about her behaviour towards Katherine Parr. She now realised that, in sending her away, Katherine had been acting for the best.

Elizabeth remained on good terms with the Queen and the Admiral throughout that spring and summer, and corresponded with them regularly. Two of her letters to Katherine Parr survive. In June, fearful that the Queen thought ill of her, she wrote,

> Although I could not be plentiful in giving thanks for the manifold kindness received at Your Highness's hand at my departure, yet I am something to be borne withal, for truly I was replete with sorrow to depart from Your Highness, especially leaving you undoubtful of health. And albeit I answered little, I weighed it more deeper when you said you would warn me of all evilnesses that you should hear of me; for if Your Grace had not a good opinion of me, you would not have offered friendship to me that way, that all men judge the contrary. But what more may I say, than thank God for providing such friends for me, desiring God to enrich me with their long life, and me in grace no less thankful to receive it than I now am glad in writing to show it; and although I have plenty of matter [i.e. news], here I will stay, for I know you are not quiet to read.
>
> From Cheston [*sic*], this present Saturday.
> Your Highness's humble daughter, Elizabeth.

On Wednesday, 13 June, the Queen and the Admiral moved to Sudeley Castle in Gloucestershire, recently presented to them by the King. They planned to stay there until the birth of the Queen's child, which was expected in late August. Both were still in touch by letter with Elizabeth. She had asked that the Admiral perform some small unspecified service for her, but he had been unable to oblige and had written to apologise. She replied,

> My Lord, you needed not to send an excuse to me. For I could not mistrust the not-fulfilling of your promise to proceed for want of good will, but only opportunity serveth not. Wherefore I shall desire you to think that a greater matter than this could not make me impute any unkindness in you, for I am a friend not won with trifles, nor lost with the like.

It seems that Elizabeth had come to terms with what had happened and was contriving to behave as normally as possible, whatever she felt underneath. She was genuinely concerned to learn from the Admiral that Katherine Parr had been ill as a result of her pregnancy, yet overjoyed to hear that the Queen was now better and missing her company, and on 31 July, she wrote again to her stepmother.

> Although Your Highness's letters be most joyful to me in absence, yet considering what pain it is to you to write, Your Grace being so great with child and so sickly, your commendations were enough in my lord's letter. I much rejoice at your health, with the well-liking of the country, with my humble thanks that Your Grace wished me with you till I were weary of that country. Your Highness were like to be cumbered, if I should not depart till I were weary of being with you; although it were the worst soil in the world, your presence would make it pleasant.

Having heard how active the Queen's unborn baby was, Elizabeth hoped that the Admiral,

> shall be diligent to give me knowledge from time to time how his busy child doth. If I were at his birth, no doubt I would see him beaten for the trouble he has put you to.
>
> Master Denny and my lady, with humble thanks, prayeth most entirely for Your Grace, praying the Almighty God to send you a most lucky deliverance.
>
> Written with very little leisure, this last day of July.
>
> Your humble daughter, Elizabeth.

Lady Jane Grey had gone to Sudeley with the Queen. The Dorsets had threatened to remove her from the Admiral's guardianship because there was still no sign of an approaching royal marriage for her, but Seymour had sweetened them with 'earnest persuasion' and a large, interest-free loan to free them from yet another financial crisis.

That summer, Elizabeth suffered what was possibly a nervous reaction to the traumatic events of the spring. Until now, she had enjoyed robust health, apart from infant teething problems, yet the onset of puberty and adolescence, coupled with the emotional disturbance of an illicit affair, seem to have triggered a series of chronic illnesses that were to overshadow her teens. Her symptoms usually included migraines, pain behind the eyes, irregular or absent periods, anxiety states and panic attacks. By the time she was twenty, her menstrual problems were notorious, and a matter of concern to foreign ambassadors come to negotiate for her hand in marriage to their masters.

Elizabeth was ill throughout the summer of 1548 and again in the autumn. In July, Ascham had planned to visit his friends in Cambridge, but Elizabeth refused to let him go, saying she needed the comfort of his presence. 'She never lets me go anywhere,' he grumbled to his colleagues at the university. She had made such progress in her studies that he had hoped to return to Cambridge for good in September, but this would only be possible 'if I can get my lady's permission, which I can hardly hope, for she favours me wonderfully'. He was right: Elizabeth insisted he stay on as her tutor and friend, for she depended upon him utterly.

The sources are silent as to the nature of Elizabeth's illness that summer. It has been suggested by several people, in her own time and now, that it was the result of a miscarriage. She was 'first sick about midsummer', about a month after arriving at Cheshunt. It is therefore possible that she could have conceived a child by the Admiral in the spring. The very lack of information about her symptoms and condition could be the result of a cover-up exercise on the part of those attending her, who would very naturally be anxious to avoid a scandal. Yet it must be stressed that there is no other evidence of a miscarriage and that the theory rests on supposition alone. The illness lasted until late autumn, and Mrs Ashley later stated that throughout its duration Elizabeth had not gone more than a mile from the house.

Whilst she lay secluded at Cheshunt, the Reformation was proceeding with vigour. Latin had been banned from the Chapel Royal services and those at St Paul's; the government had ordered the removal of the images of saints from churches, and forbidden the carrying of candles during services, the bearing of palms, and creeping to the Cross on one's knees on Good Friday. Gardiner, having publicly preached against these changes, was now in the Tower.

At Sudeley, on 30 August, Katherine Parr gave birth to a daughter, to the disappointment of her husband and secret glee of the Somersets. The infant was called Mary. At first, the Queen seemed to make a good recovery after a difficult labour, but after a day or so she developed puerperal fever and subsided into delirium, accusing her husband of delivering 'many shrewd taunts' to her. On 5 September she died.

Clad in deepest black and purple mourning, ten-year-old Lady Jane Grey acted as chief mourner at the ceremonial funeral in the castle chapel. Etiquette prevented the bereaved husband from attending. The Admiral appears to have genuinely mourned the woman he had so wronged, and himself confessed in a letter to Dorset that he was 'so amazed' (confused) that he had no regard to himself or his actions. He did, however, send a messenger to Cheshunt to break the sad news to Elizabeth. The man first sought out Mrs Ashley and told her that his master 'is a heavy man for the Queen'. Ashley, however, realising the significance of the Admiral becoming a free man, was already beginning to scheme. She had, after all, always had a soft spot for him, and genuinely felt that he was the ideal match for Elizabeth. Elizabeth, she fondly supposed, would feel the same way.

Elizabeth was 'sick in her bed', yet – according to the State Papers – the governess, making little of the tragic death of Queen Katherine, whom her charge had loved, announced, 'Your old husband, that was appointed unto you after the death of the King, is free again. You may have him if you will.'

Elizabeth was silent, but she flushed. At length she spoke.

'No,' she said.

'Yes,' said Ashley excitedly. 'Yes, you will not deny it, if my Lord Protector and the Council were pleased therewith.' But Elizabeth refused to show any enthusiasm for the idea. Ashley tried another tack, thinking that, if the Admiral were prompted to show his interest, Elizabeth's reaction might be very different. She told the girl that her stepfather was 'the heaviest man in the world', and that it would be a kindness to write him a letter of condolence. Elizabeth, however, refused to believe that the Queen's demise could occasion him so much grief, and said she 'would not do it, for he needed it not'. Nor did she wish him to think she was chasing him.

The Admiral was in fact more preoccupied with what was going to happen to Lady Jane Grey. With the Queen dead, she could not remain in his household without a chaperon, and her parents had summoned her home to Dorset House. Jane, wrote her father, was too young to rule herself without a guide, and for want of a bridle might take too much head and be forgetful of the manners and good behaviour taught her by the Queen. Her parents wanted her returned to her mother's care, to be 'framed and ruled towards virtue', humility, sobriety and obedience. Jane must have shuddered at what that meant.

This was not the real reason why Dorset wanted her back. Now that his royal wife was dead, Seymour appeared to have lost what little influence he had, and it was quite obvious that his plan to marry Jane to the King was unrealistic. Dorset knew his daughter's worth, and was confident he could do better for her elsewhere, perhaps by marrying her to Lord Hertford, Somerset's heir.

But the Admiral was loath to let her go. Because of Jane, he had retained his wife's maids-of-honour, and invited his mother, old Lady Seymour, to come and take charge of the household at Sudeley. Jane, he promised, would be 'as dear unto her as though she were her own daughter'. Once he had freed the King from the clutches of Somerset – he did not specify how this would be achieved – he had no doubt but that His Majesty 'shall marry none other than Jane'. And he gave Dorset another instalment of £500 against the £2000 required for Jane's wardship. According to Dorset, the Admiral was 'so earnestly in hand with me and my wife that in the end, because he would have no nay, we were contented she should again return to his house'. By the end of October 1548, Jane, who had briefly and reluctantly gone home, was back in the Admiral's household, then at Hanworth. On her arrival, Seymour confided to his gentleman, Harington, who had been her escort, that she 'should not be married until such time as she should be able to bear a child, and her husband to get one'. He was playing for time, meaning to retain custody of this important little personage to enhance his own status and prosperity, whilst he plotted for more than just a royal marriage.

One day the Admiral spoke of Jane to Thomas Parry.

'There hath been a tale of late. They say now I shall marry [her]. I tell you this but merrily! *Merrily!*' he emphasised. He had his eyes on a bigger fish.

By the autumn of 1548, Seymour's lust for power was becoming all too evident. Freed from Katherine Parr's restraining influence, he began to scheme in earnest to overthrow his brother, voicing loud criticisms of Somerset's government to anyone who would listen, and secretly canvassing support for his cause. The Protector heard of the Admiral's complaints and did his best to effect a reconciliation between them, but without success. Seymour was bent on Somerset's destruction, and was far more interested in satisfying his ambitions than in preserving family ties. Nothing less than the protectorship would please him.

He set about building an affinity of supporters. Dorset was asked what friends he could rely upon to support the Admiral's planned coup; Seymour advised him to suborn the freemen among his tenants with 'a flagon or two of wine or a pasty of venison, and use familiarity with them, for so shall you cause them to love you and be assured to have them at your commandment'. He offered similar suggestions to his brother-in-law, William Parr, Marquess of Northampton, and to Henry Manners, Earl of Rutland, telling the latter, 'I wish to see the King have the honour and rule of his own doings.' Rutland was dubious, and of the opinion that the Queen's death had diminished the Admiral's status, but the latter rounded upon him furiously. The Council, he roared, 'never feared me as much as they do now'. Rutland, and the rest, remained unconvinced.

Abusing his powers as Lord High Admiral, Seymour travelled to the western ports to ensure that the fleet would be loyal to him in the event of a coup. He then tried to persuade or bribe his neighbours in the West Country to support him. Back in London, he drew up 'a chart of England' and produced it at every opportunity, bragging about the strength of his tenantry and 'how far his lands and dominions did stretch, and what shires and places were for him'. He was anything but discreet about his intentions.

Naturally, his thoughts turned to remarriage. When power was his, he could take his pick of the available royal ladies. Briefly, he considered the Lady Mary, but quickly rejected the idea, probably on grounds of religion. Lady Jane Grey was too young at present. That left the Lady Elizabeth. Already there was gossip about them, not because anyone had found out what had happened at Chelsea and other places, but because some people preferred to believe that the Admiral had retained the services of his wife's maids because he meant to marry Elizabeth very soon. After all, she was the most eligible of the princesses, and of the right religion.

In October, Elizabeth moved from Cheshunt to Hatfield. The Admiral sent his kinsman, John Seymour, to escort her, but could not resist asking him to pass on a message to her, commending John to her and enquiring 'whether her great buttocks were grown any less or no'. History does not record Elizabeth's answer.

When the princess arrived at Hatfield, she found that her household had heard the rumours linking her name to Seymour's and was a-buzz with gossip. Worst of all was Mrs Ashley, who had set herself up to champion the Admiral's cause and did not pause to think of the possible consequences. She could not resist extolling his charms and brilliant prospects to Elizabeth, and insisted it would not be long before he came to pay his addresses to her. Henry VIII, she declared, had wanted the match, and the Admiral had been good enough for Katherine Parr. Why should Elizabeth quibble at marrying him? It would be a good match for her. Now that the Queen was dead, she lacked a powerful protector. Seymour would fill that role perfectly.

To begin with, Elizabeth 'would ever say nay, by her troth' to Ashley's propaganda. But there was no one else in her household to whom she could turn for guidance and advice, and gradually she began to succumb to her governess's persuasions. Seeing her about to capitulate, Ashley told Elizabeth that the Admiral loved her 'but too well. For he is the noblest unmarried man in this land.'

Elizabeth considered. 'Though he himself would peradventure have me,' she said, 'yet I think the Council will not consent to it.' They had, after all, refused permission once before, after her father's death, and would probably do so again. Ashley had to agree, but offered the bright if impractical suggestion that Elizabeth wait until the King came of age and was able to give permission for the marriage himself. But that would not be for at least six years, and the Admiral was unlikely to wait so long for her.

Despite the obvious difficulties, Ashley had succeeded in awakening Elizabeth's interest in the idea of marriage with Seymour. Whenever his name was mentioned, she would blush and show 'a glad countenance', and before long she could not resist talking about him to whoever would listen. Yet her fear of being at the centre of a scandal persisted, and when she was away from home she took care not to display her feelings or give herself away by any other means. At home, encouraged by the vicarious romantic fantasies of Mrs Ashley, she could indulge herself. Once, playing a game called 'Drawing Hands', she 'chose my lord [Seymour] and chased him away'. Ashley teased her 'that she would not refuse him if the Lord Protector and the Council did bid her'. Her answer, 'Yes, by my troth,' proves that she was thinking seriously of marriage.

John Ashley had seen evidence of her feelings and was furious with his wife for encouraging her. Seymour had not proposed, nor even made any move in Elizabeth's direction as yet, and even if he did the Council would be bound to forbid the match. John Ashley spoke sternly to Kat, bidding her on several occasions 'to take heed, for he did fear that my Lady Elizabeth did bear some affection to my Lord

Admiral. She seemed to be well-pleased therewith,' but John was sure that Seymour's plans 'would come to naught' and forbade his wife 'to meddle in anything touching him'. But it was too late. The damage had been done.

By late autumn, the Council had heard the rumours linking the Admiral's name to Elizabeth. The Protector, however, dismissed them as mere gossip, being preoccupied with other matters. On 24 November, Parliament met to approve yet more religious reforms. The clergy, hitherto bound by a vow of celibacy, were to be allowed to marry, and a new Book of Common Prayer, written by Archbishop Cranmer, was to be placed in all churches.

The Admiral attended the Parliament, riding in procession with the Lord Privy Seal, Lord Russell, behind Somerset to the state opening. Russell had heard the gossip about Elizabeth and took a dimmer view of it than Somerset.

'My Lord Admiral,' he opened, 'there are certain rumours bruited of you which I am very sorry to hear.' Without beating about the bush, he warned Seymour that if he 'made means' to marry either of the King's sisters, he would 'undo yourself and all those that shall come of you'.

Seymour, astonished, denied 'that there was any such thing attempted on his part, and that he never thought to make any enterprise therein'. But Russell's censure rankled, and when he saw him again a few days later, Seymour was less conciliatory.

'Father Russell,' he said, 'you are very suspicious of me. It is convenient for princesses to marry, and better it were that they are married within the realm than in any foreign place. And why might not I, or another made by the King their father, marry one of them?'

'Any Englishman,' replied Russell, 'who attempts to marry them will procure unto himself the occasion of his utter undoing.' Seymour, 'being of so near alliance to the King's Majesty', would face the death penalty. The King, like all the Tudors, had a suspicious mind, 'and, as often as he shall see you, to think that you wish for his death', would turn upon him with a vengeance. And how, he demanded to know, would the Admiral maintain his estate on a marriage portion of £10,000, even if permission for the marriage were permitted.

'They must have £3000 a year as well,' retorted Seymour.

'By God, but they may not!' exclaimed Russell.

'By God,' swore the Admiral, becoming heated, 'none of you all dare say nay to it!'

'By God!' rejoined Russell. 'For my part. I will say nay to it, for it is clean against the King's will.'

The warning could not have been clearer, but the Admiral never would brook any opposition. Rashly, he wrote to Elizabeth, hinting at his intentions. With commendable sense, she declined to reply.

Parliament, meanwhile, continued with its business. In December, Archbishop Cranmer and his bishops publicly announced their rejection of the doctrine of transubstantiation, and a new Bill of Uniformity banning the Catholic mass was drawn up and submitted to the assembly. The Council expressed concern over the Catholic ceremonial and display that attended the celebration of mass in the Lady Mary's household. Mary had just taken up residence at Newhall after visiting Norfolk. 'I understand,' wrote van der Delft's secretary, Jean Dubois, 'that she was much welcomed in the North [*sic*], and wherever she had power she caused the mass to be celebrated and the services of the Church performed in the ancient manner.' Clearly, this could not be tolerated by the Council, which in December sent a delegation to wait upon her and request her to exercise discretion in the practice of her faith. Somerset feared her influence and popularity, but dared not censure her too openly for fear of offending her powerful cousin, the Emperor Charles V.

Mary refused to agree to the Council's request, but her position was precarious, and in January Charles V, having learned of the Bill of Uniformity, instructed van der Delft to warn the Council that he would not tolerate any pressure being put upon Mary to conform to it. Mary was safe for the moment.

Elizabeth, on the other hand, was treading a precarious path. Two weeks before Christmas she was planning to visit her brother in London and stay at Durham House on the Strand, a property left her by her father. However, it transpired that the Protector had forgotten this and was now using the building as a mint. Rather rashly, she sent Thomas Parry to Seymour Place in London, to ask the Admiral if he knew of any house that she could use during her visit.

Parry was a busybody, fawning and often hot-tempered, and puffed up with his own importance. The Welshman was bowled over by the genial welcome extended to him by the Admiral, not realising that Seymour was already scheming to use him as a go-between and wished to ingratiate himself with him. Expansively, the Admiral declared that Seymour Place and all its 'household stuff' would be at Elizabeth's disposal whenever she needed it, which impressed Parry. Seymour then said that he would very much like to see Elizabeth again. Perhaps, when she next moved to Ashridge, he could visit her, since it was on the way to his country estates. He also suggested that, when she arrived in London, Elizabeth ask for the Duchess of Somerset's help in finding a new town house.

Having convinced Parry that he had Elizabeth's best interests at heart, the Admiral began to question the cofferer closely about her financial affairs. How many servants did she keep? What houses and lands had been assigned to her? Had her title to them been confirmed by King Edward? To this last, Parry replied that Letters Patent had not yet been issued, at which the Admiral suggested that Elizabeth ask the Duchess to help her exchange her lands for better ones, preferably 'westward or in Wales', near to his own estates. He himself, he said, would put in a good word on her behalf. He had, after all, much to gain, for the uniting of his properties with hers in the west would have resulted in a formidable concentration of landed power.

How much did she spend on household expenses, he wanted to know. When told, he made several suggestions as to how she could economise, telling Parry 'what was spent in his own house'. Parry was so flattered at being taken into the Admiral's confidence that he did not pause to think before divulging so much information; it was obviously a preliminary to a proposal of marriage, and he was only too happy to assist.

When, on 11 December, Parry returned to Hatfield, and told Elizabeth of Seymour's 'gentle offer' of a town house, she took it 'very gladly, and accepted it very joyfully and thankfully', but she was not so pleased when her cofferer urged her to consider marrying Seymour, if the Council gave permission.

'When that shall come to pass,' she said, 'I will do as God shall put into my mind.' She wanted to know why Parry had made such a suggestion: 'Who bade him say so?' He answered that no one had; he had just gained the impression that 'my lord was given that way rather than otherwise'.

Elizabeth was further angered when Parry repeated Seymour's suggestion that she exchange her lands for others that lay near his. What did the Admiral mean by such a suggestion? Parry said he did not know, 'unless he go about to have you also'. Nor would she consent to be a suitor to the Protector's wife for favours, and ordered Parry to inform the Admiral that she would have nothing to do with that insufferable woman.

Sensibly, Elizabeth ordered Parry to acquaint Mrs Ashley with what had transpired in London, 'for I will know nothing but she shall know of it. I cannot be quiet until ye have told her of it'. That way, she could not be accused of secretly conspiring with the Admiral through Parry. If she were to marry the Admiral, it could only come about with the consent of the Council; she would not defy them. Nor would she consent to allow the Admiral to interfere in her financial affairs. She intended instead to follow the astute advice of Mr William Cecil, a young, Protestant, Cambridge-educated lawyer and member of Parliament, who had just been made secretary to the Protector. Elizabeth had been in touch with him since August, and respected his intelligence and political acumen. It was the beginning of an historical partnership that would last for half a century.

Shortly after Parry's return, Mrs Ashley also went to London, where she heard gossip that alarmed her. Some related to the Admiral's political activities, some to his interest in the Lady Elizabeth. Mrs Cheke and Lady Tyrwhit, a relative of Katherine Parr, told the governess that it was still supposed that he had retained the Queen's maids for Elizabeth's benefit, and many were saying openly that he would soon be paying court to her.

Then the Protector's wife summoned Kat to court and berated her soundly for becoming over-friendly with the Admiral. She found great faults with Mrs Ashley because she had heard that, some time before, whilst they were still in the Queen's household, the governess had allowed Elizabeth to accompany Seymour on an evening trip down the Thames by barge without a chaperon.

'You are not worthy to have the governance of a king's daughter,' she shrilled. 'Another shall have your place.'

Much chastened, and not knowing if the Duchess would carry out her threat to replace her, Ashley hurried home to Hatfield. What she had heard and experienced in London had finally convinced her that now was not the time to urge a marriage between the Admiral and her charge. She told Elizabeth that such a thing might not be possible 'till the King's Majesty came to his own rule', for it appeared that neither 'my Lord Protector's Grace nor the Council would suffer a subject to have her'. It would be better therefore if she did not set her mind on this marriage, 'seeing the unlikelihood of it'; instead, she should 'hold herself at the appointment of my lords of the Council'. But Elizabeth had already decided upon this course; one scare had been enough for her, and she was well aware of what was at stake. But would Mrs Ashley follow her own advice?

3

A Royal Scandal

By December, the Admiral's schemes were maturing well. Having discovered that the vice-treasurer of the Bristol mint, Sir William Sharington, by clipping and debasing the coinage and doctoring the account books, had defrauded the King of huge sums of money in order to finance lavish improvements to his house, Laycock Abbey in Wiltshire, he blackmailed the man into handing over a share of the profits to pay for mercenaries to fight for him during the coming coup. Sharington produced £10,000 in total.

'A man might do something withal,' declared the Admiral.

Then, although his duties as Lord High Admiral included guarding the kingdom against piracy, Seymour was actively encouraging gangs of pirates to plunder English ships, giving them the freedom of his lands in the Scilly Isles as a safe haven, and receiving in return a large portion of their loot. He also demanded bribes from the masters of ships sailing on their lawful business to Ireland, as the price of their safe passage.

Meanwhile, he had done his best to poison the young King's mind against the Protector, and was now planning to remove Edward from Somerset's control even if it meant kidnapping him. With Fowler's connivance, he had counterfeit keys made for the gates to the royal privy garden, and a stamp of the King's signature forged. His nephew, however, was growing tired of his uncle's tirades: 'I desired him to let me alone,' he said later. But Seymour, in his blinkered way, believed that Edward was irritated with Somerset, not himself. He still planned to marry the boy to Jane Grey once he was in power, and told Sharington, 'For her qualities and virtue she is a fit marriage for the King. I would rather the King should marry her than the Lord Protector's daughter.' Edward, of course, given his way, would have chosen neither.

The Admiral, however, was fond of bragging to anyone who would listen about how well his plans were developing, and was careless about who was listening. 'I have more gentlemen that love me than my Lord Protector has,' he boasted. Therefore by early December 1548 the Protector and Council knew he was plotting some mischief. Spies in his household had told them he was amassing weapons at Sudeley. Yet support among his aristocratic friends was weak. Dorset had stated categorically that he was unable to afford the expense of bolstering a coup, while Northampton had warned Seymour that the whole enterprise would fail. Seymour ignored him, as he ignored Thomas Wriothesley, Earl of Southampton, when he cautioned, 'Beware what you are doing. It were better for you if you had never been born, nay, that you were burnt quick alive, than that you should attempt it.'

Christmas passed uneventfully, a tranquil spell before the tempest that was about to unleash itself. Elizabeth had decided that it might be prudent not to go to London after all, and Mary too was absent from court; in fact, throughout his reign, Mary rarely journeyed to London to visit her brother, but remained on her estates. Ascham travelled to Cambridge to spend the festival with his old friends, returning in January, and the season was marked with the usual festivities at Hatfield.

On 5 January, the evening before Twelfth Night, Mrs Ashley and Thomas Parry sat talking by the fire. Naturally, the conversation came round to the subject of Seymour's interest in Elizabeth. Parry said he had noticed 'there is goodwill between him and Her Grace', of which he had learned 'both from him and Her Grace also'.

Ashley confirmed that 'she knew it well enough', but coyly said she dared not speak of it because she had suffered such a 'charge' from the Protector's wife. Instead, she began praising the Admiral. Parry, who had heard the rumours, said it was his belief that Seymour would not be a fit husband for Elizabeth, but Kat was still harbouring romantic notions, and retorted that she was extremely pleased that the magnificent Seymour purposed to marry her charge.

'I would wish her his wife of all men living,' she declared, and stated her belief that Seymour 'might compass the Council if he would'.

Parry's response was disappointing; he did not think the Admiral had behaved at all well towards the princess. He had heard 'much evil report' of Seymour, 'that he was not only a very covetous man and an oppressor, but also an evil, jealous man; and how cruelly, how dishonestly, and how jealously he had used the Queen'.

'Tush! Tush!' flustered Mrs Ashley. 'I know him better than ye do, or those that so report him. I know he will make but too much of Her Grace, and that she knows well enough. He loves her but too well, and has done so a good while.' She then became confidential and revealed to Parry that the late Queen had been jealous of the Admiral's interest in Elizabeth, telling him how Katherine had found them in an embrace, and explaining that this was why Elizabeth had been sent to Cheshunt.

Parry was astounded.

'Hath there been much familiarity indeed between them?' he asked.

But Mrs Ashley was realising she had said too much, and 'seemed to repent that she had gone so far'.

'I will tell you more another time,' she said, and made him promise several times never to repeat a word of their conversation to anyone, 'for Her Grace should be dishonoured forever, and she likewise undone'.

'I would rather be pulled [apart] with horses,' Parry assured her.

Two days later Parry was again in London, visiting the Admiral in his chamber at court. But he found Seymour in a very different mood on this occasion, 'in some heat, or very busy, or had some mistrust of me'. In fact Seymour had just learned that word of his proposed visit to Elizabeth at Ashbridge had reached the Protector, who had icily declared that he would send his brother to the Tower if he attempted to go anywhere near her.

In fact, the shadow of the Tower was looming ever nearer. Only the day before Parry saw the Admiral, government officers raided Sharington's palatial house and uncovered documentary evidence of his forgery and his treasonable coalition with Seymour. Sharington confessed to his crimes, but admitted only to having appropriated about £4000. Because he had turned King's evidence and implicated the Admiral, he was later pardoned, restored to his house and lands, and appointed Sheriff of Wiltshire.

Somerset dispatched an urgent summons to his brother to come and explain his actions in private, but Seymour sent word that the time was inconvenient. The Protector therefore had no alternative but reluctantly to lay the facts about his brother's 'disloyal practices' before the Council, who at once ordered the interrogation of all those involved. Thus began the most extensive of all Tudor treason enquiries.

Fowler confessed all, in great detail. Even the King was questioned about his uncle's activities, although his deposition remained confidential; it would not have helped Seymour anyway, for it contained incontrovertible evidence of his designs. But the Admiral, with his peculiar talent for impulsive action, soon signed his own death warrant.

On the night of 16 January, accompanied by a party of armed supporters, Seymour used his forged key to enter the King's rooms at Hampton Court via the privy garden, intending to kidnap Edward VI. As he unlocked the door leading from the antechamber into the royal bedroom, Edward's spaniel leaped at him, barking furiously. Seymour drew his handgun and shot the dog dead. The report of the gun brought an officer of the Yeomen of the Guard running, demanding that the Admiral explain his presence, armed, outside the King's bedchamber.

As Edward stood, pale and terrified in his nightshirt, beside his dead dog in the doorway, the Admiral blithely explained that he had come to test how well the King was guarded. The dog had turned on him and he had killed it in self defence. The guard thought this a likely tale, and although he allowed Seymour to go home, he reported the matter immediately to the Council.

That august body met early the next morning and decided 'to commit the Admiral to prison in the Tower of London, there to remain until such further order be taken with him as the case shall require'. Later that day, after dinner, Seymour spoke with Dorset in the gallery at Seymour Place, saying he was 'much afraid to go to the Council'.

'Knowing yourself a true man,' reassured Dorset, 'why should you doubt to go to your brother, knowing him to be a man of much mercy?'

But Seymour would not. If Somerset ordered his arrest, 'By God's precious soul, he would thrust his dagger into whosoever laid hands on him'. These were empty words. He went meekly enough when he was apprehended that night on a charge of attempting to murder the King, merely protesting his innocence and averring that 'no poor knave was ever truer to his prince'.

On the following day, 18 January, the Council gave orders that anyone known to have associated with Seymour be questioned as possible accomplices. Mrs Ashley and Thomas Parry were suspected of being among their number, and officers were dispatched to Hatfield that same day. By 20 January, Fowler, Sharington and John Harington were with Seymour in the Tower. As the pile of depositions mounted, the full extent of the Admiral's 'plain sedition', as Somerset put it, became clear. The Protector was satisfied that his brother had 'devised and almost brought to pass a secret marriage between himself and the Lady Elizabeth, in such sort and order as he might easily (and so it appeareth intended) have taken into his hands and order the person of the King's Majesty and of the Lady Mary, and have disposed of His Majesty's whole Council, at his pleasure'.

News of the Admiral's arrest reached Hatfield within hours. Then, on 20 January, Thomas Parry, hearing the clatter of horses' hooves, saw a party of richly-attired horsemen riding through the palace gates. In a panic he fled through the house in search of his wife.

'I would I had never been born, for I am undone!' he mourned, ashen-faced and trembling. Then he 'wrung his hands and cast away his chain [of office] from his neck and his rings from his fingers'. Minutes later, the Council's representatives, Sir Anthony Denny and Sir Robert Tyrwhit, led by William Paulet, Lord St John, Great Master of the Household, strode into the palace and demanded to see the Lady Elizabeth.

It was Denny, her old friend, who questioned her about her relationship with the Admiral. She gave careful answers, painting the friendship as entirely innocent and platonic. Denny did not pursue the matter further. Without telling her, he arrested Ashley and Parry and rode back with them to London, where they were confined in the Tower the following day, pending questioning about their involvement with Seymour. Mrs Ashley seemed unaware of her peril, but Parry feared the coming interrogation because he knew very well that if the Council obtained proof that Elizabeth had consented to be Seymour's wife, her life itself might be in danger.

Back at Hatfield, Sir Robert Tyrwhit gathered the household together and announced that the Admiral had been committed to the Tower on a charge of high treason. He had plotted to overthrow his brother the Protector, schemed to marry the Lady Jane Grey to the King and make the Lady Elizabeth his own bride, and purposed to rule the kingdom himself.

Tyrwhit's instructions from the Council were that he was to take charge of the Lady Elizabeth's household and try to obtain enough evidence of treason to ensure that the Admiral went to the block. If the Lady Elizabeth was incriminated by such evidence Tyrwhit was to persuade her to lay the blame on her servants, Ashley and Parry. But, of course, if she was deeply implicated in the Admiral's crimes, then the Council would have no alternative but to impose the penalty provided for by law – death by beheading or burning.

After dismissing the household to their duties, Tyrwhit saw Elizabeth alone and told her that her governess and cofferer had been taken to the Tower. She showed herself 'marvellously abashed, and did weep very tenderly a long time', pleading fruitlessly for their release. She asked whether either had confessed anything, but Tyrwhit would say nothing; he just left her alone for the present. He would talk with her again when she had composed herself.

On 22 January, Elizabeth sent for him, saying she had remembered certain matters she had forgotten to tell Sir Anthony Denny. Tyrwhit listened keenly, but learned nothing more interesting than that the princess had written several letters to the Admiral about mundane things, such as soliciting his help in recovering Durham House. She also disclosed that, in view of the gossip, Mrs Ashley had written to Seymour, advising him not to visit Elizabeth 'for fear of suspicion', but Elizabeth had been cross with Kat for taking such a liberty.

As he listened, Tyrwhit grew restive. He had expected that the interrogation of this young girl would lead swiftly and easily to the desired results, but he sensed that Elizabeth was playing with him and that beneath the demure exterior there lurked a very formidable brain indeed. He reported to the Protector,

> I did require her to consider her honour and the peril that might ensue, for she was but a subject. I further declared what a woman Mrs Ashley was, saying that if she would open all things herself, all the evil and shame should be ascribed to them [i.e. Ashley and Parry], and her youth considered both with the King's Majesty, Your Grace and the whole Council. But in no way she will not confess any practice by Mrs Ashley or the cofferer concerning my Lord Admiral; and yet I do see it in her face that she is guilty, and do perceive as yet she will abide more storms ere she accuse Mrs Ashley.

Elizabeth realised she was fighting for her honour and reputation, at the least, and she knew enough of statecraft to understand that if she was implicated in the Admiral's crimes her very life was at stake, not to mention the lives of her servants, whom she was determined to protect. She was alone, without friends or advisers, and she had to deal with a clever politician, for Tyrwhit was a man many years her senior both in age and experience. She told him firmly that there had never been any secret understanding concerning marriage between herself and the Admiral, neither had Mrs Ashley suggested that there be. She herself would never consider marrying anyone without the express consent of the King and Council. In her opinion, neither Ashley nor Parry had ever schemed to have her married to the Admiral without such consent.

Under questioning, Elizabeth was cool and self-possessed, and – despite himself – Tyrwhit was impressed, though he had got precisely nowhere. But he could afford to wait; he knew that Ashley and Parry were being questioned in the Tower at that very moment, and meant to await the arrival of any statements extracted from them. Meanwhile, he looked through Parry's account books, grumbling that they were 'so indiscreetly made, it doth appear that he had little understanding to execute his office'.

On 23 January, Tyrwhit had another session with Elizabeth, using what he called 'gentle persuasion' to make her confess she had agreed to marry Seymour. All she would say was that, when Parry returned from visiting the Admiral in London, the marriage had been discussed as a possibility only, and that Seymour had offered to lend her his London house 'for her time being there to see the King's Majesty'.

'I do begin to grow with her in credit,' reported Tyrwhit with satisfaction. 'This is a good beginning. I trust more will follow. I do assure Your Grace she hath a good wit, and nothing is gotten of her but by great policy.'

But nothing was 'gotten of her' throughout the week of intensive questioning and subtle coercion that followed, and Tyrwhit began to despair, feeling distinctly peeved because he was certain he was being outwitted by a clever young woman, whom he was convinced was concealing information crucial to the case against Seymour. Yet Elizabeth remained impervious to threats, persuasion, or any of the other methods of questioning employed by her interrogator. Nor did she say a word to implicate her servants.

'I verily do believe,' wrote Tyrwhit, 'that there hath been some secret promise between my lady, Mistress Ashley and the cofferer, never to confess to death. And if it be so, it will never be gotten of her, but either by the King's Majesty or else by Your Grace.'

Only when Tyrwhit informed Elizabeth that rumour had it she was already in the Tower and pregnant with Seymour's child did her composure break, for above all she desired the good opinion of the people and the preservation of her honour.

'These are shameful slanders!' she cried angrily.

At this point Tyrwhit produced a letter written to her by Somerset, who urged her 'as an earnest friend' to disclose everything she knew. After reading this she was 'more pleasant' to Tyrwhit 'than she hath been at any time since my being here'. But the slanderous gossip that was being spread about her rankled, and on 28 January she wrote to the Protector, desiring him to 'declare how the tales be but lies' since 'no such rumours should be spread of any of the King's Majesty's sisters, as I am, though unworthy. My lord, these are shameful slanders, for the which I shall most heartily desire your lordship that I may come to the court that I may show myself there as I am.' Elizabeth also reiterated in

her letter the innocuous details of her dealings with the Admiral that she
had already disclosed to Tyrwhit.

As for the alleged plan to marry her to the Admiral,

> Mrs Ashley never advised me unto it, but said always (when any
> talked of my marriage) that she would never have me marry,
> neither in England nor out of England, without the consent of the
> King's Majesty, Your Grace's and the Council's. [Ashley and
> Parry] never told me they would practise it. These be the things
> whereof my conscience beareth me witness, which I would not
> for all earthly things offend in any thing, for I know I have a soul to
> save, as well as other folks have.

She ended by promising to keep Somerset informed through Tyrwhit
if she remembered anything else of importance.

Her letter made little difference. The Protector lifted not a finger to
help her, and Tyrwhit subjected her to yet another week of
interrogation, using 'all means and policies' to persuade her to reveal
the information he was convinced she was withholding. But she stuck
to her story, and warned that those who ventured to speak ill of Mrs
Ashley in her presence would 'fare the worse'. In desperation, Tyrwhit
urged the Council to intensify their efforts with the governess. If a
signed deposition of her guilt could be obtained, Tyrwhit was
confident of making Elizabeth 'cough out the whole'.

Ashley and Parry had at first been lodged in relative comfort in the
Tower, yet this did little to allay their terror. For more than a week,
both were subject to the most rigorous examination, and when this
failed to elicit incriminating evidence against Seymour and Elizabeth,
Ashley was confined in a deep dungeon, so cold and so dark that she
could neither sleep nor tell if it were night or day. Yet it was not this that
broke her, but a confrontation with Parry, who, faced with the
prospect of a similar cell, made a written confession of everything he
knew. Because Ashley had made him her confidante, it was damning,
particularly the details about Elizabeth being caught in an embrace with
the Admiral.

The Council were convinced that if Mrs Ashley were brought face
to face with Parry, and shown his signed confession, she too would
break her silence, and they were right. Parry told her what he had done
and, while she bitterly reviled him as a 'false wretch', she now had no
choice but to confess also, bewailing her 'great folly' in gossiping about
the Lady Elizabeth's marriage. Out came all the sordid details about the
Admiral's outrageous behaviour and Ashley's encouragement of his

suit to the princess; the governess admitted that she and Elizabeth had spoken of Seymour often 'and hath wished both openly and privily that the two were married together'. But neither she nor Parry had ever thought to bring it about behind the backs of the King or the Council. Nevertheless, the Council were satisfied, for they now had enough evidence to convict the Admiral.

Ashley's confession was signed on 4 February 1549. On 5 February, both depositions were delivered to Hatfield and shown by a triumphant Tyrwhit to the Lady Elizabeth. When she saw them she was 'much abashed and half breathless' with shame. Yet although they did her reputation no good, there was nothing in them to incriminate her of treason, for there was no evidence that she had ever plotted or consented to be Seymour's wife. Elizabeth pointed out to Tyrwhit that Ashley had been foolish and indiscreet but had committed no crime. Tyrwhit, however, was of the opinion that neither Ashley nor the princess had revealed all they knew. As for Parry, he was a man who had broken his word, for he had sworn to be torn apart by wild horses rather than betray his mistress. Elizabeth sprang to his defence.

'It was a great matter for him to promise such a promise, and to break it,' she retorted.

Tyrwhit remained unimpressed. 'They all sing one song,' he wrote to Somerset on 6 February, 'and so I think they would not do unless they had set the note before.' In other words, he believed they had colluded to tell the same tale.

The next day, Elizabeth confirmed in writing what Ashley and Parry had written, embellishing her statement with a few innocuous details, admitting only that she had known through others that the Admiral desired to marry her and that there was gossip about them. The recent malicious rumours of her pregnancy were false and ought to be publicly refuted. Then she signed her name, knowing that this deposition could hurt no one. She had called Tyrwhit's bluff, and he knew it. So did the Council, when they received her statement and realised it would be of no help to them whatsoever as far as the incrimination of Elizabeth and her servants was concerned. 'She will in no way confess that our Mistress Ashley or Parry willed her to practise with my Lord Admiral either by message or writing,' fumed Tyrwhit in his accompanying letter.

Elizabeth then wrote at least four times to the Protector in a determined attempt to salvage her reputation and good name. Terrified lest public opinion turn against her, she urged him repeatedly to have her innocence publicly proclaimed and the rumours refuted.

Tyrwhit was ever ready to offer advice as to how to phrase her letters, but this Elizabeth 'would in no wise follow, but writ her own fantasy'. Consequently, he took some pleasure in telling her that the Protector had taken her letters 'in evil part'. She pointed out that Somerset had asked her to be candid with him, and she had written nothing but the truth. She was disappointed that, in his reply to her, he had ignored her complaints concerning the rumours of her 'lewd behaviour'. 'However,' she replied on 21 February, 'you did write that if I would bring forth any that had reported it, you and the Council would see it redressed; which thing, though I can easily do it, I would be loath to do, because it is mine own cause.'

'Nevertheless, if it might seem good to your lordship and the Council to send forth a proclamation into the countries [counties] that they refrain their tongues, declaring how the tales be but lies, it shall make both the people think that you and the Council have great regard that no such rumours should be spread. Howbeit, I am ashamed to ask it any more, because I see you are not so well-minded thereunto.'

Somerset, who was reluctantly impressed by Elizabeth's masterly grasp of affairs and political astuteness, and now believed her innocent of all complicity in the Admiral's schemes, promised her he would indeed issue such a proclamation, though he had no intention of doing so.

Tyrwhit was now running the Hatfield household, and he had decided, despite Elizabeth's protests, that neither Ashley nor Parry were fit to return to her service. Instead, his wife would act as her governess. Lady Tyrwhit had no desire to do so, guessing what Elizabeth's reaction would be, but was overruled by her husband. Tyrwhit himself broke the news to the princess, informing her that the Council had pronounced Mrs Ashley 'far unmeet' to be her governess and wished her to 'thankfully accept' Lady Tyrwhit in her place. Elizabeth, devastated at the prospect of losing Kat, who had been as a mother to her, replied that 'Mrs Ashley was her mistress and she had not so demeaned herself that the Council should now need to put any more mistresses unto her'.

Lady Tyrwhit, who was present at the interview, pointed out that, 'seeing she did allow Mrs Ashley to be her mistress, she need not be ashamed to have any honest woman to be in that place'. But Elizabeth could not come to terms with the prospect of a change and 'took the matter so heavily that she wept all night and loured the following day', when Tyrwhit wrote to Somerset,

All is no more. She fully hopes to recover her old mistress again. The love she beareth her is to be wondered at. If I should say my fantasy, it were more meet that she should have two [governesses] than one.

Elizabeth was also writing to the Protector to express her dismay at Lady Tyrwhit being appointed her governess, because 'people will say that I deserved through my lewd demeanour to have such a one'. She expressed concern at the continuing rumours about her and Seymour, and claimed she knew the names of some of those who were spreading them; however, she would not disclose who they were because she would not have it said she was eager to see them punished. All the same, she was 'loath to have' the ill will of the King's subjects, and repeated her request for her innocence to be proclaimed to the world.

Somerset, however, was unsympathetic, and dispatched a glacial reply in which he reprimanded her for being pert and obstinate. Lady Tyrwhit was duly installed as governess and Elizabeth had no choice but to put up with her.

If Elizabeth had suffered miseries as a result of the Admiral's arrest, so had Jane Grey, whose parents had immediately brought her home to Bradgate Manor. Disappointed of a royal match for their daughter, they took out their frustrations on her as if she had personally been responsible for the failure of Seymour's plans. They also hastened to lay before the Council evidence of the Admiral's suspicious behaviour, so as to clear themselves of all association with it.

Jane remained at Bradgate for the next three years, suffering ill-treatment from her parents. Her only consolation was the time she spent in the company of her beloved tutor, John Aylmer, whose teaching enabled her to escape into a charmed world of literature, philosophy and theology.

The Admiral, meanwhile, had been invited to answer the charges brought against him before the Council. He declined, and no persuasion would make him change his mind. He meant to have an open trial so that he could air his grievances to the world.

On 22 February the Council met to discuss the charges and draw up an indictment against him: thirty-three counts of treason were listed, including plotting to marry the Lady Elizabeth 'by secret and crafty means, to the danger of the King's person', whose throne, 'following the example of Richard III', he meant to usurp; having sought to seize control of the King and turn his mind against the Lord Protector; having tried to woo Parliament by 'plain sedition'; having gathered 'a great multitude' at Sudeley Castle to help him take the realm by force;

and even having murdered Katherine Parr, which was absurd. The veracity of the other charges, however, sounded all too probable, and the Council concluded that 'the Lord Admiral was sore charged' with 'high treason, great falsehoods and marvellous heinous misdemeanours against the King's Majesty and the Royal Crown'.

On 23 February, the Lord Chancellor went to the Tower and read out the indictment to the Admiral, asking him if he could clear himself of the charges, 'or show some excuse, if he had any, whereby he could think to purge himself of them'. But he refused to answer them unless his accusers were 'brought before him, and except he were brought in open trial, where he might say before all the world what he could say for his declaration'. The Chancellor had no choice but to leave him 'in his old custody'. Somerset expressed his intention of going to visit his brother to add his persuasions, but John Dudley, Earl of Warwick, persuaded him to change his mind.

The next day, the Council agreed that formal proceedings against the Admiral should commence. There was to be no trial. Parliament 'should have the determination and order thereof' by passing an Act of Attainder against Seymour. All that would then be needed to condemn him would be the King's signature on the Act. The councillors were unanimous in their decision, even Somerset, who, 'declaring how sorrowful a case this was to him, said that he did yet rather regard his bounden duty to the King's Majesty than his own son or brother, and could weigh more his allegiance than his blood'.

After dinner, the Council waited upon the young King, who signified his approval of the proceedings to be taken against his uncle, declaring that the charges 'tend to treason, and we perceive that you require but justice to be done. We think it reasonable, and we will that you proceed according to your request.' When they heard these words, 'coming from His Grace's mouth of his own motion', the councillors 'marvellously rejoiced, and gave His Highness most hearty praise and thanks'.

When the Admiral was informed that there was to be no trial, he did at last speak out and hotly denied that he had ever meant to usurp his brother's position or kidnap the King. Yes, he had sent the King pocket money through Fowler, and had looked for 'certain precedents' dividing power fairly between the King's uncles during the minority, but he had at length become 'ashamed of his doings, and left off that suit of labour'. This said, 'he would answer no more'.

On 4 March, the Bill of Attainder adjudging Seymour guilty of high treason, which had been rushed through Parliament, received the royal assent, condemning the Admiral to death and forfeiture of lands, titles and goods. The Protector, after some hesitation prompted by fraternal affection, signed the Bill on the King's behalf. Now he had to decide what should be done with his brother and, not unnaturally, he stalled over signing Seymour's death warrant. Yet there were no such scruples over the Admiral's lands, which were distributed amongst Somerset's supporters, while the household at Sudeley was disbanded.

News of the Admiral's attainder reached Hatfield before 8 March, when Tyrwhit reported to the Protector that the Lady Elizabeth 'beginneth now a little to droop, by reason she heareth that my Lord Admiral's house be dispersed. And my wife telleth me now that she cannot bear to hear him discommended but she is ready to make answer therein; and so she hath not been accustomed to do, unless Mistress Ashley were touched, whereunto she was very ready to make answer vehemently.'

Distressed as she was by the Admiral's impending doom, Elizabeth was still fighting for Mrs Ashley's release from her grim prison, even more so now because, with Seymour attainted for treason, Ashley and Parry might be in greater danger as his accomplices. Furthermore, their continuing imprisonment imputed guilt to herself. In a letter to Somerset written on 7 March, Elizabeth conceded that Ashley had been irresponsible, and emphasised that she herself had no desire 'to favour her evil-doings', but there were three reasons why she was interceding on her behalf:

> First, because she hath been with me a long time, and many years, and hath taken great labour and pain in bringing me up in learning and honesty, and therefore I ought of very duty to speak for her. The second is, because I think that whatsoever she hath done in my Lord Admiral's matter as concerning the marrying of me, she did it because, knowing him to be one of the Council, she thought he would not go about any such thing without he had the Council's consent thereto. For I have heard her say many times that she would never have me marry in any place without Your Grace's and the Council's consent. The third cause is, because that it shall and doth make men think I am not clear of the deed myself, but that it is pardoned to me because of my youth, because she that I loved so well is in such a place.

This time, the plea was successful. Shortly afterwards, the Protector authorised the release of Ashley and Parry from the Tower, although neither was allowed to return to Elizabeth's service.

Somerset had weightier matters on his mind. A week had elapsed since his brother had been attainted and a death warrant had been drawn up, but he still had not been able to bring himself to sign it. Warwick, who had ambitions of his own which were blocked by the Seymour brothers, had meanwhile been urging his colleagues on the Council to force the Protector to do what was clearly his duty. On 10 March, the councillors had another audience with the King and asked him for permission to carry out the sentence on the Admiral 'without further troubling or molesting in this heavy case either His Highness or the Lord Protector'.

As Somerset stood beside him, helpless to intervene, Edward replied, 'I thank you, my lords, for the great care you have taken for our surety,' and granted permission for them to proceed according to the law.

Five days later, the Admiral was warned to prepare himself for execution on 20 March. In view of his gentle birth, the King had graciously commuted the sentence of hanging, drawing and quartering to the less brutal decapitation. Seymour spent his last night on Earth writing desperate messages to both Mary and Elizabeth with a rough pen made from 'the aglet of a point that he plucked from his hose', begging them to be wary of Somerset's power over the King and 'enforcing many matters against him to make these royal ladies jealous of him'. He then had his servant stitch the notes into the sole of his velvet shoe, for removal and dispatch after his death.

On the morning of the 20th, Seymour was escorted to Tower Hill. As he mounted the steps of the straw-strewn scaffold, he bade the servant in a murmured aside 'speed the thing that he wot [knew] of'. His guards overheard him. The servant afterwards confessed what his instructions were, and the letters were discovered and destroyed.

The Admiral, said Hugh Latimer, Bishop of Worcester, in a sermon preached shortly afterwards, 'died very dangerously, irksomely, horribly'. The Almighty had obviously forsaken him. 'Whether he be saved or no, I leave it to God, but surely he was a wicked man, and the realm is well rid of him.'

According to Leti, who is not the most reliable source, when the news of Seymour's death was broken to Elizabeth, she remained calm and would only say, 'This day died a man of much wit and little judgement.'

The bitter experience of loving and losing the Admiral has been adjudged by many historians to have had a traumatic effect upon Elizabeth's emotional and sexual development, occurring as it did when she was at a highly impressionable age. Some have gone so far as to blame it for Elizabeth's life-long avoidance of marriage, suggesting that, with the executions of Anne Boleyn, Katherine Howard and Thomas Seymour in mind, she had come to equate marriage with death. This did not affect her desire to flirt and court male interest, but it prevented her from ever making the final commitment in any emotional relationship. This is an interesting theory that may well have some basis in truth, though there is no contemporary evidence for it, only post-Freudian supposition. At the very least, the fate of Thomas Seymour taught Elizabeth a salutary lesson about the benefits of keeping one's own counsel and concealing one's feelings, and she never forgot it. For the rest of her brother's reign she would maintain a low public presence, leading a quiet, exemplary life and so repairing the damage caused by the Seymour affair to her reputation.

Elizabeth was not the only one to suffer as a result of the Admiral's death. Somerset was overcome with guilt that he had lifted no finger to save his brother, and blamed Warwick for dissuading him from seeing Thomas while he was in the Tower. In 1554, Elizabeth told her sister Mary that she had overheard the Protector say that if he had not been prevented from speaking to his brother, Seymour would 'never [have] suffered, but persuasions were made to him so great that he was brought in belief that he could not live safely if the Admiral lived. And that made him consent to his death.'

Little Mary Seymour was an innocent, unknowing victim of her father's death. His attainder had left her a pauper, for all that she was the daughter of a queen, and at seven months of age she was given into the unwelcoming custody of the young Katherine Willoughby, Dowager Duchess of Suffolk, who was soon complaining of the high cost of maintaining 'the Queen's child and her company' and writing furious letters to Somerset demanding a regular allowance for the baby . There is no record of his granting one, nor any reliable testimony to Mary living beyond her first birthday.

Throughout the spring and early summer of 1549, gossip about the Admiral and the Lady Elizabeth continued. Jane Dormer remembered a country midwife alleging that around this time a gentleman had called upon her in the middle of the night and taken her blindfolded, riding pillion, to a great mansion that she had never seen before, there to attend to 'a very fair young lady'. When the child was born, the man caused it to be 'miserably destroyed'. Many believed, then and later, that the young mother was none other than Elizabeth, although there is no other evidence for it and the midwife herself could not be sure of the identity of her patient.

Elizabeth herself had gradually become more tolerant of Lady Tyrwhit. She had not complained when Sir Robert informed her that she would have to make economies because Parry had left her finances in such a mess. She asked him only that Parry's position remain vacant, to which he replied that one of his own clerks would fill it on a temporary basis, saving her £100 per annum. The spirit seemed to have gone out of her; she was weary and showing signs of nervous strain. Often, she felt so ill she could not leave her bed for several days. Clearly, the events of recent months had taken their toll.

Lady Tyrwhit was fond of collecting proverbs and mottoes and applying them to everyday situations. 'Be always one,' she would say to Elizabeth, quoting a particular favourite. This caught the girl's imagination so much that, says Camden, her earliest biographer, 'she took this device unto herself', translating it into Latin as '*Semper eadem*'. It would be her motto for the rest of her life.

4

'The Most Unstable Man in England'

In March 1549, Parliament passed the new Act of Uniformity, in which it was decreed that the services in Archbishop Cranmer's Book of Common Prayer were to be used in all churches. In future it would be an offence to use any other service, and any priest caught celebrating mass according to the Roman Catholic form would be committing a crime, for which he could be first fined and then, if he persisted in his disobedience, imprisoned for life.

The Lady Mary had braced herself to deal with inevitable attempts by the government to force her into renouncing her faith and conforming to the new laws. She had already decided that she would rather face death than do so, and was indeed ready to set herself up as a champion of the Catholic religion. On the day she learned that the new Act had become law, she showed her defiance by ordering her chaplains to celebrate a particularly ceremonial mass in her presence in the chapel at Kenninghall in Norfolk. And whereas she had hitherto attended two masses each day, she now made a point of going to three and inviting the local people to join her. She also wrote to Charles V, begging him to take steps to ensure that she would be able 'to continue to live in the ancient faith and in peace with my conscience. In life or death I will not forsake the Catholic religion of the Church our mother, even if compelled thereto by threats or violence.'

Charles's reply was somewhat disappointing, for he told her that, whatever she did, she must avoid making an enemy of Somerset. If it came to her being forbidden to hear mass, she could submit with a clear conscience because she was acting under compulsion.

Before long, Mary received the expected letter from the Council, warning her that when the Act of Uniformity came into force at

Whitsun, she – like all other subjects – would be expected to conform to the new laws. Bravely, she replied, in a letter to Somerset:

> It is no small grief to me to perceive that they whom the King's Majesty my father (whose soul God pardon) made in this world of nothing, and at his last end put in trust to see his will performed, whereunto they were all sworn upon a book, to see how they break his will, what usurped power they take upon them in making (as they call it) laws, clean contrary to his proceedings and will, and also against the custom of all Christendom, and in my conscience against the law of God and His Church, which passeth all the rest. But though some among you have forgotten the King my father, yet God's commandment and nature will not suffer me to do so, wherefore with God's help I will remain an obedient child to his laws as he left them, till such time as the King's Majesty my brother shall have perfect years of discretion to order the power that God had sent him, to be a judge in these matters himself, and I doubt not he shall then accept my so doing, better than theirs, who have taken a piece of his power upon them in his minority.

Throughout the dispute that was to follow, Mary doggedly adhered to this viewpoint; Edward was too young to decide for himself in matters of religion and she would await his majority before accepting any changes to the laws made by Henry VIII. Unfortunately for her, her assertion that he was too immature to make up his own mind irked the fiercely Protestant Edward, who became increasingly determined to make his sister see the error of her ways.

That March, Mary was a guest at the christening of the latest of Warwick's large brood of children, and in the church she found herself placed next to van der Delft, the Emperor's ambassador. Later, she sought an opportunity to tell him of her troubles, communicating in a variety of languages so that the other guests should not guess what they were talking about. He was deeply moved by her dilemma and, after she had written to him several times after their meeting, he resolved to help her by taking up her case with the Emperor.

On 30 March, with the Council's knowledge, van der Delft visited Mary to pass over a letter from Charles V. When the formal audience was over, she took him into a private chamber and they had a confidential conversation in which she 'complained bitterly of the changes brought about in the kingdom, and of her private distress, saying she would rather give up her life than her religion'. She feared that a confrontation with the Council was unavoidable and was candid about being frightened of the consequences. When she asked if Charles was doing anything to help her, van der Delft passed on an oral message that his master was determined to stand by her. Mary was so overcome at this that she could not speak. When she found her tongue she told the ambassador that the Emperor was her only solace and support, for which she was profoundly grateful, and she would try to be worthy of him. She then produced a much-fingered, yellowing letter from her pocket, confiding to van der Delft that Charles had sent it to her in 1537 and, as it was her most treasured possession, she always carried it on her person.

'Her life and her salvation are in Your Majesty's keeping,' van der Delft wrote to the Emperor after the interview, and Mary said much the same thing in a letter she herself sent a few days later, in which she pleaded with her cousin to intervene on her behalf with the Council. Charles responded on 10 May by instructing van der Delft to extract from the Protector a 'written assurance, in definitive, suitable and permanent form, that notwithstanding all new laws and ordinances made upon religion, she may live in the observance of our ancient religion, as she has done up to the present, so that neither king nor Parliament may ever molest her, directly or indirectly, by any means whatsoever'.

When van der Delft repeated the Emperor's demand to the Protector, Somerset refused at first to consider it; he disliked Charles's peremptory tone, and argued that he could not override the laws made by Parliament. More to the point, 'If the King's sister, to whom the whole kingdom was attached as heiress to the Crown, were to differ in matters of religion, dissension would certainly spring up.' However, after a long discussion with the ambassador, Somerset did at length give a verbal undertaking that, as long as Mary was discreet, did not publicise what she was doing, and heard mass only in her own chamber, 'she shall do as she pleases until the King comes of age'. Of course, the Duke had no authority to give such an assurance, and indeed he was later to deny that he had ever given it, but for the present it was enough for Mary.

It so happened that Somerset, at this time, had graver matters on his mind. People were appalled at what they regarded as an act of fratricide, and denigrated him as a murderer, a blood-sucker or worse, and many were saying openly that he had let his brother go to the block without lifting a finger to save him. Some of his colleagues, notably Warwick and his supporters, saw this as evidence of the Protector's weakness, and were wondering how effective the Duke would be if he had to save himself from similar charges of treason. And would the King, who had so calmly accepted one uncle's death, care any more about what happened to his other uncle, towards whom he was so antagonistic? In the spring of 1549 it looked to van der Delft as if the fall of one brother would be the overthrow of the other.

Many of his colleagues resented Somerset's power and his policies, and he had also alienated many of his supporters by being unable to keep his promises to eradicate what many people believed to be the current evils in English society, such as rising inflation and the enclosure of common land. Some thought the Duke had gone too far in his religious reforms, while many felt he had not gone far enough. Most of his colleagues resented his overbearing, haughty manner, and Paget warned him that 'his great choleric fashions' were intolerable in a subject.

On Whit Sunday the Act of Uniformity took effect, causing several storms in the process. Many objected to the simplified English liturgy on the grounds that it debased Christian worship, making it 'like a Christmas game', while in the West Country there were risings to protest at the outlawing of the ancient rites.

Van der Delft, unaware that the Council did not know of Somerset's promise, had taken it upon himself to remind the Council that Mary should be left alone to practise her religion in private, but the lords refused to agree, asserting that Somerset had given no such undertaking. Mary must conform like all the King's other subjects. Van der Delft wrote at once, informing Mary that a deputation from the Council was coming to see her; she should stand her ground but, in order not to antagonise them, it was advisable to deny their requests pleasantly. She must remember always that the Emperor would support her, and if her own chaplains were too intimidated to say mass, she could call upon the services of the ambassador's priests at need.

That same Whit Sunday, Sir William Petre and Lord Chancellor Rich waited upon the Lady Mary at Kenninghall and informed her that she and her household were subject to the new Act. They had come, they said, to give her and her household instruction in the new rites. But Mary, in the most pleasant manner, refused categorically to listen, declaring that she would not conform to the new Act and would never use the Book of Common Prayer. Even when the councillors threatened to punish her servants for defying the law, she remained obdurate.

'My servants are my responsibility, which I will not shirk,' she said firmly, intimating that the interview was at an end.

The Council was not at all pleased to learn of Mary's disobedience. They viewed her as a threat to their religious reforms because already there were signs that Catholics were looking to her, the heiress to the throne, as their champion. On 16 June, the lords wrote her a stern letter, advising her to 'be conformable and obedient to the observation of His Majesty's laws, to give order that mass should be no more used in her house, and that she should embrace and cause to be celebrated the Communion'.

Six days later an indignant Mary responded: 'I have offended no law, unless it be a late law of your own making for the altering of matters of religion, which, in my conscience, is not worthy to have the name of law. When His Majesty comes of age he shall find me his good and obedient subject in this, as in every other matter, but until then I have no intention of changing the practices dictated by my conscience.'

She was ill, she said, and probably had only a short time to live, but while she lived she intended to obey her father's laws, which 'were all consented to without compulsion by the whole realm, so that it was an authorised law'. In her view, the recent changes would only result in 'the displeasure of God and the unquietness of the realm'.

The Council ignored Mary's letter, retaining it only as evidence of her subversive attitude. Instead of replying, they decided to undermine her defiance by threatening her servants. On 27 June, her controller, Sir Robert Rochester, her chief chaplain, Dr John Hopton, and Sir Francis Englefield received a summons to appear before the Council for questioning.

Mary was furious. Referring again to 'the short time I have to live', she scribbled another letter of protest: 'I thought verily that my former letters should have discharged this matter, not doubting but you do consider that none of you all would have been contented to have been thus used at your inferiors' hands.' She needed her servants, she stressed.

The chief charge of my house resteth upon the travails of my controller, who hath not been absent from my house three whole days since the setting up of the same, so that if it were not for his continual diligence, I think my little portion would not have stretched so far. My chaplain, by occasion of sickness, hath long been absent, and is not yet able to ride; like as I cannot forbear my controller, and my priest is not yet able to journey, shall I desire you, my lords, that having anything to be declared to me, except matters of religion, ye shall either write your mind or send some trusty person, with whom I shall be contented to talk, but ensuring you that if any servant of mine, either man or woman, or chaplain, should move me to the contrary of my conscience, I would not give ear to them nor suffer the same to be used in my house.

In other words, there was little point in suborning her servants.

The Council did not reply, and it was not long before Mary learned why. There were fresh rebellions against the Act of Uniformity in Oxfordshire and the Home Counties. The former was crushed by Dorset, but early in July there were riots around London, which seriously frightened the councillors. At the same time an even greater revolt erupted in Norfolk, led by Robert Ket, a landowner. Ket's rebels were incensed at rising food prices and rents, and fondly believed that the 'Good Duke' of Somerset would sympathise with their grievances. At least 12,000 men assembled on Mousehold Heath near Norwich, news of which sent the Council into a panic.

Somerset, under pressure from his colleagues, reluctantly agreed to use German mercenaries – hired for a war against Scotland – against the rebels, but in order to preserve his popularity with the people he made sure that the avenging army was led by Warwick, whose military reputation was impressive, and Northampton. The Protector also sent the lords Herbert and Russell to crush the rebellion in the West, which was still simmering.

Concern was expressed in the council chamber that the Lady Mary might have been encouraging the rebels; after all, she was at her house at Kenninghall at that time, in the heart of rebel territory and only twenty miles from Norwich. Many lords were convinced that she had sent agents to help foment the rising. In fact, Mary regarded Ket's followers as traitors and had refused to become involved with them. They had not risen in defence of their religion, but for economic reasons with which she, as a landowning magnate, could not sympathise, and when the Council wrote warning her not to traffic with the rebels, she replied that if those who were accusing her of doing so cared to look, they would find her so-called agents in her household, where they belonged, not meddling with traitors. The Council remained sceptical. They arrested her servant, Thomas Poley, on the grounds that he was consorting with 'the worst sort of rebels', but he was soon released and allowed to return to Mary's service. Mary, meanwhile, had furnished van der Delft with a full statement of her dealings with the Council over the matter, which he passed on to the Emperor.

On 30 July 1549, the Earl of Northampton took the city of Norwich and drove out the rebels. Seven days later Russell relieved Exeter, which had been under siege for six weeks. By 17 August, most of the rebels had scattered, leaving only a committed contingent outside Norwich determined to fight to the bitter end. On 23 August, Warwick appeared before the city, and four days later the remainder of Ket's army – reportedly 3000 strong – was butchered at Dussindale. Ket himself was captured and later hanged on the ramparts of Norwich Castle. A serious threat to the government had been eliminated, and Warwick was the hero of the hour, receiving praise from every quarter for his bravery, his military expertise and his merciful handling of prisoners. Only nine rebels were hanged; when his officers urged him to make an example of the rest of the survivors, Warwick replied, 'Is there no place for pardon? What shall we then do? Shall we hold the plough ourselves, play the carters and labour the ground with our own hands?' He could afford to be merciful; the magnate class had been seriously shaken by the rebellions, but the status quo had now been restored.

Rumours of Mary's involvement with the rebels had resulted in her being recognised by Catholics as the leader of an opposition group, already being referred to as 'the Marian faction', according to a letter sent by Sir Thomas Smith to William Cecil at this time. Smith thought Mary and her supporters 'a greater threat than rebels. The matter torments me greatly, or rather it nearly terrifies me to death. Pray God of His mercy avert this evil.'

When Ket's rebellion was at its height, Somerset had had a private discussion about Mary with van der Delft and had complained that she was 'increasingly making a public spectacle' of her mass: 'We have not forbidden the Lady Mary to hear mass privately in her own apartments, but whereas she used to have two masses said before, she has three said now since the prohibitions, and with greater show.' He hoped she would be more discreet in future, especially as he had heard that one of her chaplains was suspected of being involved with the rebels. The threat was clear, but Mary paid no heed to it.

The Council responded by again summoning Rochester, Englefield and Hopton before them, enjoining Mary not to neglect her duty to the King by preventing them from going. She knew she had no choice in the matter, but was determined to go down fighting, and in a letter to the Council she berated them for the inhuman treatment 'shown to my poor sick priest' and their lack of respect for herself, 'not doubting but you do consider that none of you all would have been contented to be thus used at your inferiors' hands; I mean, to have your officer, or any of your servants, sent for by force, knowing no just cause why. Your friend, to my power, though you give me contrary cause, Mary.'

Rochester, Englefield and Hopton suffered gruelling questioning by the Council. Rochester refused to interfere with his mistress's beliefs, but Hopton was more easily browbeaten, and was compelled to return to Kenninghall with a document outlining Mary's obligations and strict instructions for implementing the new law. Hearing what had happened in London, and fearful of what might be done to Hopton if he did not obey the Council's orders, Mary allowed him to relay their commands to her household.

Van der Delft, meanwhile, had received further instructions from the Emperor, who, having heard that the Council would not support Somerset's verbal promise about Mary's freedom to worship as she wished in private, required the ambassador to obtain the Protector's assurance in writing. Van der Delft reminded Somerset of his promise, accusing him of having broken it by allowing the Council to deal so roughly with Mary's servants. He then threatened that, unless the Duke honoured his promise, the Emperor would be obliged to take action against him rather than keep sending verbal demands. Somerset had too many problems just then to risk adding a war with Charles V to them, so he backed down and agreed that Mary might 'do as she pleases quietly and without scandal'.

Charles, however, was dissatisfied with this, not trusting Somerset to keep his promises, and again urged van der Delft to obtain a written undertaking from him. Shortly afterwards, the ambassador received a visit from two councillors, Sir William Paget and William Paulet, Lord St John, who referred to the princess in tones of the greatest respect, lamenting only that 'such a wise and prudent lady, the second person in the kingdom', was so stubborn in her opinions that she could not obey the King's new law without doing violence to her conscience. They regretted that they were unable to give van der Delft the written undertaking requested by the Emperor, but they were prepared to give a verbal promise that Mary 'should freely and without hindrance or interference continue divine service as she had been accustomed to have it celebrated in her house, and that her priests and the members of her household should incur no risk'.

Van der Delft was left feeling angry and frustrated, but Mary declared herself satisfied with the Council's assurances, believing that 'if letters were accepted they might amount to a recognition of the laws against religion, which she would always deny, for these innovations were no laws, nor had they the force of laws, for they were contrary to God, to her father's will, and to the welfare of the realm'. She would pray daily 'that matters might be restored as they were when the King her father left them', and remitted the whole matter to the Emperor's judgement.

Charles, who believed the English incapable of keeping their word, continued to press for the Protector's promise to be enshrined in Letters Patent signed by the King. In the autumn, Somerset seems to have had such Letters drawn up, permitting Mary to have mass celebrated by her own priests and attended by up to twenty named members of her household. When the document was laid before the King he signed it without protest, but added a plea that his wayward sister would seek instruction from 'some godly and learned men' in order to rid her of her 'grudge of conscience' and thus retain 'the good affection and brotherly love which we bear towards you'. There is no evidence that Mary ever received these Letters Patent, but whether she did or not, she was left unmolested for the present, and continued to practise her religion in peace.

Since midsummer, the Lady Elizabeth had suffered miserable ill-health. Her ailments were various and included painful periods, stomach problems, migraines and jaundice. Although she followed a frugal and sensible diet and avoided alcohol, she remained debilitated and often bedridden.

Now that the scandal over the Admiral had died down, Somerset was more sympathetic, and, learning that she was so sick, dispatched the King's physician, Dr Thomas Bill of St Bartholomew's Hospital, to try to cure her. Within weeks the princess was better and on her feet again. When Dr Bill returned to court she wrote to thank him most gratefully for his services.

Her main desire now was to be rehabilitated in the eyes of the people. She had not committed any crime, nor been found guilty of complicity in the Admiral's plots. Her only fault had been to fall victim to the charms of a practised scoundrel when she was hardly out of childhood, and she felt aggrieved that her good name had become tainted with scandal as a result. She therefore set herself to win back the good opinions of her brother and his subjects by cultivating the image of a sober and virtuous Protestant maiden who cared little for the frivolities and fleshly delights of the world. John Foxe, the Elizabethan martyrologist, recalled how she 'had so little pride of stomach, so little delight in glistering gazes of the world, in gay apparel, rich attire and precious jewels that she never looked upon those that her father left her'.

The Protector and Council, concerned with the subversive activities of her sister, were now inclined to view Elizabeth in a more favourable light. They were impressed by the care she took in informing them of all her doings and seeking their approval whenever she deemed it appropriate. Her quiet and blameless existence at Hatfield or Ashridge and her irreproachable behaviour soon gave the lie to the scurrilous rumours that had been circulating about her.

Dr Bill may well have recommended that Mrs Ashley be returned to Elizabeth's service. Having been deprived of her stepmother and her beloved governess in the space of a few months, let alone being at the centre of a scandal and a treason enquiry, it was small wonder that the girl's health had been undermined, and the restoration of Kat Ashley would undoubtedly benefit her. The governess returned to Elizabeth by August, having sworn to the Council that she would never again 'speak nor whisper of marriage, no, not to win all the world'. Thomas Parry was also allowed back, resuming his old duties in September, although a study of Elizabeth's household books for the next few years reveals that she herself audited his accounts, signing each column after she had checked it.

Gradually, her life returned to normal. On 7 September, she celebrated her sixteenth birthday, and shortly afterwards she was visited at Hatfield by the Venetian ambassador, who rode to the hunt and talked with her. However, anxious lest the Council should suspect she was intriguing with him, Elizabeth commanded Parry to write to William Cecil, asking him to inform Somerset that 'not for that the talk did impart weight, but that Her Grace will neither know nor do in matters that either may sound or seem to be of importance without doing of my Lord's Grace to understand thereof'.

She was still troubled by spells of cluster headaches or migraines, which were on occasion so bad that she could not read or write, nor even dictate a letter to her brother. She was obliged to beg Edward's pardon for neglecting to write to him, saying the reason was 'not my slothful hand but my aching head'. Such letters as she did send during this period are full of references to 'my evil head', 'the pain in my head' or the 'disease of the head and eyes'. Ascham's curriculum involved a great deal of reading, which did not help the problem, and may well have caused eyestrain, although there is no record of Elizabeth ever wearing spectacles, which had been introduced in the previous century. She also suffered miseries from catarrh. After a time the headaches began to occur less frequently, and then Elizabeth was able to write more often to the King, assuring him again and again of her love and respect, lamenting the fact that she rarely saw him and craving the favour of his portrait, referring to herself as 'I, who from your tender infancy have ever been your fondest sister'. Edward warmed to her letters, and it was clear that she would very soon be publicly restored to favour.

As Elizabeth's star brightened, Somerset's dimmed. His rule had brought nothing but troubles. By trying to follow a middle road in his religious policies, he had offended both diehard Catholics and strict Protestants. His economic policies, especially his aversion to enclosures, had alienated the lords who should have been his friends and allies. His fellow councillors had no patience with his liberal views, and blamed them for the recent rebellions and the perilous state of the realm. Law and order were breaking down, the Crown was nearly bankrupt, the price of food had almost doubled since Henry VIII's reign, religious dissensions raged throughout England, and there were fears that the peasantry would rise again in revolt to protest against the combined effects of all these evils.

The Duke's insufferable arrogance had led him to reserve to his own judgement decisions that should have been taken by the Council as a body, and he would not always heed the advice of his colleagues. Paget told him, 'Unless Your Grace will debate with other men and hear them say their opinions, that will ensue whereof I would be right sorry, and Your Grace shall have first cause to repent.' A king who discouraged his advisers to 'say their opinions frankly, receiveth thereby great hurt and peril to his realm. But a subject, in great authority, as Your Grace is, using such fashion, is likely to fall into great danger and peril of his own person.'

Somerset had paid no attention to such warnings. His disastrous conflict with Scotland, his alienation of the Emperor by his Protestant policies, and his failure to prevent Henry II of France from seizing Boulogne (which had been taken by Henry VIII in 1544), precipitating a war between England and France, only made matters far worse. Moreover, the Duke's reputation had been irrevocably besmirched by what many people preferred to call an act of fratricide: his dispassionate attitude at the time of his brother's execution made it seem as if he had welcomed it. The young King now made no secret of his dislike of his uncle and was beginning to grow restive against the strict regime which the Protector imposed upon him.

The country not only needed a scapegoat for all the ills that had befallen it, but also a new ruler who could put matters right. John Dudley, Earl of Warwick, now seized the chance he had been waiting for.

Born in 1501, John Dudley was the son of Edmund Dudley, a lawyer whose main talent had been extortion and who had been one of Henry VII's most unpopular ministers. When Henry VIII came to the throne, he had Edmund Dudley attainted and beheaded in order to demonstrate to his subjects that he did not intend to rule as his father had done. This earned him great popularity, but left young John and his family destitute. The boy, however, was adopted by Sir Richard Guilford, a prominent courtier, and in 1520 married Guilford's daughter and heiress, Jane, by which time the attainder on Edmund Dudley had been reversed. In 1523 John was knighted during a French campaign, and from that time his rise was steady. A protégé first of Cardinal Wolsey and then Thomas Cromwell, who both recognised his extraordinary abilities, he served Henry VIII in several capacities – privy councillor, Master of the Horse and Lord High Admiral, eventually being raised to the peerage as Viscount Lisle. His brilliant career as a soldier led to his being appointed Lieutenant General of all the King's forces in 1546, by which time he was one of the most powerful men on the Council.

At around this time he appropriated Dudley Castle in the West Midlands from his cousin and transformed it into a palatial residence, building a great hall and a new range in the Renaissance style, with classical decoration. Here, and at his London house, Ely Place in Holborn, he lived in magnificent state with his wife, who bore him thirteen children, seven of whom survived, including five sons, John, Ambrose, Henry, Robert and Guilford. The young Dudleys were often allowed the privilege of playing with the royal children, Edward and Elizabeth, and Elizabeth and Robert seem to have become particular friends. No breath of scandal attached itself to Dudley's private life; he did not drink, gamble, or womanise. His wife and children were affectionate and loyal, united in their common interests, and their household was harmonious, its peace uninterrupted by dissension.

Despite all this, John Dudley was arguably the most evil statesman to govern England during the sixteenth century. He was greedy and rapacious, corrupt, cruel and unscrupulous. His dark good looks and charismatic virility were often marred by a cold and arrogant manner, although he could exercise charm when he wanted to; the adolescent King was one of those who quickly succumbed to his blandishments.

Dudley desired power and he meant to have it by any means at his disposal, notwithstanding those who might be in his way. He had been one of the councillors who had profited as a result of the Henrician Reformation, and he was greedy for more. He was cunning and clever, with a particular talent for intimidation, and, according to Sir Richard Moryson, 'had such a head that he seldom went about anything but he had three or four purposes beforehand'.

Even with his family he was ever the statesman. He regarded the death of his seven-year-old daughter Temperance as more of an inconvenience than a tragedy, explaining to William Cecil with terrifying heartlessness that it would prevent him from attending Council meetings for a few days in case he was infectious. In his letter, he cold-bloodedly described the child's body – 'between the shoulders it was very black'. There was no evidence of any grief. Nevertheless, as a father he performed his duties punctiliously, arranging for his sons to receive a fine education under Dr John Dee, the famous astrologer and alchemist, who taught them the principles of statecraft and politics, grooming them for a powerful future as their father's heirs.

After his promotion to the earldom of Warwick, Dudley continued to consolidate his position on the Council. His energy and talent for sheer hard work commended him to his colleagues, who succumbed to his dynamism and his persuasiveness. Beyond the walls of the council chamber he won acclaim for his prowess at athletics and in the tiltyard, and in Edward VI's presence he was the perfect courtier, treating the boy with deference and respect. Behind this urbane façade he was quietly but steadily undermining the Protector's influence, predicting to the French ambassador that 'within these three years we shall see an end to [his] greatness'. It was Dudley's ambition to rule in his stead.

Events played into his hands. His masterful suppression of Ket's rebellion increased his standing amongst the people and made his colleagues on the Council regard him with increased respect. With Somerset's popularity waning, it was not difficult for Warwick to discredit him by various and subtle means. By September 1549 most of the Council, including Cranmer, Southampton, Arundel, Paulet and Cecil, were united behind Dudley and ready to overthrow Somerset.

Warwick wished to be assured of the support of the heiress to the throne before attempting a coup, and in September Mary received a message from him asking her to back a move for Somerset's impeachment before Parliament. Mary did not trust Dudley. He had converted to Protestantism years before, but it appeared that his religious views were chiefly dictated by pragmatism, for he had told the French ambassador that he loathed the reformed faith. She therefore refused to become involved, although those around her viewed the invitation as the beginning of an upsurge in her fortunes and significant in that it acknowledged her political importance.

Warwick was indeed making it his business for the time being to cultivate religious conservatives, knowing that they would be more zealous against Somerset than anyone else. Other magnates were not so reluctant to join him, because many believed that the Protector's policies had been detrimental to landed interests. Warwick, however, in his devious way, had no intention of setting up a Catholic administration because he was in no doubt that the King, who would come of age in a few short years' time, had by now firmly and passionately embraced Protestantism. Dudley's England would be the kind of Protestant state that Edward wished it to be, if that was what it would take to keep Dudley in power. Edward would be forever grateful and the Earl's future dominance assured.

Warwick returned from Norfolk in mid-September. The Council then sent a letter secretly to the Emperor expressing dissatisfaction with the recent religious changes in England, in order to earn his sympathy, and informing him of the coming coup. Unfortunately, the Protector saw the letter and accused Warwick and his colleagues of high treason. But he knew it was already too late for a counter attack and, in a desperate attempt to ensure his safety, he fled with 500 troops to Hampton Court, where the King was in residence. With the person of the sovereign in his power, he could dictate terms. Once at Hampton Court, he sent out broadsheets to be distributed through the streets of London, appealing to the people for their support.

Warwick's response was to summon his confederates with their armed tenantry and the remnants of the forces used to defeat Ket to meet him at Ely Place. The Londoners, meanwhile, fearing a bloody confrontation, were arming themselves. Word of what was happening soon reached an anxious Somerset at Hampton Court, and on 6 October he dispatched a messenger to Warwick, demanding to know what he was doing. The messenger did not return, although the Duke spent the whole day pacing the corridors and looking out for him, unhappily aware that he was in a vulnerable position since the palace lacked fortifications and had not been designed for siege warfare.

That evening word came from the city that the 'London lords' were on the march to Hampton Court. The King was already asleep, but the Duke could afford to wait no longer. Dragging Edward out of bed between eight and nine o'clock, he had him dressed and escorted down to the courtyard, which was lit by flares and filled with the Protector's troops. At his uncle's behest, the King raised the toy dagger, brilliant with jewels, given him by his father, and enjoined the soldiers to follow him against his enemies and all traitors. With one voice, they responded: 'God save Your Grace! We would all die for you!' That night, Edward recorded in his journal, 'With all the people at nine or ten o'clock, I went to Windsor,' which was solidly fortified against an attack. The journey took hours.

For all his brave words, the King was furious with his uncle. He was no fugitive, and he resented being made to behave like one. He also hated Windsor Castle. 'Methinks I am in prison here,' he wrote after his arrival. 'Here be no galleries, nor no gardens to walk in.' Nor had anything been made ready against his arrival. Windsor had not been a favoured royal residence in recent years and had suffered some neglect. The rooms were bare, stripped of their furnishings, and the decor was old-fashioned. This was nothing like the splendour that Edward was used to, and to make matters worse he developed a heavy cold the morning after his arrival.

Seeing his nephew looking so ill and sullen, Somerset lost his nerve. What if the King were to die as a result of his impulsive flight? Perhaps, after all, he had acted rather precipitately. His confidence was further eroded by news that the Londoners had risen in droves in support of Dudley, and when he received a demand from the Council requiring him to surrender his office of Protector peacefully, he did just that, knowing that if he tried to resist the kingdom would be plunged into civil war. He sent back a message that he would agree to the Council's terms if they promised to spare his life.

Somerset was shortly afterwards arrested on a charge of conspiring against the lives of his fellow councillors. There is reason to believe that the evidence for this was obtained under torture or by the false depositions of 'accomplices' who were later pardoned and rewarded by Warwick. In his journal, Edward VI recorded that Somerset had threatened that 'if he were overthrown, he would run through London and cry "Liberty! Liberty!" to raise the apprentices and rabble'. Somerset denied he had ever said such a thing, but no one would gainsay the King's word. The Duke was committed to the Tower, whilst his erstwhile colleagues decided what his fate should be.

Mary and Elizabeth remained quietly in the country during the week of the coup, siding with neither Somerset nor Warwick. After the Protector's arrest, the Council wrote to both princesses, and to the Emperor, detailing Somerset's crimes and informing them that he would be deposed from his office – he was actually stripped of his title in the January following. Mary was told that Somerset had been prevented just in time from accusing her of treasonably conspiring with him to set herself up as regent for her brother. Foreign observers certainly believed that, because Warwick had shown favour to the Catholic nobility before the coup, he would, once in power, restore the ancient faith and indeed set up the Lady Mary as regent. Mary heard these rumours but paid them little heed. Warwick and his associates were motivated by 'envy and ambition only', she told van der Delft, and in her opinion, 'The Earl of Warwick is the most unstable man in England. You will see that no good will come of this move, but that it is a punishment from Heaven and may be only the beginning of our misfortunes.'

That October, Warwick set himself up as Lord President of the Council and effective ruler of England. The office of Lord Protector was to be allowed to lapse. Those whose loyalty was suspect, such as Arundel and Southampton, were later dismissed and placed under house arrest.

Warwick already exerted a charismatic influence over the young King, and he now built upon this by relaxing the strict regimen imposed by Somerset, allowing Edward more money and letting him have more say in matters of state. The King responded with gratitude and enthusiasm, and it was not long before he would refuse Warwick nothing. As a result, by the end of November 1549, Dudley was governing England in Edward's name without reference to Parliament or Council, ruling as a dictator under the royal mandate.

Although Warwick initially restored some Catholic lords to the Council and for a matter of days allowed mass to be celebrated once more in churches, he knew that his future success depended on allying himself with the radical Protestant faction, headed by extremists such as John Knox and John Hooper, Bishop of Gloucester. There is no doubt that Dudley embraced such doctrines, not only to gain favour with his young master, but also as a means of feathering his nest, for the radicals were demanding the closure of chantries and shrines, and there were rich pickings to be had. The records show that Warwick and his allies did indeed enrich themselves liberally as a result of these measures and the sale of church treasures.

It was the Catholic lords who first discovered which way the wind was blowing, as it became more obvious with each day where Dudley's sympathies lay. Even Archbishop Cranmer found himself marginalised because his planned reforms were not extreme enough to satisfy the Lord President, while Bishop Latimer offended because he preached that the rich had obligations towards the poor. Most of the other bishops, fearful in case Dudley should take it upon himself to abolish bishoprics altogether and appropriate their wealth, went along meekly with his policies. Soon, Protestants were hailing Warwick as an 'intrepid soldier of Christ [and] the thunderbolt and terror of the Papists'.

His chief supporters were William Parr, Marquess of Northampton, and Henry Grey, Earl of Dorset, as well as other 'new men' grown rich on the spoils of the Reformation, and Protestant fanatics. He ruled by a mixture of manipulation, for which he had a deft talent, and intimidation, which came easily to a man with such a forceful and domineering personality. Nevertheless, he had many enemies, not least among the people, and before long he was governing without popular support. His government was corrupt, unconstitutional and unjust, and there were many to criticise it, though for the moment they did not do so openly.

Initially, Warwick had courted Mary's good opinion, but it was not long before she learned where his true affinities lay. If life had been difficult for her under the moderate Somerset, it might be far more so under Warwick. Therefore, whilst maintaining friendly but non-committal relations with the Council, Mary made plans to escape from England, sending Charles V a ring in token of her distress. The Emperor, however, realised that once Mary left her native land, she might as well renounce for good any chance of ever becoming queen, something that would be quite contrary to Habsburg interests. Neither did he want the expense of supporting her household in exile. He urged van der Delft to dissuade her from following through her plan, explaining that it would be too dangerous to smuggle her out of England.

Mary was distressed. She told van der Delft she was waiting 'not without apprehension' to see how Warwick would deal with her. She had learned from the ambassador that the Council suspected her of gathering a Catholic faction around her, believing that 'she was the conduit by which the rats of Rome might creep into their stronghold', and feared they might make this an excuse to proceed against her. With Somerset in the Tower, all their previous assurances to her about the practice of her religion in private were worth nothing.

The only other escape route for Mary was via marriage to a Catholic prince. Since 1536, there had been intermittent discussions about the possibility of marrying her to Dom Luis of Portugal, and recently Dom Luis had renewed his suit. Mary told van der Delft that, if the Emperor approved of the match, she would accept the proposal, but she would really prefer some other means of escape. If the Emperor could not arrange for the marriage to take place very soon, he must grant her safe refuge in Flanders, for she feared for her safety if she stayed in England.

Van der Delft agreed with the Emperor that there were too many risks involved in an escape attempt: if it failed, the consequences might be terrible; if it succeeded, it could lead to war or at the very least could prejudice diplomatic relations between the Empire and England. Yet the princess was so obviously distressed and desperate about her plight, confiding her fears that, if the King died, the Protestant extremists might put her to death rather than allow a Catholic to take the throne. More than a crown and sceptre, she desired to escape to some country where she could practise her religion in peace. Van der Delft reluctantly agreed to convey her concerns to the Emperor once more.

Parliament met on 4 November. Throughout that month, according to Bishop Hooper, 'the papists [were] hoping and earnestly struggling for their kingdom' and the reformists were 'greatly apprehensive of a change in religion'. Rumours reached van der Delft that the Catholic bishops Gardiner and Bonner were to be released from the Tower, but both he and Mary were 'unable to believe that religion is to be restored while the common people are so infected'.

They were right. By the end of the month Warwick had excluded the Catholic faction from the Council, and Parliament had upheld the enforcement of the Act of Uniformity, introducing further legislation for the removal of idolatrous images and 'superstitious books' from churches. After just one week of religious freedom, mass was no longer said in churches, and a letter signed by the King was circulated to all the bishops, deploring the fact that 'evil disposed persons' had permitted 'such vain and superstitious ceremonies, as if the setting forth of the [Book of Common Prayer] had been only the Duke's [Somerset's] act'.

Edward invited both his sisters to join him at court for Christmas, but Mary would not go, pleading illness and remaining at Newhall with her loyal friends and servants. 'They wish me to be at court so that I could not get the mass celebrated for me and that the King might take me with him to hear their sermons and masses,' she told van der Delft. 'I would not find myself in such a place for anything in the world.'

Distressed by recent events, she believed that God was about to take revenge upon England. 'He hath hardened the hearts of the privy councillors as He did Pharaoh's,' she warned the ambassador, reminding him of the plagues loosed upon Egypt. 'I long to escape from the wrath to come.' Van der Delft reported her concerns to his master, adding that there was good reason to take them seriously.

Mary went on to say that she intended to spend four or five days in London in the new year, staying in her own house. She could then visit her brother without arousing too much controversy. It had come to her knowledge that Edward was now being encouraged to set himself up as an authority on matters of religion, and she feared he was very hostile to the ancient faith. There was no doubt that Warwick was responsible. Already, she regarded Warwick as a dangerous enemy.

★

Elizabeth, on the other hand, had been glad to accept the invitation to court, being anxious to appear completely rehabilitated after the Seymour scandal. Warwick had made a point of cultivating her support. As soon as he came to power, he had issued Letters Patent conferring upon her the lands willed to her by her father, and because she had been brought up in the reformed faith, there was every hope that the new regime would continue to treat her with respect and favour.

On 19 December, recorded van der Delft, 'The Lady Elizabeth arrived at court and was received with great pomp and triumph, and is continually with the King.' There was no doubt now as to which of his sisters was in favour with Edward.

Elizabeth was sixteen, old enough, it was felt, for her formal education to cease. That was as well, because after Christmas, Roger Ascham was asked to resign. The alternative, as he confided to John Cheke, was ignominious dismissal.

Ascham had not been as contented or fulfilled as he had expected to be in Elizabeth's service. He had accompanied her to court and hated it there, despising the pomp and the vainglorious etiquette, so tawdry, he felt, in comparison with the life of a scholar at Cambridge. Apart from this, 'a coolness [had sprung] up between himself and his mistress' as a result of his quarrelling with Thomas Parry, who may have been jealous of Ascham's influence over Elizabeth and seems to have told tales about the tutor to her, which she appears to have believed. Because of this seeming betrayal, Ascham was not sad to leave the princess's household. He felt 'shipwrecked', he claimed in a letter to Cheke, 'overcome by court violence and wrongs'.

In January 1550 Ascham returned to Cambridge to continue his studies. Soon afterwards, however, he accepted the post of secretary to Sir Richard Moryson, England's ambassador to the Emperor, who was stationed in Flanders. Before he left, Ascham accepted an invitation to stay with the Dorsets at Bradgate Manor.

As he rode across the park in the depths of winter, he could see in the distance a hunting party which included the Marquess and Marchioness. At the house, he was informed that only Lady Jane Grey was available to receive him, and he was shown into the parlour where she was reading. There they had a revealing conversation. Jane knew a great deal about Ascham from his friend, her tutor John Aylmer, and before long began to unburden herself to him about her miserable existence. His account of their talk appears in his book *The Schoolmaster*, published in 1570.

Ascham was impressed to see that Jane had been reading Plato's *Phaedo* 'with as much delight as if it had been a merry tale of Boccaccio'.

'Why, madam, do you relinquish such pastimes as going into the park?' he asked her curiously.

'I wis all their sport is but a shadow to that pleasure I find in Plato,' Jane answered. 'Alas, good folk, they never felt what pleasure means.'

'And how attained you, madam, to this true knowledge of pleasure?' pursued an interested Ascham. His hostess was, after all, only twelve years old. 'What did chiefly allure you to it, seeing that few women and not many men have arrived at it?'

'I will tell you,' she replied, 'and tell you a truth which perchance you will marvel at. One of the greatest benefits that God ever gave me is that He sent me, with sharp, severe parents, so gentle a schoolmaster. When I am in the presence of either father or mother, whether I speak, keep silence, sit, stand or go, eat, drink, be merry or sad, be sewing, playing, dancing or doing anything else, I must do it, as it were, in such weight, measure and number, even as perfectly as God made the world, or else I am so sharply taunted, so cruelly threatened, yea, presented sometimes with pinches, nips, bobs [slaps] and other ways – which I will not name for the honour I bear them – so without measure misordered, that I think myself in hell, till the time comes when I must go to Mr Aylmer, who teacheth me so gently, so pleasantly, with such fair allurements to learning, that I think all the time nothing whiles I am with him. And when I am called from him I fall on weeping, because whatever I do else but learning is full of great trouble and misliking unto me. And thus my book hath been so much my pleasure, and more, that in respect of it all other pleasures be but trifles and troubles to me.'

Jane won Ascham's 'highest admiration. She so speaks and writes Greek that one would hardly credit it.' He could not but deplore her parents' cruelty to her, although he said nothing to them in reproach during his visit. Like most people in Tudor times, he accepted that parents had every right to discipline their children as they pleased. He may also have noticed the tension between the Dorsets and John Aylmer, who had spoken out against their love of gambling. Jane had sided with her tutor, which did not endear her to her parents and gave them further cause for complaint.

When Ascham left, Jane promised to write to him, thus instituting the famous correspondence between herself and a circle of reformist scholars. 'It was the last time I ever beheld that sweet and noble lady,' Ascham wrote later.

Back in London, van der Delft was informing the Emperor that Mary was very dejected and in a highly anxious frame of mind. The ambassador now believed her to be in imminent danger of persecution. 'As things are now they safeguard themselves against her, who is in their power.' Fanatical Protestant preachers were already inveighing against her influence in public. Escape, he urged, was her only remedy. The Emperor, however, was deaf to such hints. If Catholicism was to be restored in England, Mary must remain. He would bring pressure to bear on the Council on her behalf, but he would not welcome her as a refugee.

In February, Somerset, having admitted his faults, was released from the Tower and shortly afterwards allowed to resume his seat on the Council. Chastened by his experiences, he had no choice but to support Warwick's policies, and joined with him in an uneasy coalition. The King treated his uncle courteously and cordially, but there was no mistaking his dislike. However, he consented that Somerset House be restored to the Duke, and Warwick cemented the precarious alliance by marrying his son, John Dudley, to Somerset's daughter Anne. Though Warwick would have preferred to get rid of his former rival, he was not yet in a position to do so.

Edward VI continued to be fascinated by Warwick, who gave the boy further cause to love him by staging at court a series of tournaments for his enjoyment and involving the King more in the process of government. Edward thus came to believe that he was exercising some executive power, though in reality it was Dudley who was manipulating him as a puppet.

Warwick did not court publicity or acclaim. He appeared rarely in public, and, under the pretext of ill-health, conducted much business at his home, whither the councillors repaired 'to learn his pleasure'. Yet there was no mistaking who was in power. 'He is absolute master here,' van der Delft informed the Emperor. 'Nothing is done except at his command.' Nor was the ambassador now in any doubt as to Warwick's religious policy, which portended disaster for Mary: 'The most dangerous crime a man can commit [in England] is to be a good Catholic and lead a righteous life.'

5

Keeping the Faith

After Christmas, Elizabeth, fully restored to favour, returned to Hatfield. Within days a letter arrived from her brother, requesting her portrait, which she dispatched to him with a graceful letter:

> The face, I grant, I might well blush to offer, but the mind I shall never be ashamed to present. For though from the face of the picture the colours may fade, yet the other nor time with her swift wings shall overtake. And further, I shall most humbly beseech Your Majesty, that when you shall look on my picture, you will witsafe to think that, as you have but the outward show of my body afore you, so my inward mind wisheth that the body itself were oftener in your presence.

In March she again visited the King, attended by a large retinue, and that spring she came into possession of her inheritance from Henry VIII, acquiring also the palace at Hatfield, Ashridge House and Enfield Palace. She was now a landed magnate like her sister, and of great consequence in the kingdom. In order to ensure the efficient administration of her estates, she appointed William Cecil as her surveyor at a salary of £20 per annum. It was a wise choice, for he carried out his duties with skill and sound business sense. It may have been in response to his advice that Elizabeth started saving money at this time against an uncertain future.

By April, Roger Ascham was forgiven and back in her service, not as her tutor but as a friend with whom she could share her intellectual pursuits. That month he sang her praises as loudly as ever in a letter to Johann Sturm, rector of the Protestant University of Strasbourg:

My illustrious mistress the Lady Elizabeth shines like a star. So much solidity of understanding, so much courtesy united with dignity, have never been observed at so early an age. She hath the most ardent love of the true religion and of the best kind of literature. No apprehension can be quicker than hers, no memory more retentive. Nothing is more beautiful than her handwriting. She is as much delighted with music as she is skilful in the art.

After praising his mistress's skill at languages, Ascham concluded: 'I am not inventing anything, my dear Sturm. It is all true, but I only seek to give you an outline of her excellence.'

Basking in royal favour and her newly-acquired financial independence and reconciled with Ascham, with whom she now read the classics daily, Elizabeth began to enjoy life again.

Not so her sister Mary, who was still planning to escape from a situation that was fast becoming intolerable. Her hopes of marrying Dom Luis of Portugal faded that spring when it became clear that Warwick was unwilling to meet the expense of her dowry.

She was still celebrating mass in her own houses, employing up to six chaplains at any one time for the purpose. Her steadfastness to her faith was no secret, and the Catholic nobility and gentry looked to her as an inspirational figurehead for their cause, and sent their daughters to serve her. Jane Dormer recalled that 'In those days this house of the princess was the only harbour for honourable young gentlewomen given any way to piety and devotion. It was a true school of virtuous demeanour, and the greatest lords in the kingdom were suitors to her to receive their daughters into her service.'

The Emperor, who had banned the Book of Common Prayer throughout Spain and the Empire, did not cease to demand that the Council allow Mary the freedom to continue practising her faith. Van der Delft was instructed to remind them that Somerset had assured her of this. However, they would only concede that his promises applied to Mary herself and two or three serving women hearing mass in her private chamber. Even this pandering to her ignorance and incapacity was conditional upon her not causing a scandal by permitting her entire household to be present at the services, and it was only to be permitted for a limited period 'to succour her imbecility'. When she learned to embrace the Protestant faith, the concession would be withdrawn.

'She can never be brought to burden her conscience by forsaking the ancient religion,' van der Delft replied with spirit.

'You talk a great deal about the Lady Mary's conscience,' retorted

Warwick with passion. 'You should consider that the King's conscience would receive a stain if he allowed her to live in error.' So saying, he rose in fury, and would have done the ambassador some harm had not his colleagues restrained him. He would not sanction the issue of letters assuring Mary of freedom of worship, even on a temporary basis. Other councillors told van der Delft that he had no right to interfere in the domestic affairs of the kingdom.

The future looked ominous for Mary. On 29 March, the Treaty of Boulogne brought peace between England and France. Warwick made it clear he had no intention of pursuing a similar alliance with the Emperor, not only because Somerset had advocated it, but also because of Charles's support for Mary. Already England's reputation and standing throughout the rest of Christendom were waning because of her internal political and religious dissensions, and she would remain a third-rate power for as long as Dudley remained in the ascendant. Already he had begun to realise he was building a house of cards that might topple at any moment, but all he cared about was the continuance of his power, by whatever means. That spring, taking advantage of the fact that the soldiers arrayed for the war with France were no longer needed, he created his own standing army under the command of men he could trust, and paid for by funds appropriated from the royal treasury. After that, he felt stronger and safer.

In April, Mary learned through van der Delft of the Council's inflexible attitude, but paid no heed to their censures. Her conscience told her that it was her duty to allow faithful Catholics to come to her house to hear mass, even if she had to defy the Council to do so. There were official complaints about this, and before long Warwick was contemplating firmer action against the princess. Mary protested through van der Delft that he was reneging on the assurances given by Somerset, but her protests fell on deaf ears.

She also wrote forcibly to the ambassador of her fears: 'If my brother were to die, I should be far better out of the kingdom, because as soon as he were dead, before the public knew it, they would dispatch me too. There is no doubt of that, because you know that there is nobody in the government who is not inimical to me.'

Around this time, Mary received a proposal of marriage from the Margrave of Brandenburg, a Protestant prince. Fearful lest the Council consent to the match, she wrote saying that she considered the Emperor to be as a father to her and would do nothing without his consent. Yet, anxious in case this should not be sufficient reason to deter them, and desperate to escape by some means or other, she summoned van der Delft to visit her in late April at her modest manor house at Woodham Walter, two miles from Maldon in Essex, and asked his advice. He told her to wait and see what happened and to reflect on the matter at leisure. Mary felt this was not good enough, and reminded the ambassador sharply of the godlessness of the Council, saying she believed they meant to make a martyr of her.

'It is evident to all that such people fear no God and respect no persons, but follow their own fancy,' she cried vehemently. 'My cause is so righteous in God's sight that if His Majesty [Charles] favours me, I need take no further justification in delaying, until I am past all help.'

She revealed that 'some good friends' had warned her that she would shortly be forced to conform to the Act of Uniformity. She had resolved to refuse. 'When they send me orders forbidding me the mass, I shall expect to suffer as I suffered once during my father's lifetime.' She must escape soon because,

> They will order me to withdraw thirty miles from any navigable river or seaport, and will deprive me of my confidential servants, and having reduced me to the utmost destitution, they will deal with me as they please. I will rather suffer death than stain my conscience. I beg you to help me, so that I may not be taken unawares.
>
> I am like a little, ignorant girl, and I care neither for my goods nor for the world, but only for God's service and my conscience. If there is peril in going and peril in staying, I must choose the lesser of two evils.

Van der Delft marvelled at her 'wise and prudent' words, yet repeated all the Emperor's arguments in an attempt to dissuade her, though he soon realised it was useless and that 'she is quite determined not to wait here until the blow falls, for any consideration whatever'. He wondered if Charles V might be persuaded to reopen marriage negotiations with Portugal once more. Failing that, he agreed with Mary that she should be secretly 'evacuated' from England as a matter of urgency. As soon as she was safely in her cousin's dominions, Charles's agents could orchestrate a revolt in which the 'righteous' Catholics in England would overthrow Warwick and his evil associates. Van der Delft sympathised deeply with Mary's predicament; as he told the Emperor, she seemed to cling to him, and his chivalrous instincts were aroused. Before the audience had ended, he and the princess had worked out at least two plans for her escape.

It was almost fortuitous that van der Delft was to be recalled to Brussels as a result of declining health. Either Mary could find some means of sailing in disguise out to his ship, which would be waiting in the Thames estuary, or he could send a boat into Maldon, ostensibly for trading purposes, which she could board at a convenient time. Mary wanted to bring her ladies-in-waiting with her, but van der Delft vetoed this on the grounds that escaping would be dangerous enough without them.

The next day, van der Delft dispatched his secretary, Jean Dubois, to Woodham Walter to see if Mary was still firm in her resolve to escape. Dubois confirmed that she remained so, and the ambassador sent word at once to the Emperor, impressing upon him that Mary stood in real danger of persecution or even worse. Some days later, he heard again from Mary, who informed him that she was eagerly awaiting the arrival of the boat which he was sending to rescue her.

Eventually, the Emperor was persuaded, and reluctantly gave his consent to her escape. He also enlisted the aid of his sister, Mary of Hungary, Regent of the Netherlands, in consultation with whom it was decided that the second plan should be pursued as the one involving the least risk of Charles's ambassador being incriminated, should the escape plot be foiled.

Van der Delft was officially recalled in mid-May 1550. One imagines that he was relieved to be going home, not only on account of his health, but also because of the difficult nature of his duties in England. In 1550 he reported to Charles V that, although King Edward was 'naturally gifted with a gentle nature', he was being steadily 'corrupted' by extreme Protestant fanatics, whose views he was adopting with alarming fervour, by the scandalous behaviour of his self-seeking councillors, and by his helplessness to resist being manipulated by Warwick and his minions. He had been taught to 'say only what he is told to say', and was powerless to resist, even though there were occasions when he would clearly have liked to.

Roger Ascham saw Edward VI at this time and was vastly impressed by his intellectual powers.

> The ability of our prince equals his fortune, and his virtue surpasses both. In eagerness for the best literature, in pursuit of the most strict religion, in willingness, in judgement, and in perseverance, he is wonderfully in advance of his years. I consider him fortunate in that he has had John Cheke as the instructor of his youth. Latin he understands and speaks, and writes with accuracy, propriety and ease. In Greek he has learned Aristotle's *Dialectic*, and now is learning his *Ethics*. He has made such progress in that

language that he translates quite easily the Latin of Cicero's philosophy into Greek.

Yet the King's life was not entirely made up of academic pursuits. In April 1550 he recorded in his journal that he 'lost the challenge of shooting at rounds, and won at rovers'. The following month he was tilting at the ring, but the umpire acted unfairly, he felt, because 'my band touched often, which was counted as nothing, and took never, which seemed very strange, and so the prize was of my side lost'. Warwick took care to keep him entertained, with a military display on 19 June calculated to inspire in him a desire to excel at warfare, and a water tournament on the Thames, in which he saw 'the boar hunted in the river, and also wild-fire cast out of the boats, and many pretty conceits'.

On 30 May, van der Delft officially took his leave of Edward VI, intending to sail for Flanders at the beginning of June. However, this was not the best time to be planning an escape attempt, since the authorities in Essex had heard rumours that a local revolt was about to erupt, and had arranged for all coastal villages and towns to be placed in a state of alert, and ordered all householders to challenge anyone found on quiet back roads, especially at night. The country at large was still in a state of unrest, not only as a result of the recent rebellions, but also because of fears that the Emperor might be planning an invasion on Mary's behalf. Consequently there was a substantial military presence in East Anglia and an increased number of constables guarding the roads. Van der Delft was aware of these security measures before his departure, and regarded them as a serious threat to the escape plan. 'There were no roads or crossroads, no harbours or creeks, nor any passage or outlet that was not most carefully watched during the whole night,' he wrote. Mary shared his consternation, knowing that she had no choice but to walk to Maldon, heavily disguised, with her luggage and only one or two companions. She might be challenged at any time. Nevertheless, she did not shrink from the prospect.

Van der Delft had one last interview with Mary before his departure. He informed her that the new ambassador, a Fleming called Jehan Scheyfve, had been told nothing of the escape plan, so that he could truthfully plead ignorance of it if questioned by the Council. Mary seemed more than eager to leave, begging van der Delft to send any boat, even a fishing smack, to convey her out to sea. Promising to do this and to come back for her as soon as possible, the ambassador left for home.

Mary never saw him again. Almost as soon as he reached Flanders his health deteriorated alarmingly, and he died on 21 June, spilling out all the details of the escape plot in his delirium. On that same day the Emperor formally authorised the escape attempt. When he heard of van der Delft's death, he instructed the ambassador's secretary, Jean Dubois, who was about to return to England to serve Jehan Scheyfve in the same capacity, to carry out the plans laid by van der Delft, to which Dubois was privy. Dubois was well-known to Mary, and Charles had complete confidence in his discretion. The following July, Dubois wrote a full account of what followed, which remains the chief source for these events.

At the end of June, a small fleet of ships, comprising four great imperial warships and four smaller boats, under the command of the Imperial Admiral Cornille Scepperus and Vice-Admiral van Meecke-ren, sailed across the Channel in stormy weather and made for Harwich, ostensibly looking for pirates in the North Sea. On the evening of 30 June four of the smaller vessels dropped anchor off Maldon, whilst the larger ships, under the command of van Meecke-ren, lay off Harwich.

Dubois had disguised himself as the master of a merchant ship bringing corn from the Netherlands to Maldon, and sailing under the protection of the men-of-war because of threats from Scottish pirates. The plan called for Dubois to be rowed in one of the smaller ships, laden with corn, up the River Blackwater into Maldon, where he would sell his cargo, smuggle Mary on board, and return to the waiting fleet. The princess would then be conveyed to Antwerp or Brussels.

Late in the afternoon of 1 July, Dubois's boat glided along the Blackwater towards Maldon, preceded by a smaller boat carrying his brother-in-law, Peter Merchant, whose brief was to travel ahead to Woodham Walter and inform the Lady Mary that rescue was at hand.

Dubois arrived in Maldon harbour at two in the morning on 2 July. As soon as he docked he wrote a note to Mary's controller, Sir Robert Rochester, informing him that all was ready.

Mary, however, was not. She had not packed anything and had panicked at the thought of what lay ahead. She was also now beset by doubts as to whether she was doing the right thing. In an agony of indecision she sent a servant, Henry, to inform Dubois – under cover of buying corn for the household – that she was not leaving after all.

Dubois was plunged into consternation by this news, and wrote a further note to Rochester: 'I am obliged to write now to point out to you that there is danger in delay.' He had no choice, he said, but to sail with the next tide. If he remained any longer, he risked discovery. 'I must add that I see no better opportunity than the present one, and this undertaking is passing through so many hands that it is daily becoming more difficult, and I fear it may not remain secret.'

By dawn Henry was back with Rochester's reply. The controller wished to discuss matters with Dubois, and was on his way, wearing a disguise. Dubois was horrified; suspicion would certainly be aroused if people saw through the disguise and he was seen conferring with Rochester. If they were caught plotting Mary's escape, both would face the death penalty, Rochester as a traitor, Dubois as a spy. However, the servant was insistent, and at length Dubois consented to meet the controller in the yard of St Mary's Church in Maldon. From there the two men went into the house of a trusted contact of Rochester's called Schurts, who showed them into his garden, where they could talk undisturbed.

It soon became clear to Dubois that Rochester was opposed to Mary leaving the country, for the man made many difficulties, pointing out that the increased watch made the escape plan doubly dangerous, that he believed there were spies in Mary's household who had got wind of the plot, or were ever vigilant, even that escape was not really necessary because the princess was not in any imminent danger. He put forward the old argument that, by leaving England, Mary would forfeit her place in the succession. Astrologers whom Rochester had recently consulted had predicted that the King would be dead within the year, though of course it was treason to cast a royal horoscope or to speak openly of such matters. Dubois wanted to know if these concerns were shared by Mary. Rochester confirmed that they were, but the secretary was dubious, since Mary had seemed so anxious to leave the last time he saw her, before van der Delft's departure. His scepticism was obvious, for Rochester pleaded with him 'not to judge me thus, for I would give my hand to see my lady out of the country and in safety, as I was the first man to suggest it. If you understand me, what I say is not that my lady does not wish to go, but that she wishes to go if she can.'

Dubois pointed out that there was little time left for deliberation. Mary must make up her mind now whether to go or stay. And to help her do so, he sent one of his servants back with Rochester to urge her to make a speedy decision. He would not abandon the plan until the princess specifically commanded him to do so. Rochester assured Dubois that he would send for him when he knew her mind in the matter. The secretary then spent a tense hour bickering with customs officials over the clearance of his corn, for import and sale. Matters were amicably resolved when he reluctantly confirmed he had already sold the corn to Rochester for the Lady Mary's household. The officers then became quite friendly, saying they 'held my Lady Mary's Grace as high in esteem as the King's person'. Dubois then entered into a dispute with the bailiff of the port about the price of his corn, which lasted for several hours, during which time he became increasingly agitated about the tide turning.

Back at Woodham Walter, Mary had begun to pack at last, arranging for her belongings to be stowed into hopsacks, but this did not mean that she had finally made up her mind to go. She was well aware that any decision she made now was crucial, and was desperate for some good advice. She told Rochester to go and fetch Dubois. Perhaps he could allay her anxieties.

At sunset Rochester conducted Dubois 'by a secret way' to Woodham Walter. On the way the controller's behaviour was decidedly odd, and he dropped ominous hints. 'Neither [her Grace] nor you see what I see and know. Great danger threatens us,' he warned darkly, but would not be drawn further.

At the house, Dubois found Mary in a highly agitated state, still supervising her packing. However, observing protocol, she expressed the hope that the Emperor and the Regent Mary were in good health, and thanked Dubois for everything that he and Admiral Scepperus were doing on her behalf. However, she had not yet decided whether to go ahead with the escape plan. 'I am yet ill prepared,' she told him, indicating the hopsacks. 'I do not know how the Emperor would take it if it turned out to be impossible to go now, after I have so often importuned him on the subject.'

Dubois suspected that Rochester had, for good reasons of his own, put Mary off the idea of flight, but he merely answered that, if she was satisfied to stay, the Emperor would be content. If she did not wish to accompany him, he would leave England discreetly, but if she was coming, then she must not delay any further.

If he left without her, Mary asked, would he take her rings and jewellery with him to safety? 'You might as well go with them,' he answered.

At this point Rochester reminded Mary of the astrologer's prediction that her brother would soon be dead and that, if she was still in England then, she would become queen. Torn by indecision, Mary was distraught. She spent several minutes conferring with Rochester and Susan Clarencieux, who were keeping watch by the door, and then came back. She definitely wished to escape, she declared, but she was not ready yet. Could Dubois wait another two days, until Friday 4 July, when she could be waiting with her ladies on the beach at four a.m., when the watch went off duty and the coast would literally be clear? Knowing that this would be courting extreme danger, the secretary urged her to leave everything and come at once. The Emperor would provide all that was needful. Dubois had sold his corn and had no excuse for remaining in Maldon any longer. To do so would arouse the deepest suspicions. If the attempt was to take place at all, it would have to be now.

Mary considered. 'It is more than time that I was hence,' she said thoughtfully, 'for things are going worse than ever. A short time ago they took down the altars in the very house my brother lives in.'

At that moment there was a knock at the front door. Rochester left the room, then returned looking worried.

'Our affair is going very ill,' he announced. 'There is nothing to be done this time, for here is my friend, Master Schurts, who has ridden hard from Maldon to warn me that the bailiff and other folk of the village wish to arrest your boat, and suspect you of having some understanding with the warship,' now off nearby Stansgate.

Dubois was visibly shaken, as was Mary. 'What shall we do?' she cried. 'What is to become of me?'

'My friend here says there is something mysterious in the air, and that you had better depart at once, for these men of the town are not well-disposed,' replied Rochester. He suggested that Schurts escort Dubois back through the woods. There was no question now but that the escape attempt would have to be abandoned for the present.

'They are going to double the watch tonight,' Rochester went on, 'and post men on the church tower, whence they can see all the country round, a thing that has never been done before.' There were also plans to light a great beacon to warn the inhabitants of the surrounding countryside that there was danger afoot.

'What is to become of me?' Mary wailed again, and Dubois reminded her that he had risked his life to help her, and that the best way he could serve her now would be by leaving her house immediately. But still Mary delayed him, suggesting that another escape attempt take place after she had left for Newhall in a few days' time, and promising she would send a messenger to him with instructions to rendezvous with her at Stansgate. It was a wild, impossible plan, but Dubois was diplomatic. Promising that he would not abandon her, he made haste to depart, leaving her in tears and still repeating, over and over again, 'What will become of me?'

Having returned through the woods to Maldon with Schurts, and bribed a band of twenty watchmen to let them pass, Dubois was disconcerted to discover that there was no sign of hostility towards himself. The town was quiet and all seemed as normal. As he was rowed along the Blackwater, he looked back and discovered that there was no one in the church tower. He could only conclude that Rochester, in collusion with Schurts, had invented his tale in a final attempt to dissuade Mary from escaping. However, it was too late now to go back, and by morning he had rejoined van Meeckeren.

The Imperial fleet remained in the Channel, immobilised by storms, for five days. By the time the battered ships sailed to the Netherlands on 7 July, the Council had received reports of the foreign visitors to Maldon, guessed that an abortive escape attempt had taken place, and ordered that precautions be taken to ensure that the Lady Mary never left England. When Charles V learned what had happened, he too vetoed any further plans for her escape, deeming such a thing to be too fraught with danger to succeed. The Regent Mary drily expressed the hope that Mary would be sensible enough not to suggest it again.

Rumours of Mary's intended flight were circulating by the middle of July, and to calm the people the Council issued a statement saying that the Emperor, wishing to marry the heiress to the throne to his son Philip and so claim England for the Habsburgs, had indeed tried to kidnap Mary, but had failed in the attempt. The official stance was one of shocked incredulity that Charles should contemplate such a thing, and English ambassadors in Europe were ordered to express their indignation and the Council's justifiable anger at such dishonourable behaviour.

On 13 July, Sir John Gates rode into Essex with a band of armed horsemen 'to stop the going away of the Lady Mary'. A week later Sir William Petre and Lord Chancellor Rich were appointed to interview the princess. There followed a 'long communication' of letters between them, in which Rich constantly pressed her to come to court to discuss her recent conduct, and she, equally determined, declined to do so, having no intention of placing herself in Warwick's clutches. However, when she moved from Woodham Walter to Newhall an incident occurred that gave the Council the excuse they were looking for to move against her.

On the day of the move, Mary sent her chaplain, Francis Mallet, ahead to prepare to celebrate mass on her arrival. But she was delayed, and when she did not arrive he performed the rite without her, in the presence of most of her household. There were undoubtedly spies in Mary's entourage, and word soon reached the Council that the law had been flouted. William Parr, Marquess of Northampton, was also Earl of Essex, and in that capacity he constrained the Sheriff of Essex to have Mallet and another priest, Alexander Barclay, proclaimed offenders against 'the King's edicts and statutes concerning religion'.

Barclay ignored the Council and remained in Mary's household, saying mass as usual, but Mallet went to ground. The Council, however, had no intention of allowing matters to rest, and in August ordered the princess's chaplains to cease holding illegal services. They backed this up by a strong military presence in the vicinity of Newhall and an increased watch on East Anglian ports. The King of France was informed that the Council meant to guard Mary more strictly than before because, in the light of her recent conduct, her nonconformity would no longer be tolerated. 'She would have to put up with the new religion introduced by the King or she might rue it.'

Mary herself communicated her fears and her indignation to Jehan Scheyfve, the new Imperial ambassador, but he was hampered by his lack of English in his attempts to help her. 'The people fear that a war may follow,' he reported. 'Everybody is in great perplexity.' The Regent Mary warned him that rumours of war were being spread by the councillors themselves, to gain the people's approval for whatever action they planned to take against Mary. On 4 September the Emperor instructed Scheyfve to insist that the Council give an unconditional assurance that Mary be allowed to worship as she pleased: 'You will persist in your request at all costs. Give them plainly to understand that, if they decide otherwise, we will not take it in good part, or suffer it to be done.' The ambassador, however, made no headway at all with the Council.

Mary, meanwhile, had taken up the cudgels on her own behalf and demanded in a letter to Warwick that she be allowed to practise her faith, pointing out that she had received official permission to do so. Warwick denied that any such assurance had ever been made to her, which made her very angry, and Scheyfve cautioned her to write in a less imperious tone to the Lord President, but this only irritated her further. She was in the habit of writing 'roughly' to him, she declared; if she adopted a meeker approach, he might think she had capitulated.

In August 1550, Warwick reorganised the Council – thereby subtly extending his power still further – and announced that Edward VI would attend its meetings. Edward was flattered that his youthful judgement and interests should be considered so important by Warwick: Somerset had never found time for archery practice with his nephew, but Warwick did, and Edward was captivated by the Duke's sporting feats and looked upon him as a hero.

Warwick's reorganisation of the Council led him to employ William Cecil as his secretary. This suited Elizabeth very well, for Mr Cecil was most zealous to do her service, and it was helpful to have a voice to speak for her in high places. However, she was still suffering from various ailments, and that autumn was so poorly that she could hardly wield a pen. When she wrote to Warwick to request permission to visit her brother, her handwriting was very uneven. She could not even scrawl a note to William Cecil. 'Write my commendations in your letter to Mr Cecil,' she told Parry, 'that though I send not daily to him, that he doth not daily forget me.'

The Dorsets also visited the King that October, whilst he was on progress at Oxford. They were staying at the homes of various friends, among them the Willoughbys at Tilty in Essex, where they remained for two months 'with all their train'. Whilst they were there the Lady Mary came to dinner, which was followed by a masque performed by strolling players and actors employed by the Earl of Oxford. Afterwards Mary invited the Dorsets to visit her. They could not go immediately, though, because Jane Grey was unwell.

After she had recovered, they proceeded to Newhall. All the party were of the reformed faith, but Jane in particular was appalled by the regular masses that were celebrated in the chapel there, regarding such practices as superstitious idolatry. One day, passing through the chapel, Jane watched one of Mary's ladies curtsey to the Host on the altar.

'Why do you do so?' she enquired. 'Is the Lady Mary in the chapel?'

The gentlewoman was astonished at such ignorance. 'No, madam,' she replied. 'I make my curtsey to Him that made us all.'

Jane could not restrain herself. 'Why, how can He be there that made us all, and the baker made him?'

The other was so shocked by this unpardonable rudeness that she reported it at once to Mary. Up until this time Mary had had a good opinion of Jane and had performed several kindnesses for her. Now she grew cool towards the girl, and 'thereafter did never love the Lady Jane'. Relations between them were only made worse when Mary learned that Jane had called the Catholic God 'a detestable idol, invented by Romish popes and the abominable college of crafty cardinals'.

The Council had not referred to Mary's abortive escape attempt, nor to her communications with the Emperor, yet pressure was still being brought to bear upon her to come to court. She had resisted it firmly, pleading chronic ill health; fortunately, her autumnal spells of sickness were notorious. In one of his many hectoring or cajoling letters, Lord Chancellor Rich urged Mary to co-operate with the Sheriff of Essex in bringing her chaplains, Mallet and Barclay, to justice for defying the law, but she replied that she and they had been given the Council's assurance that they might worship God as they pleased. Rich denied that any such assurance had ever been given, and repeated his demand that she come to court.

At length, Mary agreed to meet with him and Sir William Petre at the priory at Leigh-on-Sea. Here, the two men presented her letters of credence signed by both King and Council, guaranteeing her safety whilst at court. The Council felt it was imperative to move her away from the coast, in case she made another attempt at flight, but Mary was clearly unwell and quite adamant in her resolve to remain at Newhall.

Rich and Petre returned to court, but the Chancellor soon resumed writing to Mary, suggesting this time that a change of air might actually be beneficial to her health. Late in November she replied: 'The truth is that neither the house nor air is herein to be suspected, but the time of the year being the fall of the leaf, at the which time I have seldom escaped the same disease these many years.'

Rich, having tried every other ruse he could think of, now thought to move Mary by kindness, visiting her at Newhall with his wife and taking her hunting with them. But when he invited her back to his own house, she refused to go, again citing her illness as an excuse. The Council, and – it seems – the King, now lost patience. On 1 December, as altars were removed from all churches in the land and the death penalty for heresy was reintroduced, Mallet and Barclay were summoned to appear before the Council.

Warwick had travelled far along the road of radical religious reform, ignoring all his critics, amongst whom Somerset was one of the most vocal. That year Dudley had the Anabaptist heretic Joan Boacher burned, much to the King's consternation. 'How can I send her to the Devil in all her error?' he cried, when Cranmer brought the death warrant for him to sign. It was not her torment in the fire that Edward shrank from, but the prospect of her never attaining Heaven.

Mary was determined to protect her servants from such persecution. On 4 December, she protested to the Council that the promises made to her encompassed her servants also. If the councillors did not recall such promises being made, she would know that they were liars: 'You, in your own consciences, know it also.' There was no question of her allowing her priests to appear before the Council and, anyway, neither were staying in her household at present.

On Christmas Day, the Council sent her a long, lecturing letter. They conceded that she had received some form of undertaking about her private worship, but insisted that it applied only to herself and a couple of servants attending mass in her closet or private chapel. It did not apply to the rest of her household, nor to services held in her absence, and if anyone flouted the rules they would be prosecuted. The letter ended with a summons to Greenwich Palace, which Mary knew she had no choice but to obey if she wished to protect her chaplains from persecution.

Just after Christmas Elizabeth arrived in London with a large retinue, escorted by a hundred mounted troops provided by the King. Scheyfve reported that 'She was most honourably received by the Council, who acted thus in order to show the people how much glory belongs to her who has embraced the new religion and has become a very great lady.'

Scheyfve had recently heard a rumour from a 'safe source' that Warwick was planning to 'cast off his wife and marry my Lady Elizabeth, with whom he is said to have had several secret or intimate personal communications, and by these means he will aspire to the crown'. However, nothing more is heard of this plan from any other source, and it seems that Scheyfve was either reporting mere gossip or got his facts wrong. The rumour, however, shows just how important Elizabeth had become and how her every act was invested with significance. Because she rarely showed herself in public the people flocked to see her, and they were impressed with what they saw.

At seventeen, Elizabeth was pale and dignified, wearing her hair loose and unadorned – John Aylmer praised her for so plain a style, unlike the crimped curls of the court ladies. She did not use any cosmetics, save a little marjoram scent, nor appear, as they did, 'dressed and painted like peacocks'. Instead she set an example for Protestant gentlewomen by wearing severely cut gowns in black and white, which made her look demure and meek. Her only vanity was her hands, with their long tapering fingers. Although one court wit had it that she was doing her best to live down the Seymour scandal, most people had forgotten her part in it, seeing only a virtuous, Protestant princess. Aylmer claimed that 'she never meddled with money but against her will, but thought to touch it was to defile her pure hands consecrated to turn over good books, to lift up unto God in prayer, and to deal alms to the poor'.

In fact, Elizabeth lived the life of a wealthy magnate, spending £400 per annum on her servants' wages and indulging her own pleasures. Her account books show frequent payments to drummers, pipers, minstrels, lute players and harpists, and also to child actors and singers from the royal household. Although there were many abortive plans laid to marry her off to foreign princes, she kept herself aloof and steered clear of the company of men. And while many Protestants saw her as the hope of the future, she betrayed no interest in playing such a

role. Although Elizabeth was high in the King's favour and corresponded with him regularly, relations between them remained formal,
at least in public. He might still address her as his 'sweet sister
Temperance' but she had to kneel or sit bolt upright in his presence,
and always signed herself 'Your Majesty's most humble sister and
servant'. Later Protestant writers would present the relationship
between brother and sister as close and affectionate, based on shared
religious interests, but this was an idealised picture. The gulf between
monarch and subject was wider than that between princely siblings.

Elizabeth had no desire to become involved in the dispute between
Edward and Mary, and as soon as the New Year festivities had ended
she returned home. She cannot have been unaware that for some
months now Edward had been in correspondence with his elder sister,
urging her most forcefully to abandon her religion and conform to the
reformed faith, as all his other true subjects had done. Mary did not
believe that her brother was capable of writing such letters, and was
persuaded that Warwick and his cronies had written them for him. The
King's own journal shows otherwise, however, and even if he did not
actually write his letters himself, he was fully in agreement with what
was written in his name.

By now, Mary's attitude infuriated Edward. At thirteen, he
considered himself old enough and wise enough to make his own
decisions. Had he not recently offered – to Cheke's delight – to rewrite
the new prayer book? Therefore, when some councillors suggested
that his sister's disobedience be tolerated in order to pacify the
Emperor, he retorted, 'Is it lawful by Scripture to sanction idolatry?'

A bishop replied, 'There were good kings, Your Majesty, who
allowed the hill altars, and yet were called good.'

'We must follow the example of good men when they have done
well,' the boy declared loftily. 'We do not follow them in evil. David
was good but David seduced Bathsheba and murdered Uriah. We are
not to imitate David in such deeds as these. Is there no better Scripture?'

The bishops looked blank.

'I am sorry for the realm, then, and sorry for the danger that will
come of it,' concluded the King. 'I shall hope and pray for something
better, but the evil thing I will not allow.'

At his insistence, the Council composed a letter to Mary condemning her 'wayward misunderstanding', to which he added some
sentences in his own hand. Addressing her as 'our nearest sister' who
should be 'our greatest comfort in our tender years', he denied that she
had ever been granted official permission to continue attending mass in
her house, and complained that, as his sister, her offence was the more

heinous for she was setting a pernicious example to his people. He went on:

> It is a scandalous thing that so high a personage should deny our sovereignty. That our sister should be less to us than any of our other subjects is an unnatural example. In our state, it shall miscontent us to permit you, so great a subject, not to permit our laws. Your nearness to us in blood, your greatness in estate, the condition of this time, maketh your fault the greater. To teach you and instruct you we will give order and so procure you to do your duty willingly, that you shall perceive you are not used merely as a subject, and only commanded but as a daughter, a scholar and a sister, taught, instructed and persuaded. You shall err in many points, such as our father and yours would not have suffered, whatsoever you say of the standing still of things as they were left by him. Truly, sister, I will not say more and worse things, because my duty would compel me to use harsher and angrier words. But this I will say with certain intention, that I will see my laws strictly obeyed, and those who break them shall be watched and denounced.

Mary was devastated to receive this stinging admonition, since it could only herald an end to her hopes that Edward would set matters right upon attaining his majority.

His cold and imperious tone made her feel bereft, and she did not hide her desolation in her reply, saying that his letter had occasioned her 'more suffering than any illness, even unto death'. She had never done him any harm, and would never bring injury upon himself or his kingdom. However, her first duty was to God: 'Rather than offend Him or my conscience, I would lose all I have left in the world, and my life too.' Death seemed a likely end to her troubles anyway, for her health was 'more unstable than that of any creature', and she felt so ill that she could barely lift the pen. His Majesty, she insisted, had been misled by wicked and vindictive advisers. 'Although, our Lord be praised, Your Majesty hath far more knowledge and greater gifts than other of your years, yet it is not possible that Your Highness can at these years be a judge in matters of religion.' He would know better when he reached 'ripe and fuller years'. In the meantime, she did not intend to rule her conscience according to the dictates of the Council.

Again, Mary appealed to the Emperor and to Mary of Hungary for help, though Scheyfve had advised her not to call the King's authority into question. Then, on 16 February 1551, acting on Charles V's instructions, he stood before the Council and demanded that they cease molesting Mary and permit her to celebrate mass with her household. After a long argument, in which the councillors insisted that the concession extended only to the princess and her personal chamber servants, the ambassador withdrew, defeated. In a letter to the Regent Mary, he confided his fears that Warwick intended to bring even greater pressure to bear on Mary.

Isolated in the country, Mary still received news of what was happening at court, and some of the things she heard disturbed her greatly. It was said, on good authority, that the Lady Elizabeth, whilst at court, had been made much of by Warwick. They had attended a bull-baiting with the French ambassador and the conversation between them had been so lively that they had seemed not to notice the sport. Warwick, Mary heard, had become so security conscious that he had increased the palace guard by over a thousand men; it was not that he feared for the King's safety, but for the continuance of his own power in the face of a growing opposition party at court, headed by the Earls of Derby and Shrewsbury and the Duke of Somerset. Mary feared she might be ousted from the succession as a result of a coalition between Warwick and Elizabeth, and for this reason, as well as the imperative of defending her faith, she decided at last to obey the summons to court.

On 15 March, Mary arrived at her London lodging, the Hospital of St John at Clerkenwell, attended by 'fifty knights and gentlemen in velvet coats and chains of gold afore her, and after her four score gentlemen and ladies, everyone having a pair of beads of black'. Not only had the princess come as a great magnate, but she was also – by ordering her attendants openly to carry their rosaries – proclaiming herself a defiantly Catholic one. As she neared the capital, throngs of citizens ran joyfully to greet her. 'The people ran five or six miles out of town,' Scheyfve recorded, 'and were marvellously overjoyed to see her, showing clearly how much they love her.' Four hundred people followed her into the city.

Two days later she went in procession to Whitehall, where the King was in residence. Again, she caused such a stir among the people that she could hardly make any progress through the crowds. Warwick, angered by her popularity, was determined that her official reception should be modest, thereby reflecting official disapproval of her behaviour. At Whitehall Palace, Sir Anthony Wingfield, Controller of the King's Household, received her and escorted her to a gallery where Edward waited to receive her in the company of the entire Council. Here, Mary fell to her knees. She had been unable to come before, she explained, because of chronic ill-health. Edward raised her, kissed her, then replied pointedly that God had sent her illness whilst granting him health. He then led her into an adjoining chamber, followed by the councillors. The door closed in the face of Mary's ladies. She was alone.

For the next two hours she valiantly defended her views in the face of heated arguments. According to Scheyfve, Edward began by saying 'he had heard a rumour that Mary habitually heard mass'. She later told the ambassador that when she perceived 'how the King, whom I love and honour above all other beings, had been counselled against me, I could not contain myself and exhibited my interior grief'. At the sight of her tears, Edward wept also, saying 'he thought no harm of her', but the religious gulf between them was so great that there was to be no common meeting ground. And the last thing the Council wanted was a reconciliation. One by one the councillors hectored Mary, accusing her of breaking the King's laws by maintaining the old faith; by defying her brother, she was told, she was disobeying the will of her father.

Mary, often weeping, repeatedly insisted that Protector Somerset had assured van der Delft that she might follow her religion within the privacy of her household, but her claims were as vigorously denied. Mary assured the councillors that there was no subject more humble or obedient than she was, but they must surely realise that the King could not expect her to change her religion at her age. Turning to her brother, she asked if he knew anything of Somerset's promise, and he had to say he did not since 'he had only taken a share in affairs during the last year'. In that case, Mary answered, he had not drawn up the ordinances on the new religion; therefore she was not bound to obey them. Nor had she infringed the terms of her father's will, which merely obliged her to consult the Council before marrying. It was Henry's executors, the councillors, who had betrayed him, for they had been enjoined to order two daily masses and four annual obsequies for his soul, and had failed to do so. Finally, she appealed to the King, begging him to allow the matter to rest until he was of an age to reach a mature judgement in matters of religion.

Edward, however, replied cuttingly that Mary too might have something to learn – 'no one was too old for that'. He was not so much concerned about her religion as her conduct, he went on. She was his subject and must obey him, lest 'her example might breed too much inconvenience'. He then informed her that his Master of Horse, Sir Anthony Browne, had just been incarcerated in the Fleet Prison for twice attending mass recently at her house. Unless he saw a change in her, he informed Mary, 'I could not bear it.' Mary answered that 'her faith she would not change, nor dissemble her opinion with contrary doings'.

By this time tempers were becoming rather short. Continuing to assert her view that the new laws were not of the King's making, Mary declared that her father had 'cared more for the good of the kingdom than all the members of the Council put together'. This was too much for Warwick.

'How now, my lady?' he growled. 'It seems that Your Grace is trying to show us in a hateful light to the King our master without any cause whatsoever.' That, replied Mary, was not her intention, but since they were pressing her, she had no choice but to tell the truth.

'There are two things only, body and soul,' she said. 'Although my soul belongs to God, I offer my body to the King's service; might it please him to take away my life rather than the old religion.'

Edward made a 'gentle answer', hastily assuring her that he had no desire for such a sacrifice, and told her she could go back to Clerkenwell whilst he discussed her case with the Council.

'Give no credit to any person who might desire to make Your Grace believe evil of me,' begged Mary, and assuring him that she 'would remain His Majesty's humble, obedient and unworthy sister', took her leave.

When she had gone and the King had withdrawn, the councillors broke into a heated debate. Many were for having her arrested and sent to the Tower, but were fearful of Edward's reaction, while others felt it might be politic to turn a blind eye to her disobedience for the present. In the circumstances they did not reach any agreement as to what they should do next.

The following day, Scheyfve received a letter from the Emperor, informing him that if Mary were forbidden to attend mass, he would declare war on England. Without delay, he laid this ultimatum before the Council. It was a bluff, because the ambassador knew very well that Charles was too busy suppressing heresy in Germany to start a war with England just then, but he knew also that the English were in no position to involve themselves in war either. Privately, the Emperor had told Scheyfve that Mary must be satisfied with hearing mass 'privately in her own house, without admitting any strangers; for her conscience cannot be hardened by submisson to outside violence'. Beyond that, she must obey the law.

'A good source' had confided to Scheyfve that many councillors 'intended to use [Mary] very roughly, keeping her here in this town if she refused to conform with the new religion, and taking away her servants, especially those whom she trusted, in whose place they would have set others of their way of thinking'. The princess herself was aware that, 'had the Council only had to deal with her, they would long ago have deprived her of the mass'. But now they had a threat of war on her behalf to contend with, and it was this, Scheyfve was convinced, that turned the tables in Mary's favour. Before the day was out, he was aware of a change in the Council's attitude.

In fact, because a war with the Emperor would prohibit access to a large arsenal of English weapons then in safe-keeping in Flanders, the councillors had hurriedly decided not to put any further pressure on Mary for the moment, while Sir Nicholas Wotton was to be sent to the Emperor with instructions to be conciliatory.

The only voice to be raised in protest was the King's. His tutors, he told the Council, had brought him up to believe that it was a sin to license a sin, and he would be committing a sin if he permitted his sister to continue hearing mass. Archbishop Cranmer, Nicholas Ridley, Bishop of London, and John Ponet, Bishop of Rochester, all assured him that the sin of attending mass might be 'winked at' if the over-riding interests of the realm required it, and with that Edward had to be content, although he confessed to some moral reservations.

The following morning, Mr Secretary Petre waited upon Mary at Clerkenwell to inform her that she might leave court without hindrance and assure her of 'the most cordial affection' of His Majesty and his Council. Mary, however, was unwell, confined to her bed with an illness that was almost certainly a nervous reaction to the strain of her visit to court. Petre informed her that the King would without doubt be distressed to learn of her condition, and would not wish to trouble her further. Nevertheless, he did ask again if she would give up the old faith, repeating all the arguments cited two days earlier.

'Pray excuse the brevity of my reply,' groaned Mary, raising herself on the pillows, 'but my soul is God's; my body is the King's to command.' Petre did not press her further, but respectfully withdrew. A few days later, Mary left London for Newhall.

Mary had been granted a few months' respite from persecution, but she felt bitter towards those who had subjected her to such an ordeal. Soon after her return home, she wrote to the Council, 'To the King's Majesty my brother I confess myself to be his humble sister and subject, but to you, my lords, I owe nothing beyond amity and goodwill, which you will find in me if I meet with the same in you.'

Thereafter she visited her brother but rarely. Whenever they did meet, Mary told Jane Dormer, Edward would 'burst forth in tears, grieving matters could not be according to her will and desire'. When he grew older, he promised, he would 'remedy all'. This interpretation of his words may have been wishful thinking on Mary's part, yet she was deeply touched by his concern for her, by his reluctance to say goodbye and his insistence on giving her some parting gift, such as a tiny jewel. It grieved him that he could not give her something more valuable. It was Mary's firm belief that the Council prevented them from meeting more often because she had been told that her presence 'made the King sad and melancholy, and affected him too deeply for his good'.

Mary might now be exempt from persecution, but her priests were not. Late in March, Robert Rochester was summoned to appear once more before the Council to answer questions concerning the activities of his mistress's chaplains. It had not been forgotten how Dr Mallet had celebrated mass in Mary's absence. Shortly afterwards a Master Benett of Ware told the Council that he had heard of a Catholic conspiracy headed by the Earl of Shrewsbury; he believed that the Lady Mary would join it. Mary, of course, was not involved, but the councillors were fearful that her house might become a focus for disaffected Catholic nobles. It was mainly for this reason that they did not want outsiders to be admitted to mass.

Late in April 1551, Dr Mallet was arrested and sent to the Tower. Mary wrote to the Council, demanding his release, but was told by way of reply, 'We are sorry to perceive Your Grace so ready to be a defence to one that the King's law doth condemn.'

Nothing daunted, she wrote again and again, but achieved nothing by it. Mallet remained a prisoner.

Edward VI, meanwhile, was growing up fast and excelled at riding, running and shooting, despite increasing short-sightedness. Consistently striving to emulate Henry VIII, he was becoming more and more like his father. Hands on hips, he would imitate Henry's straddling pose, and emit 'thunderous oaths' in his high, imperious voice. By calculated displays of wrath and coldness, he sought to make men fear him as they had his father. By now a fanatical Protestant, he was fond of lecturing those around him in the articles of his faith, a role which sat oddly with his youth. His councillors and courtiers were already in awe of him. 'He will be the wonder and terror of the world if he lives,' declared Bishop Hooper that year.

Of course, there was no reason to suppose that Edward would not live to beget a whole line of Tudor sovereigns, but throughout that summer England was in the grip of an epidemic called the sweating sickness, of which there were several visitations during the sixteenth century. The last great outbreak had been in the 1520s, but this was worse. Fifty thousand people died in it, some of them servants at

Newhall, which caused Mary to uproot precipitately and move to another of her houses.

Marriage was also in the air that summer. On 19 July, the King signed a treaty with France, renouncing his betrothal to Mary, Queen of Scots, who was now affianced to the Dauphin, and contracting himself to marry the Princess Elisabeth of France, daughter of Henry II. Elisabeth was a Catholic but Edward doubtless believed he would be able to change her opinions.

The Lady Elizabeth's marriage also came under discussion. The French Duke of Guise suggested his brother as a possible husband, and Elizabeth arranged to have her portrait sent to him. Guise also suggested the sons of the dukes of Ferrara and Florence, but one was only eleven years old. Most councillors objected to these matches on the grounds that all these princes were Catholics; they were more amenable to a suggestion made later in the year that Elizabeth marry the King of Denmark's eldest son, who was a Protestant. Negotiations for this union were opened in November, but no one expected them to be speedily concluded.

The new French alliance meant that France was soon at war with the Empire and that there could be no question now of Charles declaring war on Mary's behalf. In June, he had told Wotton that he would not suffer her to be 'evil-handled' by the Council, but the truth was that he now had no means of preventing it. In July, at Augsburg in Germany, he used threatening language to the English ambassador, and said that 'If death were to overtake the princess for this cause, she would be the first martyr of royal blood to die for our holy faith.' He would never, he said, permit her to be deprived of the mass.

To Scheyfve, he wrote in a less intransigent manner. The ambassador must urge Mary not to provoke the Council too far. Even if her priests were forbidden to celebrate mass, even if she was forced to conform to the new laws, she would be committing no sin, because she would be doing so under duress. This view was reinforced by a letter from Mary of Hungary, who assured the princess that a 'victim of force' would be 'blameless in God's sight'. Mary, however, was preparing for martyrdom.

In August 1551, Edward VI began attending Council meetings on a regular basis. Already he was beginning to flex his political muscles and wield a degree of royal power, having his say in affairs and helping to make decisions. One of his first edicts was to order the name of his father's ship 'The Great Harry' to be changed to 'The Great Edward'. His tutors were dismissed that same month, which meant that his formal education was considered to be complete. He was now to devote his time exclusively to the learning of statecraft. Edward was interested in affairs of state and in the administration of government, and began by drawing up plans for improving the efficiency of the Council.

Foreign ambassadors were impressed, not only by the young King's command of Latin, French and Greek, but also by his intelligent grasp of affairs and his athletic accomplishments. It was noticed, however, that Edward did not excel in the tiltyard as his father had done, and for this reason there were few tournaments staged. Concern was also expressed for the King's 'thin and weak' physique, and Bishop Latimer was worried that he was coming too much under the influence of 'velvet coats and upskips' – frivolous and upstart courtiers who fawned upon the boy.

Perhaps influenced by the King, the Council decided, early in August, that it could 'wink at sin no longer'. On 9 August, the councillors reached a decision to prohibit Mary from attending mass at all. They summoned her servants Rochester, Englefield and Walde-grave, whom they considered to be 'the chief instruments and cause that kept the princess in the old religion'.

When the three men presented themselves before the Council at Hampton Court, they were ordered to convey the King's decision to Mary at her house at Copt Hall in Essex. From now on, her chaplains were forbidden to say mass, and everyone else was forbidden to hear it. Her officers were informed that it was their duty to persuade her to conform in her own interests. Rochester protested that in matters of religion, Mary 'asked nobody's advice and, what was more, not one of her ministers dared broach the matter in her presence'. It was not seemly for them, as servants, to instruct their mistress how to run her household. The councillors retorted that they were required to do as they were ordered upon their allegiance to the King, which no loyalty to Mary ought to obstruct.

On 16 August, Rochester, Englefield and Waldegrave arrived back at Copt Hall, where they sought out their mistress. Guessing what had happened, Mary forbade them to repeat anything of what had been said to them by the Council. If they did, she said, she would not listen. She then wrote to the King, complaining that the new constraints came not from him but from 'such as do wish those things to take place which be most agreeable to themselves'. As for the orders given to her officers, 'I find it very strange and unreasonable that my ministers and servants should wield such authority in my house'. She then sealed the letter and sent Rochester and the others back to Hampton Court with it.

As spokesman, Rochester told the Council that he and his colleagues dared not approach Mary with their orders a second time, for she would not listen to them. Asked if he was going to do as he had been commanded, he flatly refused. On the 23rd, he, Englefield and Waldegrave were committed to the Tower, while the King drafted a letter to Mary to say that Somerset's promise to van der Delft had only applied for a short time while she came to see the error of her ways. That time had now expired, and he required her to obey his laws like all other true subjects. If she and her chaplains broke the law, the same penalties would apply to them as to everyone else. Some councillors would have liked to summon Mary to London to answer personally for her disobedience, but most were fearful of provoking a Catholic demonstration. It was decided, therefore, to send a delegation to deliver the King's letter to her at Copt Hall.

On the 28th, Lord Chancellor Rich, Sir Anthony Wingfield and Sir William Petre rode into the courtyard there. Mary came out to meet them, her attitude defiant and cool, her tone high and harsh, so as (she later told Scheyfve) not to betray any womanly weakness. Her greetings, however, were mannerly, and she fell on her knees to receive the King's letter, 'saying she would kiss [it] because the King had signed it, and not for the matter contained therein, which was merely the doing of the Council'. She then rose and broke the seal, reading the letter there and then in the courtyard without asking the lords into the house. As she read, she murmured, 'Ah, good Mr Cecil took much pains here!' – making plain her belief that Edward had not composed the letter himself. Then she looked up.

'I am the King's most humble, most obedient subject and poor sister,' she declared, 'and will obey him in everything, my conscience saved,' but rather than adopt the reformed faith 'I will lay my head on the block and suffer death, although I am unworthy to die in so good a quarrel. When His Majesty is old enough to judge these things I will obey him in religion, but now, in these years, although he, good, sweet king, have more knowledge than any other of his years, yet it is not possible that he can be a judge in these matters.'

The councillors retorted that His Majesty's patience with his sister was exhausted. From henceforth, no service must be said in her house except that authorised by law. If she wished, they would tell her the names of those at court who were opposed to her celebrating mass.

'I care not for the rehearsal of their names, for I know they are all of one mind therein,' Mary cried. 'Rather than use any other service than that ordained during the life of my father, I will lay my head on the block.' If her priests were silenced, she would have no choice but to endure it, but 'none of your new service shall be said in any house of mine, and if any be said in it, I will not tarry in it an hour!'

Rich then informed her that her officers had been imprisoned. Astonished, she exclaimed that they were 'honester men' than she had believed them to be. It only went to prove how foolish it had been to send her own servants to browbeat her, 'for, of all persons, I am least likely to obey those who have been always used to obeying me implicitly'.

When the councillors attempted to clarify Somerset's assurances to her, Mary grew even more heated. She had in her possession a letter from the Emperor, she said, which made the position very clear, and she gave it more credence than any of their words. They professed scorn at this but Mary was undeterred.

'Though you esteem little the Emperor,' she went on, 'yet should you show more favour to me for my father's sake, who made the more part of you out of nothing.' The Emperor's ambassador 'shall know how I am used at your hands'.

Rich ignored this, choosing this moment to offer to appoint 'a trusty, skilful man', whom he had brought with him, as Mary's new controller. But she would have nothing to with this substitute.

'I will appoint my own officers for my years are sufficient for that purpose; and if you leave your new controller within my gates, out of them I go forthwith, for we two will not abide in the same house.' Then, as a parting rejoinder to the Lord Chancellor, she added, 'I am sickly, and yet I will not die willingly, but I will do the best I can to preserve my life. But if I should chance to die, I will protest openly that you of the Council be the causes of my death. You give me fair words, but your deeds be always ill towards me.' So saying, she turned round and swept past him, back into the house.

After he had composed himself, Rich summoned all the members of her household into the courtyard and informed them that mass was no longer to be celebrated in the Lady Mary's houses, on pain of imprisonment. Speaking to her three chaplains, he warned them that, if they used any prayer book but the Book of Common Prayer, they would be deemed guilty of treason. Fearfully, each priest promised to comply, though next day, Mary would dismiss them all from her service in order to spare them the agony of having to compromise their principles. Meanwhile, Rich's men were searching the house for another priest they believed to be hiding there, but he was nowhere to be seen.

Whilst the councillors were waiting for their men to return, Mary sent to us to speak one word with her at a window. When we were come into the court[yard], notwithstanding that we offered to come up to her chamber, she would needs speak out of the window, and prayed us to speak to the lords of the Council, that her controller might shortly return, for, says she, 'Since his departing, I take the account myself of my expenses, and learn how many loaves of bread be made of a bushel of wheat, and ye wis my father and mother never brought me up with baking and brewing, and, to be plain with you, I am weary of my office, and therefore if my lords shall send my officer home, they shall do me pleasure. And I pray God to send you to do well in your souls and bodies too, for some of you have but weak bodies.'

So saying, she withdrew from the window, leaving the councillors to make their departure. When they had gone, Mary's fourth chaplain came out of his hiding place; having not heard Rich's announcement in the courtyard, he could truthfully say that he personally had never been forbidden to say mass. And say it he did, in the greatest secrecy, during the months and years to come, for the Council did not lift the ban on Mary's mass; it was she who defied it, choosing to live in fear of betrayal and punishment rather than be deprived of the consolations of her faith. 'Unknown to more than three of the most confidential persons at the utmost', according to Scheyfve, the princess continued to attend regular services in her private chamber, despite the danger.

Early in September, Nicholas Ridley, Bishop of London, was in residence at his manor house at Hadham, three miles from Hunsdon, where Mary was staying, and took it upon himself to pay her a private visit. Despite their widely differing views on religion, Mary knew Ridley to be a sincere man, if somewhat ardent in his views, and a fine orator, and she welcomed him in a friendly and courteous manner, remembering how amiable he had been towards her during the years when he had served her father as chaplain.

For a while their conversation centred upon general matters, then Ridley, primed perhaps by the Council, offered to come to Hunsdon the following Sunday and preach to Mary's household. He also offered to lend her some reformist books and tracts.

Mary told him firmly that she would not listen to a Protestant sermon.

'Madam, I trust you will not refuse God's Word,' he replied.

Mary bridled. 'I cannot tell what ye call God's Word,' she retorted. 'That is not God's Word now that was God's Word in my father's days.'

'God's Word is one in all times, but hath been better understood and practised in some ages than others,' returned the Bishop smoothly.

'You durst, not for your ears, have avouched that for God's Word in my father's days that now you do!' exclaimed Mary. 'And as for your new books, I thank God I never read any of them. I never did nor ever will do.' So saying, she rose, indicating that the audience was at an end.

'My lord,' she said as they parted, 'for your gentleness to come and see me, I thank you; but for your offering to preach before me, I thank you never a whit.'

Scheyfve had wasted no time in reporting recent events to the Emperor and Charles instructed him once more to make a formal protest to the Council over their treatment of Mary. Warwick listened to this courteously enough, but then he said that he could not pronounce on so weighty a matter without laying it before the King. If his excellency would care to wait . . . So saying, he withdrew to the royal apartments and was gone for some time. When he returned, he said the King had insisted that his laws be obeyed; no one, least of all Mary, might be excepted. In his, Warwick's, judgement, the King had as much authority as if he were a man of forty. Scheyfve wisely pointed out that it was not his brief to discuss the King's authority.

Nevertheless, if the Council had learned what was going on in Mary's household, they did nothing. Fear of reprisal by the Emperor was still a consideration; whatever the extent of Charles's military commitments, he still had far greater resources than England and might choose to divert them there rather than against France if sufficiently provoked. There was, therefore, a tacit official assumption that Mary was obeying her brother's edicts and conforming to the law. In March 1552 Rochester, Englefield and Waldegrave were quietly released from the Tower and allowed to return to Mary's service. It was Mary's private belief, as she would confide to a future imperial ambassador, that Edward's Privy Council knew very well that she was continuing to attend mass.

6

Pining Away

As the sweating sickness raged in that summer of 1551, councillors and courtiers, among them the Duke of Somerset, fled to their country houses to escape the contagion. In Somerset's absence, the remaining lords of the Council planned a new distribution of titles and honours amongst themselves and fretted over rumours of rebellions against Warwick's regime. It was said that Somerset was plotting some new mischief, and to counteract these threats the Council further strengthened the royal guards by employing 500 foreign mercenaries. The other enemy at the door was rising inflation, which Warwick unthinkingly sought to cure by debasing the coinage, but this did little to bring down prices, which had tripled since Henry VIII's time.

The King's sisters remained on their estates. We know something of Elizabeth's lifestyle at this time because her household book for the year from October 1551 survives. She was still suffering intermittent ill-health, but this did not prevent her from checking and signing every page of her accounts. For a princess she lived modestly, economising where she could. Her table was supplied mainly from her estates. Veal, mutton, boar, beef, poultry, eggs, barley and wheat were delivered in vast quantities to her kitchens by her huntsmen and farmers, and were supplemented by little luxuries sent by friends – a sturgeon, young swans, or some plump partridges, or gifts from local people, such as apples from a poor woman, or a basket of peas.

Elizabeth's clothes were made by a tailor called Warren, to whom she paid £26 for velvet cloaks and £78.18s (£78.90) for liveries for her servants. He also supplied her that year with a pair of silk-lined bodices, twenty and a half yards of velvet, ten yards of black velvet for a pair of sleeves, two French hoods with partlets (veils), lining for kirtles, lengths of damask, crimson satin and silk, cauls and linen cloth. During this period Warren also made up 'divers robes for Her Grace'.

Other purchases were few. Mrs Ashley bought Holland cloth for making new towels, and Elizabeth paid a carpenter 44s.9d (£2.24) for making a walnut table. She also bought some gilt plate for New Year's gifts, at a cost of £32.3s.8d (£32.18). In all, she dispensed only £7.15s.8d (£7.77) on alms for the poor.

Music was her greatest indulgence.In February 1552 she paid over £7 to the King's drummers and pipers and Master John Heywood's troupe of child performers, who came to visit her by royal command. The accounts also record payments to other entertainers, Farmor the lutist, More the harper, and Lord Russell's minstrels. Seventeen shillings went on replacement lutestrings for Elizabeth herself. Her greatest pleasures were playing her lute or virginals, reading or sewing. She still hunted daily if her health and the weather allowed it; if not, she would pace restlessly up and down the gallery, or lie listless and frustrated in her bed.

That autumn, the ruling clique rewarded its supporters. On 11 October, Warwick was created Duke of Northumberland, the first man not of royal blood to bear a ducal title in England. At the same time, Dorset was promoted to the dukedom of Suffolk, which he held in right of his wife, whose brothers had died of the sweating sickness; the accommodating William Paulet was made Marquess of Winchester, and William Herbert, another of Northumberland's cronies, was created Earl of Pembroke. Several other members of the Duke's following, relatives, tenants and soldiers, received knighthoods. By creating this new affinity, Northumberland was extending his power base and consolidating his hold upon the Council by identifying the interests of his supporters with his own.

Somerset viewed this unprecedented distribution of honours as a threat to his own position, for all of those recently ennobled were his enemies. Already, he knew, Northumberland was preparing to move against him, determined to crush the voice of opposition. Aware that bribes had been offered to those who might be prepared to speak falsely against him, he turned for advice to his former secretary, William Cecil, who gave him cold comfort.

'If Your Grace be not guilty, you may be of good courage,' he said.'If you are I have nothing to say but to lament you.'

On the morning of 16 October, when the sweating sickness had abated and most councillors had returned to Whitehall, Somerset came late to a Council meeting. Before he could sit down, the Lord

Treasurer accused him of treason and conspiracy, at which Northumberland summoned the guard and had him arrested and conveyed to
the Tower. Shortly afterwards, the Duchess of Somerset joined him
there in custody.

Northumberland had now gathered enough material to charge his
rival with treason. It was alleged that Somerset had meant to seize
control of the Tower and use its arsenal of weapons to establish his
ascendancy over the capital. He would then orchestrate risings in
various parts of the country, whilst he himself arranged the poisoning of
the entire Council at a state banquet. It sounded preposterous but it
would serve to condemn the Duke.

Whilst the Council was busy amassing more evidence, as it was
pleased to call it, the court was preparing for a state visit by Mary of
Guise, Queen Regent of Scotland, who was travelling back to Scotland
after a visit to France. The Lady Mary was invited to attend the official
reception but declined on the grounds of 'constant ill-health, which at
present is worse than usual'. The real reason for her staying away, she
told Scheyfve, was her fear of being subjected to further questioning on
matters of religion.

Mary heard, however, that her young cousin, Jane Grey, was to
attend the reception with her parents, and kindly sent Jane 'some
goodly apparel of tinsel cloth of gold and velvet, laid on with
parchment lace of gold', to wear for the occasion. The austere Jane
preferred simple clothes in black and white and identified courtly
finery with the trappings of the Roman faith.

'What shall I do with it?' she asked Mrs Ellen in dismay, as the nurse
unwrapped the gown.

'Marry, wear it, to be sure,' Mrs Ellen replied.

Jane was horrified.

'Nay, that were a shame to follow my Lady Mary against God's
word, and leave my Lady Elizabeth, which followeth God's word,' she
answered piously. But her parents made her wear the gown, knowing
that the King loved such finery, and would himself appear decked out
in robes of cloth of gold, white velvet and silk, sparkling with
diamonds, emeralds and rubies. Elizabeth, however, stuck to her
sartorial principles and 'altered nothing, but kept to her old maiden
shame-fastness,' according to John Aylmer, cutting a striking figure at
court in her severely-cut garments.

Somerset's enemies now moved in for the kill. Northumberland,
aware that Edward VI had little love for his uncle, made sure of the
King's support by promising to implement more of the kind of radical
religious policy that Edward favoured, and had little trouble in

convincing the boy of Somerset's guilt. This much is evident from Edward's journal.

On 1 December the former Lord Protector was tried in Westminster Hall, found guilty and sentenced to death. Northumberland told the condemned man that he willingly forgave him and 'will use every exertion in my power that your life may be spared'. The public, however, voiced such extreme displeasure at the sentence that it had to be deferred for fear of provoking riots, and the 'Good Duke' was returned to the Tower, surrounded by crowds crying 'God save him!' to wait until the furore had died down. Arundel, implicated in the plot, was also imprisoned. He would be released within a year, but would emerge determined to have his revenge upon Northumberland.

With the traitors satisfactorily dealt with, Northumberland held 'a great muster of men-of-arms' in what is now Hyde Park, attended by most of his colleagues on the Council. This show of strength was calculated to warn the people not to provoke their rulers.

Mary, meanwhile, had received a letter from the Emperor castigating her for not attending Mary of Guise's reception at court. As heiress to the throne, he pointed out, it would be wiser if she showed herself there at every opportunity. Mary replied that she was planning to visit her brother in the New Year; however, she had heard a rumour that she was to be forced to attend Protestant services, and she had no intention of submitting to any 'outrageous rite'. The Council were still bullying her priests into submission, and she had complained about this but got nowhere. When he read her letter, the Emperor instructed Scheyfve to make another formal protest to the Council on Mary's behalf, but when the ambassador eventually saw them in January, he was told that King Edward, like Charles V, insisted on having his laws obeyed. To argue was futile.

The court observed Christmas with the usual festivities, and on this occasion, to please the King, Northumberland revived the ancient office of Lord of Misrule. A Mr Ferrers was chosen to act the part, and, garbed in a gorgeous costume of carnation satin striped with silver, he kept great state, having his own officers, including heralds, magicians, and fools, some of whom were dressed as cardinals. The cost – over £300 – was astronomical, but the King loved it. He also enjoyed masques and plays featuring Henry VIII's former fool, Will Somers.

Neither of the King's sisters was at court for the festivities. Elizabeth stayed at Hatfield, while Mary kept the festival with the Suffolks and Lord Willoughby at Tilty in Essex, where there were banquets and masques for her entertainment. On Twelfth Night gifts were exchanged, and Mary presented Jane Grey with a beautiful necklace of pearls and rubies.

After Christmas, Northumberland put pressure on King Edward to sign Somerset's death warrant, but the boy was reluctant to send his uncle to the block, confiding to the French ambassador his hopes of preventing the execution. Edward was not yet his own master, however, and Northumberland's will prevailed. On 22 January 1552, Somerset walked from his prison to Tower Hill through tumultuous crowds who were protesting vociferously against the sentence. Suddenly, some soldiers were seen hastening in the direction of the scaffold, and the cry went up, 'Rescue! Reprieve!' However, the men were only guards arriving late for duty, and the disappointed mob would have carried off the prisoner to safety had he not been so heavily guarded.

Somerset proceeded calmly to the scaffold, and begged the people to cease their clamour.

'Through your quietness, I shall be much quieter,' he said. Then, after asserting his loyalty to the King, he knelt for the blow. After it had fallen, there was a rush for the scaffold so that people could dip their handkerchiefs into the blood of a man whom many supposed to be a martyr. If Northumberland had been unpopular before, he was hated now, and many believed he was planning even greater wickedness. As for the King, he made a brief, laconic entry in his journal: 'The Duke of Somerset had his head cut off upon Tower Hill between eight and nine o'clock in the morning.' There was no word of regret for a kinsman, no betrayal of any emotion.

Northumberland had eliminated his worst enemy and removed a focus for an opposition party. By cleverly manipulating the King and making Edward believe that he was *de facto* ruler, the Duke contrived to exercise absolute control over the government. Edward was susceptible to flattery, and Northumberland laid it on heavily, deferring cleverly to the King's desire for religious change. That spring a revised version of the Book of Common Prayer was authorised, which was to form the basis of the present Anglican liturgy; it was heavily influenced by the teachings of the Swiss reformer, Ulrich Zwingli, whom the King much admired. Meanwhile, numerous chantries were being closed and their wealth appropriated by Northumberland and his supporters. So zealous was the Duke that Bishop Hooper acclaimed him as 'that most faithful and intrepid soldier of Christ'.

That February, inspired by a sermon by Bishop Ridley that drew his attention to the plight of the poor, the King established two charitable foundations in empty religious houses in London. In the priory of St Thomas at Southwark, he founded a hospital for the sick, and in the convent of the Grey Friars at Newgate, a school for the children of the poor, called Christ's Hospital.

In fact, Edward was bursting with plans, and frustrated that his power was still too limited to carry them out. He wanted to strip the Order of the Garter of its association with St George and have its knights pledge themselves to 'the truth wholly contained in the Scripture'. He was determined to streamline the Council into committees, one of which was to govern 'the state', the first suggestion of cabinet government in England. He meant to continue his father's policies. In fact, he could not wait to exercise his prerogative in every respect, and put so much pressure upon his advisers that, in the spring of 1552, the Council, with Northumberland's blessing, agreed that the King should attain his majority and assume responsibility for the government of his realm when he reached the age of sixteen in October 1553. This announcement met with everyone's approval, and there were celebrations to mark it.

On 17 March the Lady Elizabeth rode into London to lodge at St James's Palace, bringing with her 'a great company of lords, knights and gentlemen' as well as 200 ladies and gentlewomen on horseback, and a company of yeomen. Two days later she went in procession through St James's Park to Whitehall Palace, followed by dukes, lords and knights, and ladies and gentlewomen in great company, and so she was received into the court goodly'. The warm welcome accorded her marked the esteem in which she was held, in stark contrast to the treatment meted out to her sister Mary, the Catholic heiress, whom Northumberland both despised and feared. As for the King, he was always pleased to welcome his 'sweet sister Temperance' to court.

At the beginning of April 1552, shortly after Elizabeth had gone home, Edward 'fell sick of the measles and the smallpox', as he recorded in his journal. This was probably just a bad attack of measles, rather than the disfiguring smallpox, and the King appeared to make a full recovery. On 21 April, Elizabeth, having heard he was better, was writing to express her relief to learn of his 'good escape out of the perilous disease, and that I am fully satisfied and well-assured of the same by Your Grace's own hand. I must needs give you my humble thanks, assuring Your Majesty that a precious jewel at another time could not so well have contented as your letter in this case has comforted me.'

On 23 April, Edward was sufficiently recovered to take part in the St

George's Day service in Westminster Abbey, clad in his heavy velvet Garter robes, and for a while thereafter he carried out his royal duties as normal, though it seems that his constitution had been irrevocably undermined by his illness.

At the end of April the court moved to Greenwich Palace. Here Edward enjoyed tilting at the quintain and running at the ring, hawking, evening revels and musical recitals, or trips along the river on the royal barge. He attended 'a goodly muster of his men-at-arms' on Blackheath, watched the acrobats and high-wire artistes that he loved, and a play written for him by Nicholas Udall, entitled *Ralph Roister Doister*. In June the Lady Mary visited Greenwich with 'a goodly company'. Edward received her warmly and tactfully avoided the subject of religion.

on 27 June, the King rode through London before departing on his annual progress – a tour of part of his kingdom, enabling him to meet his subjects and be seen by them. He and his huge retinue would be accommodated in the houses of great nobles who lived along the route, often at a crippling cost to these hosts. Edward had been eagerly anticipating his progress, which this year would take him through the southern and western counties, and left London in cheerful mood, but some observers noticed that he was looking thin and pale.

Unfortunately, his advisers had arranged a punishing schedule, which required him to perform all kinds of public duties, such as inspecting the naval dockyard at Portsmouth, and to be constantly on show, as a king and as a guest. There was plenty of 'good hunting and good cheer', with lavish entertainments laid on for him at the great houses along the way. John Aubrey, the seventeenth-century diarist, once met an old woman who recounted that, as a girl of sixteen, she had been out walking in the Wiltshire countryside when she met a well-dressed youth on horseback. He told her he had been hunting but had lost his way. As she gave him directions, a party of horsemen galloped up, and by their deferential manner she knew that he was the King, even before they addressed him as such.

By August, the strain was beginning to show. According to a Spanish observer, 'It was observed on all sides how sickly he looked, and general pity was felt for him by the people.' Edward appeared exhausted, but he would not give in.

The lords with him, however, decided it might be best to curtail the progress, on the pretext that funds for it had run low. They did not want to provoke a political crisis by admitting that the King was ill.

At Salisbury, Northumberland, who had remained in London, rejoined the King, and was shocked by the change in him. Edward, he decreed, must return to London and consult a physician. He then summoned the Italian doctor and astrologer, Girolamo Cardano.

Edward returned to Windsor on 15 September. He hated the castle but had been too ill to travel further. Dr Cardano arrived shortly afterwards and professed himself highly impressed by his royal patient, praising his 'excellent virtues and singular graces, wrought in him by the gift of God. Nothing can be said enough in his commendation; [he is] such a worthy prince, although but tender in years, yet for his sage and mature ripeness in wit and all princely ornaments, I see but few to whom he may not be equal.'

Cardano was therefore distressed to discover that this paragon appeared to be afflicted with all the symptoms of consumption, or tuberculosis, a serious wasting disease of the lungs for which there was then no cure. Prior to his visit, the doctor had secretly – and at great danger to himself, for it was against the law – cast Edward's horoscope, in which 'I saw the omens of a great calamity.' Now he saw clearly that the King bore 'an appearance on his face denoting early death. His vital powers will always be weak.'

Summoned before the Council, Cardano did not dare reveal his true diagnosis, for it was treason to predict the death of the King. Instead, he mouthed soothing platitudes, saying that rest was all that was needed for his patient to recover his accustomed vigour.

But a rest from royal duties made little difference. Throughout the autumn and winter of 1552, the King's health declined steadily. He developed a harsh, racking cough, was laid low by spasmodic fevers, could not face food, and had to endure an unsightly bloating of his body, like dropsy. By the time he returned to Hampton Court to celebrate his fifteenth birthday, he was suffering agonising paroxysms of coughing which made him spit blood, and his doctors could do nothing for him. By Christmas, it was obvious that what the Elizabethan antiquarian John Stow refers to as a consumption of the lungs was well-established, and that the King's days on earth were numbered.

Northumberland, however, chose to act as if all was normal, arranging especially elaborate entertainments for Christmas and pretending that the King would soon recover. Edward's death would put an end to all his schemes, for it would bring Catholic Mary to the throne, and Mary would not look kindly upon a heretic who had bullied her mercilessly over religion. Already, Northumberland was devising in his mind ways of preventing Mary from ever succeeding, while at the same time making friendly overtures to her as if he were deferring to his future sovereign.

Mary had heard that her brother was unwell, but can have had no idea how serious his illness was because of the conspiracy of silence that surrounded him. Therefore she was astonished when she began to receive respectful, conciliatory letters from Northumberland, inform- ing her of affairs of state and news of the court, and suggesting she resume the coat-of-arms she had borne back in the 1520s as her father's heiress. Then she was granted £500 for repairs to ruinous dykes on her Essex estates. It was all rather perplexing.

Elizabeth did not receive such courteous treatment. Northumber- land feared her astuteness, and when she demanded to visit the King, he forbade it, refusing to heed her protests. The Duke almost certainly feared that her influence over Edward might ruin his future plans, and began systematically to poison the boy's mind against his sister.

By January 1553, foreign observers had noticed that Edward's cough was 'tough, strong [and] straining', and he himself had confessed to a 'weakness and faintness of spirit'. It was proving impossible to keep his condition a secret, and rumours of his illness – and even his imminent death – were beginning to circulate. On 20 January, Scheyfve warned the Emperor that a crisis was approaching; he had discovered that Northumberland was hoarding huge sums of money and, having removed Winchester from the treasury, had placed himself in control of it.

In Essex, Mary heard the rumours about the King's health and was alarmed. She had received an invitation from Northumberland to attend a Candlemas masque performed by a troupe of child performers, and on this occasion had no qualms about accepting, being determined to see for herself how her brother was. In February, according to the diarist, Henry Machyn, she rode to London 'with a great number of lords and knights and ladies, to the number of two hundred horse'; Northumberland himself received her, with a display of courtesy and ceremony, an hour's ride from the city, accompanied by Lord William Howard and a hundred mounted gentlemen. He then escorted Mary to the Priory of St John at Clerkenwell, where she was to stay.

The King, Northumberland explained, was too ill to receive his sister, being in bed with a high fever, but he might be better on the morrow. Next day, Mary rode to Whitehall, where she was welcomed at the palace gate by Northumberland and the entire Council, who accorded her so much respect that she might have been a reigning queen. By now, it must have occurred to her that her brother was very ill indeed and that, to all appearances, her accession was expected. However, she did not trust John Dudley; for all she knew he might be plotting some new villainy.

For three days, while Edward was too ill to see her, Mary remained at court, where wild rumours were circulating. She was told that the King was the victim of 'a slow-working poison', or that he was already dead. It was therefore with some relief that she was finally admitted to his bedchamber. What she saw there left her profoundly shocked, for Edward looked so thin and ill that it seemed he must surely die of whatever disease was ravaging his poor body. She was assured that he was on the mend, however; he did seem pleased to see her, and they exchanged pleasantries, both avoiding the topic of religion. But he was soon exhausted, and Mary was not surprised to learn, later that day, that the masque had been cancelled and the children sent home. She too went home, troubled in her mind, not only about her brother, but about Northumberland's intentions. Did he really mean to welcome her as Queen when the time came, as come it surely would? Or was he dissembling, trying to lull her into a false state of security?

Elizabeth was angry when she heard that Mary had been to court; she too had been 'determined about Candlemas to come to see the King's Majesty', but Northumberland had put her off with excuses, saying she could come another time.

A week after Mary had left, Edward's bouts of coughing became so violent that his doctors thought he was dying, and warned the Council that he was in peril of his life. If he caught any other malady he would undoubtedly succumb to it. Edward himself feared the worst, but he was more concerned about what would happen to the Protestant cause in England if he were to die now. He remained in a grave condition for more than a week, then suddenly rallied and was able to leave his bed. Throughout the crisis, Northumberland had issued daily bulletins about the King's health, trying to conceal the mortal nature of his illness, but even he could not prevent rumour and gossip from crying abroad the truth.

An unknown well-wisher had sent Edward some books to while away the hours spent in his sick bed. After the worst was over, John Cheke wrote to the donor to say that his master had received the books

kindly and courteously. His Majesty, debilitated by long illness, is scarcely yet restored to health. Should a longer life be allowed him, I prophesy indeed that, with the Lord's blessing, he will prove such a king as neither to yield to Joshua in the maintenance of true religion, nor to Solomon in the management of the state, nor to David in the encouragement of godliness. It is probable that he will not only contribute very greatly to the preservation of the Church, but also that he will distinguish learned men by every kind of encouragement. He has long since given evidence of these things, and has accomplished at this early period of his life more numerous and important objects than others have been able to do when their age was more settled and matured.

On 21 February, the King had sufficiently recovered to open in person a new Parliament, summoned urgently by Northumberland, but people were shocked to see how weak and exhausted he was. Parliament confirmed the new date for the King's coming-of-age. So confident was Northumberland of his hold over Edward that he did not doubt that his young master would continue, if he lived, to defer to him. If he did not live, then he could be relied upon to take the Duke's advice on the appointment of a successor who would ensure the future welfare of the realm and the maintenance of the Protestant religion.

When Parliament rose, Edward departed for Greenwich, firmly believing that Northumberland had both his and the kingdom's interests at heart and could safely be left to govern the country to the King's satisfaction. As for himself, he was of the opinion, according to Scheyfve, that his illness was not as serious as had been thought, and that he would soon be restored to health. A few peaceful weeks at Greenwich, enjoying the fresh air, would effect a cure. God must surely spare him for the great task that lay ahead of him.

In his will, confirmed by the Act of Succession of 1544, Henry VIII had left the crown of England to his son Edward and his heirs. If Edward died childless, Mary and her heirs were to succeed, then Elizabeth and her heirs. If these lines died out, then the heirs of Heny VIII's younger sister, Mary Tudor, were next in succession. Mary Tudor had died in 1533, and her heir was Frances Brandon, Duchess of Suffolk, mother of Jane Grey.

Northumberland knew that, if Mary succeeded, it would mean the end of his own power and probably his life. It would also herald a Catholic revival and the outlawing of the reformed religion. By the middle of March 1553, Northumberland had decided that the succession must be altered to exclude not only Mary, but also Elizabeth, who was likely to prove unamenable to his tutelage. When Edward died, the crown should pass, not to the forceful Frances Brandon, who would be no one's puppet, but to her daughter, a fanatical Protestant who would promote the reformed religion, but who was also young enough to be in awe of Northumberland and manipulated by him. It was the Duke's intention to marry Jane to his youngest son, Guilford Dudley, in order to cement the bond between the two families and thereby create a royal dynasty of Dudleys, of which he, Northumberland, would be the founding father.

The Duke had no doubt that he was in a position to bring such an audacious plan to fruition. He ruled as a dictator, and the King was in his control. Edward would surely see the virtue in the arrangement and would give it his blessing. He could then make a new will, disposing of the crown and disinheriting his sisters. Such a process was in fact illegal, for the King, as a minor, had no right to alter his father's arrangements for the succession since they had been confirmed by Act of Parliament. Furthermore, Parliament had granted Henry VIII the power to bequeath the crown to whomsoever he pleased; it had not extended that right to his successors. But Northumberland had no time for the niceties of the law. Suffolk, when approached, was more than willing to support him, and delighted that he was at last to realise his ambition of seeing his child on the throne; he was certain that his wife would waive her right of succession in favour of her daughter. As for Jane, she was not consulted; daughters were expected to obey their parents.

Yet Northumberland was not in such a strong position as he believed himself to be. Many of his fellow councillors resented his power, his greed, his pride, and his shameless promotion of his sons. They were angry at the imperious way in which he summoned them to Ely Place to conduct business, or had secret night-time conferences with the King, and made decisions without reference to their opinions. They muttered that he was, after all, the son of a traitor. Under his rapacious rule, England had advanced steadily towards bankruptcy as the Duke feathered his own nest and those of his supporters, and her prestige in Europe had been brought lower than ever before. He had hurried through radical religious reforms without pausing to consider the fact that most people in England were not ready for them, had, indeed, only just accustomed themselves to the religious settlement established by Henry VIII, and were largely Catholic in sympathy, even if they did outwardly conform with the recent religious changes. It did not occur to Northumberland that this latest scheme to place Lady Jane Grey on the throne would not be tolerated by a populace that loved and respected both Mary and Elizabeth as the late King Henry's daughters. He could only see the advantages it would bring to himself.

Northumberland divulged his plans to no one outside his immediate circle, but Scheyfve for one guessed that trouble was brewing, and that the Duke would do his utmost to prevent Mary from succeeding to the throne: 'They are evidently resolved to resort to arms against her, with the excuse of religion among others,' he reported. Nevertheless, the Duke continued to treat Mary with deference, and acted as if there was nothing seriously wrong with the King, speaking of Edward's coming marriage with Elisabeth of France and his hopes that their union might be fruitful. The strain of maintaining this pretence told on him, however; he became short-tempered and, if thwarted, responded with violent outbursts of rage. He confided to William Cecil that he retired each night 'with a careful heart and a weary body'. Fear of the future, and the stress of retaining a firm grip on affairs whilst plotting a daring coup, had a predictable effect on his health: he was, he told his secretary, 'as ill at ease as I have been all my life. What comfort think you may I have, that seeth myself in this case after my long travail and troublesome life, and towards the end of my days?'

Mary was also in a state of high anxiety that March. She did not trust Northumberland and feared that, if the King died, he would arrange for her to be done away with before she could assert her right to the throne. She was aware that others besides Northumberland were horrified at the prospect of her becoming queen. She was strongly identified with the Catholic cause and with Imperial interests, and had throughout her life taken no decisions without first seeking the advice of her cousin Charles V or his ambassadors. There were many influential people who had much to lose if Mary came to the throne, or who simply feared foreign interference in English affairs.

Edward VI's condition was steadily deteriorating, which meant that Mary's accession seemed a near-certainty. At the end of April Scheyfve reported: 'I hear from a trustworthy source that the King is undoubtedly becoming weaker as time passes, and wasting away. The matter he ejects from his mouth is sometimes coloured greenish-yellow and black, sometimes pink like the colour of blood.' One of the royal physicians confided to the ambassador that Edward would be dead by June. The Council had also been told this grim prognosis, but continued to issue reassuring bulletins for the benefit of the public. Northumberland did not want Mary to have time in which to make plans and perhaps arm her supporters. Yet the public were suspicious, wondering why they had not seen the King for so long, and in London in particular there was rampant speculation as to what was going on behind the palace doors.

Edward himself realised he was dying, and was racked with anxiety as to what would happen after his death. If Mary succeeded him, all his plans for the establishment of a Protestant state would be undone – it was an appalling prospect. Seeing his distress, Northumberland took care to play on his fears by predicting the destruction of his religious policies by Mary, and consequently had no difficulty in convincing him that it would be wise to consider altering the succession; indeed, Edward may even have suggested it himself.

While the dying King agonised over the future of England, Northumberland finalised plans for the marriage of his son Guilford to Lady Jane Grey. Jane was already betrothed to Edward Seymour, Lord Hertford, the fifteen-year-old son of the late Duke of Somerset, but her parents had no qualms about breaking this precontract; fond as they were of Hertford, this new match held far more glorious prospects for themselves and their daughter.

Jane was now fourteen. Battista Spinola, a Genoese merchant who saw her at this time, described her as being

> very short and thin, but prettily shaped and graceful. She has small features and a well-made nose, the mouth flexible, the lips red. The eyebrows are arched and darker than her hair, which is nearly red. Her eyes are sparkling, her colour good but freckled. In all, a charming person, very small and short.

The French ambassador, Antoine de Noailles, pronounced Jane to be 'well made' and spoke admiringly of her cultivated spirit and meritorious modesty. Fluent in Latin and Greek, she frequently corresponded with reformist scholars in Switzerland, and was learning Hebrew in order to read the Old Testament in its original text. Already she was famed throughout European intellectual circles for her erudition. As well as being very clever, Jane was proud of her lineage and family, but she was also contemptuously intolerant of those who held different beliefs from herself, and insensitive to the beliefs and feelings of others.

As yet, Jane knew nothing of her betrothal being broken, nor of the plan to marry her to Guilford Dudley. Born in 1536, Guilford was Northumberland's fifth and youngest son, and his mother's favourite. The Duchess had spoiled him, and he was now a vain, foolish, self-indulgent youth, who still ran to his mother whenever anyone denied him what he wanted. He was fair-haired, with a tall, elegant physique, aristocratic good looks, and a courteous manner, but he appeared both petulant and disagreeable. Like all the Dudleys, he was ambitious, and the prospect of a royal bride appealed to his vanity.

Lady Jane was not interested in young men, preferring to pursue her intellectual interests. Left to herself, she would not have married, but she accepted that princesses of the blood royal had no choice in the matter. However, she hated the Dudley family, and when, at Suffolk

Place, her parents informed her that she was to marry Guilford Dudley, she refused to do so. Suffolk and his wife were incredulous that their daughter should dare to defy them, and erupted in fury, but Jane quietly pointed out that she was already contracted to marry Lord Hertford, and was not free to marry anyone else. Her protest did her little good. Shouting and swearing at her, the Duke and Duchess insisted she obey them; when she persisted in her refusal, they responded with blows and curses. This did not work either, so the Duchess gave her errant daughter a whipping, and thus she and her husband 'succeeded in concluding' the betrothal. A contract was drawn up and a sullen Jane gave her reluctant consent to it. Thereafter she behaved politely but coolly towards her future husband whenever they met. Their betrothal was announced late in April 1553.

By this time, the King's condition was critical. Confined to his bed at Greenwich with a high temperature, he lay coughing up foul-smelling sputum and wincing at the pain caused by ulcers that had erupted all over his body. Northumberland was still issuing optimistic bulletins but no one took them seriously any more, and there were frequent reports that the King's death was imminent or that he was already dead. When they could catch the rumour-mongers the Council had them put in the pillory, but they could not trace the persons who claimed that Northumberland was steadily poisoning Edward.

Gossip was further fuelled by the King's failure to appear at the wedding of Lord Guilford Dudley and Lady Jane Grey, which took place on Whit Sunday, 25 May 1553, at Durham House in the Strand. It was actually a double wedding, for Jane's sister Katherine was also being married, her bridegroom being William, Lord Herbert, the son of the Earl of Pembroke, an ally and friend of Northumberland. These were just two of several marriage alliances made at this time by Northumberland in order to extend his power base. The joint wedding ceremony was conducted with great pomp and splendour to underline the importance of the occasion. Durham House had been refurbished with new tapestries, Turkish carpets and new hangings of crimson and gold tissue. The King sent magnificent jewels for the young couples, and commanded his Master of the Wardrobe to supply all the wedding finery, including cloth of gold and silver tissue and rich clothes. Lady Jane wore a gown of gold and silver brocade embroidered with diamonds and pearls. The entire Council attended the wedding, but the wedding banquet and the masques and jousts that followed it were held in private, with no foreign ambassadors being invited. However, the festivities were marred by an outbreak of food poisoning, caused by a cook carelessly selecting the wrong leaves for a hot salad. Guilford Dudley was one of those affected.

After the celebrations were over, Jane returned with her parents to Suffolk Place, while her sister Katherine was sent to live with her new husband at Baynard's Castle, the riverside town house of her father-in-law. It had been agreed by the Suffolks and Northumberland that the marriages should not be consummated just yet. If the coup were to fail, then they could easily be annulled. Jane, with some relief, went back to her studies, while Katherine and William Herbert were given separate bedchambers. William was all for defying their parents and creeping into his wife's room at night, but his fear of Northumberland's wrath prevented him from doing so. History does not record whether or not either couple had any affection for each other; in Jane and Guilford's case, it is more likely that they were merely indifferent.

For a month after her wedding Jane was ill. She believed that her father-in-law was trying to poison her, although he had no obvious motive for doing so. Her parents took her to the former monastery at Sheen to recover. While they were there, a former monk, embittered at having been turned out of the foundation by Henry VIII, did his best to frighten them away. One day, when the Duke and Duchess were walking in the gallery, a bloody hand brandishing a dripping axe thrust itself out of an aperture in the wall. No sources record what happened to the monk who perpetrated this hoax.

After the weddings were over, Northumberland hastened back to Greenwich to be with the King. Thereafter, he rarely left Edward's side. As May drew to a close, the boy grew weaker, and his doctors predicted he would not last two weeks. Some gave him only three days to live. In alarm, Northumberland realised he had very little time left in which to bring his plans to fruition.

The first step he took was to persuade the Duchess of Suffolk to relinquish her claim to the throne in favour of her daughter. He then ordered Jane and Guilford to consummate their marriage, which they did shortly afterwards. Jane had still not recovered from her illness, and in June her mother-in-law sent her to recuperate at Katherine Parr's former home at Chelsea. Here she was joined by the Duchess of Suffolk, but not by Guilford. His duty done, he preferred to remain with his mother.

Late in May, John Banister, a student doctor attached to the royal household, recorded that the King was

> steadily pining away. He does not sleep except when he is stuffed with drugs. The sputum which he brings up is livid black, foetid

and full of carbon; it smells beyond measure. His feet are swollen all over. To the doctors, all these things portend death.

The physicians had given up hope, and Northumberland, knowing they could do nothing more for their patient, sent them away, and in their place installed a female quack who claimed she could cure the King. With Northumberland's blessing, she began giving Edward daily doses of a potion that almost certainly contained arsenic, which prolonged his life but caused him intense pain and suffering. It seems likely that Northumberland knew what the effects of this drug would be, but he was desperate for more time, and consequently indifferent to the agony suffered by his young master.

The Duke now faced the task of persuading the King to change his father's will and disinherit his sisters. He told him that 'It is the part of a religious and good prince to set apart all respects of blood where God's glory and the subjects' weal may be endangered. That Your Majesty should do otherwise were, after this life – which is short – to expect revenge at God's dreadful tribunal.' Faced with the prospect of eternal damnation and an England returned to the Catholic faith, the King agreed that Mary should never succeed. But he could see no reason why Elizabeth should not. Northumberland answered that Mary 'could not be put by unless the Lady Elizabeth were put by also'. A female sovereign would marry a foreign prince and would 'abolish all the ancient rights and immunities' of the realm, until her husband finally 'extinguished at last the name of England. Your Majesty should consider again, and again. Kings owe protection to their subjects to defend them from injury.'

Edward suggested that the Duchess of Suffolk succeed him, but Northumberland summoned her to Greenwich where, in the King's presence, she formally relinquished her claim to the throne. When she had gone the Duke spoke at length of the 'matchless qualities' of Lady Jane Grey and

> the agreeableness of her conversations with His Majesty's own affections. She hath imbibed the reformed religion with her milk, and is married in England to a husband of wealth and probity. Your Grace had always an affectionate sympathy for that excellent lady. You are bound by your duty to God to lay aside all natural affections to your father's house.

The Duke pointed out that both Mary and Elizabeth had been declared bastards by Act of Parliament and never formally legitimised.

Jane had been born in lawful wedlock. Moreover, there was a precedent for her succeeding in her mother's lifetime, for had not Henry VII acceded to the throne whilst his mother, Lady Margaret Beaufort, still lived?

Having laid all his arguments before the King, Northumberland instructed Edwards's closest friend, Henry Sidney, to 'entertain' his master as often as possible with 'continual discourses of Lady Jane [and] the high esteem in which she was [held] for her zeal and piety'.

Edward did not need much convincing. Believing that he would soon stand before the dreadful Seat of Judgement, he commanded Northumberland to draw up a will entitled 'My Devise for the Succession', which he copied out in his own trembling hand. This vested the succession in 'the Lady Jane's heirs males'. The Duke assured Edward that, even though Jane was married to his son, 'I do not consider so much mine own interest as the benefit of the whole kingdom'. Around 10 June, the King made an alteration to the draft Devise in his own hand, leaving the crown to 'Lady Jane and her heirs males', and after them to Jane's sisters and their heirs. Edward's own sisters were described in this final version as 'illegitimate and not lawfully begotten' and 'disabled to claim the said imperial crown', being 'but of the half blood'. It was His Majesty's pleasure that his sisters 'live in quiet order, according to our appointment'.

On 11 June, as Scheyfve was reporting that Northumberland meant to make himself King, the King summoned Sir Edward Montague, the Lord Chief Justice, together with the Solicitor General and the Attorney General, to his bedside and commanded them to draw up Letters Patent incorporating his Devise for the Succession. The judges protested that to do so would be treason, for the will of the King could not overturn an Act of Parliament, and Henry VIII's Act of Succession had made it high treason to even attempt to alter its provisions. Northumberland insisted that obedience to the King's will could never be treason. But, said the Lord Chief Justice, a deed of settlement would have no validity in law. At this, the King had his attendants raise him from his pillows, and croaked, 'I will hear of no objections!' Montague begged for time to study the Devise at leisure, which Edward granted, and thereupon the judges rode back to London, greatly troubled in their minds. After a day or two of study and debate, they agreed with each other that to do as the King and Northumberland asked would be an act of treason.

Informed of this, Northumberland summoned the judges to Ely Place, where they found him 'in a great rage and fury, trembling with anger, and amongst his ragious talk [he] called Sir Edward traitor, and further said that he would fight in his shirt with any man in that quarrel'. The Lord Chief Justice and his fellow judges were 'in dread that the Duke would have stricken one of them'. King Edward was also furious that his order had not been obeyed, and on 15 June commanded Montague 'with sharp words and angry countenance' to 'make quick dispatch', at which Montague was 'in great fear as ever he was in his life before, seeing the King so earnest sharp and the Duke so angry'. Without further argument, he and his fellow judges retired in tears and arranged for a deed of settlement to be drawn up under the Great Seal of England.

On 21 June, when this document had been signed by the King, the Council were required by Northumberland, in Edward's presence, to give their consent to the new order of succession. Some showed great reluctance to do so, believing this new development to be entirely Northumberland's doing – as most people would erroneously come to believe. In fact it was the King who, on his sickbed and hardly able to speak, vehemently insisted that all his councillors approve his Devise. He looked so ill and distressed that no one dared refuse him, and by the end of the day, over a hundred councillors, peers, archbishops, bishops, members of the royal household, secretaries of state, knights of the privy chamber and sheriffs had appended their signatures to the document. Cecil later claimed he had signed only as a witness; Archbishop Cranmer, the last to sign, was the only man who did so 'unfeignedly'. Many lords had deep forebodings as to how the common people would react to this change to the succession, and most were aware that it was illegal, since the 1544 Act of Succession had not been repealed and the King, as a minor, was not legally capable of making a valid will. Moreover, Northumberland was generally disliked, even detested, and few wanted to see him remain in power. For all this, nearly every man present agreed to sign a second document, an 'engagement' drawn up by the Duke, in which they promised to support 'Jane the Queen to the uttermost of their power and never at any time to swerve from it'.

Foreign ambassadors had not as yet been told of the change to the succession. Northumberland knew that if Scheyfve heard of it he would warn Mary what was afoot. Of course, Scheyfve had guessed that something was going on. 'On every side there are plans and preparations,' he told the Emperor, but what they were for he was not certain. On 19 June, the ambassador received a request from a worried Mary that he would ask the Emperor's advice as to what she should do. Charles responded by telling her to accept whatever offer was made to her; if it was not the crown, then he regretted he could not help her, for he had not the manpower or resources to fight for her right to the succession. But by the time this message reached her, Mary would have taken matters into her own hands.

By the end of June, Scheyfve had discovered that Northumberland had succeeded in altering the succession, although he knew no details. He told Charles V,

> The Duke's and his party's designs to deprive the Lady Mary of the crown are only too plain. He will dissemble with the princess till the King dies, and then make a *coup d'état* and kidnap her. He will say that her accession may bring ruin and establish popery. When it comes to the truth, Northumberland's party may desert him. He is hated and loathed for a tyrant, while the Princess is loved throughout the land. With her help, Northumberland may be worsted.

This appeared, however, to be a vain hope. Further confirmation of the way things were moving came on 23 June, when an order went out for prayers for the King's sisters to be omitted from church services.

Concerned about the situation in England, and worried about Mary's safety, Charles V dispatched three special envoys who would later replace Scheyfve. Simon Renard, a native of Franche-Comté whose mother-tongue was French, was by far the most accomplished and able of the three. He and his colleagues faced a difficult task. Ostensibly in England to convey the Emperor's commiserations to King Edward over his illness, their actual brief was to assure Northumberland of Charles's friendly intentions towards him whilst doing their best to persuade him to alter his plans for the succession. They were also to protect the interests of the Lady Mary, allaying the fears of the English by saying that the Emperor believed she should marry an Englishman and not a foreigner. Finally, they were to make contact with Mary and urge her to issue a declaration that she did not intend to make any sweeping changes with regard to foreign policy or religion, and that she would pardon all those councillors who had given her cause for offence during Edward's reign. If Mary agreed to take this advice, those who had objected to her succeeding on the grounds of religion or marital alliance, or simply through fear for their own skins, would have no further cause for opposition.

In the opposite camp, the French ambassador, de Noailles, was doing everything to assure Northumberland of his support. His country was at war with the Emperor, and he knew that Charles would try to thwart the Duke's plans. De Noailles promised that his government would do all that was needful to keep the Emperor fully occupied when the time came for the King's Devise to be put into effect. Guessing that the French would meddle in this way, Charles instructed his ambassadors to make use of every opportunity to counteract French influence at the English court.

Scheyfve knew that Northumberland meant to have Mary disinherited, but – like everyone else outside the Privy Council and the royal household – he had no idea who was to rule in her stead. It occurred to him that it might be Lady Jane Grey, but he rejected the idea on the grounds that she was too young. On 27 June he informed the Emperor that Northumberland probably meant to make his son Guilford king. The Duke's 'designs are obvious. God wishes to punish this kingdom.'

The next day, Northumberland concluded a secret treaty with France; in return for money and troops, it is believed that he promised to give back Calais, all that remained of England's lands in France. At the same time, the Duke forced the London merchants to lend him £50,000, and sent his captains and armed forces to man the chief strongholds thoughout the kingdom in case the populace should rise in Mary's favour when Jane was proclaimed queen.

By 2 July, the King was suffering agonies as a result of arsenical poisoning, and using his remaining strength to beseech God for a speedy release into the next world. His skeletal body had swollen like a balloon, and 'all his vital parts were mortally stuffed'. His pulse was weak and irregular, his skin was beginning to discolour, his extremities were being eaten away by gangrene, his hair and nails were falling out, his breathing was painful, and he could barely speak.

Northumberland had no further need to keep the King alive, so he dismissed the female quack who had been attending him, and recalled the royal doctors. Some historians believe the woman was murdered, since she disappears from the records at this date, but there is no evidence to support this.

Rumours abounded that the King was dead or dying, yet Northumberland had been issuing bulletins announcing that His Majesty was recovering and out of danger, and was able to walk in the galleries and gardens at Greenwich. When a prayer for his recovery was displayed on church doors in London, it provoked many citizens to make their way to Greenwich on Sunday, 2 June, demanding to see their sovereign. A gentleman of the bedchamber tried to fob them off by telling them that 'the air was too chill' for the King to come out and greet them, but they refused to go away until they had seen him, and, fearing their mood might turn ugly, Northumberland ordered the King's attendants to hold him up at a window. Seeing him 'so thin and wasted', the people were shocked, and 'men said he was doomed'. After this, no more optimistic bulletins were issued.

On or about 3 July, the Duchess of Northumberland visited Lady Jane Grey and Frances Suffolk at Chelsea.

'If God should call the King to His mercy,' she told Jane, 'it will be needful for you to go immediately to the Tower. His Majesty hath made you heir to his realm.'

Jane could not take this in; her mother-in-law's words, 'being spoken to me thus unexpectedly, put me in great perturbation and greatly disturbed my mind', she said in a statement afterwards. 'But I, making little account of these words, delayed to go from my mother.' Her refusal to leave Chelsea provoked a furious quarrel between the two duchesses, which resulted in Jane being sent to Durham House to await her accession. She was back three days later, however, having fallen sick once again.

Northumberland had provided Mary with regular false bulletins as to the state of the King's health. It was part of his plan to lure both her and Elizabeth to London, where they would be neutralised and rendered incapable of resistance; at best they would be imprisoned, at worst executed. To this end, on 3 or 4 July, the Council issued both sisters with summonses to Greenwich to attend upon the King. At the same time, Northumberland wrote to Mary at Hunsdon, telling her that her presence would be a great comfort to her brother during his illness. Thanks to Scheyfve, Mary was aware that Edward's condition was critical. She was also distrustful of the Duke's intentions, for Scheyfve had warned her that Dudley's attentions to her had been paid only in order to make himself out to be a disinterested party. At the same time, Mary was painfully conscious of the fact that she was a lone woman, in a precarious state of health, with little political influence and few powerful friends. She had no means of knowing that there were several councillors who were heartily sickened by Northumberland's misrule and would have welcomed her accession. She was 'in sore perplexity'. How should she respond to the summons?

At length, she decided to go to Greenwich. If Edward was indeed dying, it was her duty as a sister to go, and she left Hunsdon on 4 or 5 July. In London, Scheyfve waited anxiously to see what she would do. He believed that, if she went to Greenwich, she would be walking into danger. 'It is to be feared that, as soon as the King is dead, they will attempt to seize the Princess,' he told the Emperor. Then on 4 July, the ambassador found out that Lady Jane Grey had been named as Edward's successor.

If Northumberland was anxious to have Mary in his power, he was even more determined to lay hold of Elizabeth and prevent her from seeing her brother. Knowing how fond Edward was of her, and how clever she was, he was afraid that once she saw him she would persuade him to set aside the King's Devise and name her as his heir. And if that happened, it was farewell to John Dudley, for Elizabeth was not the type to allow him to rule her. Only a few weeks before, Elizabeth had set out from Hatfield, determined to visit the King; Northumberland's men had intercepted her and sent her back. She had then bombarded Edward with letters, expressing her concern for his health and begging him to let her come to him. The Duke ensured that none of them reached him.

It is not recorded that anyone warned Elizabeth that a trap awaited her at Greenwich, but when she received the summons to go there, she at once took to her bed and gave out that she was too sick to travel. Possibly her friend Cecil had counselled her secretly to remain where she was. Just in case the Council should enquire further, she made her doctor issue her with a letter certifying she was ill. Much as she would have liked to bid farewell to her brother, self-preservation took priority.

There was no doubt now that the King's last hours were approaching. The fearful progress of his disease was horribly apparent to all who approached him. Prolonged bedrest had resulted in an outbreak of bedsores; he had ulcers all over his body and a grossly swollen stomach. His digestive system had broken down, he vomited with alarming frequency, and coughed unceasingly. The 'suppurating tumour' on his lung gave him much pain, and he lay in a feverish delirium, reliant on opiates to relieve his sufferings and help him to sleep. His doctors prescribed new medicines they had concocted for him, but knew they would not work. One included nine teaspoonfuls of spearmint syrup, red fennel, liverwort, turnip, dates, raisins, mace, celery and pork from a nine-day-old sow. When William Cecil was told by a friend what was in it, he exclaimed, 'God deliver us from the physicians!'

The public now believed that Northumberland was deliberately killing the King with poison, for word of his employment of the female quack had spread. In vain, he tried to counteract the gossip by giving out that the Lady Mary had 'overlooked' her brother with the evil eye of witchcraft on her last visit.

On the afternoon of Thursday, 6 July, the Imperial ambassadors arrived at Greenwich and were 'bid welcome in the King's name' by Sir John Mason, a gentleman of the King's bedchamber, who made them 'courteous offers of entertainment'. It was a stormy afternoon, with the sky so dark that it seemed like night.

At three o'clock the King woke from a drugged sleep and began to pray: 'Lord, Thou knowest how happy I shall be may I live with Thee for ever, yet would I might live and be well for Thine elect's sake.' Then his eyes fell on one of his physicians, Dr Owen, sitting beside him. 'I had not thought you had been so near,' he murmured before drifting off once more into slumber.

When he awoke again, it was approaching six, and the storm was still raging, with thunder rumbling, lightning streaking across the sky, and hailstones red as clotted blood raining down. Dr Owen was still there, with Dr Wroth, the King's valet Christopher Salmon, and the ever-faithful Henry Sidney. When Sidney took his frail body into his arms, Edward knew that his life was ebbing away.

Too weak to cough or speak, he whispered a last prayer, one he had composed himself:

> Lord God, deliver me out of this miserable and wretched life, and take me amongst Thy chosen; howbeit, not my will but Thy will be done. Lord, I commit my spirit to Thee. O, Lord, Thou knowest how happy it were for me to be with Thee; yet, for Thy chosen's sake, send me life and health, that I may truly serve Thee. O, my Lord God, defend this realm from papistry, and maintain Thy true religion, that I and my people may praise Thy holy Name, for Thy Son Jesus Christ's sake, Amen.

At six o'clock the young King's terrible sufferings finally ended. After his eyes had closed for the last time, the tempest raged on. Later, superstitious folk claimed that Henry VIII himself had sent it, and had risen from his grave in anger at the subversion of his will.

Part II
Jane and Mary

7

'Jane the Queen'

On the evening of 6 July, Mary Tudor reached Hoddesdon, where a sympathiser intercepted her on the road and warned her that the summons to Greenwich was a trap; she should stay away from the court and ride north without delay to one of her East Anglian strongholds, where she would be surrounded by men of her affinity and the tenantry of the Howards, England's premier Catholic peers.

Mary did not hesitate. It appears that she scribbled a hasty note to Scheyfve, informing him of her intention to proclaim herself queen as soon as she heard that the King was dead, and another to Northumberland informing him that she was ill and unable to travel, before riding through the night for her castle at Kenninghall in Norfolk, accompanied by only two of her ladies and six gentlemen of her household. If her bid for the crown failed, then at least Kenninghall was well placed for her to make her escape to Flanders by sea.

Sir Nicholas Throckmorton, a court official based at Greenwich, afterwards claimed that it was he who sent the warning, although it could just as well have been William Cecil, Throckmorton's colleague, or even Mary's goldsmith, Robert Raynes, acting on Throckmorton's behalf.

Back in London, Northumberland was taking stock of his position whilst keeping the King's death a secret. On the morning of the 7th, just as the Imperial envoys were preparing to ask for an audience with Edward VI, they heard a rumour that he had died the previous evening. Such stories were common, however, and they took little notice of it. Later that day, Scheyfve's spies learned the truth, which Renard duly reported to his master. When, the next day, the ambassadors were informed that His Majesty 'was unable to grant us audience as his indisposition kept him most of the day in bed', they knew that a great deception was being maintained.

Northumberland was in control of the treasury, the navy, and the Tower, which housed an unequalled arsenal of weapons and the royal mint. He appeared to hold the Council in the palm of his hand, and had his garrisons in strongholds throughout the shires. He also enjoyed the reputation of being 'the best man of war' in the kingdom. He now gathered about him a large number of lords, had Windsor Castle stocked with arms and a great quantity of provisions and prepared for a siege, ordering that the guns of the Tower be placed at battle stations.

According to the chief source for this period, the anonymous contemporary *Chronicle of Queen Jane and Two Years of Queen Mary*, from which most of the unattributed quotations in the pages that follow have been taken, a fleet of seven great warships had been refitted and now waited off the eastern coast, in case Mary should try to flee the kingdom. Access to London was restricted and, as the palace guards were doubled, the French ambassador was reminded of the aid promised by his country.

When Northumberland was told that Mary had retreated to Norfolk, he sent his son, Lord Robert Dudley, after her with a troop of four hundred horse, but he failed to catch up with her. Nevertheless, no one believed that Mary stood any chance of prevailing: 'All the forces of the country are in the Duke's hands, and my lady has no hope of raising enough men to face him,' wrote Scheyfve gloomily, and Charles V, when he learned of her desperate gamble, wrote urgently to his ambassadors, advising them to beg the Duke to be merciful with her. Scheyfve had already sent Mary a letter, begging her to abandon her foolhardy plans and submit to Dudley.

Only Northumberland himself knew how precarious his own situation in reality was. He was aware that most of his colleagues were waiting to see what happened before committing themselves, and, knowing that he could count on the loyalty of no one save his own family, the Suffolks and the Parrs, he knew that the success of his plans depended upon speedy, decisive action. Mary must be caught, and soon, for at large she was a focus for opposition. Meanwhile, the King's death must be concealed for as long as possible.

There remained, however, the problem of what to do with the body. The Duke had hoped for a fortnight in which to gather his resources, but, since the weather was warm and the corpse already beginning to decay, this proved untenable. He could not leave the body in the King's bedchamber, yet nor could he risk an autopsy –

which, in view of the current rumours, his colleagues might suggest –
which might reveal the arsenic in Edward's body.

We do not know for certain what happened to Edward VI's corpse.
A letter written a few days later by one of Northumberland's sons states
that the Duke had not dared to let the late King lie in state but had
'buried him privately in a paddock adjoining the palace, and substituted
in his place, to be seen by the people, a young man not very unlike him,
whom they had murdered'. Was this the body delivered to the
embalmers, the body that was shortly afterwards carried in a coffin to
Westminster Abbey by twelve peers of the realm, who watched over it
in turn 'without torches or tapers', as a French observer noted in
shocked tones? If so, then it is an impostor who rests today in the altar
tomb in the Henry VII Chapel, while the pathetic remains of the true
Edward VI lie somewhere in Greenwich Park.

Northumberland managed to keep the King's death secret for nearly
two days. Then, on 8 July, in order to quell the rumours that were
circulating in the city, he summoned the Lord Mayor and aldermen of
London to Greenwich and announced to them that Edward VI had
died. He then swore them to secrecy and informed them that his late
Majesty had appointed the Lady Jane Grey as his successor by his Letters
Patent. He confided that he had just learned that Mary had 'gone
towards Norfolk and Suffolk, being the coast opposite Flanders, with
intent to involve the kingdom in troubles and wars, and bring in
foreigners to defend her pretensions to the crown'. Intimidated by the
Duke, the city fathers promised to serve Jane as their lawful sovereign.

Later that day Northumberland placed the Tower under the control
of Lord Clinton, and ordered that three important Catholic prisoners
who had been incarcerated there for most of Edward's reign – the
Duke of Norfolk, Bishop Gardiner and Edward Courtenay, a
descendant of the Plantagenets – be told to prepare for immediate
execution. Prominent Catholics such as these would not be given a
chance to support Mary. The Duke then wrote to Elizabeth informing
her of her brother's death.

Mary, meanwhile, had spent the night of 7 July at Sawston Hall near
Cambridge, the manor house of John Huddlestone, a prominent
Catholic gentleman, who welcomed her warmly and had mass
celebrated in her presence. In the morning, after she left, word leaked
out that she had stayed at the house, and some zealous Protestants from
Cambridge set fire to it, thinking she was still inside. Riding over a
hilltop, Mary could see the blaze; turning to a dismayed John
Huddlestone, who had offered to escort her some of the way, she
promised that when she was queen she would build him a better house

on the site as compensation for his loss. She then rode on to Bury St Edmunds, where she was heartened by the warm reception extended to her by the inhabitants.

That night Mary slept at Euston Hall near Thetford, the home of her friend, Lady Burgh, a widow. While she was there Robert Raynes, 'her goldsmith, a citizen of London', arrived with news of King Edward's death. Raynes said he had been sent by Sir Nicholas Throckmorton, which made Mary very suspicious. Why should Throckmorton help her? Was the news true? Or was this another bait with which to trap her? It might be that Northumberland was provoking her to declare herself queen while her brother still lived, in which case she would be guilty of high treason. It would be better to keep the news to herself and continue on her way, hoping for confirmation from another source.

At Norwich, the people shut their gates against her, and she was warned that Lord Robert Dudley and his men were closing in on her. Disguising herself as a serving maid, she rode pillion behind a man left by John Huddlestone to guide her until she was well on the way to Kenninghall. Soon she was intercepted, not by Robert Dudley, but by a courier sent by Scheyfve, who confirmed the report of her brother's death and warned her that she could not hope to prevail against Northumberland; nor could she escape from England because the way was barred by the ships stationed off the eastern coast. The Duke had sent men after her, and it would be wiser to negotiate terms while there was still time. Mary answered that she would respond to Scheyfve's message when she had had time to think about it.

She arrived at Kenninghall on Sunday, 9 July, having been joined by about thirty loyal gentlemen on the way. During Henry VIII's reign, the Duke of Norfolk had built himself a magnificent brick manor house beyond the moat of the ancient castle. When the Duke was attainted in 1547, Kenninghall passed to the Crown, and presently to Mary. The spacious accommodation included a great chamber, hung with fourteen tapestries depicting the labours of Hercules, a long gallery boasting twenty-eight portraits of 'divers noble persons', an armoury well-stocked with weapons, and a chapel made resplendent with six tapestries, each nine yards square, illustrating the story of Christ's passion.

No sooner had she arrived than Mary received news via Dr Thomas Hughes that confirmed the report from Scheyfve. Knowing that there was no longer any doubt that King Edward had died, Mary took counsel with her chief officers and then summoned every member of her household into the great chamber and proclaimed herself the rightful Queen of England 'by divine and human law'. Her servants responded with heartfelt cheers, but Mary knew that there were almost insurmountable obstacles to be overcome before she was queen in deed as well as title. First of all, she must inform Northumberland of her intentions, and to this end she dispatched her man Thomas Hungate to the Council with a letter bearing the unmistakable tone of royal command:

> My lords, we greet you well, and have received sure advertise-
> ment that our dearest brother the King is departed to God, which
> news, how they be woeful unto our heart, He wholly knoweth to
> whose will and pleasure we must and do humbly submit us and
> our will.
>
> But in this lamentable case, that is to wit now after his death,
> concerning the crown and governance of this realm of England,
> what has been provided by Act of Parliament and the last will of
> our dear father, the realm and all the world knoweth, and we
> verily trust that there is no good true subject that can or will
> pretend to be ignorant thereof. And of our part, as God shall aid
> and strengthen us, we have ourselves caused, and shall cause, our
> right and title in this behalf to be published and proclaimed
> accordingly.
>
> And albeit this matter being so weighty, the manner seemeth
> strange that, our brother dying upon Thursday at night last past,
> we hitherto had no knowledge from you thereof. Yet we
> considered your wisdoms and prudence to be such that, having
> eftsoon amongst you debated, pondered and well-weighed this
> present case, we shall and may conceive great hope and trust and
> much assurance in your loyalty and service, and that you will, like
> noble men, work the best.
>
> Nevertheless, we are not ignorant of your consultations and
> provisions forcible, there with you assembled and prepared, by
> whom, and to what end, God and you know, and Nature can but
> fear some evil. But be it that some consideration politic hath
> hastily moved you thereto, yet doubt you not, my lords, we take
> all these your doings in gracious part, being also right ready to
> remit and fully pardon the same freely, to eschew bloodshed and
> vengeance. Trusting also assuredly you will take and accept this
> grace and virtue in such good part as appeareth, and that we shall
> [not] be enforced to use the service of other our true subjects and
> friends, which in this, our just and rightful cause, God, in whom
> our whole affiance is, shall send us.

Wherefore, my lords, we require and charge you, for that allegiance which you owe to God and us, that, for your honour and the surety of your persons, you employ yourselves and forthwith, upon receipt hereof, cause our right and title to the crown and government of this realm to be proclaimed in our city of London and such other places as to your wisdoms shall seem good, not failing hereof, as our very trust is in you. And this letter signed with our hand shall be your sufficient warrant. Given under our sign[et] at our manor of Kenninghall, the 9 July 1553, Mary.

Copies of this letter were sent to cities and towns throughout the kingdom, and to many men in public office.

Bearing in mind the Emperor's advice to dissemble, Mary then made it known that she would maintain the religion of England as established by her brother and make no drastic changes. This was a popular move and encouraged several local gentlemen with their tenantry to join her at Kenninghall. At the same time, Mary sent out letters to towns as far away as Chester and messengers throughout East Anglia 'to draw all the gentlemen of the surrounding countryside to do fealty to their sovereign', and was astounded at the speed with which they responded to her summons; it was almost as if they had been waiting for it. The first to arrive was Sir Henry Bedingfield of Oxburgh Hall in Norfolk, whose father had been Katherine of Aragon's gaoler in the 1530s; then came the wealthy Sir Richard Southwell, who brought with him men, arms, money and provisions, and after him John Bourchier, Earl of Bath (whose kinswoman, Lady Bryan, had been Elizabeth's governess) and Henry Ratcliffe, Earl of Sussex, each with men of their affinity.

Meanwhile, at Paul's Cross in London on that Sunday, Nicholas Ridley, Bishop of London, acting on Northumberland's orders, preached a sermon in which he branded both Mary and Elizabeth as bastards, at which 'the people murmured sore' and shouted so loudly in derision that Ridley had difficulty in making himself heard. The Lady Mary, he cried, was a papist who would be swayed by foreign influence, but the crowd would not listen. Elsewhere, Bishop Latimer thundered from the pulpit that it would be better if both princesses were taken by God than that they should endanger the true religion by marrying foreign princes.

At this stage, the councillors appeared united behind Northumberland even if some of their number – among them Northampton, Arundel, Huntingdon and Pembroke – had qualms about the legality

EDWARD VI: 'The most godly and virtuous king that ever reigned in England' died at fifteen before he could fulfil his early promise.

Below left EDWARD SEYMOUR, DUKE OF SOMERSET: He was 'a dry, sour, opinionated man' whose ideas were too liberal for his noble colleagues.

Below right JOHN CHEKE. A renowned Greek and humanist scholar, he became chief tutor to Edward VI.

THOMAS SEYMOUR, LORD
SUDELEY: The Lady Elizabeth
described him as 'a man of much wit
and very little judgement'.

THE LADY ELIZABETH shortly
before her liaison with Admiral
Seymour.

KATHERINE ASHLEY: Elizabeth's
governess was an educated but rash
woman who loved her devotedly and
took 'great labour and pain in bringing
her up in learning and honesty'.

THOMAS PARRY: Along with
Katherine Ashley, he was sent to the
Tower for his loyalty to the Lady
Elizabeth.

HATFIELD PALACE: All that remains of Elizabeth's favourite residence; it was at Hatfield that she learned of her accession.

CHARLES V, HOLY ROMAN EMPEROR: Mary Tudor relied on his self-interested advice throughout her life. This painting shows him dividing his empire at the time of his abdication.

Left JOHN DUDLEY, DUKE OF NORTHUMBERLAND He 'seldom went about anything but he had three or four purposes beforehand'.

Right LADY JANE GREY: A formidable intellectual and fanatical Protestant, she was 'ready and glad to end her woeful days' at the age of sixteen.

MARY I: She was 'good, easily influenced, inexpert in worldly affairs, and a novice all round.' Yet later generations would call her 'Bloody Mary'.

PHILIP OF SPAIN: 'He treats the Queen very kindly and well knows how to pass over the fact that she is no good from the point of view of fleshly sensuality.'

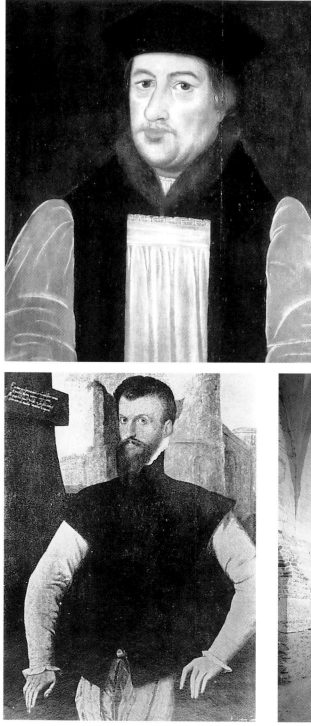

STEPHEN GARDINER, BISHOP OF WINCHESTER. Harsh and stern, he was nevertheless 'an unmatched royal servant' and tried to mitigate the religious persecution on which Queen Mary was determined.

EDWARD COURTENAY, EARL OF DEVON: Although he had 'neither spirit nor experience', he was seriously mooted as a husband for both Mary and Elizabeth.

THE BELL TOWER, TOWER OF LONDON: Both the Lady Elizabeth and Edward Courtenay were held prisoner here.

THE OLD PALACE, WOODSTOCK: The Lady Elizabeth was held under house arrest here in 1554-5.

The Remains of Woodstock, as they appeared in 1714.

[E]LIZABETH I AS PRINCESS: [n]eurotic and brilliant, she had 'a spirit of [en]chantment' and the Spanish [am]bassador Renard thought her 'greatly [to] be feared'.

REGINALD POLE, ARCHBISHOP OF CANTERBURY: He had high ideals, but little real understanding of the religious changes that had taken place in England during his twenty-year absence.

SIR WILLIAM PAGET: He made himself indispensable to four Tudor monarchs thanks to a talent for turning his coat without scruple.

Below left WILLIAM PAULET, MARQUESS OF WINCHESTER: He was one of four lords who gave Queen Mary away at her wedding; he also escorted the Lady Elizabeth to the Tower.

Below right SIR WILLIAM PETRE: He served as Secretary of State to Henry VIII, Edward VI, Mary I and Elizabeth I, only narrowly avoiding ruin for having supported Lady Jane Grey.

of his plans. Knowing that Mary was still very much at large, Northumberland stressed the urgency of having Jane proclaimed queen without further delay. Since the councillors 'were as afraid of Northumberland as mice of a cat', they concurred in this, having been suborned 'by terror and promises'.

On the afternoon of the 9th, the Duke sent his daughter Lady Mary Sidney to Chelsea where she informed Jane 'that I must go that same night to Syon House to receive that which had been ordered for me by the King'. Jane was still recovering from what she believed had been an attempt to poison her, and protested that she was too sick to travel.

'It is necessary for you to go with me,' answered Mary firmly and with 'extraordinary seriousness'. Jane allowed herself to be led to a waiting barge and taken by water to Syon House, Northumberland's mansion at Isleworth on the Thames, where her husband and parents were waiting for her with Northumberland and other members of the Council. However, none of these people were in evidence when the two girls arrived, and they were shown into the great hall of the former convent, now hung with rich tapestries, and asked to wait. Neither spoke.

What happened next is recorded in Jane's own account, preserved in the pages of Girolamo Pollini's history, and in the near-contemporary account of John Florio, the London-born Italian translator of Montaigne, and René Aubert de Vertot, a Frenchman. Presently Northumberland led the Council into the hall. For a short while those present stood around in small groups, exchanging pleasantries, but the atmosphere was tense. Jane was astonished when, before engaging her in conversation, Pembroke and Huntingdon knelt and kissed her hand: 'with unwonted caresses they did me such reverence as was not at all suitable to my state'. She realised 'they were making semblance of honouring me', but despite having been forewarned, she still had no idea of what Northumberland's purpose was in bringing her here, and when she overheard someone referring to her as 'their sovereign lady' she became confused and alarmed.

At length, Northumberland escorted Jane to the Chamber of State, followed by Mary Sidney and the councillors. Inside, she was confronted by her parents, her mother-in-law and Guilford, with other noble persons, all standing in order of precedence before the empty throne, which waited beneath a canopy of estate. Relentlessly, the Duke led Jane on towards the dais, but when she saw the whole company bow or curtsey as she passed, she began to shake with fright.

'As President of the Council,' Northumberland announced, 'I do now declare the death of his most blessed and gracious Majesty, King

Edward VI.' There was a pause for the news to sink in, while the Duke spoke in pious tones about how his late master would be sorely missed, not only by himself, but by the whole realm.

> We have cause to rejoice for the virtuous and praiseworthy life that His Majesty hath led, as also for his very good death. Let us take comfort by praising his prudence and goodness, and for the very great care he hath taken of his kingdom at the close of his life, having prayed God to defend it from the popish faith and to deliver it from the rule of his evil sisters.
>
> His Majesty hath weighed well an Act of Parliament wherein it was already resolved that whosoever should acknowledge the Lady Mary or the Lady Elizabeth and receive them as heirs of the crown should be had for traitors, one of them having formerly been disobedient to His Majesty's father, King Henry VIII, and also to himself concerning the true religion. Wherefore in no manner did His Grace wish that they should be his heirs, he being in every way able to disinherit them.

There was another pause, so that the assembled company should have time to digest the import of this pack of lies. At this point Lady Jane was observed to shudder. Then, to her horror, Northumberland turned to her.

'His Majesty hath named Your Grace as the heir to the crown of England,' he declared. 'Your sisters will succeed you in the case of your default of issue.'

The slight, fifteen-year-old girl at his side seemed dazed and uncomprehending. Later, she confessed to feeling 'stupefied and troubled'. Speech was beyond her. Taking her silence for assent, the Duke informed her that

> this declaration hath been approved by all the lords of the Council, most of the peers, and all the judges of the land. There is nothing wanting but Your Grace's grateful acceptance of the high estate which God Almighty, the sovereign and disposer of all crowns and sceptres – never sufficiently to be thanked by you for so great a mercy – hath advanced you to. Therefore you should cheerfully take upon you the name, title and estate of Queen of England, receiving at our hands the first fruits of our humble duty – now tendered to you upon our knees – which shortly will be paid to you by the rest of the kingdom.

At his words, everyone in the room knelt in reverence, while Northumberland assured Jane that each one would shed their blood for her, 'exposing their own lives to death'. Jane, however, was hardly listening. She felt sick and faint with shock, and suddenly collapsed to the floor. Her loss of consciousness was brief, however, and as she came to, she realised that not one person had come to her assistance. This made her cry. It then struck her forcibly that what Northumberland was doing was wrong, very wrong, and she wanted no part in it. Her situation so appalled her that she made no attempt to get up but lay there on the floor, sobbing her heart out. She was alone, so alone, and no one would understand how she felt, or help her. These powerful men meant to use her for their own ends, and she was unable to stop them.

The watching lords and ladies waited politely for their new queen to compose herself, believing that she wept for the late King, since between sobs she had muttered something about 'so noble a prince'. After a while Jane calmed herself and rose to her feet, bracing herself to make a stand against what she knew to be tyranny.

'The crown is not my right,' she stated flatly, 'and pleaseth me not. The Lady Mary is the rightful heir.'

Northumberland flared, 'Your Grace doth wrong to yourself and to your house!' while Jane's parents reminded her of her duty to them, to her father-in-law, to the late King's will, and to her new subjects, ordering her, as an obedient daughter, to do as she was told. But Jane was immovable. Guilford then spoke, 'sparing her neither prayers nor caresses', but made no impression either. All she would agree to do was pray for guidance. She then fell to her knees, while the august company stood by, barely concealing their impatience. Jane begged God to tell her what she should do, but He did not give her any sign. She took this to mean that she should obey her parents, as the Scriptures enjoined, and accept the crown. Then, 'humbly praying and beseeching', but with grave misgivings, she said aloud, 'If what hath been given to me is lawfully mine, may Thy Divine Majesty grant me such spirit and grace that I may govern to Thy glory and service, and to the advantage of the realm.'

She then rose and seated herself on the throne. Northumberland, expansive with relief, came forward to kiss her hand, and everyone else followed suit, swearing allegiance 'even to the death'. Inwardly, though, Jane was convinced she had done the wrong thing: 'It did not become me to accept; [it resulted from] a want of prudence.'

That evening, the Council informed the new queen of the arrangements for her state entry into London on the following day. She was to lodge in the Tower prior to her coronation, and there she would find the royal apartments ready for her. Instead of travelling in procession through the streets, as was customary, she would go by water in the royal barge, preceded by a flotilla of other barges bearing the councillors and the chief officers of her household.

At seven o'clock on the morning of 10 July, after Northumberland had ordered a strong military presence into the city, Jane was proclaimed queen in Cheapside and other places in London by the royal heralds. The citizens received the news stony-faced, no one cheered, and only a few voices cried, 'God save her!' To break the embarrassing silence, the trumpeters blew resounding fanfares but failed to arouse any enthusiasm. One Gilbert Potter, who worked as a tapster in an inn, openly stated that the Lady Mary should be queen. His master, the innkeeper, denounced him to the authorities, and he had his ears cut off the next day, but when the innkeeper drowned whilst shooting the piers of London Bridge that very evening, people called it a just punishment on him, and said it indicated that God wanted Mary to be queen. However, most people realised that there was little hope of that happening, and when Jane was again proclaimed at mid-day, at the Tower, St Paul's and Westminster, and again in Cheapside at seven o'clock in the evening, they made no protest.

In the glorious, sunny afternoon, Jane arrived at the Tower, where she was greeted by a resounding salute from the guns along Tower Wharf. With Guilford, dazzlingly robed in white, gold and silver, at her side, paying her 'much attention' and bowing low to her each time she addressed him, she landed at the court gate, followed by her mother, who was acting as her train-bearer, and surrounded by six noblemen carrying a canopy of estate above her head. Wearing a green damask kirtle, a bodice in the Tudor colours of green and white, heavily embroidered with gold thread, a gem-encrusted French hood, and three-inch high chopines – wooden platform shoes – to increase her height and thus enable the people to see her, Jane walked in stately procession through the crowded Tower precincts to the main entrance to the royal apartments, where the Marquess of Winchester waited with the Lieutenant of the Tower, Sir John Bridges, and a detachment of the Yeomen of the Guard to receive her. Winchester, on his knees, offered Jane the great keys of the Tower, but it was Northumberland who took them, himself passing them over to Jane. Then the procession passed into the White Tower where Suffolk, the councillors, and a great number of peers, including Lord Herbert and his wife, Lady Katherine Grey, the Queen's sister, were waiting to receive Jane. When she had seated herself on the throne in the presence chamber,

Northumberland and Suffolk fell on their knees to bid her officially welcome. The court then proceeded to divine service in the Norman chapel of St John high up in the keep.

Back in the presence chamber, Jane seated herself again beneath the canopy of estate, flanked by Guilford, her nurse Mrs Ellen, her gentlewoman Mrs Tilney, and other attendants. The crown jewels were brought to her, having been conveyed from the Jewel Tower at Westminster by the Marquess of Winchester, the Lord High Treasurer; however, when Winchester offered to place the crown on her head, Jane remembered that 'the crown had never been demanded by me or by anyone in my name', and angrily rebuked him, refusing to wear it. He excused himself, saying he had only wished 'to try whether it became me or no. The which, with many excuses, I refused to do.'

'Your Grace may take it without fear,' replied Winchester smoothly, and at length Jane allowed him to place the diadem on her head to see how it fitted. The very act of wearing the crown made her feel faint again, and she paid little attention when Winchester said that another crown would be made to fit Guilford. She did not answer, but later became very thoughtful, for she had registered his words 'truly with a troubled mind, and with ill-will, even with infinite grief and displeasure of heart'.

That evening, there was a great banquet in the Tower, but during the feast Thomas Hungate arrived with Mary's letter, which was read aloud to the assembled company. There followed a stunned silence, which was broken by the lamentations of the duchesses of Suffolk and Northumberland. The Queen said nothing. The Duke of Northumberland was furious to learn that Mary had evaded capture, and haughtily scornful of her orders. Both he and the other councillors assured Queen Jane and each other that Mary – a woman alone, with no friends and no influence – posed no serious threat to their plans. Yet for all their bravado, the banquet had been ruined. The unfortunate Hungate was thrown into a dungeon, and the councillors speedily withdrew in order to draw up a document repudiating Mary's claims, to which twenty-three of them appended their signatures.

Later on, when Jane and Guilford were alone in the state bedchamber, Jane informed him that he would never be king consort. The crown was hers alone, and she had no right to make him king. Instead, she would create him a duke. Guilford, who had happily anticipated the pleasures of kingship, flew into a temper at this, and raged at his wife, 'I will be made king by you, and by Act of Parliament!' When Jane made it plain she had no intention of changing her mind, he tried different tactics, bursting into tears and running off to find his mother. The Duchess of Northumberland soon sailed into the room in a fine temper, demanding that her daughter-in-law accede to Guilford's very reasonable request, but Jane was impervious to threats or tears. She would make her husband a duke, she repeated, but she could not make him king unless Parliament asked her to.

'I will not be a duke, I will be king!' wailed Guilford, at which his mother ordered him to abstain from the bed of such an undutiful wife; he should return to Syon House with her. She then swept out of the room, her son in tow, and ordered her servants to prepare to leave the Tower that night. Jane, however, forestalled her, sending Arundel and Pembroke to prevent Guilford from departing.

'I have no need of my husband in bed,' she declared crushingly, 'but by day his place is at my side.' Guilford had no choice but to obey, but he continued to sulk, even in public. Jane, too, felt badly done by, for she had been 'deceived by the Duke and the Council, and ill-treated by my husband and his mother'.

Meanwhile, London was quiet; there was no rejoicing, as was usual upon the accession of a new monarch. Not a single bonfire was lit in the streets, and one German eyewitness reported that 'the people showed nothing but grief'.

That evening Northumberland sent a messenger to Scheyfve and Renard, formally announcing to them the King's death and Queen Jane's accession. That he did not inform them personally was taken by them as a marked slight, especially since de Noailles, the French envoy, was riding high in favour with Northumberland. On that day, Mary had written from Kenninghall to the Imperial ambassadors to say that she had decided not to take their advice but instead advance her claim to the throne. Enclosed with her letter was a copy of the text of her proclamation speech. When Scheyfve and Renard received this missive they were horrified at what they regarded as an impulsive and ill-judged action on Mary's part; in their opinion she could not hope to succeed. They could not reply to her letter as all the roads were blocked, and so they wrote to the Emperor, begging to be recalled without delay, since they were under such a cloud of suspicion that they could do nothing further on Mary's behalf. Charles V refused their request, and commanded them to do everything in their power to urge Mary to acknowledge Jane as queen, since what she had embarked upon was a suicidal course. Unable to communicate with the princess, the ambassadors could only request the Council to be lenient with her when she was inevitably apprehended.

★

During the first three days of her reign Queen Jane settled quickly into a routine. In the mornings the Council met in the White Tower, but she did not attend; instead, Guilford presided over the meetings, seated at the head of the table. It was Northumberland, however, who made all the decisions.

At noon, dinner – the main meal of the day – was served with great formality, and lasted for two hours. Jane sat beneath a canopy of estate between her mother and mother-in-law, with Guilford and the lords of the Council further along the table. During the afternoon, Suffolk and Winchester would inform Jane of decisions made in her name and give her documents to approve, to which she appended her signature 'Jane the Queen'. Throughout the day she remained mainly in her private apartments, often in fear that Northumberland was plotting to have her poisoned, for she was aware that she had displeased him by her unwillingness to accept the crown. She had heard the rumours that accused him of bringing about the late King's death by poisoning; now she attributed the falling out of 'all my hair' and the peeling of her skin – conditions probably brought about by stress – to the same thing. She had only limited power as sovereign; all she had done had been to promise that she would be 'most benign and gracious to all her people, and to maintain God's holy word and the laws of the land'. In every other respect she was Northumberland's puppet, at his mercy.

Jane was aware that Northumberland was hated by the people, but did not know that he had already alienated several councillors. Arundel was bent on revenge because the Duke had had him imprisoned after Somerset's fall; he also believed that Northumberland's arrogance would be infinitely greater as father-in-law to the Queen than it had been when he was merely Lord President of the Council. Huntingdon was resentful of the elevation of Suffolk, and – like some other lords – suspicious of the plan to make Guilford king. Winchester had opposed Edward VI's Devise and had only signed it in the interests of self-preservation. And Pembroke had forbidden his son to consummate his marriage to Lady Katherine Grey until Jane had been crowned; if Northumberland's coup failed, the marriage could easily be annulled.

8

God's Miracle

Elizabeth was at Hatfield when she received the news of Edward VI's death, and there she remained, diplomatically ill, waiting upon events. Her biographer, William Camden, states that Northumberland sent commissioners to offer her a large bribe in exchange for renouncing her claim to the throne, but she refused it, saying, 'You must first make this agreement with my elder sister, during whose lifetime I have no claim or title to resign.' Northumberland had his hands too full with other matters to press her further.

By 11 July, Kenninghall was surrounded by an armed camp, which grew larger by the hour as gentlemen from Norfolk and Suffolk rode in with their tenants to offer Mary their support. In Berkshire, Buckinghamshire, Hertfordshire, Bedfordshire, Gloucestershire and Oxfordshire, men were arming in her favour after loyal supporters had proclaimed her queen. Not only Catholics turned out, but also Protestants, anxious to see the lawful heir restored to the throne. Yet support for Mary was not universal; in parts of East Anglia and Cambridgeshire there was a small and poorly-documented rising against her, which continued for several weeks.

The Council finally replied to Mary's letter on 11 July in a document composed by Northumberland and John Cheke:

> To my Lady Mary:
> Madam, we have received your letter declaring your supposed title which you judge yourself to have. Our answer is to advise you forasmuch as our sovereign lady Queen Jane is invested and possessed with right and just title to the imperial crown of this realm, not only by good order of old ancient laws of this realm, but also by your late sovereign lord's Letters Patent signed with his

own hand and sealed with the great seal of England in the presence of the most part of the nobles and councillors, judges and divers other grown and sage persons assenting and subscribing to the same.

We must profess and declare unto you that by divers Acts of Parliament you [be] made illegitimate and unheritable to the imperial crown of this realm. You will, upon just consideration thereof, cease by your pretence to vex and molest any of our sovereign lady Queen Jane's subjects, drawing them from the true faith and allegiance due unto Her Grace.

Assuring you that, if you will for respect show yourself quiet and obedient as you ought, you shall find us all [ready] to do you any service, that we with duty may be glad with you to preserve the common state of this realm, wherein you may otherwise be grievous unto us, to yourself, and to them.

And thus we bid you most heartily well to fare, from the Tower of London, the ix [*sic*] July. Your ladyship's loving friends, showing yourself an obedient subject.

[Signed] Thomas, Archbishop of Canterbury; the Bishop of Ely; Northumberland; Bedford; Suffolk; Northampton; Arundel; Shrewsbury; Huntingdon; Pembroke; Clinton; etc.

Twenty-one privy councillors signed; William Cecil was not of their number. He did not approve of Jane's accession, and was working in secret to restore Mary, using Sir Nicholas Throckmorton as an agent. Cecil's disaffection escaped Northumberland's notice, but inspired the watchful and resentful Arundel to work with him in secret on the princess's behalf.

On the 11th, Northumberland learned, to his dismay, that Mary was still at large, Robert Dudley having failed to capture her. The Duke knew that each day that saw Mary at liberty increased her chances of success, and realised that an armed confrontation was now inevitable. He must act swiftly if the victory was to be his, and he began by dispatching a letter in the name of Queen Jane to all the lord lieutenants of the counties: 'You will endeavour yourself in all things to the uttermost of your power, not only to defend our just title to the crown, but also to assist us to disturb, repel and resist the feigned and untrue claim of the Lady Mary, bastard daughter to our great-uncle, Henry VIII.'

Northumberland would have dearly loved to lead an army against Mary himself, but he dared not leave London, and had insufficient forces available there anyway. Instead, he spent that evening and the next day arranging a general muster of troops in Tothill Fields near Westminster, and organising the recruitment of more men 'to fetch in the Lady Mary, to destroy Her Grace'. 'The drum is beaten here to raise troops, and they are to have a month's pay in advance,' reported Scheyfve.

By Wednesday 12 July, thirty more gentlemen and their retainers had arrived at Kenninghall, and Mary decided that she should move to a larger stronghold with better fortifications. On that day she marched with her forces to Framlingham Castle in Suffolk, another Howard property that had reverted to the Crown, which was situated only fifteen miles from the coast. Framlingham was a mighty fortress, with a curtain wall forty feet long and eight thick, intersected by thirteen great towers, and enclosing a handsome brick lodging built recently by the Duke of Norfolk. Here, having found the deer park below the castle packed with local people come to offer their allegiance, Mary raised her standard, and it was variously reported soon afterwards that she was attended by between 14,000 and 40,000 men (the real figure was probably nearer 15,000), with numbers increasing daily, boosted by 'innumerable small companies of the common people', armed with whatever came to hand.

Contemporary observers, such as Robert Wingfield who was probably present at Framlingham and soon afterwards wrote a Latin biography of Mary, were certain that those who offered her their support did so out of a firm conviction of the rightness of her claim, and because of the love they bore her. There were, however, few noblemen in her army, and it appears that the loyal officers of her household, Rochester, Jerningham and Waldegrave, were in charge of organising her forces.

That night, Mary received two items of good news. The first was that Robert Dudley had been routed at King's Lynn and been forced to retreat to Bury St Edmunds to await reinforcements. The second was that Norwich, which had only days before closed its gates against Mary, had now recognised her as queen, setting an example that would speedily be followed by other cities and towns; men and supplies soon began arriving from there.

On the evening of the 12th, Northumberland had mustered 2000 soldiers, both infantry and cavalry, whose ranks were augmented by the yeomen of the guard, a number of Spanish and German mercenaries, and thirty great guns from the Tower arsenal. Henry Machyn, the contemporary diarist, recorded how that night 'was carried to the Tower three carts full of all manner of ordnance, as great guns and small, bows, bills, spears, pikes, harness, arrows, gunpowder and victuals'. In order to prevent Mary from escaping abroad the Duke ordered that five of his warships be moved up the coast to Yarmouth to guard it.

Northumberland was not unaware of the fence-sitters on the Council, and, fearing to leave London in their hands, suggested that Suffolk lead the army into East Anglia; but he had not reckoned with Queen Jane, who, weeping, insisted, 'My father must tarry at home in my company.' Northumberland himself was 'the best man of war in her realm', and it was he who should lead her forces. The councillors backed her, and although the Duke made loud and vociferous protests, he had no choice but to obey, though he was suspicious of his colleagues' motives, and with good reason. When he told Jane he would do as she asked, she thanked him 'humbly'.

'I pray you, use your diligence,' she said.

'I will do what in me lies,' he assured her.

Anxious to consolidate his already tenuous position, the Duke, ignoring Jane's refusal to allow Guilford to be king, announced that the young couple would both be crowned at Westminster Abbey in a fortnight. From henceforth, servitors should approach both of them on bended knee, and both were to be addressed as 'Your Grace'. Northumberland then dispatched an envoy, Master Shelley, to Charles V, to announce the accession of Queen Jane to her 'good brother' and declare how Mary was bent upon 'disturb[ing] the state of this realm', despite having the support of 'only a few lewd, base people, all the other nobility and gentlemen remaining in their duties to our sovereign lady'. The Emperor, still sure that Mary could not hope to prevail against the forces ranged against her, would tell Shelley that he rejoiced to hear of the accession of Queen Jane and 'King' Guilford.

It was now night-time but Northumberland's agents were still coming in with reports of how much of East Anglia had risen in Mary's favour, how the Earl of Derby had had her proclaimed in Cheshire, and how the Protestant Sir Peter Carew had done likewise in Devon. Even Robert Dudley, back in King's Lynn and unable to carry out his father's orders, had proclaimed Mary queen. Many councillors, hearing these reports, slipped quietly away from the Tower to offer Mary their support, one, Sir Edmund Peckham, the royal cofferer, even removing some of the royal treasure.

Early the next morning, Northumberland arranged for his army to muster outside Durham House in the Strand. They were going, he told them, towards Newmarket, where he hoped to intercept Mary on her march south to London.

Meanwhile, the Imperial ambassadors had been summoned before the Council. To their surprise they found Bedford, Arundel, Shrewsbury, Pembroke and the Secretary, Sir William Petre, speaking in warm terms of Mary and disdainfully of Northumberland, who had not been told of this meeting. It soon became clear to Scheyfve and Renard that the tide of opinion was turning in Mary's favour. These councillors were still waiting upon events, but it was obvious that they wanted to declare for Mary.

Later, Northumberland, wearing armour, returned to the Tower, still not happy about taking on 'the enterprise, being jealous of the fidelity of the Council to him' and fearing that 'during his absence they would more easily be wrought upon to deliver up the Queen'. In the council chamber, flanked by his sons, he spoke plainly to his colleagues, reminding them that he and those who rode with him were leaving their estates and families in their hands.

'Think not,' he warned, 'but if you mean deceit, thereafter God will revenge the same. I have not spoken to you upon this sort upon any distrust. Of your truths I have hitherto conceived a hearty confidence, but I have put you in remembrance thereof, what chance of variance might grow amongst you in my absence.' The lords assured him of their fidelity, but many of them dissembled.

Knowing that Mary's forces were far superior in numbers to his own, Northumberland asked the lords to raise reinforcements and send them after him with all speed. This they promised to do. Suffolk was to head the Council while Northumberland was away.

After dinner, the Duke received his commission from Queen Jane, and then bade a warm farewell to Arundel as he left the Tower. 'In a few days,' he declared, 'I will bring in the Lady Mary, captive or dead, like a rebel as she is.' He then returned to Durham House where his army, now 5000 strong, awaited him.

On 14 July Northumberland, wearing a rich scarlet mantle and accompanied by all his sons except Robert and Guilford, rode out of London through Shoreditch at the head of his men. Silent crowds lined the streets to watch them pass.

'The people press to see us,' the Duke observed drily, 'but no one sayeth God speed us.' As he rode north on the Cambridge road, couriers brought him news, all of it bad. Mary had been proclaimed in four more counties. Sir William Paget had changed sides and was planning to march on Westminster. At the instigation of Henry Jerningham, the crews of the five warships anchored off Yarmouth had mutinied in Mary's favour and threatened to throw their officers into the sea if they did not join them; soon 2000 sailors with 100 large cannon decamped to Framlingham. Even Bishop Hooper, a fervent Protestant, had urged his flock to support Mary. Growing increasingly desperate, Northumberland attempted to enlist more recruits from among the peasantry in the places through which he passed, but most men were conspicuous by their absence, having been warned of his coming. The common people had no love for John Dudley, whom they held to be responsible for the inflation and enclosures of Edward's reign.

As soon as Northumberland had left the Tower, Suffolk tried to stop disaffected councillors from leaving, but he could not prevent news of the mutiny at Yarmouth from seeping in. It was this that made many lords determined to defect to Mary's side, convinced that Northumberland's was a lost cause. The Treasurer of the Mint actually managed to slip away, laden with all the gold in Queen Jane's privy purse, and his escape inspired his colleagues to 'resolve to open their bosoms to one another' and discuss how they could outwit the Duke. Before long, they had made contact with Mary's supporters in the city of London.

At Framlingham, a jubilant Mary, encouraged by the loyalty of the Yarmouth crews, was reviewing her troops, riding between the massed ranks drawn up below the castle. So many had come that Wingfield had lost count of their number. As Mary passed, she was greeted by 'shouts and acclamation', with men crying, 'Long live our good Queen Mary!' or 'Death to traitors!' and firing their arquebuses into the air, with such deafening reports that Mary's palfrey reared in fright. Mary dismounted and continued her review on foot, walking the distance of a mile from one end of the encampment to the other, 'thanking the soldiers for their goodwill', while her eyes brimmed with tears at the demonstrations of love and loyalty.

Back in London, broadsheets in support of Mary's claim began mysteriously to appear in public places. One or two culprits were caught and punished by order of Northumberland's supporters on the Council, but the latter were dwindling in number. Nevertheless, they still exercised sufficient power to prevent waverers from leaving the Tower; one or two who tried to escape were forcibly brought back. Suffolk was incapable of maintaining control as Northumberland had done, and in the absence of strong leadership, Queen Jane took it upon herself to give orders and oversee the administration of government. She wrote to the imprisoned Duke of Norfolk, offering to release him if he would support her, but Norfolk, a staunch Catholic, ignored her letter. Jane also appointed a new Sheriff of Wiltshire, and then gave Bishop Ridley an audience to tell him her pleasure as to the content of the sermon he was to preach on the coming Sunday. Above all, she was planning, with chilling single-mindedness, to enforce radical Protestantism upon the Church of England.

Armed men were still to be seen on the streets of London, and tales abounded that Northumberland had sent them to spy out dissidents, but in fact many were deserting because they had not been paid; all the Duke's funds had been poured into the army he had taken with him.

On Saturday, 15 July, Northumberland was nearing Ware and still trying to recruit men, offering the extraordinarily high wage of 10d (4p) a day as bait. In London, the divisions on the Council were becoming markedly apparent; many lords believed that, if the Duke found he could not overcome Mary, he would declare for her, and abandon them all. Consequently, out of self-preservation, they sought to restrict his movements, instructing him to proceed only by their warrant. In turn, the Duke, determined that his acts should be seen to have conciliar backing, repeatedly sent messengers with requests for written approval of his decisions. These measures hampered his progress considerably, and gave Mary more time in which to prepare the defence of her position; Arundel, ready to defect, had already written to her, warning her that Northumberland was on his way.

By the time the Duke arrived at Ware, his slow progress was already having an effect on his soldiers' morale, and by nightfall men were beginning to desert in large numbers. Alarmed, Northumberland sent an urgent demand for more troops to the Council. His messenger rode so fast that he reached the Tower by midnight. The lords hastily gathered in the council chamber to discuss the matter, but all they sent the Duke was 'a slender answer'.

Afterwards Arundel had a quiet word with Cecil.

'I like not the air,' he muttered. Cecil confided that he was already in contact with Mary, using an assumed name, and the two men decided to sound out Winchester and Pembroke as to whether they were prepared to offer their allegiance to the princess.

Support for Mary was strengthened the next day when reports reached London that her army numbered over 30,000 men and was still growing, that more towns had proclaimed her, and that in the home counties there was widespread support for her. Both citizens and councillors now became bolder in voicing their loyalty. On that Sunday morning, a placard was attached to a church door at Queenhithe, complaining that Mary had been proclaimed queen in every place but London. The news from East Anglia was such that 'each man began to pluck in his home'. Suffolk was so worried about his daughter being abandoned that he had a proclamation issued in her name, stressing the justness of her title and demanding the preservation of the crown 'out of the dominion of strangers and papists'. That night, he ordered that the gates of the Tower be locked, having commanded Winchester, whose loyalty he suspected, to leave his house in the city and attend the Queen in the Tower. Many lords were beginning to realise that if Mary won they stood to be accused of high treason, for which the penalty was death. Pembroke, hitherto one of Northumberland's staunchest allies, managed to slip away to his home before the gates were locked. When Queen Jane learned of this she sent armed guards to bring him back, and commanded that the keys of the fortress be brought to her at seven o'clock each night without fail.

Earlier that day, 16 July, Northumberland had arrived in Cambridge in time to hear Dr Sandys, Vice-Chancellor of the University, preach a sermon upholding his cause, but its heartening effect was soon shattered when the Duke was informed of the mutiny at Yarmouth and given exaggerated reports claiming that Mary's army was 40,000 strong. In fact, he was so dismayed by the news that his supreme confidence deserted him. 'The Duke dares trust no one, for he has never given anyone reason to love him,' observed Scheyfve. Again Northumberland wrote, 'somewhat sharply' this time, urging the Council to send fresh troops, as his men were still deserting. Then he marched on to Bury St Edmunds with an alarmingly depleted force, while the people 'muttered against him' and resolved to declare for Mary as soon as his back was turned.

Morale in Mary's camp was high, especially after Thomas, Lord Wentworth, changed sides and rode in with his men, resplendent in a fine suit of shining armour. Mary appointed Sussex her commander-in-chief, and made Wentworth his deputy. Both men then set to deploying her army, drilling the ranks and making battle plans.

When Northumberland neared Bury on 17 July, he was within thirty miles of his quarry, but the reports reaching him told of an enemy force far too large for him to confront with his dwindling, resentful troops. The Council had ignored his desperate pleas for reinforcements, and were, if some reports were true, ready to abandon him; already the powerful Earl of Oxford had defected to Mary, whose forces now numbered around 20.000. Worse still, the bulk of his remaining army was ready to mutiny, and when his pleas and arguments fell on deaf ears, he had no alternative but to fall back on Cambridge. There, while he himself tried to canvass support from the largely Protestant university, he sent his remaining men to scour the surrounding villages for peasants willing to fight for him; they met with refusal and retaliated with an orgy of looting and burning, which the Duke made no effort to curb. Sickened by this, the chief officers in his army began to desert, which prompted hundreds of ordinary soldiers to slink away and join Mary. Those who were left stayed only because the Duke bribed them with promises of higher rates of pay.

In desperation, Northumberland sent his kinsman, Sir Henry Dudley, to Henry II in France, begging the French king to lead an army into England in return for the surrender of Calais and Guisnes, the last English possessions in France. A few days later, Dudley was arrested in Calais and found to have in his possession a great deal of plate and jewellery purloined from the treasury; under questioning, he confessed what his mission involved – proof, if it were needed, that Northumberland was a traitor to his country.

Even now, though, the Imperial ambassadors were still writing to Charles V telling him that Mary's cause was hopeless and advising him not to send her any help. 'In four or six days we shall hear whether people are rising.' Mary might be victorious, 'but this is doubtful and uncertain'. They noticed, however, that the guards around the Tower had been doubled, 'for [the councillors] know that the Lady Mary is loved throughout the kingdom, and that the people are aware of their wicked complaisance in allowing the Duke to cheat her of her right'.

By 18 July, all but three members of the Council – Suffolk, Cranmer and Cheke – had abandoned Northumberland and left the Tower; Queen Jane gave them permission to go when they told her and Suffolk that they needed to wait upon the French ambassador in order to procure his help in obtaining aid for Northumberland. Suffolk, instantly suspicious, insisted that he accompany them, but they threatened to have him executed if he abandoned the Queen. They then went straight to Baynard's Castle, the luxurious London residence of the Earl of Pembroke, where Arundel gave a spirited oration in support of Mary and persuaded his colleagues to reach a unanimous decision to abandon Northumberland and declare for her. The Duke, all were agreed, was guilty of treason against his lawful sovereign, and should be summoned back to London to account for his actions. A letter, demanding that he submit to the Council's decision and dismiss his army, was dispatched immediately. If he did not respond, Arundel was to go to Cambridge to arrest him. In the meantime, it was announced that a reward would be given to anyone apprehending Northumberland; £1000 for a peer of the realm, £500 for a knight, or £100 for a yeoman.

By now, it was dinner time, but the councillors made their way first to St Paul's Cathedral to give thanks for the kingdom's deliverance from treachery. Then, knowing it would stand them in good stead with the new Queen, who had every reason to censure or even prosecute them, they ordered that mass be celebrated in the cathedral.

Queen Jane had no idea that her short reign would soon be at an end. On the morning of 19 July, Mrs Underhill, the wife of a Tower warder related to the Throckmortons, gave birth to a son, and her husband Edward asked Jane if she would stand as sponsor to the infant at its christening, which was to take place later that day. Jane agreed, and permitted the child to be named Guilford.

Meanwhile, the councillors had waited upon the Lord Mayor and aldermen of London at the Guildhall and had commanded them to have Mary proclaimed queen in the city. Between five and six o'clock in the afternoon, the Lord Mayor went to Cheapside to do as he was bid, and found the crowds so great – word having leaked out of what was to come – that he had to fight his way to the Eleanor Cross where the proclamation was to be made. At last, Mary was acclaimed as 'Queen of England, France, and Ireland, and all dominions, as the sister of the late King Edward VI and daughter unto the noble King Henry VIII'.

London went wild. A foreign observer noted, 'As not a soul imagined the possibility of such a thing, when the proclamation was first cried out the people started off, running in all directions and crying out "The Lady Mary is proclaimed queen!" '

'There was such a shout of the people that the style of the proclamation could not be heard,' reported Henry Machyn. 'All the citizens made great and many fires through all the streets and banqueting also, with all the bells ringing in every parish church, till ten of the clock at night. The inestimable joys of the people cannot be reported!'

Foreigners looked on in amazement as the people celebrated. One Italian reported, 'I am unable to describe to you, nor would you believe, the exultation of all men.' They ran 'hither and thither, bonnets flew into the air, shouts rose higher than the stars, fires were lit on all sides, and all the bells were set a-pealing, and from a distance the Earth must have looked like Mount Etna'. It was said that no one could remember there ever having been public rejoicing such as this. 'Great was the triumph here,' wrote one anonymous Londoner. 'For my time I never saw the like, and by report of others the like was never seen. The number of caps that were thrown up at the proclamation were not to be told. I saw myself money thrown out at windows for joy. The bonfires were without number, and what with shouting and crying of the people, and ringing of the bells, there could no one hear almost what another said, besides banquetings and singing in the streets for joy.' Nearly every citizen was on the streets, celebrating in one form or another, and – as was customary on such occasions – the city fathers hastily made arrangements for the fountains and conduits to run with wine. Even the dignified aldermen and wealthy merchants, despite 'being men in authority and in years, could not refrain from casting away their garments, leaping and dancing as though beside themselves', and joining in the common people's sing-songs for joy. The feasting, dancing and drinking continued throughout the night and into the next morning, 'with good cheer at every bonfire, and everybody having everybody else to dinner, and the *Te Deum* sung in every parish church for the most part until the next day at Nones'. Nor did the church bells cease their pealing until the following evening. 'It seemed,' wrote one Spaniard, 'as if all had escaped from this evil world and gone to Heaven.'

Outside the gates of Baynard's Castle the Earl of Pembroke threw 'his cap full of angels' to the crowds and heartily acknowledged Mary as the rightful queen. He then announced that his son's marriage to Katherine Grey would be annulled, and as a token of his good faith, banished his daughter-in-law from his house that same evening, sending her to the Suffolks' house at Sheen. There 'she languished long under the disgrace of this rejection, none daring to make any particular addresses to her for fear of being involved in calamities'.

Arundel and Paget did not wait to join in the celebrations. They left for Framlingham on the evening of the 19th, in order to deliver the Great Seal of England to Queen Mary and tell her that the Council had throughout remained loyal to her in their hearts but that, due to Northumberland's pernicious influence, they had not dared to declare their allegiance for fear of provoking destruction and bloodshed. Hopefully the Queen would swallow this lame excuse and be conciliatory; she could hardly consign every privy councillor to the Tower. However, to prove their loyalty to her, Arundel and Paget were going afterwards to Cambridge to arrest Northumberland.

Sir John Mason saw the Imperial envoys that evening and gave them the news of Mary's accession, but their reaction was not what he expected. 'We thought we saw what they might be trying to do, namely to induce my lady to lay down her arms and then treacherously overcome her and encompass her death by means of a plot.' Even though they could see in the streets 'such a concourse of people as never was seen', it was several days before they were convinced of the Council's good faith, and only then did they conclude, as did Mary herself, that God had worked a miracle.

'God,' wrote John Knox, the Scottish reformer, 'so turned the hearts of the people to her and against the Council that she overcame them without bloodshed, notwithstanding there was made great expedition against her both by sea and land.' By giving Mary such an astonishing victory over her enemies, God, it was believed, had set the seal of His approval upon her accession. She was queen, not only by her own rightful title, but by God's will.

The royal apartments in the Tower were now almost deserted. The councillors had gone and only Queen Jane's attendants remained with her. Through the windows came the unmistakable sounds of celebrations, which she must have known were not in her honour. Then in the late afternoon of 19 July, the uneasy stillness in the Tower was shattered by Suffolk and a group of the fortress's officials bursting into Jane's presence chamber as she sat at supper beneath the canopy of estate.

'You are no longer queen,' the Duke told her bluntly, and began to rip down the canopy with his own hands. 'You must put off your royal robes and be content with a private life.'

Jane took the news calmly.

'I much more willingly put them off than I put them on,' she said. 'Out of obedience to you and my mother I have grievously sinned. Now I willingly relinquish the crown. May I not go home?'

The Duke remained grimly silent. In order to preserve his own skin, he had determined upon a display of loyalty to the new queen, and he intended to leave his daughter in the Tower until Mary's pleasure concerning her future was known. Abandoning Jane to her fate, he hastened out to Tower Hill, where he enthusiastically proclaimed Mary queen before going to ground with the Duchess at their house at Sheen.

Jane, left alone with Guilford in the bare and silent presence chamber, was quite composed. Retiring to her apartments, she informed her ladies of the latest turn of events, at which they burst out weeping and wailing.

'I am very glad I am no longer queen,' Jane told them quietly. Thereafter, she stayed in her rooms, while Guilford and his mother remained behind closed doors in the White Tower and ignored her entirely. Within hours guards had been posted at the doors, signifying that they were all prisoners, and therefore Jane could not attend the Underhill christening; Lady Throckmorton had to stand proxy for her.

Arundel and Paget arrived at Framlingham on 20 July and were at once admitted to Mary's presence. Falling upon their knees they saluted her as queen and informed her that she had been proclaimed in London. They then craved 'her pardon for the offence committed in the reception of the Lady Jane', and symbolically held their daggers with the points towards their stomachs. Mary forgave them readily. She had been preparing to defend her position against Northumberland, who was believed to be still at Bury. Now she realised that an armed conflict had been avoided and that she was queen by the will of the people. It was a heady, joyous moment, and nothing should mar it; all should share her elation.

With her heart full of thankfulness, Mary led her household into the chapel, where she commanded that the crucifix be openly placed on the altar for the first time in years. A *Te Deum* was sung, and everyone present thanked God for this miraculous, bloodless victory.

Northumberland was at King's College, Cambridge when, on the morning of 20 July, he heard that Mary had been proclaimed in London. In a desperate attempt to save his neck, he had his velvet bonnet filled with gold coins and then made haste to the market square in the company of one of his heralds, who proclaimed Mary queen. The Duke then tossed his bonnet into the air, crying, 'God save Queen Mary! God save Queen Mary! God save Queen Mary!' But whilst the people were scrambling after the coins, he was seen to weep uncontrollably.

The Duke then ordered Dr Sandys to celebrate mass, after which he confided, 'Queen Mary is a merciful woman. I look for a general pardon.' 'Be you assured', replied Sandys severely, 'you shall never escape death; for if she would save you, those that now rule will kill you.' Northumberland was silent.

At his lodgings he learned that his son Robert had been captured near Bury, and this prompted him to plot his escape with his remaining sons. But it was too late. The door was suddenly flung open and in strode Arundel, newly arrived from Framlingham. The Duke went pale and fell to his knees.

'Be good to me, for the love of God,' he whimpered, 'and consider – I have done nothing but by the consents of you all and the whole Council.'

Arundel took no notice.

'My lord,' he announced, 'I am sent hither by the Queen's Majesty, and in her name I do arrest you.'

'And I obey it, my lord,' answered Northumberland, 'and I beseech you, use mercy towards me.'

'My lord, ye should have sought for mercy sooner,' Arundel snapped.

Northumberland was imprisoned in his own lodgings, where he was seen pacing up and down in near-despair, while Arundel awaited further instructions from the Queen. The Duke's servants, terrified of sharing his fate, tore his badge from their arms 'in order not to be known as his men', and slipped away to their homes. Their horses and weapons were seized by Arundel's men in the Queen's name.

By 22 July, most men of rank or importance were travelling from London to pay their respects to Mary and crave her pardon for their disloyalty. Most were warmly welcomed by her and forgiven, but she refused to receive Northumberland's staunchest supporters. The Duke's sons, Sir John Gates, Sir Thomas Palmer and Bishop Ridley all found her doors closed against them. Having received the warnings sent by Scheyfve and Renard, Mary wrote back to assure them that she would not disband her army just yet, nor trust those who had so recently changed sides. In fact, for all her fair welcome, she would never trust any of them again.

Already, people were speculating on whom the Queen would marry. No one anticipated that, as the first female monarch to rule over England, she would attempt to rule without a husband to guide her. When Charles V learned of her accession, this thought was uppermost in his mind as well, and he instructed his envoys not only to congratulate Mary – he had always believed the English people would be 'led by affection' to acknowledge her title – but also 'point out to her that it will be necessary, in order to be supported in the labour of governing and assisted in matters that are not of ladies' capacity, that she soon contract matrimony with the person who shall appear to her the most fit'. If she needed advice on her choice, he would gladly offer it 'with all affectionate sincerity'. Naturally, he wanted her to contract a marriage that would benefit Habsburg interests, but in England the general opinion was that Mary should marry one of her own subjects. Edward Courtenay, still a prisoner in the Tower, was seen as the likeliest candidate. As early as 22 July, the Spanish ambassadors were reporting 'much talk here to the effect that he will be married to the Queen, as he is of the blood royal'.

Mary, however, had more important matters on her mind. First, she had to appoint a Council. All those councillors who had come to beg her pardon were reappointed to it, along with the faithful members of her household. The chief councillors, and the most experienced, were Arundel and Paget.

Then she had to make a decision about her brother's funeral. Wishing to hold a requiem mass, she had written asking the Imperial ambassadors for their opinion. They replied that she should allow Edward VI to be buried in the faith in which he had lived and died, since the Emperor 'would not wish you to make any innovations'. Mary had hoped for their support, and was disappointed not to receive it; she therefore resolved to ignore their advice.

Most important of all was the matter of religion. Now that God had seen fit to place her on the throne, she believed it was her sacred duty to restore the true faith. However, having let it be known that she intended to make no sweeping changes, she had to move carefully. Without apparently consulting anyone, she wrote, probably from Framlingham, to Pope Julius III, asking him to lift the interdict placed upon the English Church during her father's reign, and receive her kingdom back into obedience to the Apostolic See. Her letter reached Rome before 7 August, but remained secret at Mary's request. She did not trust her councillors, and feared they would violently oppose a return to Rome at this stage. They must be persuaded to it gently and diplomatically.

In the meantime, the new Queen was astonished at the backlog of state business that had accumulated since King Edward's death, and had scant leisure to think of marriage. She wished to go to London, although her advisers warned her it would be hot and stinking there, that the air was bad, and that plague was about. Some of her supporters, however, thought it would be best for her to return to the capital while public feeling was riding so high in her favour, and this she decided to do.

On 24 July, Mary, again ignoring the Imperial ambassadors' advice, discharged most of her great army and set out for London accompanied by a force of several hundred soldiers and a great train of lords, ladies, supporters and servants. At Ipswich, where she stayed that night, the city dignitaries met her outside the town and presented her with a purse containing £11 in gold coins. Crowds filled the streets and she was touched when a group of angelic-looking small boys gave her a solid gold heart inscribed 'The heart of the people'. She lodged in Wingfield House, where she received yet more turncoats come to pay homage and ask forgiveness, as well as William Cecil, who received a chilly reception and was presently imprisoned for a short while. Despite his loyal, behind-the-scenes support for Mary's cause, she believed him untrustworthy and never permitted him to hold public office under her.

That same day, Northumberland and his sons, with Northampton

and Huntingdon, left Cambridge under armed escort and were taken
to London. The following evening, at sunset, escorted by Arundel,
they were paraded through streets thronged with angry, jeering
crowds, who yelled 'Traitor!' as the Duke passed. In fact, the mood of
the people was so ugly that the guards around the prisoners had to be
doubled, though this did not deter everyone, and there were violent
scenes with halberdiers beating people off with their pikes, horses
rearing in terror, people throwing stones, rotten eggs and excrement,
and cries of 'Death! Death to the traitor!' Through it all Northumberland stared haughtily ahead, or shot black looks at the mob. Arundel,
fearing that his prisoner might be lynched, ordered the Duke to doff
first his hat and then his distinctive red cloak, but the people were not
deceived. At length, the prisoner was reduced to appealing to the
people, with great humility, for their pity, but, wrote Renard, they still
'cried out upon him'. It was a 'a dreadful sight, a strange mutation'. By
the time Northumberland reached the Tower, he was spattered with
mud and still bowing hopefully to the crowds. His eldest son, John, Earl
of Warwick, could take no more. As his father was borne off towards
the Beauchamp Tower, he burst into anguished tears.

Within a day or so Robert Dudley had joined his family in captivity,
as had Lord Chief Justice Montague, John Cheke, Bishop Ridley, Dr
Sandys, Sir John Gates, Sir Thomas Palmer and the Marquess of
Northampton. Five days earlier, on 20 July, the Marquess of
Winchester had called upon 'the pretended Queen' Jane, as the
Emperor called her, and required her to surrender the crown jewels
and other property that belonged rightfully to Queen Mary, such as
furs, velvet and sable mufflers, garters, clocks and portraits of Frances
Suffolk, Henry VIII and Edward VI. She was also made formally to
relinquish the crown itself.

Jane was then moved from the royal apartments to the half-timbered
house of Master Partridge, Gentleman Gaoler of the Tower, which
overlooked Tower Green and stood next to the Beauchamp Tower,
where all the Dudleys were imprisoned; despite their proximity, Jane
was forbidden to communicate with them. All her servants except Mrs
Ellen, Mrs Tilney, Lady Throckmorton and a page had been dismissed.
Although Renard told the Emperor that Jane was suffering ill-
treatment, she was allowed writing materials and books, among them
her Greek Testament and a prayer book bound in black velvet which
Guilford had given her.

The Duchess of Northumberland was released on 26 July and
immediately rode to Newhall, where she intended to beg the Queen
for mercy for her husband and sons. Mary, lately arrived from Ipswich

and Colchester (where she had stayed at the house of Muriel Christmas, who had once served Katherine of Aragon), refused to receive her, and the Imperial ambassadors, on their way to their first audience with the Queen, espied her dejected figure riding away sorrowfully.

Mary did grant the Duchess of Suffolk an interview. The Duke was still at large, and Frances was in a state of panic, begging the Queen to spare her husband and daughter. Northumberland, she declared, had tried to poison not only the late King, but also Suffolk. Mary demanded proof of this, whereupon the Duchess told her that an apothecary employed by Northumberland had just killed himself. Whether Mary believed her is not recorded, but she did assure her that she would harm neither the Duke nor Lady Jane, and allowed her to go home to Sheen. Suffolk was arrested there on 28 July, but spent only three days in the Tower, as Mary kept her word and granted his plea for mercy. Thereafter the Suffolks made no attempt to communicate with their daughter, nor to plead further for her life.

London was still celebrating, while the constant procession of lords, councillors, household officials and other dignitaries, bent on declaring their loyalty to Mary, yet made its way to Essex. The Queen received most in a spirit of reconciliation, and reserved her wrath only for her most hardened opponents. When news of Mary's accession reached her at Hatfield, Elizabeth wrote a warm letter of congratulation to her sister and set off at once for London in order to make her obeisance to her as queen. On 29 July, she rode into the capital accompanied by 2000 mounted men all wearing velvet and taffeta livery in the Tudor colours of green and white, and processed along Fleet Street to Somerset House, where she lodged that night.

On the evening of 29 July, Mary received the Imperial ambassadors at Newhall. Their purpose was to carry out Charles V's instructions to

> say to her that, as God has been pleased to dispose all things in so excellent a manner, we advise her to take very great care at the outset not to be led by her zeal to be too hasty in reforming, but to show herself to be accommodating. Let her dissemble for the present, not seek to order matters in a manner different from that now observed in England, but wait until she is able to summon Parliament in order to take such measures with its participation. Let her be in all things what she ought to be – a good Englishwoman, wholly bent on the Kingdom's welfare.

Mary was delighted and moved to see them. After greetings were exchanged, the conversation was mainly about Henry Dudley's arrest at Calais with incriminating evidence. Later, however, the Queen sent for one of the ambassadors to visit her in her private oratory to discuss more confidential matters, 'entering by the the back door to avoid suspicion'. Renard was the chosen one. Mary warmed at once to this charming but ambitious lawyer, who had such a wealth of diplomatic experience behind him and appeared so wise and perspicacious. An ambitious, volatile man with a large ego, he quickly gained the Queen's confidence, and she – who trusted none of her councillors – found herself wanting to confide in such a sympathetic and well-informed listener. All her life she had relied upon the Emperor's counsels, and the likeable Renard would provide a direct link between herself and her beloved mother's country. It was, of course, most unusual for an English sovereign to ask for confidential advice from a foreigner, and would have greatly displeased her advisers had they known about it, but Mary had no faith in the counsel of heretics and turncoats.

Renard, however, was feeling somewhat embarrassed, since he and his fellow envoys had done virtually nothing to support Mary's cause until they had been convinced of the success of it. He therefore made scant reference to the momentous events of the preceding month and began by passing on the Emperor's advice to go carefully in the first weeks of her reign and marry as soon as possible. Mary expressed warm gratitude to her cousin for his sage advice, confessing that, although as a private individual she had no desire to marry, she recognised that it was her responsibiltity to do so.

'After God,' she declared, 'I desire to obey no one but the Emperor, whom I have always looked upon as a father. I am determined to follow His Majesty's advice and choose whomsoever he might recommend.' She hoped the Emperor would remember that she was now thirty-seven and would not wish to marry a man she had never met.

As for religion, however, she must declare herself a Christian and carry out her duty to lead her people back into the fold of the true Church. Renard had been observing her closely as she spoke, and noticed her eyes lighting constantly upon the Sacrament which stood on the altar. There was no doubt of her passionate sincerity.

'I am determined to have a mass celebrated for my brother, to discharge my own conscience and out of respect for the will of the late King Henry, my father,' Mary went on. 'I wish to force no one to go to mass, but mean to see that those who wish to go should be free to do so.' Renard warned her that she would alienate the people by having her brother buried with Roman rites, but she 'felt so strongly on the matter of religion that she was hardly to be moved'. Renard suggested that she have Edward buried as a Protestant, absenting herself as custom demanded of a monarch's successor, and then hold a requiem mass for him in private later. Mary eventually took this advice.

She then spoke of her dissatisfaction with her councillors. 'She could not help being amazed by the divisions in the Council, whose members were accusing one another, disculpating themselves and chopping and changing in such a manner that she was unable to get at the truth of what had happened.' Renard could envisage a backlash against Spain if the councillors learned of his secret conversation with the Queen, and he urged her to reassure those who remembered that she was half Spanish by birth and believed her to be wholly Spanish in outlook. She should make it clear to the Council that she intended to rule with their advice. Mary retorted that her councillors knew her mind. They knew she had been celebrating mass in secret for years, and were expecting her to reintroduce the ancient forms of worship. 'I can do no less,' she said, 'for I must not be thankless for the favour shown me by God in choosing me, His unworthy servant, for this high office.'

The next morning Mary left Newhall for London, staying until 1 August at Ingatestone, the fine Essex home of Sir William Petre, and then riding on to Havering-atte-Bower, dower palace of the medieval queens of England. Wherever she went, the people came running to see her, cheering and calling blessings upon her.

Charles V's advice to Mary to marry an English husband had been merely a political expedient, calculated to allay English fears. In fact, he meant her to ally herself to a Habsburg husband to further Imperial interests. Like Mary, Charles wished to see the Roman Catholic faith restored in England; he also wished to revive the old Anglo-Burgundian alliance in a defensive pact against his bitter enemy, Henry II of France, and on 30 July he wrote to his twenty-six-year-old son and heir, Philip, who was just then negotiating to marry a Portuguese princess. Philip, suggested his father, might wish to consider abandoning the Portuguese match in favour of a marriage with Queen Mary.

The English, he wrote, would remember that he himself had – thirty years earlier – been contracted to marry Mary, and he felt sure that they 'would more readily support me than any other, for they have always shown a liking for me'. However, he was too old and too ill to contemplate remarrying 'and it has occurred to me that if they were to make a proposal to me, we might delay in such a manner as to suggest to their minds the possibility of approaching you'.

Philip, fired with the idea of becoming king of England, wasted no time in reaching a decision. Within days he reported to his father that he had resolved to break off the negotiations with Portugal on the grounds that the dowry offered was too mean. He went on: 'All I have to say about the English affair is that I am rejoiced to hear that my aunt [*sic* – Mary was in fact his cousin] has come to the throne in that kingdom. If you wish to arrange the match for me, you know that I am so obedient a son that I have no other will than yours, especially in a matter of such high import.' He would leave all for His Majesty to dispose of as he thought fitting. All Charles now had to do was await the right moment to broach the subject with Mary.

The Queen's arrival in London was now expected at any time, and on 31 July Elizabeth, obeying Mary's command, rode with a great train of nobles and attendants along the Strand, through the City of London, out through Aldgate, and on to the Colchester road, along which Mary would come, to receive her in triumph. The sisters had not seen each other for five years, and have been divided by more than distance. Elizabeth had openly embraced the Protestant faith and been in high favour with King Edward. The Venetian ambassador observed that during those years Mary 'had demonstrated by very clear signs' that she had no love for Elizabeth. Yet she had arranged now that Elizabeth share her triumph, and ride by her side when she entered the capital. Quite plainly, she meant to be conciliatory.

Both Mary and Elizabeth reached Wanstead on 2 August. Elizabeth dismounted and knelt in the road, but Mary alighted from her horse, raised her and embraced and kissed her with great warmth, holding her hand as she spoke to her. She then kissed all the noble ladies in Elizabeth's train, and the two great processions formed into one for the state entry into London.

Elizabeth rode at Mary's side, and onlookers could not have failed to be struck by the contrast between the two sisters. Although Renard chivalrously described her as 'more than middling fair', Mary, at thirty-seven, was small and thin, and her fresh-coloured complexion had been marred by years of anxiety and ill-health. What she lacked in looks she made up for by the richness of her attire, decking herself out in jewel-coloured velvets and damasks, embroidered and banded with gold and precious stones. Yet most striking of all was her obvious humanity and her demeanour, and what one ambassador called 'her gracious modesty, more divine than human'.

By the standards of her day, Mary was well into middle age. Elizabeth, at nearly twenty, was radiantly young, tall and sophisticated, with unblemished white skin and long, wavy red-gold hair. Still affecting her plain black and white clothes, she wore little jewellery, yet

she revelled in the fine figure she cut upon a horse. With her hooked
nose and thin, clever face, she was not conventionally beautiful – a
Venetian envoy considered her 'comely rather than handsome' – yet
she exuded a powerful charm and had inherited her mother's talent for
coquetry. Despite this, she had at all times a regal presence. 'An air of
dignified majesty pervades all her actions,' remarked another Venetian.
To the people, she represented the future, for until Mary bore a child –
and at her age that was no certain prospect – Elizabeth was her heir.
Hence they cheered for her almost as much as for Mary; Renard
remarked on how much they seemed drawn to her.

   In the late afternoon of 3 August, the Queen's procession entered
London through Aldgate, where the Lord Mayor was waiting to
surrender the city's mace 'in token of loyalty and homage', which Mary
promptly returned to him with a gracious speech of thanks, 'so gently
spoken and with so smiling countenance that the hearers wept for joy',
according to Wriothesley's Chronicle. Upon her entry, trumpets
sounded, guns were fired from Tower Wharf, the church bells rang
out, music played – 'which rejoiced the Queen's Highness greatly' –
and throngs of citizens cheered themselves hoarse, crying 'Jesus save
Her Grace!', while many wept for joy, 'that the like was never seen
before'. Every street was gaily bedecked with flowers, banners and
streamers, whilst tapestries and painted cloths hung from many
windows, and everywhere were displayed placards bearing the Latin
legend '*Vox populi, vox Dei* – The voice of the people is the voice of
God.'

   The Queen, who had changed into ceremonial clothes in a house in
Whitechapel, now wore a gown of purple velvet and satin in the
French style, covered with goldsmiths' work in gold and gems. Around
her neck was a thick chain or baldrick of gold, pearls and precious
stones, and on her French hood was a rich trimming of gems and pearls.
Her horse was caparisoned in cloth of gold, with intricate embroid-
eries. She looked tired but happy, almost overwhelmed by the ovation
given her. According to the Imperial ambassadors, 'her manner, her
gestures, her countenance were such that in no event could they have
been improved'.

   Behind the Queen rode Elizabeth, dressed in white, smiling and
nodding at the people, and after her came Anne of Cleves, once the
fourth wife of Henry VIII, the Duchess of Norfolk and the
Marchioness of Exeter, mother of Edward Courtenay and favoured
friend of the Queen. In front of Mary rode the Earl of Arundel, bearing
the sword of state, preceded by 740 men in velvet coats and 180 ladies
and gentlewomen. Sir Anthony Browne rode behind the Queen and

bore her long train over his arm. Five thousand more of her supporters had reluctantly remained outside the city after the authorities had expressed fears over the streets becoming dangerously congested. All the foreign ambassadors rode in the procession except for the French envoy, de Noailles, who prudently stayed away, having rather overtly supported Northumberland.

Outside the Tower of London, where Mary was to lodge for the next two weeks, a hundred children made an oration to her. She listened intently, but made no reply, and then passed on over the drawbridge of the fortress, as the cannon sounded continually 'like great thunder, so that it had been like to an earthquake'.

Inside the Tower precincts a crowd awaited her, but her gaze was drawn to four prisoners who knelt on the grass by the great gate – Stephen Gardiner, Bishop of Winchester, imprisoned at the beginning of Edward's reign for resisting Somerset's religious reforms; Thomas Howard, Third Duke of Norfolk, now eighty, whose neck had only been spared because Henry VIII, who had suspected him of leading a Catholic plot, had died before he could sign the death warrant; the Duchess of Somerset, widow of the Lord Protector, and Mary's long-standing friend; and Edward Courtenay, a youth whose Plantagenet blood had ensured his continued imprisonment since 1539, when most of his family had been executed by Henry VIII.

These prisoners all asked the Queen's pardon. She looked upon them with compassion, even old Norfolk, who had once – at her father's behest – spoken very brutally to her, and Gardiner, who had done his best to have her mother's marriage annulled. For all their faults, they were good Catholics, and she had need of them.

'These are my prisoners,' she announced, and commanded that they be immediately set at liberty, dismounting to raise, embrace and kiss them, her eyes brimming with tears. There and then she appointed Gardiner a councillor, and all were issued with written pardons the next day; Norfolk's attainder was reversed in Mary's first Parliament and his titles and lands were returned to him, whilst Gardiner was restored to his see. The Queen watched as Courtenay was reunited with his mother, and then withdrew with them and the other freed prisoners into the White Tower and presently to the royal apartments.

Part III
Mary and Elizabeth

9

'A Merciful Princess'

On 4 August 1553, the Privy Council made its formal submission to Queen Mary. She refused to issue immediate pardons to those who had declared for Jane, and rebuked them gently for their disloyalty, but, knowing she had no choice but to be conciliatory, she allowed them to kiss her hand. A few lords burst into tears at her magnanimity, but the Emperor's envoys expressed grave misgivings at such ill-advised mercy. On 5 August, acting on Charles's orders, Renard urged the Queen to be ruthless in punishing traitors; there were those who were a threat to her security, such as 'Jane of Suffolk', Northumberland, Suffolk and Guilford Dudley, and they should be put to death. Mary firmly refused to order Jane's execution, saying she had been the innocent tool of ruthless men, though Renard warned her that she was displaying a weakness that might have fatal results. The Queen, however was not to be moved; she would consider putting the men to death, but not Jane. Renard accepted that in most respects she had no choice but to be merciful, and drily observed that, if Mary had executed all those involved in Northumberland's coup, she would have very few subjects left.

Winchester and Pembroke had been arrested and imprisoned, but by 13 August they were at liberty and sworn again to the Council. Northampton was also released. Archbishop Cranmer had been refused a place on the Council, as had several others who had supported Northumberland, but the Queen retained twelve councillors who had served under King Edward, reappointed seven more who had served under Henry VIII, including Norfolk, and preferred twelve members of her household, who were loyal to her but lacked political experience. Her Council was therefore larger than hitherto, and hence cumbersome, as well as being riven by sometimes bitter divisions, rendering effective government difficult. As Renard put it, 'The Council does not seem to be composed of experienced men endowed with the necessary qualities to conduct the administration and government of the kingdom.' Even the Queen, with her piercing, intimidating glance and her deep, manly voice, found her councillors hard to control, and complained to the ambassador, 'I spend my days shouting at the Council and it makes no difference at all.'

Many councillors changed their religion in order to placate the Queen and retain her favour. To others she owed a debt of gratitude for their – admittedly belated – assistance in helping her overcome her enemies. Most were men of the world upon whom she was forced to rely heavily.

Gardiner – the best statesman among them – was appointed Lord Chancellor and Keeper of the Great Seal: the Queen's chief councillor. He was vastly experienced in politics and, like many bishops at that time, an ambitious, worldly man. Born a cloth-maker's son in Bury St Edmunds, he early on showed exceptional academic ability, studying canon law at university. Henry VIII had appointed him his principal secretary and entrusted him with many confidential embassies abroad and with the publication of anti-papal propaganda. Gardiner remained, however, one of the leaders of the Catholic party at court, whom later Protestant writers delighted in vilifying. It is true that he was capable of being a sharp-tongued bully, outspoken in his views and intolerant of those who did not agree with them, and that he could be difficult at times, but he was also, for all his religious conservatism, far more moderate than most, and full of wisdom and common sense. To his friends he showed loyalty, affection and humour. Above all, he loved England and worked tirelessly all his life for her benefit. He and the Queen differed on several important issues and their relations were never easy because, at heart, Mary did not like him. Yet he shared with her a common desire to restore the old faith, and because of this she was prepared to tolerate him.

Mary herself had spent most of her adult life in quiet obscurity in the country, had received no proper training to prepare her for queenship, and consequently lacked political experience and understanding. But she was determined to rule well, and demonstrated from the first a remarkable capacity for conscientious hard work, attending as many Council meetings as possible and writing many official letters in her own hand. She soon gained a reputation for being bountiful to those who came to her with petitions or grievances, and rarely turned anyone away. Her subjects high and low had already been impressed with her courage and unsuspected powers of leadership during the dark days of early July, but many at court thought her a lightweight, believing that, as a woman, she would be incapable of governing. The English had never had a female sovereign, nor had they forgotten the distant period of the Anarchy in the twelfth century when the Empress Matilda had fought her cousin King Stephen for the crown, and it had been said that God and His saints slept for nineteen years. The haughty and vengeful Matilda had briefly held power, long enough for the English to decide that they did not want another queen on the throne. Yet although they had welcomed Mary with open arms, she herself regarded her sex as a real handicap, and Renard was pessimistic about her chances of governing successfully, writing to Charles V's chancellor, Cardinal Granvelle, 'I know this queen – so good, so easily influenced, inexpert in worldly affairs, and a novice all round. I will tell you honestly my opinion, that, unless God guards her, she will always be cheated and misled either by the French or her own subjects, and at last taken off by poison or some other means.'

The Venetian ambassador had similar thoughts, and reported that real authority lay, not with the Queen, but in the hands of the Council, 'who are the lords of the kingdom'. And Mary of Hungary expressed the conventional view of a woman ruler when she opined to Charles V,

> A woman is never feared or respected as a man is, whatever her rank. In time of war it is entirely impossible for a woman to govern satisfactorily. All she can do is shoulder responsibility for mistakes committed by others.

Mary was, indeed, a political innocent, incapable of subtlety or the ability to dissemble. Unlike the other Tudor monarchs, who made a virtue of expediency, she ruled according to the dictates of her conscience, which sometimes made her a formidable person to deal with, for she could be ruthless in carrying out what she believed to be her duty. But if her conscience did not point the way, then she suffered agonies of indecision; if it did, she never lacked the courage of her convictions. An objective viewpoint was beyond her; she was single-minded to a fault. The quality she admired most in anyone was goodness, which was a quality she herself could boast. The Venetian ambassador, Giovanni Michieli, asserted 'There never was a queen in Christendom of greater goodness than this one.' People also admired her for her clemency, her integrity and the staunchness with which she had held to her faith through years of persecution and fear.

The Queen was particularly anxious to ensure that justice was dealt out fairly in her name, instructing her judges to sit, 'not as advocates for me, but as indifferent [i.e.impartial] judges between me and my people'. She was determined to rule only by the advice and consent of Parliament, and remained deaf to Renard's hints about establishing an absolute monarchy.

Mary's court was ceremonious and dignified, but it lacked the splendour and extravagance of her father's. It was also staid to the point of dullness, and generally free from scandal and licentiousness. The Queen enjoyed music, dancing and drama – during the first year of her reign she paid out over £2000 in salaries to musicians and actors. Her preferred entertainments were comedies or morality plays, but these did not compare with the sumptuous pageants and masques that had been staged in Henry VIII's early years. In fact such things had become extravagant luxuries now, since the country was almost bankrupt when the Queen succeeded. Scholars and artists did not frequent the court because Mary was not of an intellectual bent and could not afford to patronise them anyway. She did restore the choir of the Chapel Royal, where mass was said daily from 8 August 1553, and punctiliously observed the old pre-Reformation traditions, such as appointing a Lord of Misrule at Yuletide, or creeping to the Cross and blessing cramp rings on Good Friday, as well as touching sufferers of scrofula, the 'King's Evil', to effect a miraculous cure.

From the first, the Queen set an example of religious devotion, having six or seven masses sung each day in her chapel, which her councillors were zealous in attending. Her courtiers followed suit, not wishing to offend their mistress, and the court became a centre of Catholic piety.

The Queen rose early, spending several hours of each day at prayer, and the rest of the time conferring with her Council, which met each morning with Gardiner in the chair, or attending to state business. Often, she did not lay down her pen or cease reading official papers until late at night. Constant hard work took its toll of a constitution already undermined by ill-health: Mary suffered miseries from headaches and palpitations. Her doctors prescribed tonics and regular bleeding, but these had little effect.

Mary's only extravagance was her rich attire, as her Wardrobe Books testify. The Venetian envoy Soranzo commented on her 'great use of jewels, in which she delights greatly, and although she has plenty of them left her by her predecessors, yet were she better supplied with money than she is, she would doubtless buy many more'. She changed her outfits several times each day, and appeared in cloth of silver or gold even when attending to routine duties. The Queen affected extrava-gant clothes not only for the pleasure of wearing them, but also as an outward manifestation of her royal state, monarchs in that age being expected to look and dress the part. Soon after her accession she commissioned from the artist Hans Eworth a state portrait of herself, of which she was inordinately proud, and the French ambassador told Queen Catherine de' Medici that the highest compliment she could pay Queen Mary would be to ask for a portrait of her.

To her friends and servants Mary was the soul of generosity, liberal with money and valuable gifts. To the poor, she was compassionate and bountiful; once, whilst staying at the Archbishop of Canterbury's palace at Croydon, Surrey, she dressed up as a private gentlewoman and visited some humble homes incognito, speaking to the farmers and their wives with such 'plainness and affability' that they concluded she was one of the Queen's maids. Her maid-of-honour and friend, Jane Dormer, who often went with her on similar charitable missions elsewhere, remembered how, if there was a child in the house, the Queen would give the parents more money, advising them to live thriftily and in the fear of God. Dormer was 'particularly favoured and affected' by Mary, and often shared her bed at night, a privilege also extended to the Marchioness of Exeter, another close friend, during the early months of the reign. Dormer had charge of the Queen's jewels, and cut her meat – the Queen's favourite dish was wild boar – at table. Mary was so fond of her that she declared no man was good enough for her, and refused permission for her to marry on several occasions.

In public, Mary was regal and dignified. She could converse with foreign ambassadors in Latin and French and could understand Spanish and Italian too, although she could not speak either well. The Spanish envoys found her 'great-hearted, proud and magnanimous', and 'inclined to talk about her exalted station'. Her first coins bore the motto *Veritas temporis filia* – Truth, the daughter of time' as if to underline her miraculous triumph over her enemies. Soranzo tells how she was fond of saying, 'In Thee, O Lord, is my trust; let me never be confounded. If God is for us, who can be against us?'

Renard distrusted the 'enchantments' of Elizabeth, who was very popular and much admired. During the early weeks of the reign, the Queen often appeared in public with her sister in the place of honour at her side, holding her hand affectionately, but it was not long before Mary began suggesting that Elizabeth attend mass with her. Elizabeth hedged. She had no wish to alienate the Queen, yet nor did she desire to lose her Protestant supporters. Mary was aware of her reluctance, but continued to put pressure on her, becoming increasingly exasperated when Elizabeth still refused. It was no secret that she had embraced the reformed faith with fervour during Edward's reign, and she still wore a golden book, two inches square and containing her brother's deathbed prayer, at her waist. Mary was determined to bring Elizabeth back into the Catholic fold, for it was unthinkable that her heir should be a Protestant.

By the end of August, all the old antagonism between the sisters had surfaced again. Theirs could never be an easy relationship because the past would always lie like a sword between them, but now they were in open conflict about religion. Seeing this, the French ambassador, Antoine de Noailles, began to court Elizabeth's favour. De Noailles was of noble family and as wily as a cat; he retained a large network of paid informers, including the Venetian ambassador; Mary had no love for him because he had openly supported Northumberland, and suspected that he was even now working against her. Indeed, his brief was to do all in his power to discountenance her, because the French knew she was in the pocket of the Emperor, France's enemy. This meant worming his way into Elizabeth's confidence, with a view to setting her up as a rival for the crown. Not that Henry II wished to see Elizabeth on England's throne; when she had served her purpose she would be discarded, for his real aim was to secure England for his daughter-in-law, Mary, Queen of Scots. If Elizabeth could be induced to rebel against her sister, though, or even set herself up at the head of an opposing faction, that should keep Mary far too busy to consider involving England in the Emperor's conflict with the French.

Elizabeth responded favourably to de Noailles's compliments, and soon the two were great friends. Renard warned the Queen that her sister was a heretic who was intriguing with the French; Elizabeth's popularity, he said, was a threat to Mary's security. The girl was clever, ambitious and sly. Mary admitted that, despite her public behaviour and her sincere efforts to nurture fraternal affection, she found it impossible to hide her dislike for the daughter of the woman whom her mother had always referred to as 'the Concubine'. Every time she looked at Elizabeth, she saw Anne Boleyn and remembered the misery she had caused her. She would take Renard's advice and keep an eye on her.

The ambassador then counselled Mary once more to have Jane Grey executed, but still she would not hear of it. Jane and her husband would remain in the Tower, she said, until such time as it was safe to grant them pardons and release them. They would be tried and condemned, as a matter of form, but her conscience would not permit her to put them to death, even though they had technically committed treason. Renard argued that this was unwise, and Gardiner was of the same opinion, but Mary heeded neither of them. In fact, she had been very impressed by a lengthy letter sent her by Jane on 5 August, giving a full and honest account of her nine days' reign without making too many excuses for herself. What came across very clearly to the Queen was that Jane had had no choice in the matter, even though she had admitted that she had done wrong in accepting the crown and was 'ashamed to ask pardon for such a crime'.

'No one can ever say that I sought it or that I was pleased with it,' Jane wrote. 'All these things I have wished to say for the witness of my innocence and the disburdening of my conscience.' The Queen would only assure Renard that she would be watchful in case Lady Jane became the focus of any further conspiracy, and would ensure that the realm was quiet before she set her free, at which the ambassador expressed the hope that she would not regret such extraordinary clemency. He would not rest easy until she had agreed to 'the obliteration of the whole house of Suffolk'. Meanwhile, in the Tower, Jane remained busy at her books, denouncing the mass as 'the swill of strangers'.

The Emperor had urged Mary to go cautiously in religious matters, and initially she moved carefully, exhorting her subjects 'not to revile each other'. However, Mary had been out of touch with the English people for some time, and did not realise how deeply divided they were over issues of faith. She believed that their rapturous reception of her as queen was confirmation that they would also welcome the return to the Roman Catholic fold which was her dearest wish. It was her firm belief that those who had turned Protestant had done so under pressure from the government in her brother's time, and would happily revert now to the true faith.

Her next step was to declare her intention of restoring the mass and the religious settlement that had existed at Henry VIII's death, with herself as Supreme Head of the Church; she intended to surrender that title when the time was ripe for a return to Rome, but in the meantime she would make use of it to bring about a counter-Reformation. On 12 August, she told her Council, 'It is not our intention to compel or constrain other men's consciences.' All she intended was for them to be brought to the truth by God or the offices of 'godly, virtuous and learned preachers'.

However, according to Renard, English Catholics were already predicting that 'God would soon take pity on His people and the Church in England through the instrument of a virgin called Mary, whom He has raised to the throne', while extreme Protestants were taking part in rowdy demonstrations and riots in London, even hurling a dagger at a priest who celebrated mass in St Paul's. The stage was set for a bitter religious confrontation.

At nine o'clock in the morning of 8 August, Edward VI, or the body said to be his, was buried in Westminster Abbey with Archbishop Cranmer and John Scory, Bishop of Chichester, conducting the Protestant funeral service 'with scant ceremony'. At the same time, Gardiner was celebrating a requiem mass in the Queen's private chapel in the Tower. Mary had also ordered that masses be sung for her brother's soul 'perpetually and for ever'. Elizabeth did not attend either service.

When Pope Julius III received Mary's letter early in August, he expressed surprise and great delight that the Queen should seek to reconcile the Church of England to the Church of Rome, and then appointed her cousin, Cardinal Reginald Pole, papal legate to England. Pole's duties, however, were restricted for the present to doing nothing more than gathering information through his contacts about public opinion in England. The Cardinal began writing letters at once, and he also started a correspondence with the Queen which was to continue for more than a year. In his view, there was no time to lose, for souls were daily perishing, cast out from the communion of the Church, and he exhorted Mary, as a true daughter of that Church, to undo the evil her father had done. Mary would have heeded his words had not Charles V, through Renard, persuaded her that Pole was a well-intentioned idealist who was completely out of touch with English affairs; Charles wished the credit for the Counter Reformation in England to go to his son Philip, or himself, not Pole – though he of course said nothing of this to Mary. The Queen therefore wrote back to Pole, stressing that although she was zealous to do his bidding, there were political obstacles that must first be overcome. By way of reply, Pole asked if 'that other Mary' would have refused St Peter admission to her house.

Mary answered that her task would be considerably easier if he persuaded the Pope to allow all those who had profited through the redistribution of church property that had followed the dissolution of the monasteries to keep their lands, as this was the issue likeliest to make Parliament hesitate. Pole was horrified that such temporal concerns should be allowed to stand in the way of the unity of the Church and refused to consider granting her request. At this point Charles V, fearing that Pole's single-mindedness would wreck his plans whilst they were still in their infancy, began to put pressure on the Pope to keep

Pole out of England until the Queen, hopefully supported by Philip, was in a strong enough position to dictate her own terms to the legate.

Born in 1500, Reginald Pole was the son of Margaret Pole, Countess of Salisbury, Mary's beloved childhood governess, and the great-nephew of Edward IV and Richard III; the blood of the Plantagenet kings ran in his veins, and when Mary was young her mother and his had fondly hoped that they would marry. Reginald was a clever child, and Henry VIII became his patron, sponsoring his education and sending him to study for a time in Italy. The young man took deacon's orders and helped the King to canvass the universities for approval of the annulment of his marriage to Katherine of Aragon. However, Pole quickly became convinced that the King's pangs of conscience about marrying his brother's wife were inspired mainly by lust for Anne Boleyn, so he returned to Italy and wrote a furious and defamatory denunciation of the man who had been a generous benefactor to him. Henry responded with righteous anger and made it clear that, if Pole were to return to England, he would be dealt with as a traitor. Pole remained in Italy, finding favour with the Pope and being given a cardinal's hat in 1536. However, his family suffered persecution for his sake, and his mother was brutally executed on the flimsiest pretext in 1541, Pole having been attainted as a traitor at the same time. These events caused him much anguish, and he took to calling himself the son of a martyr.

Cardinal Pole had never returned home, although he wished to, but had risen to prominence in the Vatican and narrowly missed being elected Pope in 1549. A religious progressive, but never inclined towards Lutheranism, he had associated with humanists and those who wished to reform the Catholic Church from within, and had earned a reputation as a fine diplomat and an authority on church matters. However, he was no statesman.

Pole had an austere temperament, and was a talented, high-minded scholar, who had no desire to play a public role yet did so for duty's sake. He had high ideals but poor judgement and, although he claimed 'to know thoroughly the sentiments of the [English] people with regard to the Holy See', he had little real understanding of the changes that had taken place in England during the twenty years of his exile. According to Renard, Mary had more regard for Pole than for all the members of her Council put together. There was even talk that, cardinal though he was, she would marry him.

As a virgin who had lived a quiet and virtuous life, the Queen was overcome by modesty whenever her marriage came under discussion, as it did frequently in the early months of her reign. When she could be persuaded to speak of such a delicate matter, she made it clear that she would choose a husband 'as God inspired her' without having regard to 'fleshly considerations'. Her choice was naturally dictated by political and religious factors, which at that time went hand in hand, and she was well aware that, at thirty-seven, she had no time to waste if she was to present her subjects with an heir who would maintain the Catholic faith in England.

In August 1553, there were rumours that Mary would marry Cardinal Pole, who had never been ordained a priest and could easily have been released by the Pope from his deacon's vows, but Pole himself vetoed this idea, and warned Mary that her best course was to stay single. No one took any notice of this advice, and Gardiner suggested that the Queen marry the man whom Renard called 'the last sprig of the White Rose' of Plantagenet, his protégé Edward Courtenay.

Courtenay was twenty-seven, the great-grandson of Edward IV. His father, Henry Courtenay, Marquess of Exeter, had been executed by Henry VIII in 1538, and the boy had thereafter been shut up for fifteen years in the Tower of London on the grounds that his royal blood posed a threat to the Tudor dynasty. Provision had been made for a tutor for him, and he had devoted himself 'to all virtuous and praiseworthy studies', translating religious tracts from Italian into English, learning several languages and becoming a competent musician and artist. But his formative years had been spent in stultifying isolation, and when he was set free he had 'neither spirit nor experience' and was unable even to ride a horse, an essential accomplishment for a gentleman of his rank.

Foreign ambassadors were unanimous in their opinion that Courtenay was an extraordinarily handsome young man; he was fair in colouring, tall, elegant and graceful, with 'a civility which must be deemed natural rather than acquired by the habit of society'. He came, moreover, from one of the greatest Catholic families in the country and had remained true to the faith. What was not immediately apparent was that he was also shallow, self-indulgent, vain, irresponsible, weak and untrustworthy. Renard thought him 'proud, obstinate and vindictive in the extreme'. Even de Noailles – who wanted Mary to marry Courtenay, if only to wrest her from the clutches of the Imperialists – said he was 'as maladroit as can be believed', and already people at court were poking fun at his naivety and ignorance of polite society.

During his years in the Tower, Courtenay had come to know Gardiner, a fellow prisoner, well, since they were allowed to exercise together in the Lieutenant's garden, and a touching friendship sprang up between the two. The younger man came to refer to the Bishop as his father, and Gardiner certainly looked upon Courtenay as the son he had never had. There was therefore a strong element of personal gratification in Gardiner's suggestion that the Queen marry Courtenay, and some believed that 'Wily Winchester' had his own interests chiefly at heart.

It was not such a far-fetched idea, though, because most of Mary's subjects wanted her to marry an Englishman, and here was one of the ancient blood royal. No other Englishman had such excellent credentials. Gardiner spoke warmly to Mary of Courtenay's good character, and told her that by marrying him she would be bowing to public opinion, while two thirds of the Council were in favour of the match. Courtenay had been a popular candidate from the first, and rumours that the Queen would choose him had been circulating since her accession. After she granted him a fine house in London, speculation grew and most councillors expressed themselves in favour of the match. Naturally, the rumours were relayed to an alarmed Charles V, who at once instructed Renard to put Mary off the idea, saying that Courtenay was far too inexperienced. Of Courtenay's well-documented visits to brothels, where he was making up for lost time, the ambassador was to say nothing in case the Queen did marry him, in which case she would hold Renard's slanders against him.

Mary, however, had already made up her mind, telling Gardiner that Courtenay was not to her liking; he was too lowly in rank, too young and untried. Worse still, she had heard he was visiting prostitutes. Renard had added fuel to the fire by telling her that those councillors who favoured the match were in the pocket of the French ambassador; this had the desired effect of putting her off Courtenay completely.

At this point Renard received instructions from the Emperor that, during his audiences with the Queen, he was to hint at the advantages of a marriage with Prince Philip. Under no circumstances was the matter to be rushed, for the English would need time to acclimatise themselves to the idea of their Queen marrying a foreigner. Renard felt that Philip's proposal, when it came, 'would be the most welcome news that could be given [Mary]', for he had heard she 'had no wish to marry an Englishman'.

Renard said nothing to the Queen at this stage, but de Noailles had already anticipated that the Emperor would suggest a match between Mary and Philip and warned Henry II that such a marriage would result in 'perpetual calamity' for all Christendom. For his part, de Noailles would do everything in his power to promote the match with Courtenay or the claims of the Lady Elizabeth.

In the middle of August, Mary left the Tower and took up residence at Richmond Palace. The time had now come to make a statement of her intentions with regard to religion, and on 18 August, she issued a proclamation affirming her own devotion to the Catholic faith and her hope that her subjects would embrace it as fervently. However, she 'mindeth not to compel any of her subjects thereunto' until such time as a new determination was made 'by common consent' of Parliament. In the meantime, the clergy were forbidden to preach, which effectively removed the most powerful weapon of the reformers. Already, the old faith – still officially outlawed – was gaining ground, particularly outside London and, in the capital as elsewhere, altars were being set up again and crucifixes replaced. There were, nevertheless, many Protestants prepared to resist any attempt to enforce uniformity of worship upon them and disrupt the celebration of mass. The Queen, in her proclamation, was not advocating tolerance; she simply could not credit that anyone would wish to follow any faith other than hers, and her undertaking not to compel any man to go against his conscience was only an interim concession. What she did promise was that there would be no disturbance of existing titles to lands formerly belonging to the Church.

A number of Protestant priests defied the royal edict banning preaching, and many were arrested during the following weeks. Several bishops, including John Hooper, John Rogers, Hugh Latimer and Nicholas Ridley, were deprived of their sees and imprisoned. Archbishop Cranmer was arrested and sent to the Tower on 14 September for criticising the mass. Reformist printers had their presses confiscated, and many feared that the old anti-heresy laws would be revived, thus sparking a wave of religious persecution. Consequently there began a steady, but stealthy exodus of around 800 Protestants to the Continent. The government refused to issue religious refugees with the necessary passports, but initially made no effort to stop them from going, and even encouraged the more subversive among them to seek exile. One who left that year was Katherine Carey, wife of Sir Francis Knollys and first cousin to the Lady Elizabeth. Katherine's mother had been Mary, sister of Anne Boleyn. After she left, Elizabeth wrote to her:

The length of time and distance of place separates not the love of

friends. My power but small, my love as great as them whose gifts may tell their friendships' tale...
Your loving cousin and ready friend, Elizabeth,
Cor Rotto [broken heart].

On 18 August, Northumberland was tried by his peers for high treason in Westminster Hall and found guilty. The trial was presided over by the Duke of Norfolk as Earl Marshal of England, who sentenced the prisoner to a traitor's death: hanging, drawing and quartering, 'his heart to be drawn from his body and flung against his face'. The Queen mercifully commuted this to beheading. Northumberland had confessed all his crimes and had knelt, weeping and begging for mercy, but in vain. Many onlookers shed tears to see him in such a miserable state. The next day Sir John Gates and Sir Thomas Palmer were also condemned to die.

Northumberland did not believe that the Queen would really have him executed. After his plea for mercy had failed, he announced that he wished to convert to the Catholic faith, hoping that that would avert the Queen's desire for vengeance. He asked Gardiner to visit him and told the Bishop, 'I would do penance all the days of my life, if it were but in a mousehole. Is there no hope of mercy?'

'I think that you must die,' Gardiner replied gravely.

'I can be of no other faith but yours,' cried the Duke, bursting into tears. 'I never was any other indeed. I complied in King Edward's days only out of ambition, for which I pray God to forgive me, and I promise I will declare that at my death.'

His distress was so great that the crusty Gardiner broke down too, but even Northumberland's public conversion to Catholicism on 19 August did not save him. Mary, hearing of it from Gardiner, who pleaded with her to spare him, contemplated a stay of execution, but Renard, whose advice she now heeded more than any other's, insisted that she let the law take its course. On 23 August, the Duke mounted the scaffold on Tower Hill in front of 10,000 onlookers, who were in an ugly mood and had to be held back by halberdiers. He confessed to them that he was a 'wretched sinner and most justly condemned'. His conversion, he declared, had been unfeigned. As he knelt before the block, he said, 'I have deserved a thousand deaths.'

A cloth was tied around his eyes as he prayed: '*In manuas tuas, Domine...*' The cloth slipped, and he had to rise again, visibly distressed, in order to retrieve it. Then, clenching his hands together in prayer, he knelt again and bent his head. It was severed in one blow. His body was carried to the Chapel of St Peter ad Vincula within the Tower, where it was interred next to those of Anne Boleyn, Katherine Howard and the Duke of Somerset.

Lady Jane Grey had viewed her father-in-law's conversion with disgust. She was still in the Tower, but Mary had relaxed the restrictions governing her confinement, and Jane was now allowed onto the wall-walks with Guilford. She was still writing viciously anti-Catholic diatribes, yet was hopeful of the Queen's clemency. She was comfortably lodged with Master Partridge, and dined with him and his wife, sitting 'at the board's end' in the place of honour.

On 29 August, Jane was informed that she and Guilford were to stand trial, but that a royal pardon would undoubtedly follow. She received the news cheerfully, and praised the Queen as a merciful princess. Then she returned to her books and her studies, with which she occupied her time. In October, she would be sixteen.

At the end of August, Renard reported that Elizabeth was showing a more than friendly interest in Courtenay, and from that time onwards, her name was inextricably linked to his. De Noailles was undoubtedly responsible for this: he had ingratiated himself with Elizabeth, and was carefully cultivating Courtenay, frequently inviting him to supper and persuading the gullible young man that, if the Queen would not marry him, her sister might; with their Plantagenet and Tudor blood intermingled, they would stand as youthful and charismatic figureheads for both Catholic and Protestant subjects of the Queen, and, as leaders of a powerful opposition backed by Henry II, might overthrow Mary and so remove the threat of an Anglo-Imperial alliance from France.

On 3 September, the Queen restored Courtenay to the earldom of Devon, which had been held by his ancestors, and endowed him with lands worth £3000 per annum. She also gave him sumptuous clothes and a diamond ring of Henry VIII's worth 16,000 crowns.

Many now believed that Courtenay would become king consort, and courtiers flocked to pay court to him, kneeling as they addressed him. Pembroke presented him with a sword and horses costing 3000 crowns. The King of France wrote flattering letters to him, but he took care to give them to his mother, Lady Exeter, to pass on to the Queen. In order to win Mary's favour, he would only employ Catholics in his growing household, and did his best to become on intimate terms with those closest to her, calling Susan Clarencieux 'Mother' as he called Gardiner 'Father'. Before long, Courtenay was giving himself airs, throwing his weight about and rapidly becoming insufferable, boasting that at the coronation he would be wearing a splendid outfit in blue velvet with gold embroidery. He was somewhat disconcerted when, his words having been reported to the Queen, she sent him a curt message ordering him to wear another colour, as she herself was planning to wear blue velvet trimmed with ermine for her coronation.

Mary had no intention of marrying Courtenay. The most important issue in her life just then was religion, and by the beginning of September she thought she knew what she must do. Summoning the Imperial ambassadors, she informed them that it was her intention to restore the Church of England to the obedience of the Holy See of Rome, as it was 'before the changes took place'.

This was the first time since 1536 that Mary had spoken to anyone in England of her hopes for a reversion to Rome; she had never publicly expressed any desire other than to have the religious settlement that had existed at her father's death restored. Understandably, Renard and Scheyfve were alarmed at her resolve, telling her, 'We thought she should not go beyond the reinstitution of the mass and matters relating thereto, reverting to the condition in which they were at the time of the late King Henry's death.' They were even more alarmed when Mary informed them that she had been in constant contact with the Pope and that Cardinal Pole had been appointed legate and was coming to England. Renard begged her to consult Parliament before she allowed him into the kingdom, because her subjects would need reassurance on the subject of church property, and Pole's views were well known. It was also apparent to the ambassadors that Mary had not consulted the Council on this matter, and they urged her to tell no one but Gardiner what she had in mind, 'so that malicious people may not seize the occasion for worse plottings or machinations'. The last thing the Emperor wanted was a religious war in England.

Mary allowed herself to be convinced, and on 11 September reluctantly wrote to Rome, instructing that Pole should not be sent until the time was more propitious.

Meanwhile, de Noailles had heard an unfounded rumour from a courtier, of which he informed Henry II on 7 September, that Charles V had formally offered Prince Philip as a husband for Mary. Henry ordered de Noailles to do everything in his power to prevent the alliance, and the ambassador threw himself into his task enthusiastically, enlisting the support of leading Protestants and those Englishmen who were vehemently opposed to the idea of a foreign consort for the Queen. He warned whoever would listen that the Spaniards, once they had a foothold in England, would make it a satellite of the Empire and introduce the Inquisition, giving rise to the same large-scale religious persecution as was seen on the Continent. If Mary married Philip, he would not stay in England long because he had too many commitments abroad; she would be fortunate if he spent as much as a fortnight with her, and what good would that be to a queen who needed heirs? Worse still, England would be made an unwilling participant in Charles V's war with France, which she was in no position to afford. Many were ready to listen to de Noailles's warnings, and before long the ambassador found himself at the head of an anti-Imperialist faction. Gardiner also shared his views, but had no reason to trust him, knowing he was considering only the interests of France. However, since the Emperor had as yet made no formal offer of marriage, Gardiner could make no protest on his own behalf. All he could do was urge the Queen to call Parliament as soon as possible, in order to obtain support for an English match for her.

By now, however, rumours of a Spanish marriage had spread far and wide, and were being discussed in public taverns. The Council, suspicious that the Queen knew something they did not, insisted that all her audiences with the Imperial envoys take place in public. They even hinted that Renard and his colleagues should return home. Mary dealt with this by suggesting that Renard visit her in disguise, but her refusal to discuss her marriage only added to the confusion and resentment. De Noailles did not scruple to raise dissension and protest, nor to distribute anti-Spanish propaganda, while Renard, who had received no definite orders from his master, could only fret and agonise over the delay.

On 8 September, he asked Mary if the rumours about her marrying Courtenay were true. She denied it, saying she had not seen him since the day she liberated him from the Tower and that there was no one of her subjects she wished to marry. She then asked if the Emperor had made any suggestions. This was the opportunity Renard had been waiting for, and presently Philip's name was mentioned.

10

'The Marriages of Princes'

Philip of Spain had been born on 21 May 1527 at Valladolid in Spain. He had received an aristocratic education, becoming proficient in Latin, Greek, maths, geography, history and architecture, as well as the martial arts, music and painting. When he was twelve his mother, the beautiful Isabella of Portugal, had died in childbirth, and thereafter he grew up to be a reserved, stiffly-mannered youth with an anxious, melancholy and suspicious temperament. In appearance he was fair-haired and blue-eyed, more like his Flemish forbears than his Spanish ones, and he had the prominent Habsburg jaw, which he later concealed with a dapper beard. Of below-average height, he looked more imposing on horseback than standing, but he was slim and well-proportioned, and women found him attractive.

When he was sixteen, Philip was married to Maria of Portugal, but she died two years later, in 1545, in bearing him a son, Don Carlos, who grew up to be a vicious mental defective and died in 1568. Philip had been warned by his father not to indulge too often in marital sex because frequent intercourse could stunt his growth. Sex was for procreation only, and he should avoid the lusts of the flesh. In the death of his wife in childbirth the grief-stricken Philip saw only too plainly what could result from lust, and he had so far avoided marrying again. Instead, he had enjoyed a long-standing liaison with Doña Isabel de Osario, which his father chose to ignore.

In 1549, Charles V summoned Philip to Brussels to serve an apprenticeship in government in the Low Countries, and also gain the favour of the German Electors, so that when his father died they would elect him Holy Roman Emperor. Philip brought with him his musicians and his collection of paintings and professed himself impressed with the architecture and formal gardens of Flanders, but the

Flemings were disappointed in him. His rumoured arrogance and the fact that he would speak only Spanish were distinct disadvantages, and no one was sorry when he returned to Spain in 1551. Thereafter he ruled his native land in his father's stead wisely and well, displaying meticulous administrative skill; he patronised masters such as Titian, collected books, and resumed his affair with Isabel de Osario. Those who had dealings with him found him courteous but reticent.

In the spring of 1553, before Mary Tudor's accession, the Emperor had begun urging Philip to marry again, saying it was now a long time 'since the death of the Princess, and it seems to me suitable and necessary because of the progeny which I hope God may grant you'. There was a sense of urgency in Charles's words, because his health was beginning to fail and he wished to abdicate and retire to a monastery; before he could do that, he must see Philip settled and the succession assured. Thus had come about Philip's negotiations to marry another Maria of Portugal.

Undoubtedly Philip was the finest match in Europe, for he was the heir to a huge empire – Spain, the Low Countries, Austria, Sicily, Naples, parts of Germany and the Americas. Yet there were dark rumours circulating in Europe about his cruelty, his cold and calculating character, and his harsh treatment of heretics, and English envoys abroad were certainly aware of these things.

Renard, of course, extolled Philip's good qualities to the skies, telling Mary of his wise judgement and common sense, his sound experience in government, and his moderation. The Queen, however, expressed concern at Philip's youth: he was twenty-six and she was thirty-seven. Renard countered this by saying that Philip was 'an old married man' with a son aged seven. Mary seemed to be in a daze. She liked the idea of marrying Philip, but now that the suggestion had been made, she was thrown into confusion. Nervous at the prospect of marriage itself, she was reluctant to commit herself and fearful of her Council's reaction to the Emperor's proposal.

'I have never felt that which is called love,' she confessed to Renard, 'nor have I harboured thoughts of voluptuousness. I never even thought of marriage until God was pleased to raise me to the throne, and as a private individual I would not desire it. I must therefore leave all to the Emperor, whom I regard as a father.' The Emperor, she insisted, must approach the Council on this matter, as she could not face discussing such a delicate matter with them. Renard assured her that his master would do as she wished.

★

By the beginning of September, Mary was becoming less tolerant of those who persisted in what she regarded as heresy, and increasingly angered by her sister's failure to attend mass. Elizabeth had been subjected to mounting pressure to conform, and early in September the Council censured her to her face for ignoring the Queen's wishes – only to receive from the princess what Renard called 'a very rude response'. Elizabeth had also failed to respond to the Queen's heavy hints that she abandon the plain clothes that she wore to please the Protestants in favour of magnificent gowns like her own.

It was clear to Elizabeth, however, that some kind of compromise was called for. Much as she wished to remain a focus of hope for her sister's Protestant subjects, she dared not risk incurring the Queen's wrath by openly adhering to the reformed faith. She therefore requested an audience. Mary kept her waiting for two days before agreeing to see her in a gallery at Richmond Palace.

In the meantime, Renard had been poisoning the Queen's mind with his suspicions of Elizabeth. He had never trusted her, believing her to be in league with a burgeoning opposition of heretics and dissidents led by the French ambassador, a proven troublemaker. Already it was being said that the papists were having their turn but that the Lady Elizabeth would remedy all in time.

'She seems to be clinging to the new religion out of policy to attract and win the support of those who are of this religion,' he told Mary. 'We may be mistaken in suspecting her of this, but at this early stage it is safer to forestall than be forestalled.' The princess, he warned, was clever and sly and possessed of 'a spirit full of enchantment'. She should be sent to the Tower, or at the very least away from court, for her presence there was a threat to the Queen's security, and she 'might, out of ambition, or being persuaded thereto, conceive some dangerous design and put it to execution by means which it would be difficult to prevent'. Mary shared Renard's suspicions, confiding to him that 'the same considerations had occurred to her'. Nevertheless, she would not agree to consigning Elizabeth to the Tower. What she most earnestly desired was her sister's conversion to the Catholic faith, for it was unthinkable that the heiress presumptive to the throne should be a heretic.

Now, when Elizabeth came into Mary's presence, she fell on her knees, trembling and weeping, looking – according to Renard – 'very timid'.

'I see only too clearly that Your Majesty is not well-disposed towards me,' she faltered, 'and I can think of no other cause except religion.' However, she begged to be excused on this issue as she had been brought up a Protestant and 'never been taught the doctrines of the ancient religion'. She entreated the Queen to arrange for her to take instruction from a learned man and be given books, so that she might know if her conscience would allow her to be persuaded. A gratified Mary promised to grant these requests and told her that, if she went to mass, belief would surely follow. It was her pleasure, she added, that Elizabeth attend mass in celebration of the Nativity of the Blessed Virgin Mary on 8 September, after the court had moved to Whitehall. Elizabeth tried to excuse herself on the grounds that she was suffering from stomach pains, but Mary would hear no excuses.

On the appointed day, Elizabeth went in procession to chapel, but not, as Renard reported, 'without a certain amount of stir. She complained loudly all the way to church that her stomach ached, wearing a suffering air.' She even asked the Queen's ladies to rub her stomach for her, but her protests availed her nothing, and she had no choice but to go to the service, hoping that her Protestant supporters at court would notice the miniature gold book containing her brother's deathbed prayer at her girdle. The Queen, however, was overjoyed by her sister's apparent conversion, and – as was her way – lavished gifts upon her: a diamond, a ruby brooch, and a coral rosary that Elizabeth deliberately never carried.

The Queen's joy was short-lived, however; when the princess failed to attend mass on the following Sunday, all her former distrust and doubts were revived, fuelled by Gardiner and Renard, who believed that Elizabeth was merely dissembling the better to play her own game. Even de Noailles wrote, 'Everyone believes that she is acting rather from fear of danger and peril than from real devotion.'

Mary herself thought that her sister's request for books and instruction had been prompted only out of hypocrisy and summoned her to a second audience, in which she begged Elizabeth to speak freely and say 'if she firmly believed what Catholics had always believed concerning the Holy Sacrament'. Elizabeth, seemingly overcome with awe, and visibly shaken, replied that she had seen the error of her former ways and was planning to make a public declaration 'that she went to mass because her conscience moved her to it, that she went of her own free will and without fear, hypocrisy or dissimulation'. Renard, hearing about this interview from Mary, did not believe that Elizabeth's trembling was due to awe: '*We* maintain that she appears quite composed and proud,' he told the Emperor, reiterating his conviction that she was deceiving them all and lying about her conversion.

Nor had Mary's doubts been allayed. She could not bear to think that if she died before producing a Catholic heir, her throne would pass to one whose religious views were so suspect. To Renard, she protested bitterly that it 'would burden her conscience too heavily to allow Elizabeth to succeed, for she only went to mass out of hypocrisy, she had not a single servant or maid-of-honour who was not a heretic, she talked every day with heretics and lent an ear to their evil designs, and it would be a disgrace to the kingdom to allow her to succeed.' She was, moreover, 'the offspring of one of whose good fame he might have heard, and who had received her punishment'. She had inherited too many dubious characteristics from her mother to make a worthy queen. As for her paternity, Mary often claimed not to believe that Elizabeth was Henry VIII's child, but the result of the suspected liaison between Anne Boleyn and a lute-player, Mark Smeaton. She told Jane Dormer many times that Elizabeth had his 'face and countenance'.

In order to eliminate the possibility of Elizabeth ever becoming queen, it was imperative that Mary marry soon and produce an heir. De Noailles was mischievously spreading rumours that she was deeply in love with Courtenay and refusing to consider anyone else, and the Queen's prudish silence on the subject lent weight to these rumours. Gardiner and a group of pro-Courtenay councillors, including her former devoted servants, Rochester, Englefield and Waldegrave, seized this opportunity for an audience and begged Mary to come to a decision soon about her marriage, urging her seriously to consider Courtenay as a husband. The Queen, however, had been hearing alarming reports of that young man's behaviour, of his consorting with prostitutes, his vow to avenge the deaths of his family by slaying a cousin who had betrayed them, his involvement with the French ambassador, and the linking of his name with Elizabeth's. He was too young, she told Gardiner dismissively.

Renard, however, foreseeing the ruin of all the Emperor's carefully-laid plans, feared that the Queen might be open to persuasion. Even were she not, if Courtenay was in league with de Noailles and Elizabeth, as had been rumoured, then Mary's very crown might be under threat. He told Charles V,

> The Lady Elizabeth is greatly to be feared. I hear she already has her eye on Courtenay as a possible husband. This is very dangerous, and I foresee that Courtenay's friends, who include most of the nobility, are hatching some design which may later menace the Queen.

The Emperor had also heard talk that Mary would marry Courtenay, and replied that, if she had indeed made up her mind to do so, 'nothing would stop her, for she is like other women'. There was no time to lose.

In mid-September, Renard learned that Philip's negotiations with Portugal had been formally ended, and towards the end of the month a letter arrived from the Emperor himself, recalling Scheyfve and the other two envoys, and instructing Renard to obtain a private audience with Mary and formally offer her Philip's hand in marriage, asking her for a plain answer as to her own inclination. If she was not interested, Renard was quietly to drop the idea.

It was some time before Renard was able to see the Queen in private because her coronation was imminent and she was deeply involved in plans for it. By late September London was hung with tapestries and adorned with ceremonial arches, flowers and painted backdrops for the pageants that would be staged along the processional route. On 27 September, to the sound of fanfares and cannonfire salutes, the Queen, escorted by the Lord Mayor and accompanied by Elizabeth, came by barge from Whitehall to the Tower, where monarchs traditionally spent a night before their crowning. Tradition also demanded that the sovereign create new Knights of the Bath at the Tower, but this ceremony had to be performed by Arundel, as Great Master of the Household, because it was unthinkable that the Queen should participate in a ritual which demanded that the knights bathe naked with their king and kiss his bare shoulder.

On 30 September, Mary was attired in blue velvet and ermine with a glittering trellised tinsel and pearl caul on her head so weighty that she was frequently to resort to supporting her head with her hands. To gasps of admiration she went in procession in a chariot upholstered in cloth of gold through the streets of London to Whitehall, past cheering crowds, children singing and making pretty speeches, and fountains running with free wine. There had been some concern for her safety after a plot by Protestants to murder Gardiner had been discovered, and even though a fruitless search was made in the city for concealed arms the Queen was still nervous.

Behind Mary came another chariot, in which rode Elizabeth with Anne of Cleves; preceding the Queen were the new Knights of the Bath, with Courtenay foremost among them, Gardiner, Winchester, Norfolk, Oxford bearing the sword of state, and the Lord Mayor and aldermen. Forty-six gentlewomen brought up the rear of the great procession.

On the next day, 1 October, as bells pealed, trumpets sounded, the organ played and choristers sang, Mary, in a regal purple robe, was crowned by Gardiner in Westminster Abbey, which was entirely floored with blue cloth for the occasion. Elizabeth, wearing white and silver beneath a scarlet and ermine mantle, had the honour of bearing the Queen's train, and was the first to take the oath of allegiance to her. In the procession to the Abbey she rode behind the Queen with Anne of Cleves, followed by Lady Katherine Grey, who wore red velvet. The Queen, in her coronation oath, swore to keep 'the just and licit laws of England', thus neatly avoiding swearing to uphold the Protestant settlement that was still law. The solemnities began at ten in the morning and ended at five in the afternoon, when a magnificent coronation banquet was served in Westminster Hall. The Queen, seated beneath a canopy of estate, feasted on wild boar sent by Mary of Hungary amongst other delicacies; she was offered 312 dishes out of the 7112 prepared for the occasion; 4900 were uneaten and were afterwards distributed to the poor. Whilst the company ate, Derby, Norfolk and Arundel rode about the hall on horses, trapped in cloth of gold, ensuring that everything ran smoothly, and after the second course had been served, Sir Edward Dymoke, the Queen's Champion, rode into the hall and challenged any man to dispute her title, throwing down his gauntlet as he did so. Elizabeth sat with the Queen and Anne of Cleves at the high table, but Renard (whom the princess had pointedly ignored all day) later observed her deep in conversation with the French ambassador; sidling close to them he heard the princess groaning about the weight of her coronet. When de Noailles advised her to have patience, since this small crown would soon bring her a better one, Renard immediately concluded that they were hatching some conspiracy.

On 5 October, Mary's first Parliament met and, under Gardiner's leadership, cautiously began dismantling Edward VI's religious legislation, repealing nine statutes including the Act of Uniformity and restoring the ecclesiastical settlement that had existed at the end of Henry VIII's reign. This had the effect of reinstating the Catholic faith, but with the Queen, not the Pope, as Supreme Head of the Church, which was what the conservative majority wanted. A disappointed Mary was left in no doubt that Parliament was unwilling to consider reunification with Rome unless an agreement about alienated church property could first be satisfactorily reached. She disliked the title Supreme Head, which Pole had said 'misbecame her sex', and could never bring herself to write it, putting '*et cetera*' in its place.

From now on it was, however, forbidden to criticise the mass and for priests to marry, and the Book of Common Prayer was suppressed.

There was a vociferous reaction to these measures from the Protestant minority, with churches being vandalised, priests attacked and virulent propaganda tracts issued, but to little effect.

Further legislation included the reversal of several attainders, including that on the Courtenay family, and an Act of Restitution, which declared that Henry VIII's annulment of his marriage to Katherine of Aragon had been invalid and that the Queen, their daughter, was therefore legitimate. Elizabeth was still officially a bastard, but remained heiress to the throne under the terms of her father's will. Mary had asked Paget, Renard's crony, if it would be possible to disinherit her sister, but he warned her that Parliament would never agree to it. Paget knew that Mary was in favour of a Spanish marriage and he himself supported the alliance, but he also knew that it would be extremely unpopular in England. He therefore suggested that Mary marry Elizabeth to Courtenay in order to make her subjects more amenable to the idea of a Spanish marriage for herself, but Mary would not consider it.

As if to underline the legality of her parents' union, the Queen presented Elizabeth with a miniature gold dyptich containing portraits of them, to wear at her girdle. Whether Elizabeth ever did so is not recorded.

Immediately the coronation was over, Renard again sought an audience with the Queen, and in the late evening of 10 October a servant came to lead him to Mary's private chamber at Whitehall. After greeting the Queen, the ambassador wasted no time in declaring his purpose. The Emperor, he said, would gladly have offered himself as a husband for her, but he was 'a poor thing to be offered' because of his age and ill-health. He had therefore, after 'maturely examining her requirements', decided to offer as a most fitting substitute his son, Prince Philip.

Mary was silent for a while; now that the expected proposal had come, her instinct was to shrink from it, but, controlling her inner panic, she said, 'I thank the Emperor for suggesting a greater match than I deserve.' Then she marshalled her arguments against it: she was unsure how her subjects would take to a foreign consort, she did not know if the Council would consent, Philip might be too busy abroad to spend much time with her in England, and might involve the kingdom in his own wars; lastly, he was 'not as wise' as his father, and 'very young, being only twenty-six years of age'.

'A man of twenty-six,' replied Renard, 'can hardly be called a young man, but rather a middle-aged one, because nowadays a man nearly thirty is considered as old as men formerly were at forty, and few men survive to more than fifty or sixty.'

'A man of twenty-six,' retorted the Queen, 'is likely to be disposed to be amorous, and such is not my desire, not at my time of life, and never having harboured thoughts of love.' She declared she could not possibly make up her mind quickly, even though she was not contemplating marrying anyone else and had 'never taken a fancy to anyone'.

'Prince Philip,' Renard assured her, 'is so admirable, so virtuous, prudent and modest as to appear too wonderful to be human. I have in fact been minimising his qualities. Far from being young and amorous, His Highness is a prince of stable and settled character.' If the Queen accepted his proposal, she would be 'relieved of the pains and travails which were rather men's work than the profession of ladies. His Highness is a puissant prince to whom this kingdom could turn for protection and succour. Your Majesty and your Council would do well to remember that you have four certain open enemies: the heretics and schismatics, the rebels and partisans of the late Duke of Northumberland, the French and the Scots, and the Lady Elizabeth, who will never cease to trouble you while they have the means, and will even rise against you.'

Mary promised to consider the matter carefully, and then changed the subject, saying she had spoken with Courtenay, who had revealed that he did not wish to marry Elizabeth at all, since she was 'too heretic, too proud, and of too doubtful lineage on her mother's side'. The Queen had told him that, if he wished to marry, she would find him a Catholic bride with impeccable credentials, whereupon he disclosed that he had fallen in love with Jane Dormer, and wanted to make her his wife. But Mary did not wish to lose Jane's services and had told her that Courtenay was not worthy of her. Dormer had submitted meekly, and the romance came to an abrupt end. Mary informed Renard that she had decided not to permit Courtenay to marry in England; she had hinted that he should go abroad, but to no effect. Therefore she proposed to enrich him sufficiently to attract a foreign heiress.

There the interview ended, but two days later Mary summoned Renard again. Taking his hand, she begged him to confirm that what he had said about Philip was really the truth; was he indeed 'of even temper, balanced judgement and well-conditioned'?

'His Highness,' Renard reassured her, 'has qualities as virtuous as any prince in this world.'

'That is well,' answered Mary, squeezing his hand, but was he sure he was not speaking out of fear of, or affection for, Philip?

'I beg you to take my honour and my life as hostages for the honesty of my words,' replied the ambassador.

Still Mary was not reassured. Would it be at all possible for the Prince to visit her, so that she could see him before making up her mind?

No, said Renard, knowing that the Emperor would never risk a rebuff, but he was certain that Philip would come as soon as she accepted his proposal, having heard much of her great virtues. And with that she had to rest content.

Thinking over the proposal afterwards, she could see that there were great advantages to it. Philip had considerable political experience and in Spain had become used to ruling. He was wealthy and backed by the vast resources of the Habsburgs – more than a match for the unruly factions on the Council. Above all, he was her beloved mother's kinsman, and a champion of Catholicism. Yet she knew little of him as a man, other than through Renard's fulsome praises and some rather nasty rumours about his 'sinister and taciturn disposition' and his notorious promiscuity. Paget later noted that, 'In order to estrange the Queen, people have told her that His Highness is very voluptuous and has bastards.' Renard reported Mary's fears to the Emperor, who cagily replied, 'We admit there may be some youthfulness in our son, though it is far from being as grave a matter as some people have sought to make out.'

Courtenay might have told the Queen that he did not wish to marry Elizabeth, but he had by no means abandoned his hopes of marrying Mary herself. Encouraged by Gardiner, he and his supporters seized every opportunity to blacken Philip's name, and distributed pamphlets claiming that he was hated in Spain for his 'excessive pride and small wisdom'. Lady Exeter, ambitious for her son, joined forces with Pembroke to persuade Parliament to beg the Queen not to wed a foreigner. Learning of this, Mary had her erstwhile friend evicted from her lodging at court and sent her to live in Pembroke's house. The Marchioness, fearing she had gone too far, sought to regain Mary's favour by telling her that Courtenay intended to ask her permission to visit de Noailles.

'He has gone often enough without leave,' retorted the Queen icily. 'I hope he will behave prudently and do nothing inconsistent with his duty.' After a week her anger cooled and she permitted Lady Exeter to return to her old lodgings, but their friendship was never as close as formerly.

Courtenay's propaganda had its effect. Backed by a majority on the Council, Gardiner found it easy to convince members of Parliament that a Spanish marriage would not be in England's interests. At the same time, many were persuaded that a marriage between Mary and Courtenay would not be in England's interests either, which gave the Imperialists cause for hope. A number of people felt that Courtenay should marry Elizabeth. The princess herself had shown him marked favour and was often in his company; Renard believed that their friendship was a threat to the Queen, which led Mary to the conclusion that Elizabeth should be married abroad as soon as possible to a Catholic prince who would curb her ambitions. However, on 19 October, Renard reported that Elizabeth had fallen out with Courtenay 'for having spoken otherwise than she had looked for about the love that is said to have existed between them'. Six days later de Noailles heard that 'Madame Elizabeth is very discontented and has asked permission to withdraw from court'. The Queen refused it; she wanted to keep an eye on her sister's doings. Again, Gardiner and Renard, convinced that Elizabeth was working with Courtenay and de Noailles against the Queen, begged Mary to send her to the Tower, but she demurred, saying that if Elizabeth was intriguing with Courtenay, she would hear of it, because Courtenay would tell his mother, who would tell her.

Mary was still agonising over her own betrothal, unable to make up her mind whether or not to accept Philip. Her ladies-in-waiting urged her to do so, but the Queen baulked at the prospect of marriage, knowing that to run the risk of pregnancy at her age, having had a history of menstrual problems, was to court disaster. Yet she knew that it was her duty to present the kingdom with an heir. Her loyal supporters, Englefield and Waldegrave, were still trying to persuade her to marry Courtenay, but she had long ago rejected that idea. She spent hours praying for guidance, and later confided to Renard that she had spent many sleepless nights in tears before reaching a decision. The uncertainty affected her badly, and on 27 October, it was announced that the Queen was ill and would keep to her apartments.

On 28 October, Renard sought an audience of the Queen and, in the presence of Gardiner, Arundel, Paget and Petre, handed her Charles V's formal written proposal of marriage to his son. He had already shown it to Mary, so that she would be composed when she opened it in front of her councillors, but when she took it she could hardly speak for emotion and, moving out of earshot of the others, told the ambassador that she had wept for two hours that morning, and prayed God to give her guidance in her decision. She said she was almost resolved to agree to the Emperor's proposal. As she left the room, she whispered, 'Believe!'

The next evening Mary granted a private audience to Renard, with only a smiling Clarencieux present, and spoke again of the agony her indecision had caused her. Then, moving to the corner of the room where the Holy Sacrament stood on the altar, she knelt before it and began praying aloud for guidance. Renard and Clarencieux knelt also, joining her in prayer. Then Mary breathed, '*Veni, Creator Spiritus!*' Standing up, she declared that God, 'who had performed so many miracles in her favour' had now performed one more: He had inspired her to give a solemn promise before the Holy Sacrament to marry Philip. She then broke down in tears: 'My mind is made up and I can never change it. I will love His Highness perfectly and never give him any cause to feel jealous.'

Renard was jubilant, but he knew that he and the Queen had a difficult task ahead of them in persuading the Council and her subjects at large to accept Philip and all he represented. For this reason, Mary agreed that the announcement of her betrothal should await an opportune moment, while Renard immediately began making strenuous efforts to convince her councillors of the advantages of the match.

The strain of the past weeks inevitably took its toll. Early in November Mary suffered such bad palpitations that she was obliged to keep to her chamber for a week. 'They say it comes from the womb,' observed de Noailles, although Renard believed her symptoms were due to a change in the weather. By 8 November the Queen had recovered and on that day she summoned her Privy Council to hear her answer to the Emperor's proposal. 'With a royal mien, becoming modesty, a timid countenance and trembling gesture', and 'dissembling as if she had never heard the question mentioned before', Mary expressed her gratitude to Charles V and announced that she would marry his son. Although many councillors had anticipated such an announcement, the general reaction was one of shocked surprise.

The Queen had by now become quite enamoured of the idea of marrying Philip, and coyly accused Renard of making her fall in love with him, saying that His Highness might not be obliged to him for that, although she would do her best to please him in every way. 'It seems that she is beginning to understand what love is,' the ambassador told Charles V, 'for she is always overjoyed to hear His Highness spoken of.'

When the news of the Queen's betrothal became public knowledge, however, her subjects were anything but overjoyed. There was widespread dismay and alarm that England might be dragged into interminable and ruinous Habsburg wars. Courtenay's supporters resolved to warn Mary not to marry a foreigner because 'the people simply will not stand it', while Gardiner longed to speak out, but knew the Queen would accuse him of being prejudiced in Courtenay's favour.

In every strata of society objections were raised to the match. In accepting Philip, Mary had underestimated the insularity and xenophobia of her subjects, who resented Spanish monopolies in trade with the Americas and had heard terrible tales of the tortures of the dreaded Inquisition. Up until now, Mary's religious reforms had been accepted placidly by most people, but from now on they would be associated in the public mind with Spanish influence and become more controversial. Overnight, it became patriotic to be Protestant.

In London in particular, public outrage was expressed vociferously. The citizens declared they would not welcome 'Jack Spaniard' to England, for he was a proud villain notorious for his vices, his thieving and his lechery. Reformists cried that 'They would rather die than suffer Spaniards to rule this country.' In a climate of enmity and panic, many people concluded that Mary would bring 'the proud Spaniard' England as her dowry, and that it would become his property on marriage, as was the usual custom with dowries. They foresaw him ruling harshly and ruthlessly, characteristics for which the Spanish were notorious. Above all, their sense of national pride was outraged at the prospect of England becoming a satellite of the vast Habsburg empire.

Mary and her councillors were sensitive to these concerns, and took such steps as they could to allay them. The Queen told Renard, 'I will wholly love and obey him to whom I have given myself, following the divine commandment, and will do nothing against his will; but if he wishes to encroach upon the government of the kingdom, I will be unable to permit it.'

Renard understood the fears of the English, and spent most of November trying to allay them, whilst at the same time thrashing out the terms of the marriage treaty. The English councillors were determined to retain the sovereignty of their kingdom, and were resolved that Philip should be merely his wife's consort, without political influence or regal authority. Charles V, apprised of their concerns, told Renard to be as accommodating and conciliatory as possible. Nothing must stand in the way of the Anglo-Spanish alliance.

The ambassador made it his business to eliminate opposition to the marriage wherever possible. He told the Queen that she must neutralise her sister, either by putting her in the Tower under restraint or by treating her with the courtesy due to the heir to the throne. Mary still refused to imprison Elizabeth, but was almost as reluctant to show friendship to her. 'She still resents the injuries inflicted on Queen Katherine, her lady mother, by the machinations of Anne Boleyn,'

Renard explained to the Emperor. De Noailles reported that Elizabeth's position at court was such that no lady dared visit her without
Mary's permission, and she was treated as subordinate in rank to her
cousins, the Duchess of Suffolk and the Countess of Lennox.
Miserable at being so out of favour, Elizabeth again solicited leave to
retire to her estates, but the Queen still refused to grant it.

On 14 November 1553, Lady Jane Grey, Lord Guilford Dudley and his
brothers, and Archbishop Cranmer were tried at the Guildhall in
London on charges of high treason. The Queen, insisting that their
trials be fair, took steps to ensure that witnesses were allowed to speak
freely, and were not intimidated, and directed Chief Justice Morgan to
'administer the law impartially. It is my pleasure that whatever can be
produced in favour of the subject shall be heard.'

The prisoners came by barge from the Tower, then walked through
the City to the Guildhall, past crowds kept in control by a detachment
of 400 halberdiers. Jane came first in the procession, wearing a black
velvet gown and a black satin hood trimmed with jet. A tiny prayer
book was attached to her girdle, and she read from another as she
walked along, escorted by guards and followed by two gentlewomen.

The proceedings did not last long, for all the accused pleaded guilty
and all were condemned to death, Jane being sentenced 'to be burned
alive on Tower Hill or beheaded, as the Queen pleases'. She showed no
emotion and calmly walked from the hall with the ceremonial axe of
the executioner turned towards her. When she returned to her
lodgings in the Tower, her servants burst into tears.

'Remember, I am innocent,' she told them, 'and did not deserve this
sentence. But I should not have accepted the crown.'

Mary had no intention of having the sentences carried out. 'It is
believed that Jane will not die,' wrote Renard, and a few days later de
Noailles heard that, 'Her life is safe, though several people are trying to
encompass her death.' Mary was resolved to be merciful. The
condemned prisoners would remain in the Tower at her pleasure, and
when the time was right she would consider releasing them.

On 16 November, Gardiner made one final attempt at preventing the
Queen from carrying out her plan to marry Philip. Leading a
deputation comprising members of both Houses of Parliament, he
came to present a petition begging her to abandon the idea of a foreign
match and marry an Englishman. But when the Speaker began
ponderously to recite it, Mary angrily turned on him, telling him that
Parliament was not accustomed to use such language to the kings of

England, and that monarchs could marry where they chose. They could trust her to remember her coronation oath and always put her country first.

'If you try to force me to take a husband who would not be to my liking, you would cause my death, for if I were to be married against my will, I would not live three months and would have no children, and then you would be sorry!' she warned somewhat dramatically. 'Is it suitable to expect me to marry someone just because the Bishop has made friends with him in prison?'

'What will the people say?' Gardiner asked her. 'They will never stomach a foreigner who will make promises that he cannot keep.'

'My mind is made up,' answered the Queen, 'and if you, my Lord Chancellor, prefer the will of the people to my wishes, then you are not keeping your promises.'

Gardiner knew when he was defeated, and assured the Queen he would obey the man she had chosen.

'It is too dangerous to meddle in the marriages of princes,' he muttered as he withdrew. Arundel made a joke at his expense, saying 'He had lost his post as Chancellor that day, for the Queen had usurped it,' which drew wry laughter from the deputation.

De Noailles was crestfallen at the failure of Gardiner's plea. Although Mary had instructed her ambassador in Paris to reassure Henry II that, whoever she married, she intended to live in peace and amity with him, the French were pessimistic. 'It is to be remembered,' King Henry observed, 'that a husband may do much with his wife; and it shall be very hard for any wife to refuse her husband anything.' De Noailles was doing his best to whip up anti-Spanish feeling in England – no difficult task – and was busily spreading rumours that a Spanish army would shortly arrive to subjugate the people, that Philip meant to make England a mere province of the Empire, and that the Pope's authority would be forced on the English court. Public feeling was running so high, especially in London, that the Queen issued a proclamation forbidding 'unlawful and rebellious assemblies, lewd words and seditious tumults'.

Renard, fearful that Mary would bow to pressure and abandon the Spanish match, sent urgently to Madrid for a portrait of Philip. A likeness painted by Titian in 1551 was dispatched on 21 November, with a note from Mary of Hungary advising the Queen to view it from a distance as, 'on a close view, the sitter cannot be recognised'. There has been much speculation as to which portrait this was, but it seems likely that it was the one that now hangs in the Prado in Madrid. The Regent wanted the portrait returned to her as soon as Mary and Philip were married, 'as it is only a dead thing, when she has the living model in her presence'.

Renard need not have worried. Mary took one look at the portrait and declared that she was 'half in love' with Philip.

11

Heretics and Traitors

On 26 November 1553, a group of conspirators met in London to plot rebellion. Their leader was a Kentish knight, Thomas Wyatt, whose father and namesake had been a famous poet, diplomat and one-time suitor of Anne Boleyn. Wyatt the younger was a hot-headed former soldier, a staunch Catholic who had risen on Mary's behalf back in July, but who had travelled widely in Spain in his time and 'imbibed an utter detestation' of the Spaniards. Wyatt had gathered around him a group of men committed to preventing the Queen by force from marrying Philip of Spain; among them was de Noailles, who had agreed to ask his master for aid.

It seems, from the evidence available, that Wyatt himself intended merely to prevent the marriage; there is no clear proof that he meant to depose Mary and make Elizabeth and Courtenay king and queen in her place, which was de Noailles's objective and was what most people at the time came to believe. However, Wyatt certainly informed Courtenay of his plans, and he also wrote to Elizabeth, hoping to elicit her support.

The conspirators were men of some standing and included William Thomas, Edward VI's clerk to the Council, Sir Peter Carew, a swashbuckling west-country landowner, Sir Nicholas Throckmorton and several men who had served under Northumberland, among them Sir William Pickering, former ambassador to France, and Sir James Crofts, once Deputy Governor of Ireland. Most were Catholics, but all were committed to keeping the hated Spaniards out of England. William Thomas wanted to assassinate the Queen, but the rest firmly vetoed that plan.

Courtenay was willing to join the plotters, and it was decided that just before Philip's arrival in England, which they surmised would be around the middle of March, Courtenay should visit his estates in Devon and join forces with Peter Carew to orchestrate a rising in the west.

The government was already anticipating some such conspiracy, and its officers were watchful. When, in late November, Elizabeth again begged for permission to leave court and go to Ashridge, the Queen reluctantly agreed, but sent Paget and Arundel to warn the princess that 'her present unwise conduct was known; if she refused to follow the path of duty and persisted in concerning herself with French and heretical conspiracies, she would bitterly repent it'. Paget himself had heard from two of Elizabeth's servants that she had been secretly seeing de Noailles. Elizabeth protested to Paget that she would never conspire against the Queen, that she was a devout Catholic and would be taking priests with her so that mass might be celebrated at Ashridge. She would, in short, 'do all in her power to please the Queen'. Nevertheless, Mary, believing that her sister would 'bring about some great evil unless she is dealt with', had given orders that spies were to be placed in the princess's household to watch her every move.

By the end of November a draft marriage treaty between England and Spain had been drawn up. Thanks to Gardiner's efforts to safeguard England's sovereignty, this provided that Philip would enjoy the title of king and 'aid Her Highness in the happy administration of Her Grace's realms and kingdoms', but real power was to remain with Mary. If she died without heirs to her body, he would have no claim upon England, although the eldest son of the union would inherit England, Burgundy and the Low Countries – Don Carlos would have Spain and all Philip's other continental territories. The treaty also bound Philip to obey all the laws and customs of England. He would not be allowed to appoint his servants to English offices, nor involve England directly or indirectly in his father's war with France. No Spaniard was to interfere in English politics, and both Philip and Mary were to be counselled only by English ministers. These terms were accepted by the Emperor's representatives on 27 November and by the English Council on 7 December. Philip was not consulted.

On 29 November, he wrote to Mary a brief, formal note to say that he was pleased that she had accepted his suit, and that he would be coming to England whenever she was ready to receive him. The Emperor advised him to arrive by February or March, taking only those servants and officials who would give a good impression.

'It is impossible to exaggerate the importance of gaining popularity and goodwill,' emphasised Charles.

Because the Church prohibited marriages from being solemnised during Lent, Mary agreed that her wedding should take place afterwards, in the spring of 1554. Application was then made for the necessary papal dispensation, as the royal couple were within the forbidden degrees of affinity. By the time that Parliament was dissolved on 5 December, the Council appeared to be reconciled to the Spanish marriage, but others were not. On that day a dead dog with clipped ears, a rope around its neck, and its head tonsured like a priest's was hurled into the Queen's chamber at Whitehall. Mary announced that she would retaliate with severity if anything of that sort happened again, but she was unable to stop the flow of seditious pamphlets and the intermittent acts of vandalism perpetrated by nationalistic Protestants.

Elizabeth left court on 6 December. Renard had heard that Ashridge was near the Great North Road and, in view of the fact that de Noailles had asked to have 'posting houses on the road to Scotland', became suspicious. He therefore saw Elizabeth before she left and 'spoke seasonable words calculated to counteract the effects of French intrigue'.

De Noailles reported that, when Elizabeth and Mary bade each other farewell, there was a complete reconciliation between them, but Renard knew better, for he had counselled Mary to make a show of affection on parting; 'I had much difficulty in persuading her to dissemble,' he told the Emperor. The Queen informed him that Elizabeth had addressed a petition to her, 'asking her not to believe anyone who spread evil reports of her without doing her the honour to let her know and give her a chance of proving the false and malicious nature of such slanders'. Mary assured her she would not, and then presented the princess with two ropes of pearls and a warm sable hood. The sisters embraced and Elizabeth rode away. Before she reached Ashridge she sent a courier back to the Queen, asking if 'copes, chasubles, chalices and other ornaments for her chapel' might be sent on. Mary again suspected hypocrisy, but complied 'as it was for God's service'.

Even with Elizabeth gone, de Noailles was still plotting, blithely assuming that the princess would fall in unquestioningly with his schemes. On 14 December, he reported to Henry II:

> From what I hear it only requires that my Lord Courtenay should marry her and that they should go together to the counties of

Devonshire and Cornwall. Here they would find many adher-
ents, and they could then make a strong claim to the crown, and
the Emperor and the Prince of Spain would find it difficult to
suppress this rising. The [only] misfortune is that Courtenay is of
such a fearful and timid disposition that he dare not make the
venture. There are many of whom I know who would be ready to
give him encouragement and help in carrying out some plan to his
advantage, and I do not see what should hinder him, except his
weakness, faint-heartedness and timidity.

It was natural that de Noailles, Sir Thomas Wyatt, and every
Protestant in England should look to Elizabeth as the natural focus of
opposition to the Spanish marriage, but she was far too canny to
involve herself directly in any conspiracy. She knew she was watched,
and she knew too that Henry II would only court her for as long as she
was of use to him in a plot to overthrow her sister. Keeping her own
counsel had become habitual with her since the Seymour affair, and
that bitter experience had left her all too aware of the hideous
consequences of intriguing against princes. She knew that her enemies
would rejoice to see her condemned for treason, and she had no
intention of giving them that satisfaction.

The Queen had decided to wait until she was married and had
produced a Catholic heir before pardoning Jane Grey and setting her at
liberty. Despite remaining under sentence of death, Jane was well-
treated in the Tower, being allowed to walk in the gardens and even
beyond the walls to Tower Hill, escorted by guards. Guilford Dudley
was allowed similar freedoms, but the two were not allowed to meet
now. The Lieutenant of the Tower, Sir John Bridges, was a lenient and
compassionate gaoler, and Jane came to regard him as her true friend.

In December, however, with public protests against the Spanish
marriage growing ever more vociferous, and fears of risings against the
Queen becoming daily more acute, Jane was informed that she was no
longer to be allowed out of Master Partridge's house for her daily walks.
The Council believed that either she or Elizabeth might be made the
focus for a rebellion, and wanted Jane out of the public eye, but the
enforced confinement made her ill. This, and her conviction that
Elizabeth posed the greater threat, prompted Mary to command
Bridges to allow his prisoner to resume her walks in the garden at his
discretion. Renard thought this imprudent, for on the same day he
reported that the Suffolks were planning a rebellion. In the Tower,
Jane waited dejectedly for a pardon that did not arrive, and took to

carving fatalistic Latin inscriptions on the walls; these were obliterated long ago, but survive in manuscript copies. They read:

> To mortals' common fate thy mind resign,
> My lot today tomorrow may be thine.

And,

> While God assists us, envy bites in vain,
> If God forsake us, fruitless all our pain –
> I hope for light after the darkness.

Suffolk was indeed involved in the rebellion planned by Sir Thomas Wyatt. On 22 December, along with Courtenay, he joined the conspirators to plan four simultaneous risings orchestrated to take place on Palm Sunday, 18 March 1554. Wyatt was to raise the men of Kent, Crofts those of Herefordshire and the Welsh Marches, Carew and Courtenay the disaffected men of Devon, and Suffolk the commons of Leicestershire. The four rebel armies would then march on London and, with the aid of the French, rescue Mary from her evil councillors and so prevent her from marrying Philip. Afterwards it was widely believed that there was a hidden agenda to depose Mary and elevate Elizabeth and Courtenay to the throne, but at the time Courtenay was probably hoping to marry the Queen herself. So unpopular was the Spanish marriage that the conspirators had every expectation of popular support.

Renard's spies soon heard rumours that trouble was brewing, but could uncover no hard evidence. Nevertheless, the ambassador rightly concluded that 'before Easter there shall be such a turmoil in England as never was seen'. The whispers had it that some disaffected Englishmen were 'trying to induce Courtenay or Elizabeth to act as their leader', but Elizabeth 'was too clever and sly' to agree to that. She would never admit that she had been in contact with Wyatt, but around Christmas she began summoning her loyal tenants to come, armed, to protect her from her enemies. Renard was convinced she was planning something underhand.

We shall probably never know how much Elizabeth knew of the plot. One conspirator, Pickering, was a friend of hers, and they had had a private conversation in her room lasting for two hours at the end of October. De Noailles, himself involved in the conspiracy, claimed that Elizabeth was 'strongly familiar' with Sir James Crofts, who visited the princess at Ashridge that month and afterwards told the ambassador that, as soon as the rebellion began, Elizabeth intended to move out of Mary's reach to avoid being taken hostage. Crofts also told de Noailles that she had hopes of the crown, 'especially if the matters undertaken for her come to a successful end'. It may be, however, that Crofts was making this up in order to enlist French support.

There is no proof that Elizabeth ever did anything to encourage or aid the conspirators, nor is there any evidence that she ever sent any treasonable communication to them. Many would shortly try to find such evidence, but the search proved abortive. What is likely is that Elizabeth knew of Wyatt's plans but was waiting upon events and taking measures to protect herself. She later claimed that she had learned how to keep silent during Mary's reign.

There was still talk in government circles of marrying Elizabeth to Courtenay, but the Emperor put a stop to that on 24 December when he ordered Renard to do everything in his power to prevent such a match, on the grounds that it threatened Mary's security as queen. At the same time, Gardiner was doing his best to reconcile the people to the Spanish marriage, preaching at Westminster that it would lead to 'the enriching of the realm. We are much bounden to thank God that so noble, worthy and famous a prince would vouchsafe so to humble himself as in this marriage.' His words provoked an outcry of disgust and increased tension in London, to the dismay of the authorities. Thus, when Charles V's commissioners arrived on 27 December to finalise the marriage treaty, they were met with a sullen hostility and demonstrations of protest, 'so hateful was the sight of their coming in'. On 1 January, the embassy servants were pelted with snowballs by a crowd of jeering boys, while a rash of seditious placards mysteriously appeared in the capital. Hearing of these things, the Queen's ladies hastened to her in fright, fearful that a rebellion was about to break out. The 'melancholy and sadness' she felt at what they had to tell her brought another bout of illness.

The next day, the embassy from Charles V headed by Count Egmont arrived in London in bitter weather. Landing by barge at the Tower to a great peal of guns, they were courteously received by Courtenay and then escorted in state through the city, only to find a group of demonstrators outside Durham House, where they were to lodge. The Queen, furious that they had suffered such an unfriendly reception, let it be known that any person insulting the Emperor's representatives would suffer severe penalties.

Egmont had brought with him the draft articles of the marriage treaty as well as money and jewels with which to make the Council ready to offer concessions – a fruitless exercise. Renard was also given money to bribe those who might 'do harm and cause difficulties'. Renard had held de Noailles responsible for the recent disturbances in London, but the Council believed that they were a front for more treasonable activities, and had for some time been suspicious of the activities of Sir Peter Carew.

At the beginning of January their worst fears were confirmed when incriminating letters written by Wyatt and de Noaillies were intercepted, and by 2 January they knew they had to deal with a serious and widespread rebellion. Worse still, the ambassador's letter implied that Elizabeth was involved and knew of the plot. It also claimed that she had left Ashridge and moved to another of her houses, where she had already assembled her supporters, though the Council knew this to be incorrect.

At the same time, there were reports that Sir Peter Carew was inciting the people of Exeter to rise against Mary by preying on their fears of the Spaniards. The Council at once summoned him to London to account for his behaviour, and dispatched captains and lieutenants throughout southern England to recruit men in order to keep the peace. On hearing that a warrant had been drawn up for Carew's imminent arrest, Courtenay panicked, for he knew it was probable that he would be implicated.

When Philip of Spain learned of the terms that the English were insisting on incorporating in the treaty, he felt angry and slighted, and momentarily thought of withdrawing from the marriage. Yet too much was at stake for that, and on 4 January he contented himself by placing his hand on a crucifix and making a secret formal declaration that he did not consider himself bound by a treaty whose terms had been negotiated without his knowledge or approval. The Emperor, who had bent over backwards to accommodate the sensibilities of the English, almost certainly knew of his son's disclaimer, and may even have suggested it.

When Philip heard that Mary had refused to be married in Lent, he decided to delay his arrival in England until the late spring. He now found himself bombarded with advice. The Imperial envoy in Rome wrote, 'For the love of God appear to be pleased, for there is nothing that could be of greater effect in the service of God or against the French.' His father repeatedly instructed him to choose his retinue carefully, picking only mature and dignified men who would know how to behave in a strange land, and wrote, 'Though I know it is not necessary, I will ask you to be especially careful, if God favours this match, to demonstrate much love and joy to the Queen, both in public and private. And you will converse and be friendly to the English, behaving to them in a cordial manner.' He should also send Mary a ring to mark their coming betrothal.

Philip in his reply, contented himself with saying that his impending marriage was 'a source of satisfaction' to him: 'I trust the result will contribute to the service of God and the welfare of Christendom.'

On 9 January 1554, the marriage treaty was concluded at Winchester House, Gardiner's London residence at Southwark; three days later it was signed by Mary and returned to Charles V. Soon afterwards came news that the Pope had issued the necessary dispensation, and this was followed by the gift of a great diamond from the Emperor with a note telling the Queen that he now 'considered her as his own daughter'. On 14 January, the signing of the treaty was proclaimed throughout England to a frosty reception: 'each man was abashed, looking daily for worse matters to grow shortly after', and there were cries of , 'We will have no foreigner for our king!'

Mary was now eagerly anticipating Philip's arrival, and repeatedly asked Renard when he would come. When Lord Audley teased her about her feelings for the Prince, she blushed furiously. Renard now began sending frequent letters to Philip, urging him to write to the Queen or send some gift or token. The sooner the marriage took place the better, for Mary, 'being a woman, cannot penetrate the knavish tricks' of her councillors 'nor weigh matters of state'.

By 18 January, government troops had occupied Exeter and thus put paid to a revolt in the west. On that day, Renard divulged all he knew about the conspiracy to the Queen. Crofts was now making for the Welsh border and Suffolk was keeping a low profile at Sheen, while Wyatt was raising the men of Kent from his base at Allington Castle, near Maidstone. By 19 January, thirty local gentlemen had joined him. Carew had managed to evade arrest, letting it be known that he would throw the next delegation of Spaniards into the sea.

It was Courtenay, fearful for his own skin, who betrayed them. Renard had confided his suspicions of the Earl to Mary, who in turn had spoken of them to Gardiner. The Chancellor, who still looked upon Courtenay as a son and wished to save him from his own foolishness, summoned him to Winchester House on 21 January and questioned him closely as to his involvement in the rumoured conspiracy. 'This lying fool of a Courtenay,' raged de Noailles, when the young man broke down and humbly confessed everything, craving the Queen's forgiveness. Gardiner hastened to pass on the intelligence to the Council, but took care to conceal the extent of Courtenay's involvement. Courtenay was now at pains to convince everyone of his loyalty to the Queen, and told Gardiner that he would rather go back to the Tower than marry Elizabeth.

Within a day the leaders of the conspiracy learned they had been betrayed and decided to bring forward the date of their planned uprisings; the promised French aid had not yet arrived, but they could not afford to wait for it. They were too deeply implicated in the plot to abandon it, and if they were to succeed they must act now.

On 22 January, Sir James Crofts, alerted by messenger, turned back and rode to Ashridge, where he tried to persuade Elizabeth to move to her castle at Donnington, an isolated and well-fortified house near Newbury. But Elizabeth was ill with nephritis: her body was swollen and her head and arms ached. She refused to go anywhere, and Crofts was obliged to leave her and return the way he had come, making for the Welsh border. Wyatt also tried to get Elizabeth to leave Ashridge, writing that 'she should get herself as far from the city as she could, for her safety from strangers'. She 'sent him word by Sir William Saintlow that she did thank him much for his goodwill, and she would do as she would see cause'. Which was precisely nothing.

By 23 January, the government had raised 8000 men. That day, Wyatt visited Suffolk at Sheen and was promised the Duke's support on condition that the rebels would depose Mary and set his daughter Jane on the throne in her place. Wyatt then returned to Allington, while Suffolk contacted his Leicestershire neighbour, the Earl of Huntingdon, who agreed to raise his tenants at Ashby-de-la-Zouche. Huntingdon then went straight to the Council and warned them what was afoot.

On 25 January, the conspirators rose as planned, but with disappointing results. Without Courtenay as a figurehead, the people of the west were unwilling to rise, and Sir Peter Carew was obliged to flee to France disguised as a servant. Suffolk tried to take Leicester with 150 men, but was successfully resisted. He then withdrew to Coventry, only to find its gates closed against him. By then, his few supporters had abandoned him, and he was forced to go to ground. Crofts did nothing; he seems to have returned to London.

It was Wyatt who posed the most serious threat. When he raised his standard at Maidstone and issued a proclamation protesting against the Spanish marriage, his army was 3–4000 strong. Soon he was riding at the head of 5000 rebels towards London, unopposed because the authorities had been unable to muster any support in the area. Soon Rochester Bridge and a fleet of royal ships anchored in the Medway had fallen to him, yielding vital arms and ordnance. The Londoners, who had received exaggerated reports of the size of the rebel army, awaited its advance in terror.

Gardiner now heard that Elizabeth was either provisioning Ashridge against a siege, or was moving to Donnington Castle. On 26 January, the Queen, anxious to have her sister where she could keep a watchful eye on her, wrote to Elizabeth, 'We, tendering the surety of your person, which might chance to be in some peril if any sudden tumult should arise, either where you now be, or about Donnington, whither (as we understand) you are bound shortly to remove, do therefore think it expedient that you should put yourself in readiness with all convenient speed to make your repair hither to us, which, we pray you, fail not to do; assuring you that as you may more surely remain here, so shall you be most heartily welcome to us. And of your mind herein, we pray you return answer by this messenger.'

Back came a verbal message: the princess was too ill to travel, having 'such a cold and headache that I never felt their like'. Of course, Mary did not believe her, and interpreted her reluctance to come to court as evidence that she was involved in the conspiracy. This suspicion appeared to be confirmed when de Noailles's postbag was seized, on Gardiner's orders, on its way to Dover and searched and a copy of Elizabeth's last letter to the Queen found in it. Mary and Gardiner guessed that Elizabeth had sent the ambassador a copy, and concluded that she was secretly intriguing with the French. Renard was convinced that Gardiner had deliberately suppressed another letter containing indisputable evidence that Courtenay and Elizabeth were plotting to overthrow Mary, but was unable to obtain any verification of this. Mary was disgusted at her sister's conduct, and ordered that her portrait be taken down from her gallery; however, both Queen and Council were so overtaken by the events of the next fortnight that they had no leisure to inquire further into Elizabeth's activities.

On 25 January, the Council had Suffolk, Carew and Wyatt proclaimed traitors in London for having 'raised certain evil-disposed persons to Her Grace's destruction, and to advance the Lady Jane and Guilford Dudley'. Anyone bringing Wyatt to justice was promised a great estate to be held in perpetuity. On 27 January, the Queen dispatched the octogenarian veteran, Norfolk, into Kent with a sizeable force of the London trained bands to suppress Wyatt's rebels. On the 28th, the Duke mounted an attack on them on Rochester Bridge, but 500 of his men deserted to the enemy, saying they would never 'be under the rule of proud Spaniards or strangers'. The rest fled, leaving behind their guns and the money that was to finance the expedition. When Norfolk's remaining troops staggered wearily back into

London, 'their coats torn, all ruined, without arrows or string to their bows', the sight was 'heart-sore and very displeasing' to the Queen, who realised that she now faced a crisis of discouraging proportions, for nothing stood between Wyatt and the capital.

The Council was also aware of the magnitude of the threat, and there were a few among its members – according to Renard – who considered abandoning Mary and offering their allegiance to Elizabeth. Gardiner and others, more loyal, urged the Queen to leave London for the safety of Windsor, but she refused. Nor would she let Count Egmont or the other Imperial envoys fight on her behalf.

While panic mounted in London, the councillors squabbled. Mary complained to Paget that they had failed to provide her with a bodyguard, at which he fell to his knees and reminded her that he had spent two weeks recruiting men, and he had only one voice on the Council and could not do everything himself. Some councillors felt that the Queen should ask the Emperor for military aid, but she was reluctant to have him think she was unable to deal with the situation in case he had doubts about sending his son to such a lawless country. More to the point, the arrival of an Imperial army on England's shores would only confirm her subjects' worst suspicions. Bravely, she gave orders that London should be fortified. She herself would remain at Whitehall until the crisis was over. Remembering how the citizens had welcomed her as their queen, she had no doubt that she could count upon their loyalty now, though in view of recent events others were not so sure.

On 30 January, Wyatt's army arrived at Gravesend, where Sir Edward Hastings failed to halt it. At Blackheath, Wyatt commanded Hastings to demand of the Queen the surrender of her person and of the Tower, but was briskly refused. Hastings then rode at speed to London to warn Mary of Wyatt's intentions, which the Queen interpreted as a declaration of civil war.

The next day she sent for Renard, who found her very agitated because the Council had still not provided her with a bodyguard, although they were doing their utmost to raise men to fight for her. She could trust no one, she declared. Yet even as she spoke the gates of London were being carefully guarded, the drawbridge on London Bridge had been raised – for Wyatt must first cross the Thames before he essayed the city – and great guns had been positioned next to it.

On the morning of 1 February, a deputation from the Commons waited on the Queen and begged her to reconsider her decision to marry Philip. She refused, but assured them that her marriage would never interfere with their liberties. She then saw Renard and told him,

'I consider myself His Highness's wife. I will never take another husband; I would rather lose my crown and my life.'

Later that morning Count Egmont, fearing the fury of the populace, asked the Queen for leave to return to Brussels, and was impressed by her calmness in the face of danger: 'Though she had reason enough to be perplexed, she showed a firm spirit.' She had already determined to make a personal appeal to the Londoners and – ignoring pleas from the councillors to consider her safety – went in the afternoon, wearing her crown and robes of state, to the Guildhall, where the Lord Mayor and aldermen and a huge crowd gathered to hear her address them from the throne in the great hall.

'I am come in mine own person,' she began, 'to tell you that which you already see and know; that is, how traitorously and rebelliously a number of Kentishmen have assembled themselves against us and you.'

What I am yet right well know: I am your queen, to whom, at my coronation, when I was wedded to the realm and laws of the same, you promised your allegiance and obedience unto me. My father, as ye all know, possessed the same regal state, which now rightly is descended unto me, and to him ye always showed yourselves most faithful and loving subjects; and therefore I doubt not but ye will show yourselves likewise to me.

I say to you, on the word of a prince, I cannot tell how naturally the mother loveth the child, for I was never the mother of any; but certainly, if a prince and governor may as naturally and earnestly love her subjects as the mother doth love the child, then assure yourselves that I, being your lady and mistress, do as earnestly and tenderly love and favour you. And I, thus loving you, cannot but think that ye as heartily and faithfully love me. And then I doubt not but we shall give these rebels a short and speedy overthrow.

But for marriage, I will not, for mine own pleasure, choose where I lust, for I am not so desirous that I need a husband. For, God I thank him, I have hitherto lived a virgin, and doubt not that with God's grace I am able so to live still. But if, as my progenitors have done before me, it may please God that I might leave some fruit of my body behind me to be your governor, I trust you would not only rejoice thereat, but also I know it would be to your great comfort. And, on the word of a queen, I promise you that if it shall not probably appear to all the nobility and commons that this marriage shall be for the high benefit and commodity of the realm, then I will abstain from marriage while I live.

I am minded to live and die with you, and strain every nerve in our cause, for this time your fortunes, goods, honour, personal safety, wives and children are all in the balance. If you bear yourselves like good subjects, I am bound to stand by you, for you will deserve the care of your sovereign lady.

And now, good subjects, pluck up your hearts, and like true men face up against these rebels, and fear them not, for I assure you I fear them nothing at all!

Her speech – which Foxe says 'she seemed to have perfectly conned without book' – had the desired effect, as did her obvious courage, and, with many a cap being thrown in the air and many a tear shed, the citizens responded with a loud ovation, realising that their loyalty to their queen was greater than their aversion to her chosen husband. By her timely action Mary had tipped the scales of public opinion in her favour and inspired between 20,000 and 25,000 men to volunteer the next morning to fight against the rebels.

'Oh, how happy we are, to whom God hath given such a wise and learned prince!' exclaimed an impressed Gardiner.

'There never was a more steadfast lady than this queen,' commented Renard, with equal admiration.

Inexorably, the rebel army, 7000 strong by some estimates, but not as large as Wyatt could have hoped for, advanced on London. On Saturday 3 February, he halted at Southwark, dismayed to see that the citizens had now destroyed London Bridge to prevent him from crossing the Thames. He therefore encamped on the Surrey shore for three days and allowed his men to sack the Priory of St Mary Overy (now Southwark Cathedral) and the Bishop of Winchester's palace. Within the city itself there was 'much noise and tumult' as the people donned armour, shut shops and stalls, and heeded the Lord Mayor's injunction to 'stand every one at his door, what chance soever might happen'. The Queen's speech was being read out by heralds in every part of the city to inspire the Londoners with courage, but even so 'there was running up and down in every place. Aged men were astonished, many women wept for fear; children and maids ran into their houses, shutting the doors for fear.'

In the Palace of Whitehall, armed guards were packed into the Queen's presence chamber, while her ladies wept and wailed, making great lamentations and wringing their hands. But the Queen remained cool, giving orders that she was to be informed of every development, and urging her household to place their trust in God.

Mary's advisers wanted to have the Tower guns fired across the river at the rebels, but she refused to allow it in case the innocent inhabitants of Southwark were killed. Even so, it was the fear of bombardment that drove Wyatt to march his army upriver towards Kingston on 6 February. There he crossed the Thames and marched back along its northern shore in the early hours of 7 February to Knightsbridge and Tyburn, which lay outside the city walls. When news of his advance reached Whitehall, every member of the royal household, including menials, was issued with arms. Nevertheless there was panic at court, and the Council advised the Queen to make her escape by river. She refused, saying she 'would tarry to see the uttermost'. Leaving her bedchamber she went to look out of the window in the gallery over the Holbein Gate, calmly ignoring the tumult in the palace, the slamming of doors and 'the running and shrieking of gentlewomen'. At one point she even expressed a desire to be in the field in person.

The rebel march continued unchecked until it halted at St James's Park, where it was confronted by a force of cavalry led by the Earl of Pembroke and Sir Humphrey Clinton. Wyatt's men were exhausted and hungry, and it appears that both sides were reluctant to fight. After a brief skirmish in which many of his troops deserted, Wyatt managed to lead a small detachment of his men away towards Charing Cross, where there was another scuffle, this time with Sir John Gage's men, in which sixteen people were killed; the sound of gunfire could be heard in Whitehall Palace. Courtenay was with Gage, but when the fighting began, he fled in terror, crying, 'All is lost!'

One of the rebels reached the Court Gate at Whitehall and shot an arrow into the palace precincts, prompting further panic, but when Mary's soldiers came to her, crying, 'All is lost! Away! Away!', she 'never changed her cheer nor removed one foot out of the house'.

'Fall to prayer,' she told everyone, 'and I warrant you we shall hear better news anon.'

Wyatt was now making his way along a deserted Fleet Street to Ludgate, passing by locked and shuttered houses. Ludgate, however, remained firmly shut against him, and when he turned to retreat, he found that the way was barred by Pembroke's force, which had followed him as far as Temple Bar and cut off the rest of his army. He was trapped. Realising that his supporters were too few to resist such a large force, and that the Londoners were not going to support him after all, Wyatt gave himself up, and the rebellion collapsed. As his followers were rounded up and arrested, he watched dejectedly from a bench by an inn. By five in the afternoon he himself was on his way to the Tower, where he was imprisoned in the Bell Tower.

★

For the Queen, it was as if God had worked another miracle. But her councillors and Renard, all of whom had been thoroughly frightened, were at pains to point out that the rebellion was the result of her being over-merciful at her accession. This time, she must harden her heart and show her subjects that she was not to be intimidated, for her leniency had almost cost her her throne. This time, Mary took their advice. Never again would she show clemency to traitors. She told Renard, 'I will not cease to demand of the law to strike terror into all those who venture to do evil.' Nor would she tolerate heresy in her realm, for it could only lead to seditious plots against her. Renard, who had hitherto advised caution, now changed his tune and urged her to proceed firmly against all heretics.

Immediately after Wyatt's arrest, both Queen and Council decided that the leaders of the revolt should be executed as an example to other would-be rebels, and Renard expressed his gratification that the government intended to exact such a fearful vengeance. He also urged the Queen to rid herself of other persons who might become a focus for rebellion, such as Jane Grey and her husband. They had been condemned, and as long as they lived would prove a thorn in her side. The councillors were of the same opinion, for had not Suffolk made Jane's restoration a condition of his supporting Wyatt? If Jane were allowed to live, her very existence might jeopardise the Spanish marriage. In corroboration of this, Charles V, when he heard of the outcome of the rebellion, wrote: 'Let the Queen's mercy be tempered with a little severity.' He would not, he said, permit Philip to come to England until Jane was removed.

Reluctantly, Mary capitulated, and that evening Renard wrote to inform the Emperor that the execution of Jane and Guilford had been set for 9 February, two days hence, but that there was uncertainty as to whether it would take place, given Her Majesty's foolish notions of clemency. Yet, even as he wrote, Mary was signing the death warrants, and later that evening the condemned couple were told to prepare themselves for their fate. Jane simply said, 'I am ready and glad to end my woeful days.' In a prayer she composed soon afterwards she described herself as a 'poor and desolate woman, overwhelmed with miseries, vexed with temptations, and grievously tormented with the long imprisonment'.

Tempted she was, because the next day Mary sent the learned Richard Feckenham, Abbot of Westminster, to offer her a reprieve in return for her conversion to the Catholic faith. Feckenham was a kind old man, unusually tolerant for his time, and Jane warmed to him against her will. After their first interview, he asked the Queen to postpone the execution for three days as he believed that he could bring about a change of heart in her cousin in that time. Mary gladly agreed to this and repeated that, if he was successful, Jane would be allowed to live.

Jane, however, was steeling herself for the worst, for she knew she could never embrace the Roman faith, and prayed that

> I might not deny Thee, my God. Be unto me a strong tower of defence. Suffer me not to be tempted above my power. I beseech Thee that I may stand fast.

Her rooms in Master Partridge's house looked out over Tower Green, where workmen were already building the scaffold upon which she was to suffer. Resolutely, she began writing farewell letters to her family and friends. In one to her sister Katherine, she exhorted,

> Live still to die, deny the world, deny the Devil and despise the flesh. Take up your Cross. As touching my death, rejoice, as I do, and adsist that I shall be delivered from corruption and put on incorruption.
>
> Farewell, dear sister; put your only trust in God, Who only must uphold you. Your loving sister, Jane Dudley.

Feckenham was soon back at the Tower with the Queen's promise of mercy, but Jane did not rejoice.

'Alas, sir,' she said, 'it was not my desire to prolong my days. As for death, I utterly despise it, and Her Majesty's pleasure being such, I willingly undergo it. I assure you, the time hath been so odious to me that I long for nothing so much as death.'

Feckenham was deeply grieved, and asked if a public debate might help her to change her mind.

'This disputation may be fit for the living, but not for the dying. Leave me to make my peace with God,' Jane answered.

The Abbot nevertheless prevailed upon her to agree to a debate, which took place in one of the Tower chapels. Predictably, Jane remained firm in her convictions, and Feckenham sadly conceded that he had failed. She told him, 'True it is that we shall never meet [in Heaven] except God turn your heart.' He asked if he might accompany her to her execution, to which she agreed, and then he left her to complete her letters, dispose of her possessions, and select a suitable gown for her last public appearance. These preparations being completed, she fell to prayer, in which she found deep comfort.

★

Jane's father, Suffolk, had remained in hiding, but on 10 February the Earl of Huntingdon discovered him hiding in a hollow tree in his park at Astley in Warwickshire, where he had spent the past two days. The keeper who had hidden him betrayed his whereabouts. The Duke, shivering and bedraggled, crawled out of the trunk and fell at Huntingdon's feet. He was then conveyed to the Tower with his two brothers, who had turned traitor with him. At the same time, other leaders and rebels, including Sir James Crofts, were being rounded up and arrested by the authorities.

Suffolk now suffered belated pangs of remorse over the way he had treated his innocent daughter, and began sending her piteous messages begging for forgiveness. Jane replied,

> Father, although it hath pleased God to hasten my death by you, by whom my life should have been lengthened, yet can I so patiently take it that I yield God hearty thanks for shortening my woeful days. Herein I may count myself blessed that, washing my hands with [my] innocency, my guiltless blood may cry before the Lord.
>
> The Lord continue to keep you, that at the last we may meet in Heaven. Your obedient daughter till death.

She also wrote him a message in the prayer book she intended to carry to the scaffold: 'The Lord comfort Your Grace. Though it hath pleased God to take away two of your children, think not that you have lost them, but trust that we, by losing this mortal life, have won an immortal life; and I, for my part, as I have honoured Your Grace in this life, will pray for you in another life.'

Sir John Bridges was deeply saddened at the prospect of Jane's execution, and craved some small remembrance of her. She promised him that after her death he should have her miniature prayer book bound in velvet, and alongside her last message to her father inscribed it for him: 'There is a time to be born and a time to die, and the day of our death is better than the day of our birth. Yours, as the Lord knoweth, a true friend.'

While she was writing the speech she would deliver from the scaffold, Bridges came to tell her that the Queen had granted a request from Guilford to say farewell to his wife. Jane asked how Guilford was, and the Lieutenant had to tell her that he was in a state of collapse, weeping and railing against an unkind fate. Jane said she preferred not to see him, and sent a message desiring him to 'omit these moments of grief, for we shall shortly behold each other in a better place'. To comfort him, she promised to watch him take his final walk to Tower Hill, where persons who were not of the blood royal were executed.

The executions were to take place on the morning of 12 February. During the night of the 11th, Jane composed a farewell statement:

> If justice is done with my body, my soul will find mercy with God. Death will give pain to my body for its sins, but the soul will be justified before God. If my faults deserve punishment, my youth at least, and my imprudence were worthy of excuse. God and posterity will show me more favour.

Early the next morning a panel of matrons arrived to examine Jane, in case she was pregnant; had this been the case, she would have been spared the axe. But she was not, and presently she took up her place at the window of her lodging, wearing the same black dress she had worn at her trial.

Guilford had asked that a Protestant priest accompany him to the scaffold, but the Queen would not allow it. Many gentlemen felt sorry for him, and went along to support him in his ordeal. The wretched youth wept as he walked to Tower Hill, but by the time he reached the scaffold he had composed himself. He shook hands with his friends, and asked them to pray for him. Then, after a 'very small declaration' to the assembled crowds, he knelt in prayer. Suddenly, his courage deserted him, and he burst into tears again, crying, 'Pray for me! Pray for me!' over and over again, as his eyes were bandaged. The axe took off his head in one stroke.

The headsman then made his way back to Tower Green to dispatch Lady Jane. She saw him coming, as she also beheld with horror the cart returning with her husband's body encased in a bloody sheet and his head wrapped in a cloth. As it trundled past her window, taking its pitiful burden to the Chapel of St Peter ad Vincula for burial, she wept, whispering, 'O Guilford! Guilford! O the bitterness of death!'

It was now her turn. At ten o'clock, on the arm of a grieving Sir John Bridges, Jane walked the short distance to Tower Green, reading her velvet-covered prayer book as she went. Onlookers were impressed by her dignity and composure, which contrasted most movingly with the distress of Mrs Ellen and Mrs Tilney, who followed her, 'wonderfully weeping'. Feckenham followed, keeping his promise to stay with Jane until the end.

Some of the councillors and other dignitaries had gathered to witness the execution, and when the prisoner had mounted the black-draped scaffold she addressed them: 'Good people, I am come hither to die, and by a law I am condemned to the same. The fact, indeed, against the Queen's Highness was unlawful, and the consenting thereunto by me: but touching the procurement and desire thereof by me, I do wash my hands in innocency before God and the face of you, good Christian people.'

She wrung her hands, then went on, 'I pray you all to bear me witness that I die a true Christian woman. And now, good people, while I am alive, I pray you assist me with your prayers.'

Turning to Feckenham, she asked, 'Shall I say this psalm?'

He was too choked with emotion to answer immediately, but at length he said, 'Yea,' and she knelt and recited in English the nineteen verses of the 51st Psalm, the '*Miserere mei Deus*', 'in a most devout manner'.

Then she rose and kissed Feckenham goodbye, saying, 'God I beseech Him abundantly reward you for your kindness towards me. Although I must needs say it was more unwelcome to me than my instant death is terrible.' For a moment they held hands in silence.

Jane gave her gloves and handkerchief to Mrs Tilney, and her prayer-book to the Lieutenant, before untying her gown. The executioner offered to help her but 'she desired him to let her alone'. In silence she untied the scarf around her neck and took from Mrs Ellen 'a fair neckerchief' with which to blindfold herself. 'Then the hangman kneeled down and asked her forgiveness, which she gave most willingly.'

At this point the executioner asked Jane to stand on the straw in the centre of the scaffold, moving aside so that she could see the block, which had been hidden by his bulk.

'I pray you dispatch me quickly,' she said, and knelt, then asked apprehensively, 'Will you take it off before I lay me down?'

'No, madam,' was the reply.

Jane tied the blindfold and felt for the block. It was not there.

'What shall I do?' she cried in mounting panic. 'Where is it?' No one moved as she groped blindly in the air, then an unidentified bystander guided her hands to it. She laid her head down and arched her body to receive the blow.

'Lord, into Thy hands I commend my spirit,' she said clearly. De Noailles reported afterwards that the torrent of blood that gushed from her body when the axe descended was extraordinary.

The headsman picked up the head and cried, 'So perish all the Queen's enemies! Behold the head of a traitor!'

Later that day, when the crowd had dispersed, Jane's attendants laid her to rest beneath the altar pavement of St Peter ad Vincula, between the bodies of two former queens, Anne Boleyn and Katherine Howard, who had also perished on the scaffold. Nearby lay the remains of the two dukes, Somerset and Northumberland, whose ambition had shaped Jane's destiny and made her a martyr to expediency. Centuries later the Victorian historian Lord Macaulay would call this 'the saddest spot on Earth'.

12

'Much Suspected of Me'

With the rebellion quelled, Queen Mary and her councillors had time to consider the behaviour of the Lady Elizabeth, and on 9 February they dispatched three councillors, Lord William Howard, Sir Edward Hastings, and Sir Thomas Cornwallis, and two royal physicians, Dr Thomas Wendy and Dr George Owen, to Ashridge to determine whether the princess was indeed as sick as she had claimed to be. As both Queen and Council believed Elizabeth to have been implicated in Wyatt's rebellion, the doctors were under instructions to bring her to court in Mary's own litter if, in their professional opinion, she could be safely moved. Renard had his own suspicions that Elizabeth was pregnant with Courtenay's child, while the malicious de Noailles was putting it about that Mary had tried to poison her.

The physicians duly examined Elizabeth and concluded that, although she was suffering from 'watery humours' (probably nephritis), she was able 'without danger to her person' to travel to court. The princess, although 'very willing and conformable, much feared her weakness to be so great that she should not be able to endure the journey without peril of life', and pleaded for a few days' grace until she had better recovered her strength. But when told that all excuses must be set aside, she agreed to be ready to leave on 12 February.

Elizabeth had good cause to fear her arrival in London, for the Queen was coming under increasing pressure to deal with her sister as she had dealt with Lady Jane Grey. Renard repeatedly declared that he would not know any peace of mind until two more heads had fallen – those of Elizabeth and Courtenay, 'the two people most able to cause trouble to the realm. Her Majesty is absolutely determined to have strict justice done.' When these traitors had been removed, he told the Queen, 'Your Majesty need have no fear for your crown.'

Gardiner also urged Mary to proceed against Elizabeth, preaching openly before the court that, by cutting off its 'hurtful members', she would be showing mercy to the whole commonwealth. He also instructed that Wyatt be rigorously questioned in order to make him reveal Elizabeth's involvement in his conspiracy. De Noailles, however, who had been privy to the plot, and was lucky to have escaped censure by the Queen, was adamant that neither the princess nor Courtenay had had anything to do with it.

Courtenay was easily snared, for it was possible for the Queen to accuse him of treasonable negligence in failing to help prevent Wyatt's hordes from entering London. This was rather unfair, since Courtenay had received no training in the martial arts, but it served to put him safely behind bars. On 12 February, half an hour after Lady Jane's head had fallen in the straw, Courtenay was brought through the privy gate beneath St Thomas's Tower (now called Traitors' Gate) into the Tower of London, where he was given his old room in the Bell Tower. Soon afterwards he underwent five examinations by Sir Robert Southwell on behalf of the Council, and was also brought face to face with Wyatt, but all he would admit was that a servant of his had gone to France without his permission. After his arrest, his mother, the Marchioness of Exeter, was banished from court, and on 3 March, Courtenay himself was moved to St Thomas's Tower.

On that same day, at nine in the morning, Elizabeth and her escort set out from Ashridge. When the princess was led forth from the house, 'she was very faint and feeble, and in such a case that she was ready to swoon three or four times', but at last she was settled into the litter. The three councillors showed her every consideration, riding very slowly and covering only six or seven miles a day. Even so, Elizabeth was violently sick several times during the journey, and de Noailles heard later that she was 'so ill that her life was despaired of'.

On 21 February, Elizabeth and her escort spent the night at the house of a Mr Cholmley at the village of Highgate on the hills north of London, and on the 22nd they began their descent to the city. Elizabeth, who had that morning donned a white gown to enhance her alarming pallor, now had the curtains of the litter drawn apart so that the crowds who gathered to see her could see how ill she looked. 'She was a pitiful sight,' wrote de Noailles. Her face, like her body, was grossly swollen and she could not smile for the people, which prompted Renard to conclude that she was deliberately putting on a 'proud, lofty and defiant' air in order to cover her mortification at the way in which she was being treated. The ambassador believed that her symptoms were caused solely by a guilty conscience.

Upon arrival at Whitehall, most of her attendants were dismissed. She asked for an audience with the Queen, but was informed that Her Majesty would not see her until she had been closely examined by the Council concerning her recent conduct. For the present, she must remain in her apartments, which were isolated from the rest of the court and heavily guarded. The room above her bedchamber belonged to her Scots cousin, Margaret Douglas, Countess of Lennox (daughter of Henry VIII's sister Margaret), who deliberately turned it into a kitchen so that the princess would be continually disturbed by the noisy 'casting down of logs, pots and vessels'. There were rumours that Mary would set aside Henry VIII's will and name the Countess her successor, and – with her eye on the crown – Margaret Douglas seized every opportunity to denigrate Elizabeth to Mary and report every snippet of gossip that tended to confirm her guilt.

In London, the dreadful consequences of the rebellion were soon all too evident. On 14 February, forty-five rebels were hanged; more suffered at Southwark the next day. Soon afterwards thirty were marched to Kent to be dispatched there as an example to the people, although some were pardoned before they arrived. In all, more than a hundred people were executed. The Queen gave orders that their bodies were to be displayed on gibbets at every street corner, and before long the Londoners were averting their eyes from the ghastly spectacles and holding their breath to avoid the stench of rotting corpses. Above the city gates severed heads and dismembered limbs hung gruesomely. Even so, Mary felt compelled to exercise her prerogative of mercy in some cases; when the wives of 400 rebel soldiers besought her to pardon their husbands, she made a grand gesture: the condemned men, wearing halters about their necks, were brought into the courtyard of Whitehall Palace and pardoned by their sovereign. Even Jane Wyatt, Wyatt's wife, was treated with sympathy by the Queen, although there was no question of her husband being pardoned.

Most of Wyatt's rank and file were in fact allowed to return home unmolested. It was the gentlemen and nobles who were suspected of complicity that were imprisoned, among them Sir James Crofts and Sir Peter Carew, who was arrested at Antwerp and sent back to England in a fishing boat. Mary had him imprisoned in the Tower, where he stayed until his release in 1556.

On 15 February, Mary triumphantly informed the Emperor that the rebellion had been successfully suppressed, concluding, 'I trust therefore that the result will be to establish my reign more firmly than ever to enable the alliance with my lord the Prince to be concluded and to purify the kingdom by exemplary punishment inflicted on the guilty.'

Simultaneously, Renard was sending Philip a carefully-censored account of the rising, claiming it was a minor disturbance over religious issues. The ambassador, aware that Philip had made no attempt to communicate with Mary since the marriage treaty was signed, was at pains to emphasise that England was perfectly safe for Spaniards.

The Prince had actually been busy making preparations to come to England, and at the beginning of February had begun to assemble his fleet at La Coruña and to gather his household. He planned to take with him 3000 courtiers, 1500 mules and 60 ships. His father, however, continued to urge haste, and he had to abandon his plan to take such a large retinue. He assured the Emperor that he would cross to England as soon as his new ships were seaworthy, and promised to take only as many servants as were strictly necessary, for he was aware he would be expected to 'accept the services of natives in order to show them that I mean to trust myself to them, and favour them as if I were an Englishman born'. Before long, however, Philip had learned from his father of the real reason for Wyatt's rebellion, and this naturally made him less than eager to depart for England.

Others were also having second thoughts. On Mary's thirty-eighth birthday on 16 February, she received a discouraging letter from William Peto, Cardinal Pole's chief aide, urging her not to marry: 'You will fall into the power and become the slave of your husband. At your advanced age you cannot hope to bear children without peril of your life.'

Even Renard, fearful for his young master's safety, was counselling Philip to delay his arrival until the autumn, and secretly hoped that the whole matter might be re-thought. But, despite all the gloomy forecasts, Mary was determined to be married as soon after Easter as possible.

On 17 February, Suffolk was attainted and condemned for supporting the rebels, and six days later was beheaded on Tower Hill. His head fell into sawdust that had become impregnated with tannin, which preserved the head perfectly for 400 years. It was shown as an object of curiosity until the Second World War, but after that it was buried in St Botolph's Church, Aldgate, London. The rest of Suffolk's body was interred on the day of his death in St Peter ad Vincula within the Tower.

Soon afterwards, Lady Katherine Grey's marriage to Pembroke's heir was annulled and the Queen brought her to live at court, granting her an annual allowance of £80, and treating her and her hunchbacked sister Mary Grey with great favour. This led many to believe that Katherine might supplant Elizabeth as Mary's successor, and some Protestants were in favour of this because, as well as being of undoubted legitimacy, Katherine had been reared in the reformed faith. But before long it was being said she might convert to the Roman faith, which led those of that persuasion to declare that they would prefer her to the other Catholic heiresses, Mary, Queen of Scots and Margaret Douglas, because they feared the intervention of the French and the Scots in English affairs.

On 9 March, less than a month after the execution of her husband, the Duchess of Suffolk remarried, causing a scandal because her bridegroom was her impecunious, low-born master of horse, Adrian Stokes. Not only was he a poor match for a princess of the blood, but he was also, at twenty-one, half her age. Furthermore, it seems that the marriage was rendered necessary because Frances had become pregnant, for later that year she bore a daughter, Elizabeth, who died in infancy. Even though Queen Mary received the newly-wedded pair, she would not allow Frances's elder daughters to return to her care, but sent them instead to live under the guardianship of the formidable Dowager Duchess of Somerset at Hanworth. Here Katherine met the Duchess's son, Lord Hertford, who would later marry her clandestinely. As for the Duchess of Suffolk, she bore Stokes two sons who did not live, died in 1559, and was buried in Westminster Abbey.

There was still no word from Philip, apart from a formal agreement to a proxy betrothal ceremony, which took place on 6 March at Whitehall. Count Egmont, who had returned to England for the purpose, represented the groom, and knelt with Mary before Bishop Gardiner, who officiated at the ceremony, in the presence of the entire Council. Afterwards, the Queen knelt before the Holy Sacrament and called upon God to witness that she was marrying Prince Philip, not out of any carnal affection or desire, nor for any motive whatsoever but the honour and prosperity of the realm. She called upon all those present to pray that God would give her the grace to accomplish the marriage, and that He would look upon the union with favour. Egmont then placed upon the Queen's finger a ring sent by the Emperor, which she received with obvious pleasure and displayed afterwards to her councillors. The betrothal was considered binding on both parties.

The Council, meanwhile, had been doing their best to uncover evidence incriminating Elizabeth. Sir James Crofts was 'marvellously tossed and examined' by 'Mr Secretary' Sir John Bourne, but gave away nothing. On 25 February, Wyatt was also interrogated by Bourne, but the latter was obliged to tell Gardiner that, even though he had resorted to torture, he could not make the prisoner reveal anything about communicating with the princess. Later, after several agonising sessions on the rack, Wyatt admitted that he had contacted her twice, once to warn her to leave London for her own safety, and once to advise her that he had arrived at Southwark. On the first occasion she had sent William Saintlow to thank him and say she would do as she thought fit. Saintlow, however, 'stoutly denied' that any of this had happened, 'protesting that he was a true man, both to God and his prince'. Lord Russell, one of the rebel leaders, confessed to having delivered letters from Wyatt to Elizabeth, but no trace of them was ever found, nor was there any proof that she had responded to them.

On 1 March, Renard reported that Crofts had 'admitted in plain terms the intrigues of the French ambassador with the heretics and rebels', but there was no evidence to prove that Elizabeth had furnished de Noailles with the letter found in his postbag. And when Wyatt was tried and found guilty on 15 March, he would say nothing further about the princess beyond what he had already confessed. He did, however, declare that he was only the fourth or fifth man in the rebellion, claiming that Courtenay had been the prime mover.

Without proof of her complicity, there was no case against Elizabeth, but Renard could not understand why Mary and her Council were so at pains to find direct proof. 'She has been accused by Wyatt, mentioned by name in the French ambassador's letters, suspected by the councillors, and it is certain that the enterprise was undertaken for her sake. If she does not seize this opportunity of punishing her and Courtenay, the Queen will never be safe,' he fumed. However, he had discovered to his dismay 'that the law as laid down by the English Parliament does not inflict the capital penalty on those who have consented to treason if they have committed no overt act'. In the ambassador's opinion, it looked as if someone – Gardiner, probably – was being deliberately negligent 'in the hope that something may crop up to save' Elizabeth and Courtenay.

Gardiner was in fact one of those who had continually urged Mary to proceed against Elizabeth, yet he had been hampered by his concern to protect Courtenay, for it was likely that the prosecution of one would lead to the incrimination of the other. The Chancellor, however, was convinced that the removal of Elizabeth was essential, even though he had to admit that there was as yet no case against her.

'As long as she lives,' he told Renard, 'I have no hope of seeing the kingdom at peace.'

Mary felt the same. 'My sister's character is just what I have always believed it to be,' she confided bitterly to Renard, but even though she was in favour of having Elizabeth indicted for treason, she had to admit that it would be inadvisable to institute criminal proceedings against her at this stage; Paget and others had warned her that to do so might well precipitate another rebellion. However, both Queen and Council were convinced of Elizabeth's guilt and debated long and hard what to do with her. Some lords favoured keeping the princess under house arrest in the country, but no one was willing to have so dangerous a person under his roof, and the idea was abandoned.

By the middle of March, the councillors were bitterly divided in their opinions and unable to find a solution. The Queen was to leave London for Oxford shortly, and it was essential that Elizabeth be placed in safe custody, in a place where she could wreak no mischief. Gardiner urged that she be confined to the Tower and there questioned further about her activities, but this provoked a violent clash of opinions, for many lords believed that Mary would not live long after her marriage and that Elizabeth might soon be their queen; how, then, would she deal with those who had brought about her imprisonment? Gardiner, however, by sheer good sense and force of character, prevailed; the Queen agreed, insisting that her sister be dealt with fairly; and on the 16th Renard learned to his satisfaction that Elizabeth's fate had been settled.

On that Friday the princess received a visit from the Lord Chancellor and nineteen lords of the Council, who questioned her closely about her involvement in Wyatt's rebellion. Gardiner warned her that she would incur the severest penalties if she did not admit her guilt and throw herself upon the Queen's mercy. Elizabeth firmly denied that she had done anything worthy of reproach, saying she could not ask mercy for a fault she had not committed. Firmly believing that she had only to come face to face with her sister in order to convince her of her innocence, she asked for an audience with the Queen, only to be told that Mary was about to leave London.

'It is the Queen's pleasure that you should go to the Tower while the matter is further tried and examined,' she was informed, to her horror. For her, this was the worst punishment that could be devised, for in that grim fortress her mother had suffered the agonies of confinement as a condemned prisoner and died a terrible death. What else could her own imprisonment portend but a similar fate? The executions of Jane Grey, Guilford Dudley and Suffolk had been, she was sure, but a

254
The Children of Henry VIII

prelude to her own. Vigorously, and with some desperation, Elizabeth again denied having had any involvement with Wyatt, 'affirming that she was altogether guiltless therein. I trust the Queen's Majesty will be a more gracious lady unto me than to send me to so notorious and so doleful a place.'

But the councillors could offer her no reassurance on that point, and bowed out of the room 'with their caps hanging over their eyes'. An hour later, four lords returned with orders to dismiss the princess's servants and replace them with six members of the royal household who could be trusted to ensure that 'none should have access to Her Grace'. That night, a hundred soldiers in white coats were set on watch in the gardens of Whitehall, whilst a huge fire burned in the great hall as the Council appointed two of their number – the Marquess of Winchester and the Earl of Sussex – to escort the princess to the Tower on the morrow.

These gentlemen duly presented themselves in her apartments on the morning of Saturday, 17 March, and informed Elizabeth that a barge was waiting to take her to the Tower; she must come without delay for the tide 'tarrieth for nobody'. There was no charge, for the lords of the Council could not agree on one. Elizabeth, visibly distressed, was ready to try any delaying tactics, and begged them to wait for the next tide, which would allow her another day of freedom. Her request was refused, as was her plea to see the Queen. She then asked if she could write a letter to Mary before leaving for the Tower. Winchester told her that he dared not permit such a thing, which he believed would do more harm than good. Sussex, however, remembering that they were in the presence of a lady who might one day become their queen, fell to his knees before Elizabeth and said, 'You shall have liberty to write your mind and, as I am a true man, I will deliver your letter to the Queen and beg an answer, whatsoever comes thereof.' Pen and paper were fetched, and the princess sat down to write the most difficult letter she had ever been driven to compose.

If any ever did try this old saying, that a king's word was more than another man's oath, I most humbly beseech Your Majesty to verify it to me, and to remember your last promise and my last demand, that I be not condemned without answer and due proof, which it seems that now I am; for that without cause proved I am by your Council from you commanded to go into the Tower, a place more wonted for a false traitor than a true subject, which, though I know I deserve it not, yet in face of all this realm appears that it is proved.

I protest afore God, Who shall judge my truth, whatsoever malice shall devise, that I never practised, counselled nor consented to anything that might be prejudicial to your person in any way, or dangerous to the state by any means. And I therefore humbly beseech Your Majesty to let me answer afore yourself and not suffer me to trust to your councillors; yea, and afore that I go to the Tower, if it is possible; if not, afore I be further condemned. Let conscience make Your Highness take some better way with me, than to make me condemned in all men's sight afore my desert known. I have heard in my time of many cast away for want of coming to the presence of their prince; and in late days I heard my Lord Somerset say that if his brother had been suffered to speak with him, he had never suffered, but the persuasions were made to him too great that he was brought in belief that he could not live safely if the Admiral lived, and that made him give his consent to his death. Though these persons are not to be compared to Your Majesty, yet I pray God as evil persuasions persuade not one sister against the other, and all for that they have heard false report. Therefore, once again, kneeling with humbleness of heart because I am not suffered to bow the knees of my body, I humbly crave to speak with Your Highness, which I would not be so bold to desire if I knew not myself most clear, as I know myself most true. As for the traitor Wyatt, he might peradventure write me a letter, but on my faith I never received any from him; and as for the copy of my letter sent to the French King, I pray God confound me eternally if ever I sent him word, message, letter or token by any means, and to this my truth I will stand in till my death.

By now Elizabeth's handwriting was becoming less controlled; that and her frequent deletions and amendments betrayed her consuming anxiety. She had come to a halt near the top of a page; if she signed it now, her enemies might forge some incriminating statement in the space that was left, and so encompass her ruin. To prevent this she drew diagonal lines across the offending space, then concluded, 'I humbly crave but one word of answer from yourself. Your Highness's most faithful subject that hath been from the beginning and will be to my end, Elizabeth.'

Meanwhile, time had been creeping on, and the waiting councillors realised that they had missed the tide. The Thames would now be so low that it would be dangerous to attempt to steer the barge between the piers supporting London Bridge. The next favourable tide would occur at midnight, but transferring the prisoner under cover of darkness would be risky in case there was an attempt by London Protestants to rescue her. Winchester and Sussex therefore decided to wait until the next morning, which would be Palm Sunday; the journey could be made when the citizens were in church, so as to avoid any popular demonstration on Elizabeth's behalf.

When Elizabeth finished writing, she handed her letter to Sussex, who immediately took it to the Queen. The sight of it made Mary very angry, as did news of the delay it had caused, and she refused to look at it.

'Such a thing would never have been allowed in my father's time,' she raged at the quailing Sussex. 'I would he could come back, if only for a month, and give my councillors the rebuke they richly deserve!'

It rained heavily the next morning, but at nine o'clock Sussex and Winchester came to inform Elizabeth that the Queen would not see her. Instead, they were to escort her to the waiting barge and convey her by river to the Tower.

'The Lord's will be done. If there be no remedy, I must needs be contented,' she said, but as they hastened through the gardens of the palace to the river stairs, she kept looking behind her, hoping she might see the Queen at a window and attract her attention.

'I marvel much at the nobility of the realm,' she cried scornfully, 'who suffer me to be led into captivity, the Lord knows whither, for I do not.' Sussex replied that quite a few members of the Council 'were sorry for her trouble', and he was himself sorry that he had lived to see this day.

Accompanying Elizabeth were six ladies-in-waiting – three of the Queen's and three of her own – and a gentleman usher and two grooms, who all sat with her in the cabin of the barge, out of the rain. Even now, at high tide, the craft nearly capsized whilst navigating London Bridge, and as it turned towards the privy gate of the Tower of London, a shaken Elizabeth emerged from the cabin and pleaded with Winchester and Sussex to be allowed to enter the fortress through any gate other than this one, for many had passed through it and never come out again. Such a gate was not fit for a princess to enter, and she would not use it, she declared. The lords refused to listen, whereupon she grew impatient at their insensitivity, and sulked. However, seeing that she was becoming soaked, Winchester offered her his cloak, but she pushed it away 'with a good dash'.

Above the privy stairs the kindly Lieutenant, Sir John Bridges, waited with a troop of yeomen warders to receive his prisoner. But after her escort had alighted from the barge, Elizabeth refused to leave it, complaining that she would get her shoes wet, and sat glaring at the waiting guards. Winchester turned back and informed her that she had no choice but to accompany them.

Elizabeth placed one foot on the stairs and cried, 'Here landeth as true a subject, being prisoner, as ever landed at these stairs. Before Thee, O God, do I speak it, having no other friend than Thee alone. O Lord, I never thought to come in here as a prisoner!' Then, turning to address the yeomen warders, she continued, 'I pray you all, good friends and fellows, bear me witness that I come in as no traitor but as true a woman to the Queen's Majesty as any as is now living; and thereon will I take my death.'

Her speech had such an effect on the warders that a few came to cast themselves on their knees before her, and some cried, 'God preserve Your Grace!'

But at that moment Elizabeth's courage failed her. Death might well await her in this place, and the prospect was so dreadful that she refused to take a step further. Instead, she sat down on the cold, wet flagstones and would not move.

'You were best come out of the rain, madam, for here you sit unwholesomely,' said Sir John Bridges gently.

'It is better sitting here than in a worse place, for God knoweth, I know not, whither you will bring me!' cried Elizabeth, raising a tearful face to him, and for some minutes the Lieutenant's persuasions proved fruitless. Then Elizabeth's usher, moved by her plight, burst into tears. Angrily, she rose to her feet and castigated the poor man for 'uncomfortably using her, seeing she took him to be her comforter'.

'I thank God that I know my truth to be such that no man can have cause to weep for me,' she declared, and with renewed courage allowed Bridges to escort her and her retinue to the rooms prepared for her in the twelfth-century octagonal Bell Tower, which was adjacent to the Lieutenant's Lodging and had housed in its time Edward Courtenay and Sir Thomas More. It had earned its name because within its sixty-foot-high walls hung the great bell that summoned the Tower garrison to arms or sounded an alarm.

Elizabeth's quarters, which had in 1535 been occupied by the martyred John Fisher, Bishop of Rochester, and would in 1685 be allocated to the doomed Duke of Monmouth, were on the second floor, above More's former cell, and consisted of a large, circular, vaulted chamber boasting a great fireplace and lit by three tall arched windows with seats set in the thickness of the ancient walls. In this room, Elizabeth would spend her days and nights, sleeping in a tester bed, with her ladies disposed about her on pallets on the floor. Outside was a passage leading to three latrines which overhung the moat. Bridges deposited his prisoner and her ladies in the great chamber, then locked the door 'very straitly' behind them. As he did so, Sussex began weeping.

'Let us take heed, my lords,' he warned, 'that we go not beyond our commission, for she was the King our master's daughter as well as the Queen's sister. Let us use such dealing that we may answer it thereafter, if it shall so happen; for just dealing is always answerable.' Bridges and Winchester silently indicated their agreement, whereupon the lords left, deeply pensive.

Throughout her confinement in the Tower Elizabeth was treated with respect and consideration by Bridges, who never forgot who she was and what she might become. He arranged for her to take her meals with him in the Lieutenant's Lodging, which must have aroused conflicting feelings in his prisoner, for her mother had spent her last days in that house, although it had since been refurbished. Elizabeth's servants were allowed out to buy food for her, at her expense, not only to ensure that she might enjoy such luxuries as she was used to, but also to guard against any attempt to poison her.

For recreation, Elizabeth was allowed to walk along the walls, accompanied by five attendants, as far as the Beauchamp Tower. Here too were poignant reminders of Anne Boleyn, and of more recent tragedies, for the wall-walk overlooked the scaffold on Tower Green, a scaffold which might well serve for Elizabeth herself in the near future, or so she feared.

Bridges's superior, the Constable of the Tower, Sir John Gage, soon became concerned at the freedoms permitted the prisoner, and before long Elizabeth found her privileges withdrawn. Her servants were ordered to hand over their provisions at the gate, which meant that they were usually purloined by 'common rascal soldiers'. When the servants complained to Gage, he 'sware by God that, if they did either frown or shrug at him, he would set them where they should see neither sun nor moon', and stated that the princess would be treated the same as any other prisoner. Eventually, a compromise was reached: Elizabeth's servants might bring food in for her, as long as Gage was able to employ the services of her skilled cook. 'And good cause why, for he had good cheer and fared of the best, and Her Grace paid well for it.'

There were other petty restrictions, though. The princess was not allowed pen or paper because she was forbidden to communicate with anyone. Being confined to her rooms affected her health so badly that after a month Gage allowed her to walk about in the gloomy Queen's lodgings in the crumbling royal apartments, so long as the windows were closed and she did not look out. As Elizabeth continued to pine for fresh air, he was obliged to permit her to use the Lieutenant's walled garden, as long as she was escorted by an armed warder and the gate was locked.

One day, as she sat in the garden, a five-year-old boy, the son of the Keeper of the Wardrobe, accompanied by a child 'not above three or four years' called Susannah, came to the gate and offered a posy of flowers; with them was another little girl who presented Elizabeth with a miniature bunch of keys 'so that she might unlock the gate and go abroad'. Their visits became a regular occurrence until Gage became suspicious, and there came a day when, as the boy offered his floral tribute, the guard swooped, and the terrified child was borne off and questioned closely as to who had given him the flowers. Was any secret message concealed within them? Was it from the prisoner Courtenay? Of course, the posy had been an innocent, childish gift, but the boy was warned that he would be soundly whipped if he dared to speak to the princess again. Nevertheless, he bravely returned the next day and called through the gate, 'Mistress, I can bring you no more flowers now.' She smiled, but did not answer.

For all the kindness shown her, Elizabeth suffered both physically and mentally as a result of her imprisonment. She was in a ferment of anxiety as to what was going to happen to her, and went daily in mortal fear of being executed. Many years later she confided to the French envoy Castelnau that she was so desolate and despairing that she thought only of asking the Queen to have her beheaded by a swordsman, as her mother had been, because she knew it would guarantee a quick death not always afforded by the axe.

There may, fortunately, have been lighter moments. Historians have long speculated that Elizabeth's enduring romance with Lord Robert Dudley, later Earl of Leicester, who was still incarcerated in the Tower with his brothers, may have begun at this time. The two had known each other since childhood, and may have derived comfort from knowing they were near each other. However, it is unlikely that they would have been allowed to meet, and there is no evidence that they did. Besides, Robert had been married for four years to Amy Robsart, who visited him frequently; he could therefore have no legitimate interest in the heiress to the throne.

A week after Elizabeth arrived at the Tower a deputation of ten councillors headed by Gardiner came to question her, and began by 'examining her of the talk that was at Ashridge betwixt her and Sir

James Crofts, concerning removing from thence to Donnington Castle, requiring her to declare what she meant thereby'.

Elizabeth hedged. First she denied knowledge of owning such a house, but then she admitted that she did know of it, although she had never visited there and could not remember anyone advising her to do so. At this juncture Crofts was brought in to confront her with his evidence, but she insisted she had little to say to him or 'to the rest that were prisoners in the Tower'.

'My lords,' she said, 'you do examine every mean prisoner of me, wherein, methinks, you do me great injury. If they have done evil and offended the Queen's Majesty, let them answer it accordingly. I beseech you, join not me in this sort with any of these offenders.'

She then confessed that she did remember Crofts suggesting she move to Donnington, but what harm was there in that? 'Might I not, my lords, go to mine own houses at all times?' she asked.

Some of the councillors were beginning to feel rather uncomfortable, and many were at heart unhappy about Elizabeth's imprisonment. Like Sussex and Bridges, they had an eye to the future, and even Arundel, who supported the Spanish marriage, now fell to his knees and told Elizabeth, 'Certainly we are very sorry that we have so troubled you about so vain matters.'

'My lords, you do sift me very narrowly,' she replied, 'but well I am assured you shall not do more to me than God hath appointed, and so God forgive you all.' It was obvious that nothing further was to be gained from the interview, and the councillors departed without having obtained any incriminating evidence at all.

Renard, however, was still expecting to hear that Elizabeth and Courtenay were to be put to death. 'It seems to me', he told the Emperor, 'that while they are alive there will always be plots to raise them to the throne, and it would be just to punish them, as it is publicly known that they are guilty and deserve death. While the Lady Elizabeth lives it will be very difficult to make the Prince's entry here safe.' On 24 March, he told Mary as much, saying that he would not recommend Philip's crossing to England until 'every necessary step' had been taken to ensure that he was not in danger.

Mary burst into tears at this, crying, 'I would rather never have been born than that any harm should be done to His Highness.' At length, she reassured Renard that Elizabeth and Courtenay would be tried before Philip's arrival. As a precaution, she advised, the Prince should bring his own doctors and cooks.

At the end of March, Paget began assembling Philip's household, but when Renard insisted on interfering, 'venomous' disputes arose, for the English courtiers felt that this was their responsibility, not his. The Emperor, meanwhile, was urging Philip to leave for England as soon as possible, as Mary would be disappointed at any delay 'and she does not deserve that'. To the Duke of Alba, who was to accompany the Prince, Charles wrote, 'Duke, for the love of God, see to it that my son behaves in the right manner, for otherwise I tell you I would rather never have taken the matter in hand at all.'

The Council continued to debate what they should do with Elizabeth. Gardiner was all for having her executed in the interests of state security, but his was a minority voice on the Council, most of whose members were aware that her guilt was by no means established and that there was no case against her. The Queen, who agreed with Gardiner, consulted senior judges, but they too advised her that there was no evidence to justify a conviction. Gardiner urged that the princess be at least disinherited, but Paget led his colleagues in violent opposition to this idea, and suggested instead that Elizabeth be married abroad to a friendly Catholic prince. At the same time, Courtenay's friends were pressing for his release and pardon, on the grounds that he had committed no overt act of treason.

By 3 April Renard had reluctantly resigned himself to the fact that the government would not proceed against either Elizabeth or Courtenay. Nothing could be proved against them, nor was it likely that any further evidence of import would come to light, although the Queen still believed that the rebels would not have contacted Elizabeth 'unless they had more certain knowlege of her favour than is yet confessed by her'. But when Wyatt was executed on 11 April on Tower Hill, he assured the large crowds that had gathered to see him die that neither Elizabeth nor Courtenay were 'privy to my rising'. News of their exoneration by him spread fast, despite efforts by the authorities to suppress it, and provoked joy and pride in the people, in whose affections Elizabeth had always occupied a special place. After he was hanged, Wyatt's body was dismembered and exhibited in different parts of London, but his head was stolen by those who regarded him as a martyr.

Parliament had met on 2 April. There was no opposition to the Queen's marriage treaty being ratified, but an attempt to revive the old law against heresy was thwarted. There was strong feeling, especially in the House of Lords, that a Catholic revival would threaten the continued tenure of those who had been granted Church property after the Reformation. Mary and Gardiner were known to be in favour of reunification with Rome, but Paget stirred up popular feeling in

Parliament against this, and was lucky to escape arrest. Nevertheless, he was obliged to leave court in disgrace. Parliament also authorised a public dispute at Oxford between the imprisoned Protestant bishops, Cranmer, Latimer and Ridley, and a panel of Catholic theologians. At the end of three days, during which a thousand spectators jeered at and interrupted the reformers, the three were denounced as heretics and excommunicated, despite their eloquent and skilful arguments. As there was no law under which heretics could be condemned to death, the three bishops were sent back to prison.

In the middle of April there were further demonstrations in London against the Queen's impending marriage and her religious reforms. A mysterious voice in a city wall would say 'So be it' in response to 'God save the Lady Elizabeth', but when people said 'God save Queen Mary' it remained silent. Seditious pamphlets were distributed and a dead cat dressed as a priest was hung from the gibbet at Cheapside.

The councillors were still deeply divided over what to do with Elizabeth. 'What one advises, another opposes,' observed Renard. There was no justification for keeping the princess in the Tower, but because the Queen was convinced of her guilt she insisted that it would not be 'honourable, safe or reasonable' to receive her sister at court, and demanded that Elizabeth be held under house arrest in a secure place in the country, where she could be kept under surveillance. As before, few councillors were willing to undertake the responsibility of being Elizabeth's gaoler, but at length a loyal Catholic gentleman and privy councillor, Sir Henry Bedingfield of Oxburgh Hall in Norfolk, who has been one of the first to rally to Mary in July 1553, was nominated.

Gardiner and Renard wanted Elizabeth sent to the North, where most people were Catholics, perhaps to Pontefract Castle, scene of the murder of Richard II in 1400, but Elizabeth's influential uncle, Lord William Howard, opposed this, and it was eventually decided to send her to the ancient royal manor at Woodstock in Oxfordshire. Mary's chief desire was to have Elizabeth out of the way before Philip's arrival, and there may have been an element of personal jealousy as well as fear for her own security in this, in case the striking looks and coquettish manners of her twenty-year-old sister aroused Philip's sense of chivalry or even prompted him to contrast them with Mary's fading charms.

Sir Henry, a former diplomat now in his forties, was the son of Sir Edmund Bedingfield, who had been gaoler to Katherine of Aragon during her imprisonment at Kimbolton Castle in the 1530s. Sir Henry was a conscientious man with a rigid sense of principle and duty, one of little imagination who would not be swayed by the caprices of a flirtatious young woman, and he accepted his new responsibilities without question, although with a heavy heart. On 4 May, he arrived at the Tower at the head of a hundred soldiers wearing armour and blue liveries, in readiness to take charge of the princess. When Elizabeth saw them from her window she was greatly alarmed, imagining that they had come to escort her to her execution, and anxiously asked her attendants 'whether the Lady Jane's scaffold were taken away or no'. Even when they assured her that it had been dismantled, she was still convinced that her end was imminent.

Bedingfield – 'a man unknown to Her Grace and therefore the more feared' – then appeared and announced that he had come to make preparations to escort her to a more comfortable place of confinement, the royal manor of Woodstock in Oxfordshire, where he would be her guardian. Elizabeth felt sure that this was a plot to do away with her, and that once she was away from London she would be quietly murdered. Nor did Bedingfield's correct, officious manner reassure her.

'If my murdering were secretly committed to your charge, would you see to the execution thereof?' she asked, with candour born of panic. Bedingfield, shocked, answered that he would certainly not. However, the princess remained fearful, even though she was informed that Sir Henry had orders to protect her from attacks by Catholics or rescue attempts by Protestants.

Two weeks later, at one o'clock on 19 May, the eighteenth anniversary of Anne Boleyn's execution, Elizabeth – escorted by Bedingfield and Lord Williams of Thame, the Sheriff of Oxfordshire – left the Tower by barge and was taken along the Thames to Richmond Palace, then owned by Anne of Cleves. However, to Bedingfield's dismay, it soon became apparent that what had been planned as the discreet transfer of a state prisoner from one place of security to another was rapidly turning into a triumphal progress. German gunners of the Hanseatic League on the Steelyard wharf let off joyful bursts of cannon-fire when apprised that Elizabeth was passing, and crowds gathered on the banks to see her, cheer and wave.

At Richmond, the princess, believing that her end would be expedited by the demonstrations in her favour, said to Lord Williams, 'Pray for me, for this night I think to die.'

'You need have no such fears; you are safe with me,' soothed Lord Williams, and so it proved: there was no poison cup, no assassin lurking in the shadows. An intruder was found lurking in the grounds, but he turned out to be one of de Noailles's spies, and – stripped to his shirt – was packed off to London for questioning. It turned out he had heard a rumour that Elizabeth was being married off to one of France's enemies, and was trying to establish if it were true. Because of the disturbance and her fears, the princess spent a 'doleful' night.

The next day she set out in a dilapidated litter to make the journey by road to Windsor, still believing she was on her way to her doom. Again, crowds gathered to watch along the roadside, and she bade a friendly guard go over and pass a message to them: '*Tanquam ovis* – Like a sheep to the slaughter.' At Windsor, the princess and her escort spent the night at the Dean's house, and when they rode off in the morning the schoolboys of Eton College gave Elizabeth a rousing ovation.

All along the route, the story was the same. Church bells were rung to celebrate Elizabeth's release from the Tower – Bedingfield ordered that the offenders be clapped in the stocks or the lock-up – and the country folk came with their blessings and their simple offerings: cakes, wafers and bunches of herbs or flowers, which they tossed into the litter, or into the arms of the princess's attendants, who could not carry all the gifts she was given. Bedingfield was flustered and irritated by the attention paid to his charge, and did his best to ward off well-wishers, but with little success, and he sourly reported to the Queen that 'betwixt London and this place [the people] be not good in matters of religion'. For all his authority, he could not punish everyone who cried out, 'God save Your Grace!' as the princess passed, although he would dearly have liked to.

After spending the third night at Sir William Dormer's mansion at High Wycombe, Elizabeth was escorted through the villages of the Thames Valley until she was brought to Lord Williams's house at Rycote near Thame where her host held a great banquet in her honour, inviting all his neighbours and friends. Bedingfield thought this was going rather too far, and reprimanded Williams for forgetting that Elizabeth was 'the Queen's Majesty's prisoner, and no otherwise', but he was overruled and the feast went ahead as planned and 'Her Grace was marvellously well entertained.'

At last, after what seemed to Bedingfield an endless four days of unwelcome compromise, they arrived at Woodstock. Even here, a small group of well-wishers awaited them at the gates, much to his disapproval.

The old palace at Woodstock has vanished, having been demolished in 1710 to make way for Blenheim Palace, the magnificent mansion presented by Queen Anne to the Duke of Marlborough, but in its day it was a splendid royal residence. The manor of Woodstock, which was eight miles north of Oxford, had been a royal demesne since Saxon times and a favoured royal residence during the Middle Ages. Here, Henry I had established a menagerie, and legend had it that Henry II had built a maze for his mistress, Fair Rosamund Clifford, so that she could hide from his jealous queen. The Black Prince had been born here, as had numerous other royal infants, and successive kings had used the place as a hunting lodge, but although Henry VII had spent more than £40,000 on repairs and rebuilding between 1494 and 1503, little now remained of the palace's former glories. Its fabric was crumbling and many of the rooms were uninhabitable. The main house, which occupied a site north of the present bridge over the lake in Blenheim Park, was built of stone around two courtyards, but Elizabeth was informed that she was not to lodge here but in four rooms in the gatehouse, two up and two down, which had been furnished with items brought from her own houses or lent by the Queen. One room had a vaulted ceiling painted blue and decorated with gold stars. There was insufficient room for her attendants, who had to find lodgings in the village, and the princess made a great fuss about the poor accommodation, while Bedingfield made a greater fuss when he discovered that the locks did not work on three of the four doors. In fact, he became obsessed with security and suspicious of all contacts with the outside world.

The Queen's instructions to Sir Henry required him to guard his prisoner closely and 'use her in such good and honourable sort as may be agreeable to our honour and her estate and degree'. He must ensure that she had no 'conference with any suspected person out of his hearing, yet permit such strangers whom ye shall think honest to speak with her in your hearing only'. When Elizabeth walked in the gardens or orchard, he was to accompany her. Mrs Ashley was forbidden her presence, and so was Parry, although he was to look after her accounts, and pay Bedingfield's expenses, from his lodging in the nearby Bull Inn, which Sir Henry thought to be 'a marvellous colourable place to practise in', meaning that he saw it as a weak link in his security arrangements. The princess's other servants were to be thoroughly vetted, and watched at all times in case they carried messages. There was to be no cloth of estate above her chair when she dined, nor was she permitted to write or receive any letters. Her laundry was to be searched for hidden messages. Unsuitable books were to be banned. If Elizabeth had any requests, these must be referred to the Council for approval.

Bedingfield followed these instructions to the letter, endeavouring at the same time to retain the goodwill of his demanding and often capricious charge. He was unfailingly courteous to her, even when refusing her many and various requests. She wanted books: a Cicero, an English Bible and the Psalms of David in Latin. She wanted more maids to wait on her. She wanted a tutor so she could converse in foreign tongues. She wanted to walk in the park, as she had been promised. She wanted paper and ink so that she could write to the Council. She wanted to send messages to the Queen by courier. Bedingfield, who was 'marvellously perplexed' by this stream of demands, passed every one on to higher authority, telling her that he was unable to 'grant her desire or say nay'.

'I shall do for Your Grace what I am able to do,' he would say. Elizabeth became very irritated when he would not even grant the most trivial request on his own authority, but he was impervious to her complaints.

Before long, she came to realise that her life was not in danger. Fear was replaced by boredom and frustration, and she took pleasure in baiting Sir Henry or in being deliberately awkward. Often, he confessed, he could not decide 'if her meaning go with her words, whereof God only is judge'. But she never got the better of him. Although he obtained several books for her, he refused to let her have an English Bible because, he said, she was able to read Latin so well that he imagined she would take greater pleasure reading books in that language. Elizabeth took this 'not in good part', nor was she very pleased when one of her favourite ladies, Elizabeth Sands, was dismissed for her 'evil opinions'.

The princess could not bear the restrictions placed upon her, and chafed at her imprisonment, which she felt was entirely undeserved. On one occasion, when Bedingfield accompanied her on her walk in the gardens, she stood watching as he patiently locked six pairs of gates, one after the other, and then lost control of herself.

'Gaoler!' she screamed at him, but he only fell on his knees and begged her not to refer to him by that harsh name.

'I am your officer, appointed to take care of you and protect you from any injury,' he said with feeling. He saw himself as a kindly guardian, and would defer punctiliously to her rank, always kneeling to address her. He took his duties most seriously, and reported all his dealings with his 'great lady' in a series of detailed letters to the Council, which still survive. He divulged that, while Elizabeth was happy to attend mass, she preferred to have parts of the service said in English. Mary was angry to hear this, and Elizabeth had to promise to follow the Latin form, though her sister was still not convinced of her sincerity.

Elizabeth's contemporaries, John Foxe, the martyrologist, and Raphael Holinshed, the chronicler, claim that on one occasion during her captivity she took a diamond ring and scratched on a window pane these words:

Much suspected of me,
Nothing proved can be,
Quoth Elizabeth, prisoner.

Nothing had been proved against Courtenay either, despite Renard's efforts to secure his conviction for treason, but he was still seen as a menace to the Queen's security and, at Gardiner's suggestion, was sentenced to be banished from the kingdom. His house was given to the Duchess of Somerset, and on 25 May he was released from the Tower into the custody of Sir Thomas Tresham and taken to Fotheringhay Castle in Northamptonshire, a former stronghold of the Yorkists during the Wars of the Roses, now in poor repair and said to be damp. His gaoler was kindly, however, and he was allowed to go out hunting during the summer months whilst the Council debated where to send him.

With both Elizabeth and Courtenay in safe custody, and the memory of Wyatt's rebellion receding into the past, the kingdom was relatively tranquil, and the Queen began to hope for news of Philip's arrival. It seemed that nothing now could prevent their union, and de Noailles commented cynically, 'Perhaps God is permitting this marriage in order to punish them both.'

13

The Spanish Marriage

The Queen was in a fever of impatience for the coming of her future husband. 'She is nothing but a poor, love-sick woman,' de Noailles told his master. In her impatience she was becoming testy and would 'curse and accuse people' and even complain about the weather. Lord William Howard, seeing his sovereign 'wrapt in thought' after a banquet one evening, pointed to the empty throne set in readiness beside hers and whispered that he wished the Prince were with her 'to drive thought and care away'. Mary blushed and began to chide him for over-familiarity, but then she broke into laughter, in which every person present joined. It was now May, and surely she would not have to wait much longer.

Preparations for Philip's coming were well advanced in England. His household of 350 persons, headed by Arundel as Lord Steward, was complete, the Queen was having a Garter insignia prepared for her husband, a party of noblemen had been dispatched to Spain to greet him, and a fleet was now patrolling the Channel in readiness to escort his ships to Southampton. But as yet Philip had failed to send a single letter to Mary, and Renard, who was embarrassed by this unforgivable omission, complained that his silence was causing scandal and concern. Belatedly, on 11 May, Philip wrote to her and sent her three sumptuous gifts: a beautiful table diamond in a rose-petal setting, which had belonged to his mother and which would please his bride for that reason alone; a necklace containing eighteen flawless diamonds in a filigree setting; and an enormous diamond from which hung a matchless pearl called 'La Peregrina', both suspended from a long gold chain – 'the most lovely pair of gems seen in the world', which Mary would favour above any others. These items were entrusted to the Marquess de Las Navas, who was acting as Philip's messenger.

The Prince's Spanish retinue was now assembled at La Coruña, his mistress had been dismissed and sent to a nunnery, and he was awaiting the arrival of his sister, who was going to act as Regent for him in Spain, but when news came that she had been delayed by illness, he decided to make a last-minute tour of his properties in Segovia, Madrid and Toledo. He also visited his mad grandmother, Queen Juana, at Tordesillas.

Early in June, the Prince's Spanish household sailed to Southampton in a fleet of 125 ships. It comprised 9000 noblemen and servants and a thousand horses and mules, and with them was carried three million gold ducats. The Marquess de Las Navas docked ahead of the main fleet on the 11th. Five days later, upon receiving news of his arrival, the Queen left Whitehall on the first stage of her journey to Winchester, where her wedding was to take place. She met the Marquess at Guildford on 17 June and expressed the greatest delight at Philip's letter and gifts, and even greater pleasure at the news that the Prince himself would be with her in just two weeks. Nor was Mary the only recipient of Philip's bounty, for there were presents of precious stones – pearls, diamonds, emeralds and rubies – for her ladies also. The next day she travelled to Farnham, where she took up residence in the castle belonging to the bishops of Winchester, there to await the summons to Winchester to greet her prince.

Mary's happiness was such that she could even feel warmth towards her sister, and de Noailles noticed that she had had Elizabeth's portrait re-hung in her gallery. Yet she would not set the princess at liberty, nor allow any relaxation of the rules governing her confinement. The Emperor had suggested that Elizabeth be sent to the court of Mary of Hungary at Brussels before Philip's arrival, but Lord William Howard used his influence over the Council to veto this idea.

Early in June Elizabeth had fallen ill with another attack of what seems to have been nephritis. Her face and body became swollen and sore, and her recovery was hindered by an all-encompassing black depression. She asked Bedingfield if she might be bled in order to release the evil humours from her body, and particularly requested that the Queen's physicians, Dr George Owen, Dr Thomas Wendy and Dr Robert Huicke, whom she knew and trusted, might attend her. The Council, however, saw no reason why she could not be treated by local physicians from Oxford. When Bedingfield conveyed their decision to Elizabeth, she told him she would rather die.

'I am not minded to make any stranger privy to the estate of my body, but commit it to God,' she declared indignantly. Her obstinacy paid off, and on 12 June Bedingfield rendered his apologies to the Council for having been 'enforced, by the importunate desires of this great lady, to trouble your lordships with more letters than be contentful to mine own opinion'. This resulted in the royal doctors being dispatched to Woodstock, where they prescribed bleeding from the arm, which was done by a barber-surgeon under their supervision, followed by bleeding from the foot, this treatment to be repeated in the autumn to prevent a recurrence of the illness. Afterwards, Bedingfield reported, Elizabeth progressed 'reasonably well'.

For weeks now the princess had been asking leave to write to the Queen, and towards the end of June her request was granted. Sir Henry dutifully brought her writing materials, and she composed a letter which has not survived. Its contents, however, were sufficient to arouse Mary's wrath and prompt her to send a complaint to Bedingfield about Elizabeth's insolence, her haughty tone, and her hypocrisy. Her letter, reported Renard, had been couched in the most disrespectful and rude terms; she had addressed the Queen throughout as 'you' rather than as 'Your Majesty', and had also protested against the treatment she had received, denying that she had ever deserved it. Mary's reaction was to forbid Elizabeth to write to her again, saying that if she had any matters to communicate, she should use Bedingfield and the Council as intermediaries. Bedingfield understood this to mean that Elizabeth should not even write to the Council, at which she hotly objected, claiming that it left her 'in worse case than the worst prisoner in Newgate'. Nor would he write on her behalf, and when she saw that he would not relent, she became very downcast, moaning that she 'must continue this life without all hope worldly, wholly resting to the truth of my cause'.

This was on 3 July, but four days later came news that the Queen herself had lifted the ban and said that Elizabeth might 'write her mind' to the Council. Elizabeth responded with a request for an audience with her sister, but there was no reply, for the court was naturally preoccupied with the Queen's imminent marriage. For weeks, Elizabeth waited for a letter, growing ever more despondent and bad-tempered. Bedingfield reported that she was in a very contrary mood and that, although she was attending mass regularly, she would not join in when her chaplain enjoined his congregation to pray for the Queen's Majesty.

By 9 July, Mary had waited at Farnham for three weeks, and still Philip had not come. On that day, Renard noted, 'The officers appointed for His Highness's service have been living at Southampton at great expense for a long time, and are now beginning to leave that place, speaking strangely of His Highness.'

In fact, Philip's household was now running out of food, not to mention patience. Mary was troubled by this, and imagining that all manner of disasters had overtaken her betrothed. In some agitation, she moved to the Earl of Wiltshire's palace at Bishop's Waltham, two miles from Southampton. This was a large, moated house, built in medieval times but boasting more modern comforts. Here, Mary waited on, growing ever more anxious.

On Friday, 12 July, in a brisk wind, Philip embarked at La Coruña in his ship the '*Espiritu Santo*', a vessel beautifully painted to resemble 'a lovely flower garden' and having upholstery of crimson brocade and scarlet cloth. The Prince suffered miseries from seasickness and kept to his cabin during the voyage. Two days later the sea was calm again, and the coast of southern England was sighted. The ship dropped anchor three miles out of Southampton, and presently Philip was recovered sufficiently to receive a deputation of nobles led by Admiral Lord William Howard, who had arrived from the mainland in a small boat. The next day Philip was visited by a party of young noblemen craving entry into his household, and thereafter there could be seen a succession of small craft sailing back and forth from the Spanish flagship.

On 19 July, the entire Spanish fleet was sighted off the Isle of Wight, and on that day Lord William Howard escorted Philip's ship past the Needles and into Southampton harbour. On the following day the Marquess de Las Navas went on board the '*Espiritu Santo*' to welcome his master, and was followed by an official reception committee of English lords, led by Arundel, who arrived in an elaborate gilded barge. Acting on the Queen's behalf, Arundel invested Philip with the Order of the Garter, fastening around his calf a garter encrusted with diamonds, rubies and pearls. Dinner was then served on board ship, after which the Prince, wearing a suit of black velvet and white satin, was rowed ceremoniously to shore in torrential rain.

Drawn up on the quayside were a hundred drenched archers wearing his livery, and his entire English household, all craning their necks to see him. Unfortunately, Philip had had no idea that so many people had been appointed to wait on him; he had brought all the nobles and servants he needed with him, and was now very worried about how he was going to support two large establishments and keep so many people gainfully occupied.

As the Prince stepped ashore in the wet, he was greeted by a salute of cannonfire, serenaded by the Queen's consort of minstrels, and presented with a white horse richly caparisoned in crimson velvet and gold, a gift from his bride. The Emperor's envoy, Don Juan de Figueroa, bowed and informed Philip that his father had ceded to him the kingdoms of Naples and Jerusalem so that he might go to his wedding as a monarch in his own right, on equal terms with Queen Mary, 'whereat the English lords were very pleased'. Philip said he would inform the Queen of this news before making an official announcement. He was then formally welcomed to England by Sir Anthony Browne and Bishop Gardiner, who were accompanied by virtually the entire peerage of the realm. Crowds had gathered to see Philip, and several people were trampled underfoot in the crush.

The Prince knew that a difficult task lay ahead of him: he had to marry a middle-aged woman for whom he was unlikely to feel any desire, behave well at all times to his new subjects and try to win them over, oversee the reunification of the English Church with that of Rome and hopefully take the credit for it, and persuade the English to support the Habsburgs in their war against the French.

No one could have faulted his demeanour or conduct. He exerted himself to be courteous and amiable to the English, who were 'greatly pleased with his appearance', according to Figueroa. What no one knew was that Philip intended to stay in the country for a week at most; on 29 June, the fortress of Marienbourg (now Alûksne in Latvia) on the Emperor's north German border had been taken by the French, and Philip had been ordered by his father to come to his aid as soon as he decently could. The Prince had already agreed to do so, and had secretly instructed his servants not to unload the horses. Yet by no word or gesture did he betray that he was a man in a hurry.

After giving thanks in the Church of the Holy Rood for his safe arrival in England, Philip, riding his new horse and soaked to the skin, was escorted to his lodgings, which were hung with tapestries depicting the triumphs of Henry VIII. That evening, at a banquet in his honour, he delivered a speech in Latin, saying, 'I have not left my own country to augment my estate or the greatness of my power; on the contrary God has summoned me to be the husband of the Queen your mistress, and I will not refuse His divine will. For this purpose I have crossed the sea to live with that lady and with you. As long as you are faithful subjects, I will be your good prince.' There was warm applause, which increased when the Prince made a point of downing a glass of good English beer, which he appeared to enjoy. Then, to the gratification of his hosts, he turned to his Spanish nobles and told them to forget all their old customs, for from henceforth they must live like Englishmen.

The next morning was also wet. Philip was up early to receive Gardiner, who presented him with a diamond ring from the Queen. The Prince thanked him fulsomely, and then fortuitously found a ring of his own to send back to her. He stayed three days in Southampton, sleeping late in the mornings, then receiving members of the Council who came to kiss his hand. On 23 July, resplendent in a red cloak and doublet and breeches of white satin studded with diamonds and embroidered with gold, he rode off with a great retinue, again in pouring rain, towards Winchester, where he would meet his bride, and where they would be married on 25 July, the feast day of St James of Compostella, patron saint of Spain. Late in the afternoon, Philip stopped at the Hospital of St Cross outside Winchester to change into a suit of black and white velvet adorned with bugles of gold thread.

At around six o'clock in the evening the Prince's procession entered the city and wound its way to the cathedral, where Gardiner and four other bishops welcomed Philip and sang a *Te Deum*. So many people were crammed into the building that 'they were all in danger of stifling'. Afterwards, accompanied by torch-bearers, the Prince was taken to his lodgings in the nearby Dean's House, bowing to the crowds on the way. Mary was staying in Wolvesey Palace, the Bishop's residence, of which only ruins remain today.

At ten o'clock, after eating supper and changing into yet another splendid ensemble, on this occasion a suit of white kid with a surcoat embroidered in silver and gold and a hat with a long plume, Philip, described by one of his entourage as looking 'very gallant' and accompanied by twelve Spanish and Flemish gentlemen, was conducted through the cathedral grounds and the private gardens of the palace, to where Mary awaited him in the long gallery. She too had dressed herself carefully, in a gown of black velvet with a silver underskirt, 'cut high in the English style and without any trimming', and loaded herself with jewels. With her waited her ladies, her councillors and courtiers.

When the Queen heard footsteps approaching up the stairs, she almost ran to the door, and then suddenly she was face to face with her future husband. Modestly, she kissed her own hand before taking his, but he smiled and kissed her on the mouth 'in the English fashion'. 'Of visage he is well-favoured,' reported a Scottish observer, 'with a broad forehead and grey eyes, straight-nosed, and [with a] manly countenance. His face is princely, with a yellow head and a yellow beard. He is well-proportioned of body, arm, leg, and every other limb.' Mary, obviously delighted with what she saw, 'very lovingly, yea, and most joyfully, received him'. Philip took her hand and led her through to her presence chamber in the West Hall of the Palace, where, in the company of ten elderly courtiers, they sat on the thrones beneath the canopy of estate and conversed for half an hour.

What language they chose to speak is something of a mystery. Philip knew no English, so it may have been Spanish, for Mary had been taught it by her mother; however, the Venetian ambassador Michieli states that, although she understood Spanish, she could not speak it, and she certainly needed the services of an interpreter when she met the Duchess of Alba later on. She could speak French fluently, but Philip could not, although he understood it. Fortunately both knew Latin, and it may be that it was in this tongue that they communicated. Observers noticed that the Queen chatted animatedly while Philip responded quietly and courteously.

Then Lord William Howard appeared and began making bluff sailors' jokes about their imminent wedding, the bride's charms and the undoubted virility of the bridegroom. Fortunately, Mary was rescued from this banter when Philip's gentlemen came forward to be presented. Returning the compliment, she rose and took the Prince into the next room, where her ladies were waiting to meet him. They curtsied, but he raised them and kissed them all on the lips, as was customary in England.

All too soon it was time for Philip to leave, for the hour was late, but Mary insisted on detaining him for more private talk.

'No wonder she is so glad to get him and to see what a gallant swain he is,' commented a watching Spaniard. Eventually, the Prince asked Mary if she would teach him some words of farewell to say to the English lords. With obvious pleasure she whispered something in his ear, then he rose, took leave of her, and said, 'Good night, my lords all.' This made a very good impression.

Although one of Philip's Spanish courtiers reported that Mary was 'rather handsome than otherwise', others were less complimentary. Ruy Gomez, the Prince's closest friend and advisor, described her as 'rather older than we had been told. She is not at all beautiful and is small and flabby rather than fat. She is of white complexion and fair, and has no eyebrows.'

His words almost certainly reflected Philip's own impression, since the Prince often confided in Gomez. One Spaniard complained that Mary had lost most of her teeth, while another opined that, although she was 'a perfect saint', she 'dresses badly'. Gomez thought she would look a lot better if she wore Spanish dress. These comments were supported by a description of the Queen penned three weeks earlier by a Venetian envoy, who stated she was 'of low stature, red and white complexion, and very thin. Were not her age on the decline, she might be called beautiful.'

On the morning of the next day, which was the eve of their marriage, Mary sent Philip a gift of two magnificent suits to wear at the wedding ceremony. One had a surcoat of cloth-of-gold in the French style, with the roses of England and the pomegranates of Spain delineated in gold beads and seed pearls, and eighteen buttons fashioned from table diamonds. In the afternoon the royal couple met again in the vast East Hall of Wolvesey Palace, where they 'pleasantly talked and communed together, each of them merrily smiling on the other, to the great comfort and joy of the beholders'.

The crowds were out in force on Wednesday, 25 July 1554, when, at ten in the morning, preceded by his nobles, Philip went in procession to Winchester Cathedral, where he sat in a side-chapel to await his bride. He was elegantly attired in one of the outfits she had sent him, a full-length robe of cloth-of-gold lined with crimson satin and banded with crimson velvet and pearl buttons, with matching doublet and breeches, which he had chosen in preference to the other because, as he noted years later, it was too ornate. The cathedral, which had been hung with rich tapestries, was packed with courtiers and dignitaries.

At 10.30 the Queen – wearing cloth of gold, with her train borne by Lady Margaret Douglas and the Marchioness of Winchester – arrived with her Privy Council, peers and ladies, entering through the west door into the choir, where a circular wooden platform draped with purple had been erected. Here, Philip joined her, and together they ascended the five steps and knelt to be shriven by Bishop Gardiner, who then conducted the marriage ceremony in both Latin and English. The Queen was given away by the Marquess of Winchester and the Earls of Pembroke, Derby and Bedford, on behalf of the nation. According to the contemporary *Chronicle of Queen Jane and Two Years of Queen Mary*, the ring that was placed on Mary's finger was, by her own choice, 'a plain hoop of gold' because 'maidens were so married in old times'. The oak chair in which she sat during the ceremony is still on display in the cathedral.

When the marriage service was concluded, 'all the people gave a great shout, praying God to send them joy'. Gardiner then announced that the Emperor had ceded the kingdoms of Naples and Jerusalem to Prince Philip, who was also, by virtue of his marriage, King of England.

The Earls of Derby and Pembroke, bearing swords of honour, led Mary and Philip, who walked hand in hand, through the choir to the high altar, Their Majesties processing under a canopy of estate borne by four knights. High mass was then celebrated by Gardiner and five other bishops with due splendour, the office being sung by the pure voices of the Children of the Chapel Royal and the cathedral choir, accompanied by the majestic sound of the organ, 'using such sweet proportion of music and harmony as the like was never before invented or heard'. Several Spanish observers noticed that during the hour-long service, the Queen 'never took her eyes off the Sacrament'. Afterwards, to the sound of trumpets, Garter King of Arms solemnly proclaimed the rulers' new titles in Latin, French and English: 'Philip and Mary, by the grace of God, King and Queen of England, France, Naples, Jerusalem, Ireland, Defenders of the Faith, Princes of Spain and Sicily, Archdukes of Austria, Dukes of Milan, Burgundy and Brabant, Counts of Habsburg, Flanders and Tyrol.'

After leaving the cathedral at three o'clock to the sound of fanfares, the King and Queen walked, still holding hands, under a canopy of estate to Wolvesey Palace for a splendid nuptial banquet lasting for three hours, served in the East Hall, which had been decorated with hangings of cloth-of-gold and silk. Seated at the high table with Bishop Gardiner, and served by the nobility of England, Mary ate off gold plates and Philip ate off silver plates, a slight that did not go unnoticed by the King's Spanish courtiers, who hoped that it would be rectified after Philip's coronation. During the banquet minstrels played and the royal heralds distributed alms for the poor, whilst the rest of the guests ate standing up beside four long tables. Then the royal couple led the company in dancing 'after the German fashion', Mary proving by far the better dancer. At nine, they retired to their private apartments and were served supper in separate rooms, after which they made their way to the lodging that had been prepared for them. On the door, placed there by order of Gardiner, was a plaque bearing a Latin verse:

> Thou art happy, house, right blest, and blest again,
> That shortly shalt such noble guests retain.

In deference to the Queen's rank and modesty, only a few selected courtiers attended the public bedding ceremony. Gardiner blessed the conjugal bed, then he and the guests discreetly withdrew, leaving Philip and Mary, still wearing their wedding clothes and 'great quantities of jewellery', alone together for the first time. An anonymous Spaniard wrote, 'What happened that night only they know. If they give us a son our joy will be complete.'

On the morning after the wedding, Philip was up and working at his desk at seven o'clock; he attended mass twice that day and took his meals alone. When his Spanish nobles came to call on the Queen in the morning, her ladies were shocked and barred the door, protesting that it was 'not honest' to call on a bride just after her wedding night, for English custom decreed that a queen remain in seclusion until the second day after her nuptials. The Spaniards tried to explain that in their country it was traditional to greet their monarchs in bed on the morning after a royal marriage, but could not make themselves understood.

Mary, meanwhile, was writing to her father-in-law to thank him 'for allying me with a prince so full of virtues that the realm's honour and tranquillity will certainly be thereby increased. This marriage renders me happier than I can say, as I daily discover in the King my husband so many virtues and perfections that I constantly pray God to grant me grace to please him, and behave in all things as befits one who is so deeply embounden to him.'

The following days were taken up with 'such triumphs, banquets, singing, masquing and dancing as was never in England heretofore. To see the King's Majesty and the Queen sitting under the cloth of estate in the hall where they dined, and also in the Chamber of Presence at dancing time, where both Their Majesties danced, it should seem another world.' Philip spent these crucial days being shown the local sights, attending to private business, going to mass, getting to know Mary's councillors, discussing state papers and learning how the English administration worked. Fortunately, word had come that the French troops had been beaten back by Imperial forces, which meant that there was no longer a pressing need for him to leave England so soon. The Emperor wished him to remain with his wife for the present, 'busying himself with the government of England' and devoting his energies to the important task of reconciling the English Church to Rome. Nevertheless, Philip secretly arranged for a ship to be prepared in readiness for his passage to Brussels.

'Our marriage has gone off admirably,' reported Ruy Gomez. 'I am sure they will be very happy, and Our Lord will do the rest.' On the surface the auguries were good, but already there were hidden tensions. There is no doubt that Mary had fallen in love – or at the least become infatuated – with Philip, or the image he presented, the moment she saw him. Starved of affection from her childhood, deprived of the fulfilment of sexual love and children during her adult years, she was ready to lavish all her frustrated emotions on the husband she had acquired so late in life, a husband who could give her all the things she held dear: a link with her mother's country, the prospect of a Catholic

heir to England, the furtherance of her desire to be reconciled to the
Pope, and the weight of his masculine authority to make her task
easier. For the first time since she was ten, when her father's eye had
first lighted on Anne Boleyn, she was truly happy.

Mary had stressed that she had not entered into the marriage for
carnal reasons, and according to Ruy Gomez, it was as well Philip
understood this, for 'he treats the Queen very kindly and well knows
how to pass over the fact that she is no good from the point of view of
fleshly sensuality'. With his male friends the King made it plain that, for
him, this was a marriage of convenience only, and that he was not
attracted to Mary. He even complained to one gentleman that her
portrait painters had flattered her in order to conceal the truth from
him. Gomez commented, with feeling, 'To speak frankly, it will take
God himself to drink this cup.' Soon, some members of Philip's
entourage were asking, 'What shall the King do with such an old
bitch?' and alleging that Mary was old enough to be his mother. Gomez
had nothing but praise for the 'tactful and attentive' way in which his
master dealt with a wife who could offer him little in the way of sexual
satisfaction, for the royal couple gave every appearance of being
content and devoted; 'He makes her so happy that the other day, when
they were alone, she almost talked love talk to him, and he replied in
the same vein,' noted Gomez. Mary certainly had no idea that her
husband found her less than attractive, and nor had Renard, who told
the Emperor: 'The royal couple are bound together by such deep love
that the marriage may be expected to be a perfect union.'

Emotionally, it was an unequal partnership, for Philip could never
reciprocate Mary's deep devotion. Nor did he feel her equal as a
sovereign, for he was not allowed any power but what she would
permit, which he and his compatriots regarded as an intolerable and
dishonourable position to be in. Mary naturally deferred to him in most
things, and he soon replaced Renard as her chief confidant. It was also
reassuring for her to have at her side someone of equal rank to advise
her, after having to struggle alone and deal with her troublesome,
squabbling councillors. However, if she disagreed with his wishes she
could be very stubborn, and would only comply with them if they
matched her own. This was not the usual behaviour of a wife in the
sixteenth century, when women were expected to obey their husbands
without question, but then a queen regnant was a novelty also, and in
view of her position could not be expected to conform as other
women did. Nevertheless, when Cardinal Pole wrote to Mary after her
marriage, he exhorted her to pray for Philip as 'a man who, more than

all other, in his own acts, reproduces God's image, which God did send into the world in holiness and justice'.

If English gossip spoke true, then this man cast in God's image was soon indulging in 'gross licentiousness' with women of the court behind the Queen's back. One tale recounted how he had spied upon the statuesque Lady Magdalen Dacre whilst she was in her dressing room, and then attracted her notice as he reached through the door to touch her. Lady Magdalen was said to have seized a staff and brought it down painfully on the royal arm. A Protestant pamphlet claimed the King had said that 'the baker's daughter is better in her gown than Queen Mary without her crown'. These stories were probably invented by those who were anxious to discredit Philip or who feared his influence with the Queen, for they are unsubstantiated by reliable sources.

The King did indeed provide his English courtiers with cause for resentment, because he made it clear from the start that he preferred to be attended by his Spanish household. Yet there were many on the Council who welcomed him in the hope that he would advance them for their support of the Emperor or help them pay off old scores against colleagues.

The honeymoon period was not over before Mary resumed her duties as sovereign, which left her little time to spend with Philip. They usually saw each other when they dined in public or sometimes in the evenings when she would play the lute or virginals for him. Normally, she rose at dawn, did not break her fast until after mid-day, then frequently attended to state business until well after midnight. There seemed never to be enough hours in the day for all she had to do, and the strain told in headaches and palpitations. It soon became evident to the King that his wife was unable to control her headstrong councillors: 'The Queen is a good soul, but not as able as we were led to suppose, I mean as a stateswoman,' reported Gomez. Nor was Philip very impressed by the state of England's finances, and made immediate arrangements to secure loans from Spain to bolster them.

News of her sister's wedding had reached Elizabeth at Woodstock and helped to explain why her plea for an audience had not received a reply. Nevertheless, she found the waiting intolerable, and made life very difficult for Bedingfield by pestering him to allow her to write another letter. When he refused for the umpteenth time, she sneered that 'their lordships would smile in their sleeves' when they learned how scrupulous he was. Finally, on 30 July, she prevailed upon him to write to the Council on her behalf and 'make suit to your honours to be means to the Queen's Majesty [and] to beseech your lordships to consider her woeful case, that, being once licensed to write as an humble suitress unto the Queen's Highness, [she] received thereby no such comfort as she hoped to have done'. He hoped it would please the Queen 'upon very pity, considering her long imprisonment and restraint of liberty, either to charge her with matter to be answered unto and tried, or to grant her liberty to come into Her Highness's presence, which she sayeth she would not desire were it not that she knoweth herself to be clear before God'.

If Mary would not consent to these requests, then the princess begged that a deputation of councillors be allowed to visit her, so that she could protest her innocence to them and 'not think herself utterly desolate of all refuge in this world'.

The letter was duly dispatched, and the interminable waiting began again.

On 31 July, Mary and Philip left Winchester to make a leisurely progress east towards the capital. They stayed for two nights at Basingstoke and a further night at Reading before arriving on 3 August at Windsor Castle, where they were to enjoy a few days' hunting, although both were suffering from heavy colds. Soon afterwards the King, wearing a purple velvet mantle, was formally installed as Sovereign of the Order of the Garter and presided over a chapter meeting. Mary, ever anxious to please him, presented him with a jewelled dagger to mark the occasion. Renard, observing them, wrote that it was 'a great pleasure to see them together. His Highness is altogether changed from what he was when he last left the Low Countries.'

On 11 August, the royal couple moved on to Richmond Palace, preparatory to making a state entry into London. Whilst they were here news came that the French had laid siege to the Imperial town of Renty, thus prompting eighty noblemen of Philip's entourage to leave for the Low Countries to go to its defence. The Emperor, however, had expressly ordered his son to stay where he was for the present.

On 17 August, the King and Queen were informed that preparations for Philip's official welcome, which had been going on since May, were complete, and on that day they came by barge to Southwark, where Gardiner entertained them at Winchester House. After hunting in the adjoining park, they spent the night at Suffolk Place, formerly the London home of Lady Jane Grey's parents.

At two the following afternoon Mary and Philip rode across London Bridge and were welcomed by bursts of cannonfire and six lavish pageants set up at intervals along the city streets, some on sites where gibbets had recently stood. The civic authorities had spared no expense and, Spaniards or no Spaniards, the people loved a holiday and were out in vast numbers to see the procession.

There were few incidents to mar the occasion, but in one pageant Gardiner spotted a figure of Henry VIII holding a book inscribed '*Verbum Dei*' (the Word of God), and hastily commanded that it be covered with a pair of gloves. Renard reported that the Londoners had been impressed with Philip and thought him a prince 'of benign and human countenance, likely to turn out a good ruler'. The King himself was delighted with his welcome, and wrote later that he had been received 'with universal signs of love and joy', prompted no doubt by his generous distribution of largesse to the poor and the free wine that ran from the city's conduits.

At the end of the day the royal couple came to Whitehall, where they expressed delight at two wedding presents that awaited them there: tapestries embroidered with gold and silver from the Emperor, and a gold and silver portable organ, encrusted with jewels, from the Queen of Poland.

Philip now set out to establish his authority as king. His first priority was to reduce his unwieldy household. 'We are all hanging about here with nothing to do,' complained the Duke of Alba. Gomez blamed Renard for the fact that his master had too many servants, but Renard had had no idea that Philip would be bringing such a vast retinue, nor had the Council consulted him when they made their arrangements. It was not long before Renard came to resent having been ousted by Philip from Mary's confidence, and when it became clear that the King did not like him, he begged to be recalled, though the Emperor would not agree to being deprived of the services of one who understood English affairs so well.

Philip seems to have detailed personal duties to his Spanish courtiers and formal ones to his English attendants. This caused resentment on both sides, sparking bitter complaints and rivalries, which were not resolved by the King's largely unfulfilled promises to devolve greater responsibility upon his English gentlemen.

Another of Philip's chief concerns was that his coronation take place as soon as possible in the interests of underlining his regal authority. However, the marriage treaty did not provide for it and the Privy Council showed little enthusiasm for the idea. As far as they were concerned, Mary was the sovereign and he the consort; in their view he had no real authority, and the Queen herself made no concerted effort to remedy this. Nevertheless, the King did everything he could to win the affection and respect of his new subjects, deferring to English customs and traditions and being lavish with gifts and rewards to those who served him well. Recognising in the fallen Paget a good statesman and a loyal supporter, he worked to restore him to favour, but never succeeded in establishing a King's faction at court, for all his popularity with some nobles there. Gomez wrote, 'His way with the lords is so winning that they themselves say they have never had a king to whom they so quickly grew attached. The King is certainly a master hand at it when he cares to try.'

The people, however, who had no chance to experience Philip's affability at first hand, were soon complaining that he rarely appeared in public and, when he did, he could not be seen for the hordes of lords who surrounded him.

Philip's influence should not, however, be underestimated. It was accepted that in marriage, as in Nature and Divine Law, a woman was subordinate to a man, and it was as natural for Mary to defer to her husband's opinion in all matters as it was natural for her councillors – and indeed all her contemporaries – to expect her to. So although the King had no formal authority conferred by the marriage treaty or by Parliament, in reality he was perceived as being the real power in government, and respected as such. In September, an ambassador from Savoy reported, 'The King hears and dispatches all state affairs, as it befits his dignity and authority that he should. He already has the same authority as his predecessors on the throne of England.'

Charles V himself had declared that the object of the marriage was for Philip to rule England in Mary's name, but he did insist that the Queen, being an anointed sovereign, retain at least the semblance of power. Yet Mary, as we have seen, was not always willing to play a subordinate role, and this, more than sexual incompatibility, was at the root of Philip's dissatisfaction with his marriage, for it was not honourable, in his opinion, for a man to take second place to his wife, and insupportable that their reversed roles should be a matter of public knowledge.

Marriage suited Mary. Within weeks she was reported to be 'fatter and of a better colour than ever before'. Her rather staid court had also become livelier, with more entertainments than hitherto. On 12 October, Mr Francis Yaxley informed Sir William Cecil, 'The King and Queen's Majesties be in health and merry. They danced together on Sunday night at the court. There was a brave masquery of cloth of gold and silver, wherein the masquers were all dressed as mariners.' Other favoured pastimes included cards and dice, and the occasional play, a novelty at that date. One particularly favoured by Mary was

Respublica by Nicholas Udall, a celebration of her accession. Apart from the singing in the Chapel Royal, which had been revived on the Queen's orders, there was little music at court, although Philip did bring a consort of musicians from Spain.

The amount of food consumed by the courtiers was staggering. In 1554 an anonymous Spaniard reported,

> The Queen spends over 300,00 ducats a year on her table, for all the councillors eat in the palace as well as the household officers and the wives of all these gentlemen. The Queen's ladies also eat by themselves in the palace, and their servants. There are usually eighteen kitchens at full blast and they seem veritable hells, such is the stir and bustle in them. The usual daily consumption is eighty to a hundred sheep, a dozen fat beefs, a dozen and a half calves, without mentioning poultry, game, deer, boars and great numbers of rabbits, and they drink more than would fill the Valladolid River. In the summer the ladies and gentlemen put sugar in their wine, with the result that there are great goings-on in the palace!

King Philip might have won some personal popularity with the nobility, but he and the Spaniards he brought with him were hotly resented by the majority of Mary's fiercely insular subjects. This resentment began to manifest itself in a series of ugly incidents in the court and the city; as early as August 1554 knives were being drawn at court on a daily basis to settle private scores. From the first there were bitter rivalries between Philip's English and Spanish households, and in London the Spaniards found that they were always fobbed off with inferior lodgings, overcharged in shops and taverns – by as much as twenty-five times the normal price, one claimed – and insulted or jostled in the streets. The English, for their part, declared they were being made to feel like strangers in their own land, and that Queen Mary appeared to care nothing for them. In August, the Venetian ambassador corroborated this when he reported, 'The Queen, being born of a Spanish mother, has always been inclined towards that nation, scorning to be English and boasting of her descent from Spain.'

Many Spaniards were naturally homesick, and complained of the weather, the food and the women; one even claimed, wrongly as it turned out, that 'Not a single Spanish gentleman has fallen in love with one of them, nor takes any interest in them, for they are not the sort of women for whom Spaniards feel inclined to take much trouble.'

Others grumbled that the royal palaces were cramped and uncomfortable, and that there was nothing to do at court but eat and drink – 'the only pastime the English understand'. Such an attitude could, and did, cause tremendous ill feeling. The King made efforts to silence his compatriots, especially when they got into the habit of dismissing all the English as heretics and barbarians, but the damage had already been done. Even after many nobles had left to take part in the war with France, enough 'artisan and vagabond Spaniards' remained to cause trouble. Even the wives of the remaining grandees, who had come to England in defiance of the Emperor's advice, were shunned by the ladies of the court, and not only because of the language barrier. Mary was too busy to spare time for them, and when she did see the Duchess of Alba, both were so insistent on ceding precedence to the other that, rather than occupy the higher seat, they both ended up sitting on the floor. The proud Duchess found this humiliating, and stayed away from the court thereafter.

But it was in London that the worst incidents occurred. Here, Spaniards were mugged, robbed and subjected to violent attacks, and the friars in Philip's train were too terrified to go out, for on the one occasion they had done so a jeering mob had tried to strip them of their habits and crucifixes. The Venetian Michieli states that the English were invariably the aggressors, and in his diary Henry Machyn records that several Englishmen were hanged for robbing or murdering Spaniards, while the records show that others were pardoned for similar offences. In May 1555, 500 men rioted in London against the 'strangers', and there were half a dozen deaths. In June, an angry mob attacked and desecrated a church in which Spaniards were celebrating the Feast of Corpus Christi. Seditious pamphlets and malicious rumours circulated by the French did not help matters, and sometimes caused needless panic, as when it was put about that Philip intended to bring thousands more of his compatriots to England, or was proposing to garrison the Tower with Spaniards.

Mary grieved deeply over the dissensions. 'It is a matter of great sorrow to the Queen if [her subjects] maltreat a Spaniard, greater than if she herself had to suffer,' wrote one of Philip's gentlemen. By September, when most Spaniards had been offered accommodation within Whitehall Palace for their own safety, many were praying that Mary would soon be pregnant, for 'when she has children of him, it is said, the King may go home to Spain'. However, few of them believed the Queen to be capable of bearing children.

Now that her marriage had been accomplished, Mary turned her attention to what she regarded as her life's work: reconciliation with Rome. With Philip in England she felt there was no longer any need for Cardinal Pole to be detained in Rome. In June, Pope Julius III had instructed Pole to make the English mission his priority and had warned him to be conciliatory over the sensitive matter of alienated church property. If necessary, concessions must be made.

In September, Mary herself wrote a directive to the Council, commanding that the Legate be summoned from Rome to carry out an inspection of English churches and universities. Heresy must be rooted out, and the offenders burned at the stake so that others might be saved. Philip, aware that Spanish influence would be blamed for any religious persecution, warned the Queen to tread warily and use moderation, but she saw her task as a sacred mission and would not be deflected from it. Philip also advised Mary not to allow Pole to come to England until the Legate had made it clear that he would not demand the return of church property. Mary perceived this as sound advice, and a despondent Pole was soon asking Philip why, although other ambassadors were received in England, 'the Legate of St Peter's successors is alone denied admission'. But Philip had his own position to consider. If he could be seen as the man who had brought about the reconciliation with Rome without incurring loss to his new subjects, then his standing with them would surely increase tenfold. Pole, therefore, must wait.

Once back at Whitehall, Mary at last responded to Elizabeth's pleas for an audience. Granting her one was out of the question, but she assured her sister that, although she thought her complaints 'somewhat strange', Elizabeth need have no fears that she had been forgotten as 'We be not unmindful of your cause.' And that was all.

Frustrated and miserable, and seeing no end to this interminable confinement, Elizabeth took refuge in her books, and wrote in the fly-leaf of her copy of St Paul's Epistles, 'August. I walk many times into the pleasant fields of the Holy Scriptures, where I pluck up the goodlisome herbs of sentences, that, having tasted their sweetness, I may the less perceive the bitterness of this miserable life.'

Talk of a coming religious persecution reached Woodstock by September and Elizabeth wisely continued to attend mass regularly, taking care not to give the Queen cause for offence.

That September, Mary's happiness was crowned with elation and triumph when her doctors confirmed that she was pregnant. She had all the usual symptoms: her periods had ceased, her breasts and abdomen had swollen, and she suffered from nausea in the mornings. The

Savoyard ambassador wrote, 'The Queen is pregnant. I have personal reason to believe it, as I have noticed her feeling sick to her stomach.' And Renard obtained 'positive assurance' of Mary's condition from the royal physicians; 'If it were not true, all the signs described would prove to be fallacious.'

This was the culmination of all Mary's hopes, and coming at a time when reconciliation with Rome was imminent, she interpreted her conception of a Catholic heir as being further evidence of God's favour. She was therefore in a triumphant mood when she announced her pregnancy to the Council. At the beginning of October a delighted Philip ordered that a ball be held in the Ladies' Hall at Whitehall to celebrate the good news, and himself led Mary out to begin the dancing. He then wrote to the Emperor to inform him of her happy condition. Apart from the prospect of an heir, her pregnancy brought the added benefits of better relations between the English and Spanish courtiers, who now found themselves united in a common desire, and increased authority for the King, for the Queen's condition would require her to delegate much of her power to him. Her duty now was to produce a healthy child.

14

True Religion Restored

Late in September 1554, Cardinal Pole was still stranded in Brussels, unable to travel to England because he had not yet received a royal summons, and prevented from entering the land of his birth uninvited because the Act of Attainder passed against him in Henry VIII's reign had not been reversed. Technically, he was still a convicted traitor under sentence of death.

Pole's mission was two-fold. His chief task was to complete the process whereby the Church of England would be reunited with that of Rome, but he had also been instructed by the Pope to work towards a reconciliation between the Habsburgs and France. Already he had sought the Emperor's co-operation in this, but all he had succeeded in doing was antagonising him. Charles, having now had first-hand experience of Pole's attempts at diplomacy, feared that he might take an inflexible view on the sensitive issue of church property and thus jeopardise the reunification of the Church, and was consequently still seeking to delay the Legate's arrival in England. At the same time, Philip, in a series of letters, was doing his best to persuade Pole to take a more pragmatic view. Neither Philip nor Charles wanted the Cardinal usurping the King's role as the Queen's chief adviser. Mary, however, had great sympathy for Pole, and pleaded his case with both her husband and her father-in-law, eventually, with the aid of Renard, wearing down their resistance to his coming to England.

On 22 October, Renard met Pole in Brussels and gave him a letter from Mary. This, and the ambassador's arguments, as well as instructions from the Pope, at last convinced the Cardinal that it would be in the interests of everyone concerned 'to abandon all church property rather than risk the shipwreck of the operation'. Acting upon Renard's advice, both Philip and Charles agreed that the Legate could now proceed to England to carry out his mission, and on 3 November the Council authorised his admission to the country. Two days later Paget and Sir Edward Hastings were sent to escort him home.

On 10 November, a proclamation was read to all Mary's subjects, requiring them to submit to the Legate's authority 'in cases of spiritual jurisdiction, for the reformation of their souls'. This prompted a new wave of anti-papist activity and a new flood of Protestant propaganda, made possible by an efficiently organised underground movement of which little is known. Protestants were still very much a minority group, and they were perceived by the Queen and her advisers as a cancer in the body politic of the commonwealth that must be cut out lest it affect the sound members of that body.

Parliament assembled on 12 November, and was packed with members of 'the wise, grave and Catholic sort', who were prepared to push through Mary's programme of religious reforms. The King and Queen, clad in matching robes of crimson edged with ermine, went in state to Westminster for the opening ceremony, Mary in an open litter 'to expose her to the public view' and Philip riding beside her. They received a warm ovation, and it was noticed that the Queen was 'in excellent health and three months with child'. Already her gowns were too tight for her. 'She is said to be very happy, and the King is also,' reported Luis Varegas, one of Philip's gentlemen.

Once Parliament was in session Gardiner tried once more to introduce a bill disinheriting the Lady Elizabeth, but this was blocked by his old enemy Paget on the grounds that the birth of an heir to the Queen would soon neutralise her sister anyway, and that formally to disinherit the princess now might well have an inflammatory effect upon the people. There was talk of marrying Elizabeth to a 'safe' Spanish noble, such as the Duke of Segovia's son, or even Philip's own son, the nine-year-old Don Carlos, but it was felt that to send her to Spain with suspected heretical views would expose her to the unwelcome interest of the Inquisition, and the plan was abandoned. Paget came up with the idea of marrying Elizabeth to the Protestant Margrave of Baden, a German prince, but, again, religion was seen as a barrier to such a match.

King Philip, however, had put forward a number of suggestions as to whom the princess might marry, among them his distant cousin Emmanuel Philibert, Duke of Savoy, one of the Emperor's most highly regarded generals. When word of this reached the Duke, who was not well off, he was entranced at the prospect of securing an English princess as his bride, and arrived in England that November to 'pluck the fruit'. His surprised hosts arranged for him to be lodged in

Elizabeth's London residence, Somerset House, but did little to further his suit. Savoy was disconcerted to learn that his intended bride was under house arrest at Woodstock and not allowed to receive him, and after kicking his heels in London for a month, he went home, a disappointed man.

The royal child was expected in the middle of May, and with a realistic appreciation of the possible consequences of the Queen's pregnancy, Parliament passed a Regency Act, settling the government of the realm upon King Philip in the event of Mary dying and leaving the throne to an infant heir.

On 13 November, Cardinal Pole left Brussels for England, and on the 17th a Bill for the repeal of the Act of Attainder against him was introduced into Parliament, thus heralding the completion of the Counter-Reformation in England. The Bill passed rapidly through both Houses within five days without provoking adverse comment. Pole crossed from Calais to Dover on 20 November, setting foot in his native land for the first time in twenty years; he was the first papal legate to come to England since Cardinal Campeggio had arrived in 1529 to try Henry VIII's nullity suit against Katherine of Aragon.

The Legate was received with great ceremony by a deputation of councillors, and was then conveyed by litter to Gravesend, where he boarded a barge that would take him to London. Two days after his arrival, the King and Queen went in person to Parliament to give the royal assent to the Bill reversing his attainder, so that it became law before his arrival in the capital. The next day, according to Renard, Mary felt the baby move for the first time.

On 24 November, a chilly, overcast day, Pole came up the Thames to London, where he was received with great ceremony at Whitehall Stairs by King Philip, who led him into the palace. Mary was waiting to receive him in the Long Gallery, and at the sight of her cousin she was quite overcome with emotion, afterwards declaring that at the moment she caught sight of his crucifix 'the pious child had exulted and leapt in her womb, as had the unborn John the Baptist at the greeting of Our Lady'.

'*Ave Maria, gratia plena, Dominus tecum, benedicta tu in mulieribus,*' said the Cardinal, with a fine sense of occasion. 'It was the will of God that I should have been so long in coming. God waited until the time was ripe.'

As he spoke, the Queen sank into a low curtsy, as a sign of respect for the Church he represented, then Pole knelt to her as his sovereign lady. She and Philip helped him to rise, and she joyfully told him how her unborn child had responded to his arrival. Beaming, Pole continued to compare the Queen with the Virgin Mary, saying, 'Blessed art thou among women, and blessed be the fruit of thy womb.'

After conversing with the King and Queen for a time, the Legate was conducted across the river to Lambeth Palace, vacant since Cranmer's arrest, where he was to lodge. This confirmed the expectations of many that Mary meant him to be the next archbishop of Canterbury once Cranmer had been deprived of his see by the Pope.

On the Queen's orders, *Te Deums* were sung in churches in London in thanksgiving for the Legate's safe arrival in England. Then, on 28 November, a service was held in St Paul's Cathedral to give thanks for the quickening of the royal child, the text of the sermon being, 'Fear not, Mary, for thou hast found favour with God.' For the next few months, every mass that was celebrated would, by order of the Council, contain this prayer: 'Give therefore unto Thy servants, Philip our King and Mary our Queen, a male issue, which may sit in the seat of Thy kingdom. Make him in body comely and beautiful, in pregnant wit notable and excellent, in obedience like Abraham, in hospitality like Lot, in strength and valour like Samson.'

In Brussels, Charles V was happily anticipating the birth of his grandson, and appeared to Sir John Mason, the English ambassador, 'as lively as I have not of long time seen the like lustiness in him'.

'How goeth my daughter's belly forward?' Charles asked Mason.

'Sir,' the other replied, 'I have from herself nothing to say therein, for she will not confess the matter, but by others I understand, to my great joy and comfort, that her garments wax very strait.'

'I had never doubted the matter, but that God, [who] for her had wrought so many miracles, would make the same perfect by assisting of nature to His good and most desired work,' answered the Emperor. 'I warrant it shall be a man child.'

'Be it man or be it woman, welcome shall it be,' declared Mason, 'for by that shall we at the least come to some certainty to whom God shall appoint by succession the government of our estate. It maketh all good men tremble to think the Queen's Highness must die, with whom, dying without fruit, the realm were as good also to die.'

'Doubt not God will provide both with fruit,' the Emperor assured him.

English Protestants, however, were praying, not for a male heir, but that God would 'turn the heart of Queen Mary from idolatry, or else shorten her days'.

On the same day as the service of thanksgiving in St Paul's the King and Queen went to Westminster to hear the Legate address both Houses of Parliament. Seated on twin thrones beneath a cloth of estate, they watched as Gardiner presented 'the reverend Father in God, my lord Cardinal Pole' to the Lords and Commons, saying that he had 'come from the Apostolic See in Rome upon one of the most weightiest causes that ever happened in this realm'. Pole rose from his chair near Mary, and delivered an inspiring speech in a firm, authoritative voice. He spoke of England's long tradition of devotion to the Catholic faith, of the Queen's miraculous triumph over her enemies and God's purpose in preserving her, of Philip's Christian reputation, and of his mandate from the Pope.

'My commission is not of prejudice to any person,' he reassured his audience. 'I come not to destroy but to build. I come to reconcile, not to condemn. I come not to compel, but to call again. Touching all matters of the past, they shall be as things cast into the sea of forgetfulness.' In conclusion, therefore, he asked Parliament to repeal all the Acts that remained as obstacles to reconciliation with Rome, saving only those that dealt with the redistribution of church property; in accordance with the wishes of the Pope, that would not be reclaimed.

That night, in honour of the Legate, there was a lavish masque at court depicting the feats of Hercules, followed by a tournament with canes instead of lances, arranged by the King, who – splendidly attired in silver and purple – took part and performed well; the Queen, smiling, presented the prizes. Pole reported to the Pope that the King treated his wife with the respect due from a son to his mother, but it was obvious that he found it an effort to keep up the façade he was obliged to maintain.

The next day Parliament repealed Henry VIII's Act of Supremacy and drew up a petition to the King and Queen, signed by all but two of the members of both Houses, that they, being persons unsullied by heresy or schism, would intercede with the Legate so that the realm could receive absolution for its disobedience and then be reunited with Rome. The stage was now set for the public act of reconciliation that would return England to the Roman Catholic fold.

On the afternoon of St Andrew's Day, 30 November, Gardiner led the members of both Houses of Parliament to Whitehall, where, in a great chamber lit with torches, they presented their petition to the King and Queen, saying they were 'very sorry and repentant of the schism and disobedience committed in this realm against the See Apostolic', and begging to be received 'into the bosom and unity of Christ's Church'. Then Cardinal Pole rose, and the entire company, apart from Philip and Mary, fell to their knees before him. He told them that, in the name of the Pope, he welcomed 'the return of the lost sheep', and granted absolution to the whole kingdom; which he received back into the mother Church. As he spoke, an exultant Mary wept for joy, and the Lords and Commons murmured, 'Amen! Amen!' many bursting into tears and embracing each other. Then Pole announced that, from now on, each 30 November should be celebrated as a new holy day, the Feast of the Reconciliation.

This was the supreme moment in Mary's life, the triumph that made all her past sufferings seem worthwhile. Now her conscience was at peace: she had done what she believed God wanted her to do, and fulfilled her destiny. Yet it was Philip who had worked hard behind the scenes to bring this about, and who had ensured that her wishes were implemented by Parliament, and she was well aware that she owed a debt of gratitude to her husband: on 7 December, she told the Emperor in a letter that the reconciliation with Rome was largely due to the King.

On 2 December, after celebrating high mass in a St Paul's packed with worshippers, Gardiner preached to the people of London at Paul's Cross, on the text 'Now we must arouse ourselves from sleep.' Watching him from an open window were King Philip and Cardinal Pole, who had attended the service. Pole had conferred upon Gardiner the power to grant absolution, and was gratified to see 1500 people – the largest crowd ever recorded in St Paul's Churchyard – displaying 'great piety' by kneeling in the cold to receive it. 'A sight to see it was, and the silence was such that not a cough was heard,' wrote one Spaniard.

Pole now threw himself with a vengeance into the task of purifying the English Church, supported by the Queen and the Council, who did their best to rectify his inability to understand how twenty years of schism had changed the English people. Mary and Pole got on well, and she relied heavily upon his advice. Next to Philip, he was the man she trusted most. However, he undermined her confidence by his constant references to the unfitness of women for ruling, and he never became reconciled to the idea of church property remaining in secular hands. Thwarted over this issue, he concentrated his energies on trying to restore the Church to its pre-Reformation state. Mary supported him wholeheartedly in this, but of course in many respects it proved impossible to turn the clock back. Saints days were no longer celebrated; monasteries, chantries and shrines remained closed, although the Queen did found six new religious houses; people no longer went on pilgrimage, nor were saints' relics reintroduced into churches as objects of veneration. The Queen's objective was to restore the spiritual values of the Catholic Church, and she and Pole worked hard to create a religious climate in which these could flourish.

It was Mary's fervent desire that heresy should be entirely eradicated from her realm, and shortly before Christmas, Parliament, whose members were still fired with the spirit of reconciliation, prepared to carry out her wishes. Wyatt's rebellion had left the government with a conviction that all heretics were would-be traitors and that heresy must therefore be eliminated in the interests of state security. The Queen wanted the heresy laws passed by Richard II, Henry IV and Henry V in the late fourteenth and early fifteenth centuries revived, and Pole, Philip and Gardiner supported her in this. Gardiner wanted to make an example of the heretics to deter others from adopting their beliefs; Philip had been an indefatigable champion of the Inquisition back in Spain, had presided over the mass executions known as Acts of Faith, and detested heresy in any form; Pole wanted it rooted out so that his task of reforming the Church was made easier.

On 18 December, 'An Act for the Renewing of Three Statutes made for the Punishment of Heresies' became law just six days after its introduction. This gave the bishops, who were in favour of the Act being passed, the power to investigate cases of suspected heresy, and provided for the Church to hand over those found guilty to the secular authorities for burning at the stake. Each execution was to be authorised by the Queen's writ. The property of a convicted heretic would then automatically revert to the Crown.

The responsibility for the persecution that followed the passing of this legislation must be laid fairly and squarely at Mary's door. As queen, she was the person with the ultimate power to sanction the burnings that took place. Most of her advisers, including Philip and Gardiner, urged her to proceed with caution; in fact Gardiner, whom most Protestants blamed for the persecution, did not condemn a single heretic in his diocese, and soon grew alarmed at the numbers being burned elsewhere. He had anticipated that a few executions would suffice to bring the people to their senses, and when he realised that this was not having the desired result he tried to call a halt, although by then it was too late.

Mary was not at heart a cruel person; many sources testify to her kindness and compassion. Yet she believed that it was her Christian duty, as sovereign, to make the heretics suffer a foretaste of hell-fire in this world, so that at the last they would repent and be saved. She also saw it as her duty to punish those who had sinned most dreadfully against God and His laws. If she failed in that duty, she would surely incur the wrath and displeasure of the Almighty, who had so far shown her nothing but favour. Like Gardiner, she was convinced that the burnings would act as a deterrent to others. She therefore insisted that the new Act be implemented with due rigour, and issued many directives to the authorities concerned, especially in London, where Protestantism had taken root more deeply than elsewhere, urging them to be diligent in seeking out and punishing heresy, and commanding, 'Touching punishment of heretics, methinketh it ought to be done without rashness, not leaving in the meanwhile to do justice to such as by learning would seem to deceive the simple. Especially within London I wish none to be burned without some of the Council's presence, and both there and everywhere good sermons at the same.'

She would not show her customary mercy to those guilty of crimes against God, and there is not a single instance on record of her extending clemency to a heretic. Nor would she permit others, Pole included, to show lenience.

The church courts that condemned heretics came under the jurisdiction of Cardinal Pole, but he was not as zealous as Mary, and John Foxe states that he preferred disinterring and burning dead heretics to consigning living ones to the flames. There were indeed bishops and other church officers whose eagerness to punish offenders made them feared and loathed, but none, not even the notorious Bishop Bonner of London, were influential at court. In fact, Mary reproved Bonner for being tardy about bringing heretics to justice, and rebuked the Sheriff of Hampshire for sparing a heretic who had recanted as soon as he felt the heat of the fire.

The only person in the kingdom who had the authority to stop the burnings was the Queen, but she never wavered in her resolve. It seems she was sustained in her convictions by a group of Spanish clergy who came to England in Philip's retinue. These included three Dominican friars, whose Order had been famous for its efficiency in suppressing heresy since the thirteenth century. One, Bartolomeo Carranza, became the Queen's confessor. Another, Alfonso de Castro, Bishop of Cuenca, had written several books on the persecution of heretics and was considered an authority on the subject. It was he who urged King Philip, who was concerned about the effect of the burnings on his reputation in England, to be more zealous in persecuting the English heretics. But Mary needed little persuasion: she saw her duty clear, and carried it out with chilling single-mindedness.

The success of her Counter-Reformation, together with her advancing pregnancy, meant that the Christmas of 1554 was one of the happiest of Mary's life. There were splendid celebrations at court, culminating in a moving service in the Chapel Royal, in which the King's choristers joined the Queen's to create an angelic sound. And in honour of the coming heir, the great Thomas Tallis composed a new mass entitled 'Unto us a child is born', which may have been sung on this occasion.

By January, however, the discomforts of her condition and her fear of a new uprising on behalf of Elizabeth and Courtenay, fuelled by the discovery of an obscure plot to assassinate the King and Queen, had undermined Mary's health and spirits. She was so ill that she was unable to write more than a brief note in response to one of the Emperor's solicitous letters. What made matters worse was Philip's obvious restlessness. He had done his duty in England and got the Queen with child, and now he was anxious to leave for the Low Countries to fight the French. In a letter to his father written at this time he confided, 'I must confess that for some years past I have been desirous of leading a campaign, and I would like it to be as soon as possible. It will be my first campaign, my first opportunity of acquiring or losing prestige; all eyes will be fixed on me.' He certainly had no intention of delaying his departure until after the birth of his child, and made no secret of the fact.

Mary was devastated, and her distress served only to undermine her health further. Because of her age and medical history, she feared that the birth would be a difficult and dangerous one, and needed the reassurance that her husband would be near at hand. Whenever he implied that his father needed him more than she did, he provoked floods of tears and emotional scenes, which placed the royal marriage under some strain. By the beginning of February Mary was 'very melancholy' and her councillors feared she might die in childbirth, if not before. It was then that Renard took it upon himself to write an admonitory letter to the King, warning him what could happen if he left England now.

> Your Highness, it is true, might wish that Her Majesty was more agreeable, but on the other hand she is infinitely virtuous. Your Highness, like a magnanimous prince, must remember her condition, and exert yourself to assist her. Although it might be wished that the Queen were more gracious, your own virtue, goodness and intelligence leave nothing to be desired.

While Philip agonised over where his loyalties lay, the burnings began.

On 28 January, a commission headed by Gardiner condemned five persons to death for heresy, among them John Hooper, Bishop of Gloucester, and John Rogers, prebendary of St Paul's and a married priest. Rogers was the first victim of the Marian persecution. He was burned on 4 February 1555 at Smithfield in London, in the midst of an angry protest by the watching crowd, who were incensed that Gardiner had forbidden the condemned man to say goodbye to his wife and children.

Hooper suffered next, on 9 February, in his own diocese of Gloucester. The Queen, signing the writ for his execution, had ordered him not to address the spectators in case he tried to portray himself as a martyr. His death was terrible: the gunpowder bag, which was sometimes hung around the necks of heretics to ensure a speedy end, did not explode and he burned for three-quarters of an hour, pitifully begging the crowd to fan the flames in order to end his agony. In March five Protestants went to the stake in London and one, a priest, in Colchester. All died bravely.

Immediately there was a public outcry, so great that Renard feared another uprising. Far from converting the Protestants to the Roman Faith, the burnings had the effect of hardening their resolve and inflaming their anger against the Queen. The bravery of the men who had died so painfully was an inspiration to many; already they were regarded as martyrs with beliefs worth dying for. There was no shortage of men and women ready to speak out against the persecution, and the _Acts of the Privy Council_ records that unprecedented numbers were set in the pillory that spring for uttering 'horrible lies and seditious words of the Queen's Majesty and her Council'.

But the burnings went on. Over the next few years around 240 men and 60 women died at the stake. Most were popular preachers, artisans, farm labourers or poor, ignorant folk who could not recite the Lord's Prayer or did not know what the Sacraments were, and were apprehended by over-zealous parish priests; the majority came from the south and east. Some were blind or disabled; one woman, Perotine Massey of Guernsey, was pregnant. Her baby was born as she was burning, and cast back into the flames by the executioner. The 'better sort' of heretics had already escaped abroad. Compared with the thousands who were martyred on the Continent for their faith, the Marian persecution was on a very small scale, but it was unprecedented in England and therefore sufficient to inspire horror and revulsion in most people. Frequently, the executions were bungled or mismanaged by incompetent executioners, or the faggots were damp, causing the victim unnecessarily prolonged suffering. Before long, the Council ordered that there should be more guards present in order to stop the onlookers from 'comforting, aiding or praising the offender'.

As soon as the burnings began, King Philip ordered his confessor, Alfonso de Castro, to preach a sermon at court against them, hoping thereby to deflect public censure from himself. But this did not stop most people from concluding that it was Philip and his Spaniards who had made the Queen consent to this cruel legislation, though in fact it was Philip who tried constantly to curb the Queen's religious zeal.

Gardiner was soon sickened by the burnings, and when he saw that they were producing the opposite effect to that intended, he tried to persuade the Queen to adopt other methods of punishment. Cruelty, he protested, served no useful purpose. But Pole, Paget and other councillors accused him of being 'too mild and gentle' towards the heretics, who were after all guilty of a 'great atrocity' against God. Disillusioned and in failing health, Gardiner realised there was little he could do to stem the tide of persecution. The irony was that his enemies were calling him a 'man of blood' in the belief that it was he who had instigated it.

Mary had come to the throne on a tide of popularity, but the burnings cost her that and the love of many of her subjects. She was now reviled by Protestants as the cruel persecutor of martyrs, and although the epithet 'Bloody Mary' was not invented until the seventeenth century, it was not unjustified. For centuries afterwards Catholicism and persecution would be irredeemably linked in the minds of the English people, and this was certainly her doing. Many now prayed that the Queen's pregnancy would come to a calamitous end, and looked to the Lady Elizabeth to be their deliverer. Indeed, if anyone could have been said to benefit from the persecution, it was Elizabeth, who now found herself more popular than ever.

This was, in every respect, a difficult time for Mary. Throughout the January of 1555 de Noailles's brother François was plotting to marry Elizabeth to Courtenay. This came to light in February, when a plan to proclaim Courtenay as Edward VII at Fotheringhay was revealed. On 13 March, Renard commented that the kingdom would 'never be at peace till the Elizabeth and Devon matter is settled'.

Whilst Mary fretted over that, preparations for her confinement, now just two months away, were under way. Yet even this was marred by persistent rumours that she was not pregnant at all but planning to pass off a base-born baby as her heir. Mrs Alice Perwick, the wife of a London merchant, was brought before the justices in March for saying 'The Queen's Grace is not with child, and another lady should be with child, and that lady's child should be named the Queen's child.' It was also being said that Edward VI was not dead at all, but would soon return to depose his sister. Mary's repeated denials of this made little difference, for this particular rumour persisted for years.

Then, in March, Pope Julius died. His successor, Marcellus II, died after three weeks in office, to be succeeded by Paul IV, a seventy-five-year-old alcoholic who had long been antagonistic towards the Habsburgs and who professed a deep loathing of all Spaniards. This was a terrible blow to Philip, who perceived at once that all the advantages he had gained by bringing about the reconciliation with Rome were irrevocably lost. To begin with, however, the new pope proceeded carefully, confirming Cardinal Pole in his mission as Legate. Yet Pole would never enjoy with Paul the friendly rapport he had had with Julius, and from 1555 relations between the English Church and the papacy steadily deteriorated.

By early March, Philip had reluctantly told Mary that he would remain in England until after their child was born. Instead of satisfying his need for military glory abroad, he devoted himself to planning a series of tournaments at court, but Mary did not attend them, not only because of her pregnancy, but also – according to the Venetian ambassador – because she could not bear to watch her husband risking his life by attempting daring exploits in the lists.

To allay her other fears, Philip suggested that Elizabeth and Courtenay be sent abroad, to places where they could be kept under supervision, the former to Brussels and the latter to Rome. The Queen liked the idea, but the Council warned her that exiling Elizabeth now, at such a sensitive time, might provoke another rebellion, and she was forced to abandon it. Indeed, there was a small, easily-quelled rising in Elizabeth's favour that month, when a group of rebels in Hampshire, claiming to believe the rumour that the Queen was planning to foist a changeling on the realm, attempted to persuade the local countrymen to rise against her and set her sister on the throne.

Again, Gardiner urged that Elizabeth be disinherited, but Philip realised that if Mary died in childbirth, and her child with her, Henry II of France would then press the claim of his daughter-in-law, Mary, Queen of Scots, to the English throne, which was the last thing he and the Emperor wanted. If Mary Stuart succeeded then England would become a French dominion and the Habsburgs would lose all the strategic advantages they had gained by the English alliance. In the middle of April Renard submitted a detailed memorandum on the English succession to Philip, which accurately described the problems that could arise if the Queen did not survive childbirth:

Supposing the Queen is not with child, or dies without issue, there will certainly be strife and the heretics will espouse the cause of the Lady Elizabeth. If Elizabeth is married to an Englishman, she will prevail upon her husband to adopt the new religion, even if he is a Catholic. If a foreign husband is found for her, it will be necessary to make sure that he is constant and faithful to Your Majesty. There would seem to be no alliance more advantageous for her than with the Duke of Savoy.

The ambassador urged the King to see Elizabeth before he left for the Low Countries and promise to 'do what is suitable for her' in return for her good behaviour. Naturally, Philip was curious to meet his sister-in-law, who had been the cause of so much controversy since he had become involved in English affairs.

Philip therefore urged that a decision on Elizabeth's future be deferred until after the Queen's confinement, and advocated bringing her to court so that he could keep an eye on her until then. It also occurred to him that it would be wise to establish a good working relationship with her in case she did become queen. If she looked upon him with gratitude as the person who had rescued her from a rigorous confinement, then he might obtain her good will and so preserve the Anglo-Spanish alliance. Reports from Bedingfield confirmed that the princess was behaving in every respect like a good Catholic, and the King entertained hopes that her conversion might be more than mere expediency. Yet even as a Protestant, she was infinitely preferable to the Catholic Mary Stuart when it came to the question of who should succeed if Mary died childless.

When Philip suggested to his wife that Elizabeth be brought to court, Mary agreed without protest, knowing that this would prevent the princess from inciting a rebellion against him if she herself died in childbed.

One problem could be effectively disposed of: that of Courtenay. On 29 April, at Philip's instigation, 'the last sprig of the White Rose' was issued with a pardon, released from Fotheringhay and sent on a diplomatic mission to the Imperial court at Brussels, where he would be under the supervision of Charles V. 'One of the embarrassments we have been apprehending is out of the way,' observed Renard, but Courtenay had hopes of being summoned home before long, and left his house fully furnished against his return. He suffered miseries of homesickness during his exile, which brought added suffering to his sick mother, Lady Exeter, who wrote: 'If wishing might take place, you should be there.' She promised him that, although 'my years require rest', she would return to her post at court 'if my waiting [on the Queen] can do you good'. But the summons that Courtenay prayed daily for never came.

15

'A Miracle Will Come to Pass'

On 4 April 1555, which fell in Easter week, the King and Queen went to Hampton Court to await the birth of their child. Mary would have liked it to be born at Windsor, but it was felt that, given the uncertain state of the country and the temper of the people, Hampton Court afforded better security and was nearer to London and the Tower arsenal.

The Queen was well into her eighth month of pregnancy – Renard told the Emperor that the baby was due around 9 May, although some of Mary's ladies were of the opinion that she had miscalculated her dates and that it would arrive around 9 June, but as she had announced the pregnancy in late September, then a date early in May was most likely. Soon after her arrival at the palace she took to her chamber with appropriate ceremony, in the presence of her chief courtiers. Custom demanded that six weeks before the birth a queen go into 'confinement' in her apartments for forty days, with her ladies taking upon themselves the functions normally reserved for male officers of the household. It was considered improper for any men other than her husband to attend the Queen at this late stage of her pregnancy.

Preparations for the baby's arrival were completed by the middle of April. In the Queen's bedchamber stood a sumptuous cradle covered with an embroidered counterpane; Latin and English verses had been carved in the wood, and read:

> The child which Thou to Mary, O Lord of might, hast send,
> To England's joy, in health preserve, keep and defend!

Swaddling bands and wrapping cloths were laid out in readiness for 'the young master'. Mary and her ladies had stitched a beautiful bedcover and matching headpiece for the bed in which she would be delivered, and in her clothes chest were folded away four smocks of the finest Holland cloth trimmed with silk and silver braid at the neck and wrists, as well as breast binders and extra blankets. Midwives, physicians, nurses and rockers had been engaged and were already in residence, whilst the great ladies of the realm, with husbands in tow, descended upon the palace in order to comfort the Queen and be her 'gossips' when her hour was upon her.

In the birth chamber, the physicians had already assembled the equipment they would need, and tables, benches and bowls had been set there for their use, as well as bottles of scented water to sweeten the air during the delivery.

The Queen was naturally anxious, and her fears were exacerbated by news of ugly incidents and protests against the burnings in London. Because of this, King Philip summoned 'true and faithful men of the realm' to Hampton Court to reinforce the guards already on duty, and ordered that the Watch take extra precautions in the city by recruiting more men and patrolling the streets continuously through the night.

Mary was not the only person to know fear at this time. Her doctors were terrified of the responsibility entrusted to them, and were privately pessimistic as to the outcome, considering the age and mental state of their patient. They were also concerned about her poor appetite, saying that she ate so little that she could not possibly provide both herself and her baby with adequate nourishment. Some people recalled that the Queen's mother, Katherine of Aragon, had lost five out of her six children at birth or soon afterwards, and predicted that history might repeat itself, while others claimed that the Queen might not be pregnant at all, but had 'a tumour, as often happens to women'. Yet Mary had all the symptoms of pregnancy: her periods had ceased, she had experienced 'swelling of the paps and their emission of milk', according to the Venetian ambassador, and her stomach was very swollen. She had also felt the child move.

On 17 April, Sir Henry Bedingfield was relieved to receive orders to bring his illustrious prisoner to court. Elizabeth was no less pleased that her long confinement was coming to an end, believing that her innocence would at last be established once and for all, though she was to remain under close guard for some weeks yet.

They left Woodstock on 20 April in gusting winds which billowed out the ladies' skirts and repeatedly blew Elizabeth's hood off. She begged to be able to take shelter in a nearby manor house, but Bedingfield, still obeying orders to the letter, refused to allow it, and the princess was obliged to pin up her windswept hair and replace her hood in the shelter of a hedge. On the last morning of the journey, about sixty of Elizabeth's gentlemen and yeomen tried to catch a glimpse of her as she left the George Inn at Colnbrook.

On 29 April, Michieli, the Venetian ambassador, reported that the princess was expected at Hampton Court the following day; he understood that she had been summoned as a hostage for King Philip's safety, which – in the event of Mary dying – would depend more upon Elizabeth than upon any other person. Already there were rumours that Philip had earmarked her as his third wife.

She arrived privately, being still under the Queen's displeasure, and was conducted by Bedingfield into the palace 'on the back side', accompanied by only a handful of her own attendants. It was no coincidence that she was assigned apartments near to those of King Philip and Cardinal Pole. Sir Henry was soon afterwards relieved of his duties as her gaoler, and, declaring that God Almighty knew that this was the joyfullest news he had ever heard, escaped with heartfelt relief into the country. Elizabeth held no grudge against him, although, years later, when he came to her court, she told him 'with a nipping word' that if she had any prisoner 'whom we would have sharply and straitly kept, we will send for you!' Whenever they met thereafter, she referred to him affectionately as her 'Gaoler', and stayed once as his guest at Oxburgh Hall.

The absence of any official welcome to the court should have warned Elizabeth that the next few weeks were not going to be easy. The Queen had, of course, retired from public life for the present, but that would not normally have prevented her from receiving her sister. What did do so was Mary's conviction that Elizabeth would be so desperate for an audience that she would confess her involvement in Wyatt's rebellion just to obtain one. The Queen therefore sent Gardiner, Arundel, Shrewsbury and Secretary Petre to inform the princess that, if she did so confess, 'Her Majesty would be good to her'. Gardiner even fell to his knees and begged Elizabeth to submit to the Queen.

She vehemently maintained her innocence. 'Better for me to lie in prison for the truth than to be abroad and suspected of my prince,' she declared. 'In yielding, I should confess myself an offender, which I never was, towards Her Majesty, by occasion whereof the King and Queen might ever hereafter conceive of me an evil opinion.' A second visit by the councillors failed to move her, and Gardiner informed the Queen that nothing further was likely to be obtained from the princess. Mary 'marvelled that she should so stoutly stand by her innocence', and remained adamant that she would not set her sister at liberty until she had told the truth. Soon, Elizabeth discovered that she had exchanged one form of house arrest for another. She was permitted to receive visitors – although very few dared come – but was not allowed to leave her rooms.

However, Philip, according to de Noailles, could not resist seeing her, and insisted upon a meeting. Three days after her arrival, she received a curt message from Mary, ordering her to wear her finest robes and prepare to receive the King. The meeting took place in private, and consequently no record of what passed between them has been preserved, although later sources indicate that some degree of sexual chemistry sprang up between them – just what Mary had feared.

Afterwards, Philip observed that the Queen was very different from her sister, and in later years Elizabeth herself would often claim light-heartedly that Philip had been in love with her, and that she had made a most favourable impression on him when first they met. She was fond of boasting that their long-drawn-out enmity had begun with love, and that if she so chose there was no reason why they could not be friends once again. Late in the sixteenth century, William Cecil's son, Thomas, reported that Philip had said that 'whatever he suffered from Queen Elizabeth was the just judgement of God because, being married to Queen Mary, whom he thought a most virtuous and good lady, yet in the fancy of love he could not affect her; but as for the Lady Elizabeth, he was enamoured of her, being a fair and beautiful woman'.

Even as early as May 1557, Michieli was reporting that, 'At the time of the Queen's pregnancy the Lady Elizabeth contrived so to ingratiate herself with all the Spaniards, and especially with the King, that ever since no one has favoured her more than he does; for not only would he not permit, but opposed and prevented the Queen's wish to have her disinherited by Act of Parliament, which – besides affection – implies some particular design on the part of the King with regard to her.' Their first meeting may therefore have been significant in more ways than one.

As the date of Mary's expected delivery drew nearer, tension mounted at court. Renard wrote to Charles V,

> Everything in this kingdom depends on the Queen's safe deliverance. If God is pleased to grant her a safe delivery, things will take a turn for the better. If not, I foresee disturbance and a change for the worse on so great a scale that the pen can hardly set it down.

Already, letters in French announcing the birth had been prepared by the royal clerks, who had diplomatically left a gap in case *'fils'* had to be altered to *'fille'*. The Queen had commanded that her ambassadors convey news of the birth to foreign courts as soon as the child was delivered, and had signed passports for them. To hearten her, and relieve the tedium of waiting, there were brought to the palace on 24 April 'three beautiful infants for Her Majesty to see, they having been born a few days previously at one birth, of a woman of low stature and great age like the Queen, who after delivery found herself strong and out of danger'. Mary professed herself much encouraged to see them.

Childbirth was indeed fraught with dangers at that time. Forceps would not be invented for another fifty years, and if the baby could not be delivered in the normal way then midwives had to resort to butchery on either mother or child in order to facilitate parturition. The need for hygiene was not understood, and many women succumbed to the dreaded puerperal fever, brought on by bacterial infection. Many babies died at birth or soon afterwards, and often their mothers died with them. There was no effective pain relief, and labour could last for days. For an older mother, the risks – then, as now – were greatly increased.

At dawn on the morning of Tuesday, 30 April, wrote the diarist Henry Machyn, 'tidings came to London that the Queen's Grace was delivered of a prince, and so there was great ringing [of church bells] through London, and [in] divers places *Te Deum Laudamus* sung'. Royal officials in the capital confirmed the news and said that the Queen had come through her ordeal 'with little pain and no danger', and that the child, born just after midnight, was a fair boy, without a blemish. The citizens, glad of any opportunity for a celebration, declared the day a holiday, shut their shops, lit bonfires, and set tables laden with meats in the streets, whilst the city authorities laid on free wine for all, and the clergy went in procession around the city giving thanks 'for the birth of our prince'. The joyful tidings spread to the Continent by means of sailors leaving the port of London, and by 2 May Charles V and his court were 'rejoicing out of measure' at the news.

It occurred to no one in London that there had been no official announcement of the birth from Hampton Court, and the citizens were aghast and dismayed when, late in the afternoon of 30 April, their celebrations were interrupted by the arrival of messengers from the court, who had hastily come to inform the city fathers that the news was false, and that there was as yet no sign of the Queen being in labour. 'It is hardly to be told how much this dispirited everybody,' reported

Michieli. 'But it shall be when it please God,' wrote Machyn, 'for I trust God will remember His true servants that put their trust in Him.'

On 4 May, the Emperor, puzzled as to why he had received no official announcement of his grandson's birth, sent for Sir John Mason and demanded an explanation. Mason said he had heard the news from a contact in London, but had received no confirmation from the court. Charles said he was 'loath to bring the thing into any doubt', but the lack of news was certainly strange. Then came a letter from the Duke of Alba at Hampton Court, to say that the reports in London were false and that the Queen was still waiting for her pains to begin. The Emperor was therefore obliged to remain in a state of hope and expectation like everyone else.

On 3 May, there was another false report of the birth of a prince, this time in Herefordshire, where one John Gillam stated, 'Now there is a prince born, his father will bring into this realm his own nation and put out the English nation.' This was a fear he shared with most of Mary's subjects, and that it was not mere scaremongering is proved by Michieli's view that, once his heir was born, Philip would look for a complete change in his relationship with Queen and Council. Already, it was being said that the troops assembling in the Netherlands had not been recruited to fight the French but to subvert the English and enforce Philip's authority in the event of Mary's death.

Throughout the first weeks of May, the Queen remained in strict seclusion; once or twice her courtiers saw her at a window. On the 7th a curious item of news was reported by a French envoy called Boisdaulphin, who had gone to Padua in Italy to recover from an illness. He told Henry II that he had been informed that Queen Mary had been 'delivered of a mole, or lump of flesh, and was in great peril of death'. Boisdaulphin's source is not known, but any news from England would have taken at least three weeks to reach him, and therefore, if the Queen had suffered this freak delivery, it would have occurred around the middle of April, soon after she took to her chamber.

What Boisdaulphin was claiming was that Mary had been delivered of a hydatidiform mole, a condition of pregnancy caused by chromosomal irregularity, where the placenta develops into a benign tumour resembling a bunch of grapes, and deprives the growing embryo of nourishment. The embryo dies but the mole continues to grow. The woman's abdomen swells, as in pregnancy, and she may suffer nausea and high blood pressure. Eventually her body expels the mole, which resembles a 'lump of flesh'. This was not a common condition –

nowadays the incidence in the United Kingdom is about one in five hundred pregnancies.

It is unlikely, however, that Mary suffered from this condition, for two very sound reasons. When a mole is expelled, the woman suffers bleeding, sometimes very heavy bleeding, and there is no record of Mary experiencing this. Secondly, expulsion only rarely occurs later than three to four months after conception, and almost never later than five.

The other possibility raised by Boisdaulphin's evidence is that the Queen suffered an intrauterine death – the death of a viable foetus, which is sometimes referred to as a late abortion. Again, the probability is against this because bleeding is bound to have occurred when the foetus was passed, an unmistakable sign that the pregnancy had terminated, which even Mary could not have ignored.

Realistically, therefore, for either of these conditions to have occurred, someone – and the Queen herself – must have lied about the bleeding, as well as the timing in the case of a mole. This seems hardly likely in view of the available evidence and Mary's own known integrity. Boisdaulphin's report, therefore, can only have been based on unsubstantiated gossip or speculation, and may be dismissed as unreliable evidence.

On 21 May, Michieli reported that 'Her Majesty's belly has greatly declined', although this had been said by the doctors and midwives 'to indicate the approaching term'. One of Mary's physicians, Dr Calagila, announced that he expected labour to commence any day now, asserting that his royal patient was definitely in the final month of pregnancy. But by this time, Mary was so despondent about the baby's failure to arrive that she began to think that God was punishing her for not rooting out heresy with sufficient rigour, and consequently issued a written directive to all her bishops, ordering them to step up their efforts to search out and punish offenders.

On 22 May, Ruy Gomez confided in a letter to a friend that there was no sign of the birth being imminent. He had seen the Queen out walking in her privy garden, 'and she steps so well that it seems to me that there is no hope at all for this month'. Her doctors maintained that they were still expecting labour to commence at any moment, but Mary had now convinced herself that she had muddled her dates. Very soon, the physicians were concurring in this view, predicting that the birth would take place on 23 May, at the next change of the moon, or after the full moon, on 4 or 5 June.

De Noailles, however, poured scorn on this, and professed himself amused at everyone's expectations. To his certain knowledge, he announced, the Queen was not pregnant. He had spoken to a male friend of Susan Clarencieux and the chief midwife — 'one of the best midwives in the town' — to whom both ladies had confided that, apart from being 'pale and peaked' and having a swollen abdomen, Mary had none of the other signs of pregnancy. In the midwife's opinion the royal doctors were either too stupid to realise the truth, or too scared to admit it. She herself, 'more to comfort the Queen with words than anything', had spoken soothingly of an error over dates. De Noailles had a reputation for mischief-making, and certainly this particular infant's appearance would discountenance his master's ambitions. Yet at the end of May the chief midwife publicly affirmed that the Queen was indeed with child, and the ambassador told Henry II that she was practising a blatant deception.

23 May came and went with no sign of labour commencing, and on the 29th de Noailles reported that Mary was spending long hours alone, sitting in silence on cushions on the floor of her chamber with her knees drawn up to her chin, staring at the wall. Such a position he pointed out, would not be possible for a heavily pregnant woman. Yet Renard, despite a certain anxiety over the delay, remained confident and optimistic, and subscribed to the opinion that a mistake had been made over dates. Nevertheless, some courtiers were already expressing scepticism about the Queen's condition, and in Brussels, the Venetian ambassador to the Imperial court had received from an unnamed source what he believed to be reliable information that 'the Queen has given manifest signs of not being pregnant'. He was obliged to suppress such sensitive intelligence, and only reported it in confidential dispatches, whilst behaving in public as if he too expected a happy announcement from England at any time. In France, meanwhile, Henry II was diplomatically attributing the delay to 'women's ways'.

At the end of May tidings of the death of the King's grandmother, Queen Juana, reached England, and the courtiers were commanded to don mourning. The Emperor was hoping that Philip would be present at the funeral, but the King knew he could not leave England at such a crucial time and retired to his apartments, there to remain in seclusion until after Juana's obsequies were over. He would put off his mourning, he announced, 'for the joy of the delivery' of his son. His wife, however, was well aware that he was itching to be off fighting the French, and that he would depart for the Netherlands the moment the baby was safely born. Michieli reported, 'From what I hear one single hour's delay in this delivery seems to him a thousand years.'

Then, on 31 May, Mary felt what she believed were her first contractions, and the court held its breath in anticipation. It proved to be another false alarm, and despondency reigned when it was known that she had still not taken to her bed. Gomez grumbled, 'The Queen's deliverance keeps us all greatly exercised in our minds,' and reported that the doctors were now saying that 'the nine months are not up until 6 June'.

Towards the end of May Philip succeeded in persuading Mary to see her sister, and at ten one evening Susan Clarencieux came to escort Elizabeth to the Queen's apartments. The princess turned pale when she received the summons and begged her attendants to pray for her, as 'she could not tell whether ever she should see them again or no'. But Clarencieux reassured her, telling her to change into her finest dress for the occasion, and when she was ready led her by torchlight through the gardens to the side door to Mary's rooms. Once inside, they mounted the back stairs to the privy chamber and when Elizabeth saw the Queen sitting there she threw herself on her knees, burst into tears, and cried, 'God preserve Your Majesty! You will find me as true a subject of Your Majesty as any, whatever has been reported of me.'

Mary looked away and said sarcastically. 'You will not confess your offence but stand stoutly in your truth. I pray God it may so fall out.'

'If it does not, I desire neither favour nor pardon at your hands,' replied Elizabeth with passion. However, this was not the firm denial that her sister desired to hear from her lips.

'Well,' said Mary coldly, 'you stiffly still persevere in your truth; belike you will not confess, but that you have been wrongly punished?'

'I must not say so, if it please Your Majesty, to you,' answered Elizabeth carefully, knowing she trod on dangerous ground.

'Why then, belike you will to others?' returned Mary.

'No, if it please Your Majesty. I have borne the burden and I must bear it. I humbly beseech Your Majesty to have a good opinion of me, and to think me to be your true subject, not only from the beginning, but for ever, as long as life lasteth.'

Mary did not immediately reply, then she rose and murmured what sounded – according to John Foxe, who recorded this conversation – like *'Sabe Dios'* – Spanish for 'God knoweth'. This Foxe presumed to be for the benefit of King Philip, whom he says was hiding behind a tapestry, listening to the interview, and watching through a small hole in the fabric. Finally, knowing that it was futile to question Elizabeth further, Mary spoke 'a few comfortable words' to her and dismissed her.

Soon afterwards there was another meeting between the sisters, after which it became clear that 'the Lady Elizabeth is at her full liberty', and thereafter it was tacitly accepted that, thanks to King Philip's influence with the reluctant Queen, Elizabeth had been received back into favour. Nevertheless, the princess rarely left her rooms, and although the courtiers were aware that they might now visit her without fear of incurring the Queen's displeasure, 'They all avail themselves of it with great reserve.' Mary had made no secret of the fact that she would never trust Elizabeth again.

Shortly afterwards, Dr John Dee, the notable astrologer, and three of Elizabeth's servants were arrested for having conspired to cast the horoscopes of the King, the Queen and the Lady Elizabeth, it being treason to forecast the sovereign's death. Yet before the accused could be interrogated the persons who had informed on them were afflicted 'the one with present death, the other with blindness', and the charges were dropped, probably through fear of witchcraft.

Had Elizabeth, in her altered circumstances, tried to discover what the future held for her?

It was an unseasonably cold, rainy summer. In the muddy fields the corn failed to ripen, presaging a bad harvest and the prospect of famine during the winter months. 'The like is not remembered in the memory of man for the last fifty years,' commented Michieli. The machinery of government had come to a standstill as a result of the Queen's prolonged confinement, and in London, the mood of the people was ugly, exacerbated by the spurious report of a prince being born and the sickening spectacles at Smithfield. Scurrilous placards against the Queen began appearing with alarming frequency in the streets, and rumours abounded that she had died in childbirth and that the hated Spaniards had concealed her death for nefarious reasons of their own, or that she was not pregnant at all but mortally sick. There were also more wild claims that Edward VI was about to emerge from seclusion and return to the throne. Already, many people spoke with deep affection of the Lady Elizabeth, and a printed prayer to be said at her accession was circulated. So angry was the mood of the people that Philip became concerned and wrote to ask the Emperor for advice on how to handle the situation. Before long, the Council were obliged to send Pembroke at the head of a small force to keep order in the capital.

Nor was the atmosphere at court conducive to harmony. With so many people packed into a palace affording only primitive sanitation, the air was becoming foetid and tempers short. The tension between the English and Spanish courtiers was almost tangible, and fights and squabbles broke out at the slightest provocation. Blood was shed, and King Philip warned those concerned that they were to maintain silence about it so as not to provoke further incidents. Then a violent mob of hundreds of young Englishmen marched on Hampton Court and camped menacingly outside the main gates, swords at the ready to slay any Spaniard who dared venture forth. Philip ordered the palace guards to drive them away, and there was a nasty skirmish involving 500 men that left half a dozen dead. Given the political climate, the King dared not punish the offenders harshly, but contented himself with administering a stern reprimand to them about keeping the peace. This only served to convince them that he and his countrymen were afraid of them, and they withdrew to plot a more ambitious assault on the palace. Fortunately their plans were discovered and forestalled by the Council.

'Everything is in suspense and dependent upon the result of this delivery,' wrote Michieli. 6 June passed without any sign of labour, and the doctors again revised the expected date, saying that it would be around the 24th. They had almost certainly realised by now that there was to be no child, yet such was the Queen's state of mind that they, the midwives, and her ladies all kept up the pretence that the pregnancy, which had now lasted ten months, was normal. When Mary expressed fearful doubts about her condition, they reminded her that her grandmother, Isabella of Castile, had borne a child at the age of fifty-two. The delay was simply due to a muddle over dates, and given Mary's menstrual history, this seemed feasible.

Nevertheless, to be on the safe side, the Queen requested that the clergy go in procession through London daily, praying for her safe delivery. Similar intercessions were made each morning at court, with the privy councillors and courtiers processing around the courtyards of the palace, and passing below a small window of Mary's apartments, where she sat watching them and bowing slightly 'with extraordinary cheerfulness and graciousness', while they doffed their caps and bonnets in return. It was noticed that she looked much healthier and had rosier cheeks, and indeed she told her attendants that she had never felt better, but regretted that she had felt 'no movement indicating parturition'.

The delay was now causing intense embarrassment, especially to King Philip, who felt he was being exposed to ridicule by it. Abroad, English ambassadors hastened to assure foreign rulers that the non-appearance of the heir to England was due to 'the common error of women in reckoning their time'. Rumour was already rife at the Imperial court that Queen Mary was not pregnant at all, and Sir John Mason sent an urgent message to the Council begging that Her Majesty show herself just once at mass to give gossip the lie. In England, when a Polish envoy arrived to offer the King and Queen congratulations on the birth of a prince – the false report of the birth had reached Warsaw – he noticed that his Latin speech was occasioning 'laughter and amusement' amongst the throng of courtiers. By now, the Queen's pregnancy was regarded as something of a joke.

Any admission that there was, after all, to be no child would result in the monarchy being held up to ridicule and an extreme loss of face. Mary's enemies were certain that she was practising an elaborate deception, possibly to keep Philip at her side for as long as possible, and Foxe claims that on the morning of Whit Sunday, 11 June, a woman called Isabel Malt, who had just borne a son, received a visit from two lords, one of whom announced himself as Lord North and asked 'if she would part with her child, and would swear that she never knew nor had any such child'. This matter, claims Foxe, 'was rumoured among the people' to concern 'the childbed of Queen Mary', the implication being that young Master Malt was to be passed off as the heir to England. It is unlikely, however, that Mary was capable of such sustained deception, and there is plenty of evidence to show that she believed she was pregnant well after this date.

In the middle of June, there was another false alarm, but the courtiers were becoming daily more suspicious. Those who had seen Mary reported that she no longer looked pregnant, a fact that was commented upon by Ruy Gomez in private correspondence: 'All this makes me doubt whether she is with child at all, greatly as I desire to see the thing happily over.'

'The expressions on people's faces are strange,' noted Renard. 'They have a masked appearance.' Yet on 24 June he reported confidently that the royal physicians had been two months out in their calculations, and that the child was not due for another eight or ten days. Five days later he stated that Mary was as well as he had ever seen her and was undoubtedly with child.

July came in with still no sign of labour, yet still the Queen did not abandon hope. The palace was now stinking and filthy, and the fear of plague – common in summer in Tudor times – added itself to the courtiers' other frustrations. The doctors and midwives were still assuring Mary that she had muddled her dates, but with less and less conviction. When they announced that the birth might not take place until August or September, no one believed them, and it appears that even the Queen was beginning to accept that there would be no child.

Early in July, some of the items prepared for the confinement were quietly stored away, and before 10 July Mary was attending once more to official business and taking the air in the gardens, looking her usual slender self. Yet she still insisted that she was pregnant, and sent instructions to Mason in Brussels that he was to deny any report that she was not with child. Her councillors, however, took it upon themselves to inform him privately that she was almost certainly deluding herself. In London, it was being said by some Protestants that the Queen had declared that the baby would not be born until every heretic in the kingdom had been burned; others distributed seditious pamphlets claiming that King Philip was keeping company with whores whilst his wife was confined to her rooms.

As late as 25 July, when the 'pregnancy' had lasted eleven and a half months, it was still being said that 'a miracle would come to pass in this as in all Her Majesty's other circumstances, which, the more they were despaired of according to human reasoning, the better and more auspicious did the result then show itself'. The birth of her child would show the world that Mary's affairs 'were regulated exclusively by divine providence'. Yet in the taverns of London the Protestants made ribald jests at the Queen's expense and imputed her failure to produce an heir to the judgement of God. Many believed that the repeated deferment of the date of delivery was only 'for the sake of keeping the populace in hope, and consequently in check', yet most were now of the opinion that 'the pregnancy will end in wind rather than anything else'. Mary's desperation is revealed in the tear blots in her prayer book on the page entitled 'A Prayer for a Woman with Child'.

By the beginning of August the Queen had to face the bitter fact that this time there was to be no miracle for her. What finally convinced her was probably the resumption of her periods. There was no public announcement, but on 3 August, having dismissed all the nursery staff, Mary emerged from seclusion and left Hampton Court with Philip for the small royal hunting lodge at Oatlands. The reason given for her departure was that Hampton Court needed a thorough cleansing. At this signal, the great ladies who had attended her throughout her confinement departed for their estates, satisfied that their services would not be needed. The Lady Elizabeth was permitted to withdraw with her household to an unnamed residence three miles from Oatlands, and was not expected to return to court because, as Michieli reported, 'she is absolutely free'. Her eventual succession was now seen as a near certainty, and the King was making sure that she was treated with the respect due to the heir presumptive.

At Oatlands, Mary – looking surprisingly fit and well – resumed her normal daily routine, granting audiences and putting a brave face on her bitter disappointment and humiliation. Only to her lady-in-waiting and old friend, Frideswide Strelley, 'a good, honourable woman' and the only person who had not tried to raise false hopes, did she confide her anger at the flattery and lies with which those around her had sought to mislead her. Nevertheless, she had not given up hope of bearing a child, and trusted that God would at some stage grant her this favour. She never referred in public to her calamitous confinement, and when de Noailles made a slanted reference to it she cut him dead.

The strongest possibility is that Mary suffered from pseudocyesis, a rare psychological condition commonly known as a phantom pregnancy. This can occur when a woman longs desperately for a child; so desperate is the longing that the pituitary gland releases hormones that cause signs of pregnancy. Menstruation ceases, the breasts become tender, and they may even produce milk. The woman believes she is pregnant, and the resultant trauma, when she finds that this is not the case, can be very damaging to her mental health.

It is no easy task, at a distance of more than four centuries, to apply a medical diagnosis on such scanty evidence. Mary Tudor certainly longed for a child and had all the signs of pregnancy, and she clung to the pathetic belief that she was carrying a baby long after those signs had disappeared. Reliable evidence shows that her girth had declined greatly by the end of May, but despite this, the Queen continued to believe that she was pregnant, and her belief was supported by the doctors and midwives, even though the signs of pregnancy had disappeared.

De Noailles claimed that Mary's pregnancy had been a tumour in the womb, yet there is no other evidence to support this theory, and a tumour large enough to mimic a pregnancy at term would rapidly have proved fatal in those days. It would certainly not have mysteriously disappeared.

On the strength of the evidence, the symptoms presented by Mary – in as far as we can ever know them – strongly suggest that the traditional diagnosis of a phantom pregnancy is the correct one. There were a number of possible contributory factors. Firstly, given her medical history, both physical and psychological, and her almost emaciated appearance, she was quite likely to have believed that she had become pregnant when the first missed periods of an early menopause occurred. This probably resulted psychosomatically in the other symptoms of a phantom pregnancy, like abdominal distension and the emission of breast milk, which developed as a result of the enormous importance of this 'pregnancy' to the Queen.

Nowadays, the question of whether a pregnancy is genuine or not is easily determined by an ultrasound scan, but prior to the invention of such screening a phantom pregnancy was considerably more difficult to diagnose, and would have been even more so in Tudor times, when doctors would not – for reasons of etiquette – have been allowed to examine their sovereign thoroughly, and probably would not have known how to anyway.

A woman who has a history of menstrual irregularity would be more susceptible to believing herself pregnant when she was not. In fact, such women are more likely to produce unusual gynaecological symptoms under pressure than women with regular menstrual cycles.

Abdominal distension in a phantom pregnancy is caused by gas, which can dissipate at any time, and would account for the fact that Mary had regained her waistline by June 1555. Her subsequent depression and the indications that she ate very little during pregnancy may suggest that she suffered from a spell of anorexia, which also produces distension and might well have delayed the resumption of her periods until August, when she had to admit to herself that it had all been a terrible mistake.

That it was a genuine one there can be little doubt. As Michieli wrote, years later, Mary had 'all the other manifest signs of pregnancy . . . There was neither deceit nor malice in the matter, but mere error, not only on the part of the King and Queen, but on that of the councillors and the whole court.'

On 8 August, humiliated and disappointed, Philip escaped to Windsor for a few days' hunting. Many members of his household, even Ruy Gomez, had already left for the Low Countries, and the King was desperate to join them. Yet he was concerned about Mary's state of mind and how she would react when he told her of his plans, and wrote begging Gomez to advise him on 'what line I am to take with the Queen about leaving her. I must say something, but God help me!'

Soon afterwards he and Mary returned to Hampton Court, and there he plucked up the courage to tell her that his duty to the Emperor meant that he must leave England without further delay. Mary became hysterical, crying and pleading with him to stay. If she thought she had tasted the depths of despair at the abandonment of her hopes for a child, she had been mistaken: now she was in worse misery.

Philip tried to calm her by telling her that he would be gone for six weeks at the most, but she knew he was lying to her, and a bitter quarrel ensued, which resulted in the Queen giving orders that his portrait be removed from her bedchamber. She was only pacified when, to underline his good intentions, Philip promised to leave most of his household behind against his early return. Then she believed him, although many saw through this ploy. Protestant agitators accused the King of callously deserting his wife in her hour of need, yet the truth was that the Emperor had never intended Philip to remain permanently in England: Habsburg interests dictated that his presence would be required abroad from time to time, and the King was urgently needed now to help fight the French.

At length, Mary came to understand this, and having recovered her equilibrium wrote to her father-in-law, expressing her gratitude to him for having allowed her husband to remain with her for so long, yet stressing that, as there was 'nothing in the world that I set so much store by as the King's presence', it was her firm hope that his absence would be brief. Charles, however, was ailing and worn out, and his chief desire now was to abdicate in favour of his son. If that came to pass – and it was expected in diplomatic circles that it would not be long before it did – then Philip, as ruler of Spain, the Low Countries and Burgundy, would hardly have time to spare for visiting England, even if he wished to.

Before he left, Philip warned Mary that Elizabeth, as heiress presumptive, must be treated with respect, if not affection. It was obvious to Mary that he had decided to extend his protection to the princess, and despite her jealousy she promised to take his advice, realising that there were sound political reasons for it.

The King had reorganised the Council so that it had become less unwieldy and more efficient. Thanks to his moderating influence, the deep divisions that had caused such disruption in the first year of Mary's reign had been smoothed over, and the Council now functioned as a largely united body. Philip also saw Cardinal Pole, calling upon him 'very privately in person' late one night, to the Cardinal's immense astonishment, to ask him to assume responsibility for the government of the realm and the welfare of the Queen during his absence. The next day, the King told the councillors that they must defer to Pole and seek his opinion and advice on all major issues, whilst dealing with 'private and ordinary matters' themselves. Mary's role was not mentioned, and everyone assumed that from now on she was to be a mere figurehead.

On 23 August, the King and Queen left Hampton Court for Greenwich Palace, travelling through London. This was Mary's first public appearance since her confinement, and the sight of her in an open litter, with Cardinal Pole riding at her side, prompted touching demonstrations of loyalty from many citizens, who had heard rumours that she was dead. Michieli says that people were running 'from one place to another, as to an unexpected sight, as if they were crazy, to ascertain if it was her, and seeing her in better plight than ever, they, by shouts and salutations, then gave yet greater signs of their joy'. Others, however, refused to doff their caps, either for their sovereigns or for the ceremonial cross that was borne before them; Gardiner, riding in the procession, ordered his secretary to make a note of all the houses whose occupants showed such disrespect. Presently the King and Queen came to Tower Wharf, where they took their barge for Greenwich.

The Lady Elizabeth also came by water to Greenwich, but, at the Queen's command, she was conveyed (according to de Noailles) 'in a very badly-fitted boat, with only four ladies and two or three gentlemen, which has caused much discontent among the people'. Mary feared that, if her sister travelled by road, there would be demonstrations of loyalty and affection for her, and that the Queen could not have borne.

The whole court assembled to witness Philip's departure on 29 August. Mary had wanted to accompany him as far as Dartford, or even Dover, but – probably fearing more tearful scenes – he had dissuaded her, promising that he would be back in time to open Parliament on 21 October. Having said goodbye in private, the Queen formally bade her husband farewell at the top of the great staircase at Greenwich, then watched him descend and leave the palace for a ship that would take him as far as Gravesend. Although 'she expressed very well the sorrow becoming to a wife', she was quite obviously 'deeply grieved internally', though she concealed her terrible distress with commendable fortitude, 'constraining herself to avoid, in sight of such a crowd, any demonstration unbecoming her gravity'. Only when the last of Philip's gentlemen had kissed her hand did she hasten to a window in the gallery and, seating herself to watch Philip's departure, burst into tears, thinking herself unobserved. However, many people saw her there. The King had already boarded his ship and gone below decks, but when he at last emerged he too caught sight of his weeping wife at the window and waved his hat, 'demonstrating great affection'. The Queen sat there sobbing until he had sailed out of sight. She then wrote him a letter, which was waiting for him when he arrived at Canterbury, Mary having arranged to have a team of messengers, with horses ready saddled, waiting to deliver her letters post haste to the King, who, during his sojourn at Canterbury received letters almost daily from his bereft wife. Her devotion to him was the talk of the courts of Europe.

16

Bloody Mary

Mary had decided to remain at Greenwich until King Philip's return, but after his departure the court became a gloomy place, and its inhabitants took to wearing garments of dark hues, prompting one ambassador to complain that it seemed like a court in perpetual mourning.

The court reflected the Queen's mood. She was utterly desolate without her husband and spent many hours weeping inconsolably; her only comfort was found in writing him daily letters in French, telling him inconsequential items of news and begging to be reassured of his health and well-being. In these letters she addressed herself to him 'in as humble wise as possible', and signed them, 'Your very loyal and obedient wife, which to be I confess myself justly obliged to be, and in my opinion more than any other woman, having such a husband as Your Highness is.'

To escape from the pain of separation, she threw herself into her royal duties with such a vengeance that Pole feared for her health, and was moved to write to Philip,

> Her Majesty passes the forenoon in prayer, after the manner of Mary, and in the afternoon admirably personates Martha by transacting business. She has so urged her councillors as to keep them incessantly occupied, thinking that she sees Your Majesty present in their persons. She has laboured so hard as to require energy in this matter to be checked rather than stimulated. Her Majesty spends the greater part of the night writing to Your Majesty. I fear that these labours and the strain of Your Majesty's absence might make her fall sick. Your return will cure all.

The Cardinal, despite not being a member of the Council, was constantly at hand to advise and console Mary, and she made few decisions without his sanction. He had been assigned apartments near her own, so that he might 'comfort and keep her company, Her Majesty delighting greatly in the sight and presence of him'.

The Lady Elizabeth had also stayed on at court, although Mary did not delight greatly in her presence, of course, but suffered it for Philip's sake. The King wrote frequently, 'commending the princess to her care' and reminding her of his advice to treat her with kindness and respect, to which the Queen responded by receiving her sister 'with every sort of graciousness and favour', although she could barely conceal her 'evil disposition' towards her. To Michieli, it was obvious that Mary hated her sister. Whenever they met they conversed about 'agreeable subjects' only. By now, it was well known that the princess enjoyed 'a good share in the favour of the King', which provided Mary with further cause for jealousy and gave rise to speculation in private circles as to what Philip's future intentions were towards his sister-in-law.

Elizabeth took care to behave with circumspection, attending mass daily with the Queen. On 4 September, the princess began a three-day fast, for which she would receive an indulgence – a remission for temporal punishment for her sins – from the Pope. Renard was not alone in thinking she was doing it for pragmatic reasons. Cardinal Pole was cold towards her, and most courtiers still deemed it best to shun her company. The princess escaped into her studies, and that autumn welcomed Roger Ascham – now in England again after diplomatic service abroad, and acting as Latin secretary to the Queen – back into her service. He found that her mind was 'so well-stocked' that he learned more from her than she did from him, and confided to his reformist friend, Johann Sturm, that her understanding of Greek and her grasp of the political conflicts found in the pages of Demosthenes would 'strike you with astonishment'. To John Aylmer, he wrote, 'I teach her words, and she me things.'

When Philip arrived in Brussels on 8 September, the Emperor began the process of transferring power to him preparatory to abdicating, and on the 25th made his son Regent of the Netherlands. Once Philip had left England, however, his influence there diminished, despite Mary's insistence on pursuing his chosen policies. On the 26th, Simon Renard retired, at his own request, and returned home with a generous parting gift of gold plate from Mary; he was not replaced, because Philip mistakenly felt that he could rely on his friends on the Council to keep him informed of English affairs and represent his interests.

A few days later, Charles V suggested his nephew Ferdinand as a possible husband for the Lady Elizabeth, 'so that he may succeed to that crown [of England], as his Imperial Majesty [King Philip] has no hope of an heir by his consort'. But the plan was quietly dropped, possibly because Philip vetoed it, having something quite different in mind for Elizabeth.

Late in September England suffered 'the greatest rain and floods that ever was seen in England'. Men and beasts drowned, houses were flooded, and – coming on top of a poor harvest – the damage to farming and trade was immense.

Other storm clouds were on the horizon. On the 30th, the Protestant bishops Latimer and Ridley were condemned to death for heresy and in Oxford Archbishop Cranmer was tried on the same charge. His case was referred to Rome for a decision. Rumours of a rift between King Philip and the Pope caused Cardinal Pole much anxiety, and the Queen was dismayed to receive a stream of requests from members of Philip's household to join him in the Netherlands. De Noailles reported that Spanish grandees were leaving England every day, 'suspecting that their master's absence will not be a short one'. Some took with them the King's personal effects, and the same month his intentions became clear when he settled all his debts to English creditors and dismissed the crew of a ship that had been waiting to bring him back to England.

Worst of all, Philip was replying less and less frequently to his wife's letters, and when he did he wrote no comforting words of love, saying only that he had 'fair hope of soon seeing her', which she found hard to believe. On 13 September, she complained to Michieli, 'very passionately and with tears in her eyes', that she had not received a letter from the King for a week. The ambassador heard, from sources close to Mary, that, when she thought herself unobserved she appeared as one stricken with grief, 'as may be imagined with regard to a person extraordinarily in love'.

Philip had decided to use Mary's desire for his return as a bargaining counter for more power for himself in England, and began responding to her frequent letters with demands that he be crowned. Mary could not authorise this without the sanction of the Council or Parliament, and the councillors were none too keen on the idea, so she was obliged to defer agreement until Parliament met. Philip accused her of not trying hard enough on his behalf, and made it clear that he would not be returning to England until his request was complied with and he was assigned an honourable role in the government of the kingdom. On 15 October, he wrote to the Council expressing his regret that he would not after all be able to return in time to open Parliament, and on the 19th he wrote to Mary, asking her to arrange for the remaining members of his household – apart from his confessor and a few clerks in holy orders – to be sent to join him. Ostensibly they were needed to replace those servants of the Emperor who would soon be returning with Charles to Spain, but Mary was not deceived. However, she did as he asked. Rumours were circulating in England that the Emperor had deferred his abdication because he felt his son was too fond of 'masquing and amusements'. All the evidence shows that Philip was certainly enjoying himself in the Netherlands, for he is described as attending hunts, banquets, and weddings, often disguised with a mask. At court balls he would dance until the early hours of the morning with notable beauties, and then sometimes move on to another glittering function. There were reports that he and his young male companions were often drunk and too tired to attend to business the next day, and that they cared little for the opinions of others. Soon Philip was being seen in the company of a Madame d'Aler, 'who is considered very handsome and of whom he seems much enamoured'. Federico Badoer, the Venetian ambassador to the Imperial court at Brussels, says that news of her husband's infidelity was being kept from Queen Mary because 'she is so easily agitated'. But Mary heard the rumours all the same, and bravely hid her distress.

On 16 October, Latimer and Ridley went to the stake in the ditch outside the town walls of Oxford. Cranmer was compelled to watch, so as to make him recant his Protestant beliefs, which would place a powerful propaganda weapon in the government's hands. 'If he can be brought to repent, the Church will derive no little profit from the salvation of a single soul,' wrote Pole.

As they were chained to the stake, Latimer comforted Ridley with prophetic words that would ring down the centuries: 'Be of good comfort, Master Ridley, and play the man! We shall this day light such a candle, by God's grace, in England, as I trust shall never be put out.' He died quite quickly, but Ridley's sufferings were immense, for he burned for three-quarters of an hour. He was not the only one to endure such agony, for the wet weather resulted in prolonged torture for several heretics sentenced to be burnt that autumn.

By now, the public outcry against the burnings had intensified, and there were often violent demonstrations at executions. In the minds of the English Catholicism was increasingly becoming identified with brutal persecution, and many longed for the Queen to die and be succeeded by her sister Elizabeth, who would surely call a halt to the burnings and send the hated Spaniards – who were blamed as much as Mary for them – back where they belonged. Yet Mary persevered, believing that the hearts of her people had been hardened by heresy and that more examples must be made to bring them to their senses. In the eyes of the government, Protestants were enemies of the state and must be ruthlessly eradicated. It was they who were responsible for the flood of anti-Catholic pamphlets, in which the Queen was referred to as 'the Jezebel of England' and the population incited to rebellion. Alarmed by the strength of public feeling, Renard, before his departure, had advised Mary to have heretics executed in private, but she refused on the grounds that the burnings acted as a deterrent. Gardiner, another advocate of moderation, met with similar stubbornness on her part.

When Mary was preparing to return to London to open Parliament in solitary splendour, Elizabeth was granted leave to go to her house at Hatfield. Mary bade her a cordial farewell and presented her with gifts. On 18 October, the princess rode through Shoreditch on her way to Hertfordshire, and received a rapturous welcome from the citizens, but, fearing to give her sister cause for complaint, she sent some of her gentlemen into the crowds to calm and restrain them. However, she was delighted to hear the bells pealing for joy at her coming, and 'would pause and listen attentively'. For her, this was 'some hope of comfort, appearing as if out of a dark cloud'.

Mary took the precaution of setting spies in Elizabeth's household. 'No one comes or goes, and nothing is spoken or done, without the Queen's knowledge,' wrote Michieli. Elizabeth soon became aware that she was being watched, and wisely made it her business to attend confession and mass regularly. Roger Ascham accompanied her to Hatfield, and he too had to conform, as did the princess's surveyor, William Cecil, who had never held office under Mary but was proving himself a loyal friend to Elizabeth, and corresponded with her regularly. Other friends who returned to the princess's service at this time were Katherine Ashley and Thomas Parry.

During this session of Parliament, Gardiner fell mortally ill and had to be lodged in Whitehall Palace as he could not travel back to Winchester House. The members of Parliament, having heard talk that the Queen would ask to have Philip crowned, and being wary of this being a preliminary to granting him 'the absolute rule of the realm', were in a rebellious, awkward mood, and she did not dare raise the matter, even though coronations did not come under Parliament's jurisdiction. Instead, she wrote and told her husband that she hoped to defer a decision until after Parliament had been dissolved, and then, with the aid of those peers who supported him, grant his request.

So dangerous was the mood of Parliament that when, in November, a proposal to extradite from their safe havens abroad all those Protestants who had left England without permission resulted in an uproar in the Commons, the Queen hurriedly dissolved Parliament and had those who had opposed the measure imprisoned in the Tower.

That autumn the Council uncovered a number of obscure plots both at home and abroad to have Mary – 'who is a Spaniard at heart and loves another realm better than this' – assassinated, and Elizabeth set up in her place. Rumours were rife, and Elizabeth was terrified that she would be suspected of complicity. Fearful of what Mary might do to her, she wrote to her sister on several occasions, protesting her loyalty and passionately emphasising that she had had nothing to do with these conspiracies. It seemed that, no matter how hard she tried, she could not avoid being involved, either directly or indirectly, in sensitive political issues. Renard wrote warning Mary that the princess gave 'the impression that she had changed her religion [and] was too clever to get herself caught'. Mary always believed what she heard from Imperial sources, and against influences like these Elizabeth did not stand a chance. Nor could she prevent zealous but careless plotters from using her name in their ill-conceived conspiracies. 'In trust, I have found treason,' she was to say much later.

Gardiner, Mary's most able statesman, died on 12 November; as a royal servant, claimed Michieli, he was unmatched. Pole expressed the hope that he would be replaced by someone 'less harsh and stern', but in fact Gardiner had often spoken out against the persecution of heretics, and after his death the number of burnings increased.

Philip wanted Paget to succeed Gardiner as Lord Chancellor, but Mary chose Nicholas Heath, who possessed few of his predecessor's qualities; consequently it was Cardinal Pole who became Mary's chief adviser in Gardiner's stead. However, he lacked the late Chancellor's political acumen and drive, as well as his understanding of the English people. Before long, the old divisions within the Council resurfaced, for there was no one strong enough to hold the members in check.

Faced with more troubles, Mary tried other ploys to bring Philip home. She had her cooks prepare his favourite meat pies and shipped them across to Flanders; with them, however, went a letter informing him that, given the mood of the government and people, there was little likelihood of him being crowned in the near future. Philip replied that, while his chief desire was to please her, his honour would only permit him to return to England if he were allowed 'to share the government with her'. He was the absolute ruler of the Low Countries, and to accept a lesser status in England would be 'unbecoming to his dignity'. Mary swallowed her misery and struggled on alone with her mounting problems.

In November, another conspiracy – the Dudley conspiracy – was hatched in response to rumours that Mary meant to have Philip crowned. It was named after one of the prime movers, Sir Henry Dudley, a cousin of the late Duke of Northumberland. The aim of the plotters was 'to send the Queen's Highness over to the King, and to make the Lady Elizabeth queen, and to marry the Earl of Devonshire to the said lady'. Money for the uprising, to the tune of £50,000, was to be appropriated from the Exchequer, wherein Dudley had contacts. The money would be smuggled abroad to France, where the conspirators had a party of staunch supporters among the Protestant exiles, and used to hire ships and mercenaries.

Dudley and his fellow conspirators never succeeded in obtaining the support of the substantial gentry who would have lent their enterprise credibility. Many people, including the Lady Elizabeth herself, felt as strongly as the conspirators did about the state of affairs in England, but most now believed that the Queen would not live long and that the day of deliverance would soon arrive, and they were not prepared to risk their all for an ill-conceived rebellion. However, many minor gentry supported the plotters, as did some royal servants and a few minor scions of the peerage.

Dudley, having once been Captain of the Guard at Boulogne, had many friends in France, and in December visited Paris, where he was well-received by Henry II, who would normally have connived at anything that would discountenance the English government. However, after signing a truce with Philip, Henry's enthusiasm had cooled, and he sent Dudley home with only the vaguest assurances of support. De Noailles, however, enjoyed the confidence of the conspirators from the first, and aided and abetted them by constantly spreading seditious rumours and alarmist gossip.

The Queen was aware of what people were saying and in an atmosphere charged with her fear of threatened conspiracies and whispers of secret intrigues, hardly knew whom she could trust. Her ambassador in Brussels told Philip, 'When she looks round and carefully considers the persons about her, she hardly knows one who has not injured her or who would fail to do so again, were the opportunity to present itself.'

Her tribulations seemed endless. In December the Pope, having excommunicated Cranmer and formally deprived him of the archbish-opric of Canterbury, declared him guilty of heresy, and commanded that he be delivered to the secular arm for punishment. Paul then nominated Cardinal Pole as the new Primate of England 'with many kind words'. He was nevertheless ill-disposed towards Mary because she had married a Habsburg, and that very month he signed a secret treaty with Henry II against Spain and the Empire. Mary's envoys abroad guessed what was going on and alerted her, causing her and Pole the deepest concern. The last thing she wanted now was an open rift with the papacy.

Then, on 20 December, the last of Philip's household left England, most being as relieved to escape as the English were to see the back of them. Even Alfonso de Castro, the King's confessor, had gone, to Mary's profound distress. In Brussels, Badoer wrote, 'The King's confessor has reported a variety of foul language uttered by the English, indicating that ill-will towards His Majesty and the Spanish nation, and has stated that, on seeing him and the rest of the royal attendants depart, they made great rejoicing; and he has said that the Queen's wish to see the King again is very great, nay, boundless.'

Mary wrote to Philip to say that she was sorry 'for her non-adoption of any of the resolutions desired by him in the matter of the coronation', but she was 'encompassed with enemies' and knew it would be impossible to accede to his wish. She had also received a request from him for English support against the French, but protested that to grant it would endanger her throne, for she could not contravene the terms of their marriage treaty. A deadlock had been reached, and Mary now faced the fact that her husband would only return to her if she could deliver everything he was asking for, which she dared not do. She might be his wife, but she was the queen first and foremost.

The court stayed at Greenwich for Christmas, but the Queen's gloom pervaded the festivities. The New Year brought only food shortages and the fear of famine, and Mary took this to be a sign from God that she was not stamping out heresy with sufficient rigour. Until now, heretics arriving at the stake had been given the opportunity of recanting, and if they did so had been reprieved, but Mary now decreed that, as few were benefiting by example, sheriffs should not in future offer condemned heretics this choice. Furthermore, those who showed sympathy towards heretics suffering execution were themselves to be arrested. Eighty people would be burned in 1556.

By January, Dudley and his conspirators had concealed stores of arms at strategic points, suborned the Captain of Yarmouth Castle so as to ensure that a safe harbour was prepared for the coming invasion of exiles and mercenaries, and hidden the money purloined from the Exchequer 'in the water by [London] Bridge'. They had also contacted Courtenay, who was still sulking in Brussels and imagining – perhaps with good reason – that Ruy Gomez had hired an assassin to kill him, and obtained his agreement to marrying the Lady Elizabeth.

Whether Elizabeth knew anything of the plot is open to question. Her past experiences should have taught her that it would have been foolish, not to mention fatal, to involve herself in a treasonable conspiracy, yet in February 1556 the Constable of France wrote to de Noailles, warning him to take care and 'above all restrain Madame Elizabeth from stirring at all in the affair of which you have written to me; for that would be to ruin everything'. This reads as if the princess was eagerly supporting the plotters, but the Constable may have been misled by de Noailles or could have been making assumptions. Foreign intelligence could be notoriously inaccurate, but there is no doubt that people close to Elizabeth knew what was going on.

When Charles V, crippled with arteriosclerosis, finally abdicated on 16 January, Philip and Mary became King and Queen of Spain, the Netherlands, Spain's possessions in Italy and the Spanish colonies in the Americas. The German electors, however, chose Charles's brother, the Archduke Ferdinand, as the new Holy Roman Emperor in preference to Philip. The Emperor therefore ceded Austria, Burgundy, some of his territory in Italy and his German possessions to his brother.

Philip had by now lost all interest in England, save for protecting the interests of the Lady Elizabeth and treating the kingdom as a potential source of manpower for his wars. Mary was still writing to him, begging him to return to her so that their marriage might bear fruit, but he fobbed her off with meaningless promises whilst trying to persuade her that it was her duty to provide him with men for his army. The Council responded to her tentative requests by pointing out that her marriage treaty expressly forbade it, and even if it did not, England was in no financial state to contemplate a war, especially in support of the interests of a foreign power.

On 16 February, Mary reached the age of forty, but she looked older. De Noailles asserted that she had aged ten years during the past months. Her face, although still pink and white, was heavily wrinkled, and she appeared thinner than ever. Michieli was of the opinion that her ugliness was compensated for by her becoming dignity. Worsening eyesight made her peer at people with alarming intensity; her sight had suffered through her regular habit of writing to Philip by candlelight in the small hours of the morning. It was said now that she usually slept for at most four hours at night. De Noailles was told by a lady who slept in the Queen's chamber that Mary's dreams of love and passion were so vivid that she often lost complete control of herself in bed, apparently reliving the delights of Philip's lovemaking. In her waking hours, he reported, she spent her time weeping, sighing and raging against her people, and was in such 'depths of melancholy that nothing seemed to remain for her but to imitate the example of Dido', who had committed suicide. 'But that she will not do,' for suicide was a mortal sin. Instead, she told her ladies, that 'As she had done all possible to induce her husband to return, and as she found he would not, she meant to withdraw utterly from men and live quietly, as she had done the chief part of her life before she married.' In future, religion would be her chief consolation.

No one could have doubted the depths of her faith. She was punctilious in her religious observances and was attending mass nine times a day. Her obvious emotion at public church ceremonies was enough to inspire observers with awe, as when she kissed the sores of forty scrofula victims with ecstatic devotion.

Unpopular with her subjects she might have been, but those who knew her and worked for her would hear no ill spoken of her. To them, she was kindness personified, unselfish and sensible of their feelings. This consideration extended itself to her refusal to go on an annual progress in case it placed too great a financial burden on her subjects. Naturally, there may also have been an underlying fear that her reception from those subjects would not be a warm one. Religious persecution on so great a scale had now turned most of them against her.

Cranmer was formally degraded by Bishops Bonner and Thirlby on 14 February. The former archbishop wept at the loss of his primacy and when, ten days later, the Queen signed his death warrant, he capitulated and issued a series of abject recantations, having been led by the authorities to believe that his life would be spared. But the Queen 'would nothing relent', remembering not only his heretical policies and prayer books, but also the fact that this was the man who had declared her parents' marriage null and void and herself a bastard. The Council might deliberate over whether political capital might be made of making Cranmer's recantations public – in the end they were suppressed – but the former archbishop's fate was certain.

★

Sir Henry Dudley was back in France that March, raising an invasion force that would land on the Isle of Wight and march on London. Courtenay was keeping a low profile, but a suspicious King Philip had arranged for a careful watch to be kept on him in Brussels. The conspiracy was now far-flung and unwieldy, depending on too many people, and early in March one of them, Thomas White, an Exchequer official, panicked, and told Cardinal Pole all he knew. The subsequent arrests of twenty suspects were followed by a series of interrogations, some under torture, in which most of the accused confessed all the details of the plot. What did set alarm bells ringing was the number of conspirators who had connections with the Lady Elizabeth. John Bray was her neighbour at Hatfield, Sir Peter Killigrew was her friend, a number of others were her servants, and one, Sir John Perrot, claimed to be one of Henry VIII's bastards and her half-brother. 'Never is a conspiracy discovered in which either justly or unjustly she or some of her servants are not mentioned,' commented Michieli.

Several of the accused referred to de Noailles's involvement, and the Council considered deporting him 'as a plotter and contriver against the State and the person of the sovereign', but they were pre-empted by Henry II, who swiftly recalled him. Henry Dudley escaped arrest also by virtue of being in France. The ramifications of the plot seemed endless, and extended even to some of the councillors themselves. Mary was 'deeply troubled'; it seemed to the Queen as if the whole fabric of her government was crumbling, and that her authority carried little weight, and she complained in her letters to Philip that she needed his presence more than ever. She saw treason everywhere, distrusting not only her councillors but also her personal attendants, and as March turned into April she took steps to ensure that the continuing interrogations were handled only by men such as Rochester, Jerningham and Englefield, who had served her for many years and proved themselves trustworthy.

In the middle of March Mary instructed Sir John Mason to 'pray the King her consort to be pleased to say frankly in how many days he purposed returning', and to ask whether she should continue to maintain the fleet that she had kept waiting in readiness to bring him home. Mason was also instructed to urge the King 'to comfort the Queen by his presence' and remind him 'that there was no reason yet to despair of his having heirs'. Mason in fact urged haste, seeing that the Queen was now forty and would soon be past the age for bearing children.

Ruy Gomez told Mason that the King could not leave just now as he was about to tour the Flemish provinces, and made it clear that few

Spaniards had any desire to return to England after the bad treatment they had received there. The King shared their reluctance, and felt that his wife had shown him 'little conjugal affection' of late. Philip, who was preoccupied with arranging a splendid tournament on the theme 'that the women of Brussels are handsomer than those of Mechelin', told Mason to inform his mistress that it was necessary for him to remain in Brussels for the present because the King and Queen of Bohemia were expected for a state visit. When Mary heard this, she was 'beyond measure exasperated', but nevertheless replied that the royal guests would be most welcome in England. Philip ignored this, and was heard to say that England was now nothing more to him than an expensive nuisance. Nor were his courtiers any more encouraging, for they would say to Mason, 'Why should His Majesty gratify a wife who had done nothing to gratify him?'

Undeterred, Mary dispatched Paget to Brussels with letters and rings for Philip and his father. Paget, now Lord Privy Seal, was 'dear to the King' and 'very subtle', and his words might carry some weight. Philip expressed himself pleased to see Paget, and politely enquired after the Queen's health. Reporting back to Mary, Paget managed to imply that this was more than a formal courtesy. Yet soon he did have good news for her. Charles V had been present at the interview and had asked Paget how the Queen was.

'Her Majesty does indifferently well, as one might do that wanted of that you loved above all earthly things,' replied Paget pointedly. Knowing that his father would not be pleased if 'the Queen's angry remonstrances were converted into hatred', Philip hastened to assure Paget that he hoped to return to England in a few weeks' time.

'If I have not returned by the end of June,' he said, 'Her Majesty may no longer consider me a trustworthy king.'

On 20 March, Cranmer was told to prepare for death at the stake, and spent his last night writing another recantation. In the morning he was taken under guard to St Mary's Church in Oxford to read it out in public. But overnight, or on the way, realising that he must die anyway, he underwent a complete change of heart, and instead of a humiliating renunciation of all his former beliefs, the listening throng heard only a firm reaffirmation of his Protestant faith. As he finished, he promised that the hand that had signed his recantation should be the first part of him to burn, as it had so offended God. He was hustled away to his death, but already the Protestants were proclaiming him as a martyr and making political capital out of his declaration of faith, whilst his courage in the face of a terrible ordeal became a useful propaganda tool in the hands of those who were sickened by the burnings.

On the day after Cranmer's death Pole was consecrated Archbishop of Canterbury at Greenwich, and thereafter he was the chief ecclesiastical advocate of the persecution of heretics.

Early in April, having heard of Charles V's intervention with Philip on her behalf, Mary wrote to him,

> I thank you humbly for remembering me where the return of the King my husband is concerned. I implore Your Majesty most humbly, for the love of God, to do all that is possible to permit it. I cannot but deeply feel the solitude in which the King's absence leaves me. As Your Majesty well knows, he is the chief joy and comfort I have in the world. I beg Your Majesty to forgive my boldness and to remember the unspeakable sadness which I experience because of the absence of the King, which emboldens me thus to write to you, which have always shown me a more than paternal affection.

In France it was being said that the royal marriage was on the verge of breaking down, and Henry II prophesied, 'I am of opinion that ere long the King of England will endeavour to dissolve his marriage with the Queen.' It was reported in Venice that Mary had lost her temper and run amuck in her apartments, slashing at Philip's portraits, and although this may have been mere scandal-mongering, in England Susan Clarencieux was heard to say that she wished the marriage had never taken place.

That April, Michieli learned that the Queen had 'earnestly canvassed' the idea of sending Elizabeth to Spain, for she had 'conceived that by removing her bodily from hence, there will be riddance of all the causes for scandal and disturbances'. One suggestion was that the princess might make a suitable bride for Philip's son, the ten-year-old Don Carlos, but Elizabeth had heard that he was mad and declared that she would not marry him. As before, the plan to send her out of the kingdom was abandoned for fear of provoking insurrections on her behalf.

So far, none of those accused of involvement in the Dudley conspiracy had mentioned Elizabeth, yet the Council saw fit to have Somerset House searched in her absence for incriminating evidence. The searchers discovered 'seditious' books and pamphlets and a small cabinet containing 'several papers, portraits, paintings and other defamatory libels, to the great dishonour and vituperation of the Queen and her husband, together with all the bishops and ecclesiastics of her kingdom'. These items appeared to be the property of Mrs Ashley, who was arrested at Hatfield in May and taken to the Tower for questioning. At the same time, Battista Castiglione, Elizabeth's Italian master, who had been imprisoned in 1554 on suspicion of having distributed subversive literature, was also arrested, along with Francis Verney, another of the princess's servants.

Under questioning, Mrs Ashley denied all knowledge of Sir Henry Dudley's conspiracy, and stoutly proclaimed her loyalty to the Queen, adding that the Lady Elizabeth's 'love and truth is such to Her Highness that if she might prove me corrupt but in thought to Her Highness, I am sure she would never see me again'. For all her protestations, she was not believed, and was consigned to the Fleet Prison for the next three months. Castiglione likewise denied any involvement in treasonable activities. He had visited London on the princess's behalf, he said, but only to buy lute strings. He was released, but Verney could not extricate himself from the suspicion of treason, and in June was tried and sentenced to death although he was later pardoned.

At the beginning of June, the Queen sent Lord Hastings and Sir Francis Englefield to Hatfield on the pretext of apologising to Elizabeth for any disruption caused by the removal of her servants, and explaining that their arrests had been necessary because their behaviour had exposed her 'to the manifest risk of infamy and ruin'. The Queen's emissaries presented the princess with a diamond ring from her sister, and informed her that Mary knew her to be 'so wise and prudent that she would not wish to undertake anything to the prejudice of Her Majesty'. Nevertheless, Mary would have liked to have Elizabeth questioned, and even consigned to the Tower, but dared not move against her without Philip's approval, which she had sent for by special courier at the beginning of the month. 'Nothing is done without her having the King's opinion about it and hearing his will,' observed Michieli.

But instead of arresting her sister, Mary was instructed to send a kind message, with 'loving and gracious expressions to show her that she is neither neglected nor hated, but loved and esteemed by Her Majesty'. This, reported Michieli, 'has been very well taken by the whole kingdom'. Mary also invited Elizabeth to stay at court, but Elizabeth politely declined. The Queen then sent 'a widow gentlewoman' to Hatfield to replace Ashley, along with Sir Thomas Pope, 'a rich and grave gentleman, of good name, both for conduct and religion'. Pope was to act as Elizabeth's 'governor' and keep an eye on her; his presence in her household would not only set the Queen's mind at rest but prevent the princess's enemies from accusing her of subversive activities. Elizabeth realised this, and accepted his appointment without protest, even thanking Mary for her kindness.

Pope was a learned man with many interests, a lawyer who had once been a friend of Sir Thomas More; three months earlier he had founded Trinity College, Oxford. Happily married with children, and of a generous disposition, he was far more cultivated and worldly than Bedingfield had been, and Elizabeth soon warmed to him, sensing a kindred spirit. During Pope's four months at Hatfield, they would spend many happy hours discussing Sir Thomas's plans for his new college, or conversing on learned topics with Roger Ascham, and towards the end of his stay, Pope arranged – and paid for – lavish productions of masques and plays which were performed for the princess's pleasure.

Meanwhile, in London ten men were executed – against a background of public protests – for their parts in the Dudley conspiracy.

Late in June, Mary received word that Philip was ill, and sent to ask almost daily how he was progressing. Because of his illness he could not join her as planned, yet even when he had recovered he did not come, and on 15 July his wife wrote to Charles V, in an unusually caustic tone and with a shaking hand, 'My Lord, now that June is over and July drawing to an end, it would be pleasanter for me to be able to thank Your Majesty for sending me back the King my lord and good husband. However, as Your Majesty has been pleased to break your promise in this connection, I must perforce be satisfied, although to my unspeakable regret.'

During that summer Mary's state of mind gave those who knew her grave cause for concern. The anxieties and frustrations of the past months had taken their toll and there were fears that her health might break under the strain. She was deeply depressed and rarely appeared in public; the new French ambassador, François de Noailles, Bishop of Acqs and brother to the disgraced Antoine de Noailles, reported that she could not sleep, had dark circles under her eyes, and spent her waking hours in 'tears, regrets, and writing letters to bring back her husband'. Terrified of new conspiracies or assassination attempts, she had filled the palace with hosts of armed guards, consulted only a handful of councillors whose integrity she had no cause to doubt, and would only permit five trusted ladies to enter her chamber and attend to her personal needs. The ambassador reported that 'She rages against her subjects, for she is utterly confounded by the faithlessness of those whom she most trusted, seeing that the greater part are kith and kin or favoured servants of the greatest men in the kingdom.' François de Noailles was no less malicious than his brother, and took care to make Mary aware of foreign reports that Philip had applied to the Pope for an annulment of their marriage. This was not true, but fear that it might be only added to the Queen's miseries.

The support of Cardinal Pole was her only comfort, and in July she stayed with him at Canterbury, 'intent on enduring her troubles as patiently as she can'. But she felt little better for it, and on returning to London shocked her councillors by ordering the removal of a portrait of Philip from the council chamber. There were reports that she had actually kicked it out of the room. And to Lady Bray, she observed with feeling, 'God sent oft times to good women evil husbands!'

Michieli had been away from the court for some weeks, and when he returned he was concerned to see how ill the Queen looked. 'For many months now the Queen has passed from one sorrow to another,' he wrote. 'Her face has lost flesh greatly since I was last with her.'

That July, yet another conspiracy was revealed when a young Suffolk schoolmaster named Cleobury appeared in Essex impersonating Courtenay and, after journeying through East Anglia inciting rebellion, had the priest at Yaxley in Huntingdonshire proclaim from his churchyard that Queen Mary was dead and that 'the Lady Elizabeth [was] queen and her beloved bedfellow, Lord Edmund Courtenay, king.' This was hardly a serious affair – Cleobury could not even get Courtenay's name right – and it had attracted few supporters. These were quickly rounded up and arrested by local people 'without any commandment'; what the government feared was that Courtenay himself had incited them to rebel, although it soon became clear that they were acting independently. The Council instructed Sir Thomas Pope to acquaint Elizabeth with 'the whole circumstance' so that 'it might appear how far these men had abused Her Grace's name'. Even Mary did not suspect her of colluding with them this time, but Elizabeth was horrified, and on 2 August wrote to her sister:

> When I revolve in mind, most noble Queen, the reverent fear of Romans to their Senate, I can but muse for my part, and blush for theirs, to see the rebellious hearts and devilish intents of Christians toward their anointed king. It had been my part, above the rest, to bewail such things, though my name had not been in them, yet much it vexed me that the devil oweth me such a hate as to put me

in any part of his mischievous instigations. I would that there were as good surgeons for making anatomies of hearts, that might show my thoughts to Your Majesty, as there are expert physicians of the bodies. For then, I doubt not but know well, that whatsoever other should suggest by malice, yet Your Majesty should be sure by knowledge; so that the more such misty clouds obfuscate the clear light of my truth, the more my tried thoughts should glister to the dimming of their hidden malice.

Cleobury proved to be a Protestant with a criminal record for burglary and confessed that, encouraged by Henry II, a group of English exiles in France had hatched the plot and used him as a figurehead. He was hanged, whilst twelve of his accomplices were imprisoned in the Tower.

Neither Mary nor Elizabeth were well that August. Elizabeth suffered an attack of jaundice accompanied by the intermittent breathlessness that, according to de Noailles, had plagued her 'ever since the time when her sister began to maltreat her'. Mary could not tolerate the heat, and remained secluded in her apartments for most of the time, not even attending Council meetings.

Philip had sent a message to tell Mary to expect him in August, but he did not arrive; it was now a year since she had seen him. Instead of hastening to console his distraught wife, he had left Brussels for fear of the plague and was busy frequenting 'houses of pleasure' in the surrounding countryside.

Courtenay had also left Brussels and travelled to Venice, where he associated with only a select circle of friends. He knew he was watched and did his best to maintain a low profile. Late in August he took a gondola ride to the Isle of Lio in the lagoon, but was stranded there by a storm and had to wait, soaked to the skin and suffering from exposure, until a ship rescued him. Three days later he was reported to be suffering from malaria, although he insisted on travelling to Padua, twenty-five miles away, where there were excellent doctors in the medical faculty of the university. As he left, he fell down the stairs of his lodgings, and consequently found the journey he was forced to make by wagon very uncomfortable indeed.

Mary's ambassador to Venice, Peter Vannes, was in Padua when Courtenay arrived and went at once to greet him, but found him very ill with a high temperature. Vannes summoned two notable doctors, but the patient's condition worsened over the next fortnight. The last offshoot of the Plantagenet family tree died on 18 September 1556.

Vannes immediately suspected poison. Courtenay's death stood to benefit both England and Spain, and there had been several rumours that Spanish assassins had been hired to kill him. The ambassador made every one of the Earl's servants and physicians sign sworn statements that, to the best of their knowledge and belief, he had died from natural causes. It fell also to Vannes to arrange the funeral on his limited resources, and the body was placed in a plain wooden coffin, which was stored in the cloister of St Anthony's Church in Padua. Four years later it was still there, 'having neither epitaph nor any other thing to preserve it from oblivion', but by 1560 a marble monument had been built to house it in the Church of the Eremitani. This church was bombed in 1945 by the Allies, destroying the tomb.

Courtenay's death finally removed the Plantagenet threat to the Tudor throne that had hung over the dynasty since 1485, and when Queen Mary learned of it, she said, 'God has once again shown His justice.' Elizabeth was also relieved, and Philip did not trouble to hide his satisfaction. 'There was more in it of human help than divine,' concluded the French ambassador. Whether he had good cause to say so remains a matter of debate to this day.

Relations between Philip II and the papacy had steadily deteriorated during the past months. The Pope had made strenuous efforts to break the truce between France and Spain, and had adopted a provocative attitude towards Habsburg interests in Italy. Being a dutiful son of the Church, Philip had done his best to avoid an open confrontation, but when Paul made it clear he was going to join Henry II in his war against the Habsburgs – hoping that the French would help him drive them out of Italy – Philip ordered the Duke of Alba to invade the papal states, sack their towns, and hang their garrisons.

England had no part in this quarrel, but Mary was naturally very distressed by it because she felt torn by a conflict of loyalties, not wishing to be on bad terms with either her husband or the Holy See. The Pope took no action against her, but gradually England's relations with Rome became more and more strained, and finally broke down. Cardinal Pole was also much grieved by the rift between Philip and the Pope, and wrote begging the King not to make war on the Vicar of Christ. Since Philip ignored this, on 14 September the Cardinal wrote to the Pope, begging for guidance as to how he should conduct himself during the present crisis. Ominously, there was no reply.

Pole felt it would help if he could discuss the matter with Philip in person, and told Michieli that he was 'beginning to be incredulous' at the King's prolonged absence. He was also very concerned about the

Queen's state of mind. That month, whilst staying in the apartments that Pole kept in readiness for her at his palace at Croydon, Mary had one day found them strewn with broadsheets on which was printed the worst kind of subversive propaganda: she was depicted as an ugly old crone suckling Spaniards at her sagging breasts, with the legend '*Maria Ruina Angliae*' encircling the picture. She was shocked to see herself portrayed so cruelly, and was driven to write once again to Charles V.

> I wish to beg Your Majesty's pardon for my boldness in writing to you at this time, but I implore you to consider the miserable plight into which this country has now fallen. Unless the King comes to remedy matters, not I only but also wiser persons than I fear that great danger will ensue. I am not moved by my personal desire for his presence – although I do unspeakably long to have him here – but by the good of my kingdom.

It is unlikely that Charles ever received her letter. He departed from the Netherlands on 17 September, and travelled to Spain where he would spend his remaining days in comfortable retirement at the monastery of Yuste. His withdrawal from the political scene meant that Mary was deprived of his friendship, protection and advice, which had been freely extended to her for as long as she could remember.

On 19 October, however, Mary was overjoyed to learn that Philip had ordered some members of his household to return to England. To her, this meant only one thing, that he himself would soon be with her. However, that was not his immediate intention. He had decided to divert Henry II's attention away from Italy by invading northern France, and badly needed English support, but he had come to the belated realisation that he had neglected his interests in England for too long. A public relations exercise was called for, and the first objective was to recover the goodwill of the Queen. When the first Spanish grandees began arriving in London, Mary appeared much 'pacified' and was reported to be 'enduring this delay much better than she did'. Yet her health was still poor, and when Cardinal Pole led the court in a great celebration of the Feast of the Reconciliation on 30 November, she was unable to attend.

In October, Mary decided that there was no longer any reason to keep Elizabeth under close surveillance, and informed Sir Thomas Pope that his services were no longer required at Hatfield. At the same time, Katherine Ashley, who had been released from the Fleet Prison, was allowed to rejoin Elizabeth's household.

On 10 October, Badoer reported that, with Courtenay out of the way, Philip was again considering marrying Elizabeth to the Duke of Savoy. Reports of the Queen's ill health had led many people to assume that the princess's accession was a near-certainty, and – since it was unthinkable that she might remain unmarried – Philip was determined to marry her off beforehand to a Catholic prince who would be loyal to Habsburg interests. As the wife of Savoy, whose inheritance had been seized by the French, she would be unlikely to enter into friendly alliances with Henry II or attempt to restore the Protestant religion in England.

No one consulted Elizabeth on what she felt about the marriage, but she was naturally averse to it. She had little inclination to marry at all, and every intention of dismantling Mary's religious settlement as soon as she became queen.

Late in November, Mary, who was initially in favour of the match, summoned Elizabeth to London to discuss it. The princess arrived in some state, 'riding through Smithfield and Old Bailey, and through Fleet Street unto Somerset Place, with a great company of velvet coats and chains, Her Grace's gentlemen, and after a great company of [200] men', all wearing her livery of red coats slashed with black velvet. Michieli noted 'the infinite pleasure of the entire populace' at the sight of her. There was no official welcome, although Mary received her 'very graciously and familiarly', but when she spoke of her sister marrying Savoy, Elizabeth flatly refused to even consider it, and burst into tears. 'The afflictions suffered by me are such that they have ridded me of any desire for a husband,' she declared. 'I would rather die!'

Mary was moved to see her sister so distressed, but she was determined that Elizabeth should accept Savoy, and the interview ended in deadlock. The princess returned to Somerset House, where 'many lords and gentlemen of the court' came during the next few days to pay their respects.

François de Noailles had hoped to be among their number, but heard that Elizabeth was so closely surrounded by courtiers and attendants that there would be no chance of a private conversation. What he wanted to ask her was whether she would give her support to a rebellion he hoped to incite on her behalf the following summer with Henry II's blessing. The matter would have to wait, he told his master, 'until God should give me a better opportunity'.

He was surprised, therefore, when the Countess of Sussex, one of Elizabeth's close friends, visited him secretly in disguise on two successive nights, and told him that the princess's household were begging her to escape from an impossible situation by fleeing abroad.

Would it be possible for him to arrange for Elizabeth to cross to France, to seek asylum with King Henry?

De Noailles was dismayed, and advised that the princess should not consider taking such a desperate step, but should remember what was at stake. If she hoped to be queen, she must on no account leave England. The Countess, nevertheless, went to France herself, presumably to make arrangements for Elizabeth's flight, but her absence was noticed and she was questioned by the Council when she returned. Fortunately, she gave the impression that her trip had been entirely for private purposes. Elizabeth, meanwhile, took the ambassador's advice and abandoned her plans for escape.

On 3 December, after seeing Elizabeth again and finding her as adamant as ever that she would not marry Savoy, Mary sent her home, having threatened once more to have her disinherited by Parliament, or even sent to the Tower or put to death. Both, however, knew that neither Parliament nor King Philip would sanction any of these punishments. Mary herself would have preferred disinheriting her sister to contemplating her as her successor, and would spend a great deal of time that autumn searching for precedents for it, but Philip insisted that she persuade Elizabeth to marry Savoy. Mary's own enthusiasm for the match had, however, evaporated, for she knew that, once Elizabeth was married to the Duke, there would be no question of disinheriting her; she would have formally to acknowledge her as her heir, which she had until now avoided doing, having always hoped to find a more suitable alternative.

Back at Hatfield, Elizabeth settled down to as pleasant a life as she could in a house that was subject to unseen surveillance.

That December, Pole learned from his contacts in Rome that the Pope was refusing to deal with any matters concerning England because he believed the Queen was as guilty of offences against the Holy See as her husband, and that both deserved to be excommunicated. Mary was incensed at this and privately made up her mind that England should, after all, join Philip in what she was coming to perceive as a just war. Before long, secret agents were moving between the King and Queen on a daily basis, and by Christmas most of Philip's household had returned to England to await their master's coming. On 22 December the court moved from St James's Palace to Greenwich for the festivities; at Philip's request, Elizabeth was among the guests, and would remain at court until his return, but Mary now had no room in her heart for jealousy. Instead, she distributed generous gifts of plate to her sister, Pole, Anne of Cleves, and nearly 300 courtiers and servants, and was reported to be joyfully anticipating the reunion with her husband that was now imminent.

There was, however, little other cause for rejoicing. Michieli observed that the kingdom was seething with discontent and that, much to her distress, 'The Queen witnesseth the daily decline of the affection evinced towards her personally at the commencement of her reign.' The unemployment generated by the enclosure of common land, and three bad harvests in succession, had done little to improve matters, and many of Mary's subjects were now dying of malnutrition and starvation.

The country's finances were in a precarious state, and the fires of persecution were still burning. In London alone in 1557, sixty-four people would be sent to the stake. It was now obvious even to the Queen that her methods of suppressing heresy were not working, though she refused to admit it, and insisted that her officers act more rigorously in punishing offenders. Not only the common people but also the gentry were now blaming the Queen for all the ills that had befallen the kingdom, seeing God's judgement on her sins in famine and economic decline, and many were looking to Elizabeth as their deliverer. When a register of martyrs was printed in London in 1557, each list ended with the rhyme:

> When these with violence were burned to death,
> We wished for our Elizabeth.

On 11 January, Henry II broke the truce and mounted an offensive on Douai. Mary, hearing of this, summoned her Council and demanded that England go to war with Philip against the French. The councillors were horrified, and gave several reasons why it was not possible. Firstly, the country could not afford a war; secondly, the quarrel did not involve England, therefore why should the kingdom impoverish itself to support the interests of a foreign power? Lastly, and most important of all, England was not bound by treaty to support Philip in his wars. Pole supported the Council, but against Philip's influence both he and they were helpless. Declaring war was Mary's prerogative, and she had already made up her mind to it. De Noailles commented, 'She is on the eve of bankrupting either her own mind or her kingdom.'

On 2 February 1557, Philip sent Ruy Gomez to London to tell Mary that his arrival in England would be dependent on her promising to declare war on the French. Aware that she was being offered an ultimatum, Mary promised to do all she could to persuade the Council that they must agree to this. As for herself, she gave Philip her solemn promise that she would do as he asked, and sent him £100,000 in token of her good faith. On 21 February, she wrote a final letter to her husband, begging him 'not to be afraid to come'.

At last there came the news she had waited eighteen long months for. Philip had left Brussels on 8 March. He was on his way.

17

'Little Children Like Angels'

On 18 March 1557, King Philip sailed from Calais to Dover, whence he travelled to Gravesend, there boarding the royal barge for Greenwich. There, at five o'clock in the afternoon of 20 March, he landed to the sound of a thirty-two-gun salute, and received a rapturous welcome from his wife in the presence of all the courtiers, many of whom were crying, 'God save the King and Queen!' It was immediately clear, from the small size of his personal retinue, that he did not intend to stay long and had not come just to be reunited with Mary. The twofold purpose of his visit was, indeed, entirely political: to persuade the English to declare war on France, and to conclude the marriage of the Lady Elizabeth with the Duke of Savoy. It did not concern him that few people in England, not least the councillors, wanted to go to war on behalf of the hated Spaniards, nor that Mary herself by now was averse to the Savoy marriage.

The next day, on the Queen's orders, all the bells in London pealed out in celebration of the King's return, and in every church *Te Deums* were sung. Later that day, however, Machyn recorded how the citizens had been alarmed by the arrival of three ships full of Spaniards in the Pool of London. Meanwhile, at Richmond, Mary had organised a splendid festival in Philip's honour, to which Elizabeth came, arriving in a state barge bedecked with flowers.

On 23 March, the King and Queen rode in state to Whitehall, with Elizabeth at their side. Her presence evoked a resounding response from the Londoners, which neither Philip nor Mary could ignore. The King was hoping that the people would believe the princess supported England entering the war, but in this he was mistaken.

A day or so later, Philip's bastard half-sister, Margaret, Duchess of Parma, and his cousin, Christina of Denmark, Duchess of Lorraine, arrived in England, and were met by the King at Whitehall Stairs and escorted by him up to the presence chamber to be presented to the Queen. Back in 1539, the beautiful and spirited Duchess of Lorraine had, at the age of sixteen, been suggested as a bride for Henry VIII, but had refused to consider the idea, declaring that, if she had two heads, one would be at His Grace's disposal.

The Venetian ambassador in Paris heard that 'The cause of their ladyships' going [to England] was that, on their return, they might bring with them Madame Elizabeth to give her for wife to the Duke of Savoy.' De Noailles, whose master had a vested interest in preventing such a marriage, sent the Countess of Northampton secretly to warn Elizabeth, who had returned to Hatfield, what was afoot, and to urge her not even to consider taking a husband who was 'so poor and stripped of all his wealth'.

'I would rather die than submit,' Elizabeth told the Countess, who reported her words to de Noailles. The Queen, however, proved an unexpected ally, refusing to invite her sister to court or to allow the Habsburg duchesses to visit her at Hatfield.

In fact, Mary was not at all at ease about the presence of the Duchess of Lorraine at her court. What the King's attendants referred to as her 'warmed-up honeymoon' with Philip was not progressing as she had hoped. Although he treated her with unfailing courtesy, he was preoccupied, not only with political matters, but also – his wife suspected – with the fair Christina. Rumours about an affair between them had preceded Philip's return, and the Queen, whilst affecting to be unaware of them, had allocated the Duchess apartments on the ground floor of the palace, far from the royal apartments. Michieli reported that, during Philip's absence, Mary's chief fear had been that her husband might become involved with another woman. She knew he had not been faithful to her, but was not so concerned about these passing fancies. What she did dread was him falling in love with someone else, which would make her 'truly miserable'. Now she felt she had cause to speculate over what Philip felt for another woman, and she also had to suffer the humiliation of seeing him dancing with the Duchess at court balls, and entertaining her over the Easter holiday; nor could Mary complain, for these were perceived as the normal courtesies due to visiting royalty.

Philip must have noticed how much Mary had aged during his absence. Michieli, who left England that spring, described her at this time as having 'some wrinkles caused more by anxieties than by age, which make her appear some years older', and spoke of her 'grave aspect'. However, he felt she was 'never to be loathed for ugliness, even at her present age'. In character, he wrote, 'She is like other women, being sudden and passionate – rather more so than would become a queen.' Yet, 'unlike other timid and spiritless women', Mary had shown herself to be 'brave and valiant', with never a sign of cowardice. Above all, she had a 'wonderful grandeur and dignity'.

What most concerned Michieli was her recent predisposition to 'a very deep melancholy, much greater than that to which she is constitutionally liable from menstruous retention, so that the remedy of tears and weeping, to which from childhood she has been accustomed, is not sufficient; she now requires to be blooded, either from the foot or elsewhere, which keeps her always pale and emaciated'.

Generally, she was not well. She still slept badly and had recurring problems with toothache. Michieli believed that her unfruitful confinement was the most devastating thing that had happened to her. Not only was her barrenness a constant sorrow to her as a woman, but in a queen it was also a reproach, an indication that God had withdrawn His favour from her. 'No one believes in the possibility of her having progeny, so that day by day she sees her authority and the respect induced by it diminish.'

Mary's failure to produce an heir meant that she was constantly worrying about who was to succeed her. It was vital to the stability of the country that this question be resolved, yet the Queen could not bring herself to acknowledge Elizabeth as her successor. It may fairly be said that by now Mary hated her sister, and although she tried to hide it, 'it cannot be denied that she displays in many ways the scorn and ill-will she bears her'. It was anathema to the Queen 'to see the illegitimate child of a criminal who was punished as a public strumpet on the point of inheriting the throne with better fortune than herself, whose descent is rightful, legitimate and legal'.

What made matters worse was that Elizabeth, knowing herself to be in a strong position thanks to the protection of King Philip and the love of the people, seemed insensible to her inferior status. 'She is proud and haughty,' wrote Michieli, 'and although she knows that she was born of such a mother, she does not consider herself of inferior degree to the Queen, whom she equals in self-esteem. She prides herself on her father and glories in him, everybody saying that she also resembles him more than the Queen does.' To Mary, this was an intolerable insult, seeing that she herself firmly believed – and had for years done her best to convince everyone else – that Elizabeth was the daughter of Mark Smeaton, Anne Boleyn's lute player.

Yet worse than her fear of Elizabeth succeeding her, claimed Michieli, was the Queen's dread of a further separation from her husband. What she felt for him was such 'violent love' that 'she may be said never to pass a day without anxiety' on this account. 'Separation, which to any person who loves another heartily would be irksome and grievous, is assuredly so to a woman naturally tender.'

Philip had not been in England a week before he began to put pressure on Mary to demand that her Council agree to declare war on France. He reminded her that she had promised him she would do this, and threatened that if she broke that promise he would leave England forthwith and never come back. On 1 April, the Queen summoned her Council and, in Philip's presence, set out the arguments in favour of war. They listened gravely but asked for time in which to consider the matter. Two days later they told her that England could not and should not become involved in a foreign conflict. Cardinal Pole had not taken part in these discussions. He had remained at Canterbury, thus depriving the peace party at court of a powerful advocate.

The conflict with the Pope turned out to be unexpectedly to Philip's advantage, in one respect at least. On 10 April, the pontiff recalled all his legates, including Pole, from the King's realms and dominions. He also issued a brief depriving Pole of his status as legate. Then he passed sentence of excommunication on Philip II, casting him out from the Church and condemning him to eternal damnation. England would now be forced to take sides.

Sometime during April Mary bowed to Philip's demands and summoned her sister to court. The King had every intention of forcing Elizabeth into marriage with Savoy himself, and made it clear that he meant to take her back to Brussels with him as a bride, but Elizabeth, fortified by the knowledge that the Council would never allow him to do so, flatly refused to agree. Philip then tried bargaining with her, offering to ensure that her right to succeed was acknowledged in return for her agreeing to marry, but this too failed to move her. Nor did the reassurance that Savoy would be happy to come and live in England with her, having no lands of his own.

Mary was equally resistant to the match, refusing to be won over by her husband's arguments, which led him to accuse her of failing in her duty of obedience to him. At one point Mary capitulated, but changed her mind two days later, explaining that she could not make Elizabeth marry against her will or the will of the people, but Philip would not listen and ordered her to compel her sister to do as she was bid. Mary tried, but found the princess as adamant as before.

'What I shall do hereafter I know not,' she told the Queen, 'but, I assure you upon my truth and fidelity, I am not at this time otherwise minded than I have declared unto you; no, though I were offered the greatest prince in all Europe.' Torn between relief and fear of what Philip might do, Mary dismissed Elizabeth from court. Later that month she visited her at Hatfield, where she was entertained by a bear baiting, a Latin play performed by the boys of St Paul's School, and a recital on the virginals by her accomplished sister. The Savoy marriage was not mentioned.

When Mary returned, she and Philip presided over a chapter of the Order of the Garter at Whitehall and then visited Hampton Court for a few days' hunting, which were marred by tragedy: one of the courtiers was thrown from his horse and dashed his brains out against the privy garden wall. After that it was deemed best to return to London, where at the beginning of May a farewell ball was held in honour of the two Habsburg duchesses, who returned to Flanders immediately after- wards, having become 'very bored' in England. The Venetian ambassador in France reported, however, that the Queen, angry at the prolonged stay of her rival, had ordered her to leave.

The King, meanwhile, who cannot have been feeling very well- disposed towards his wife, had obliged her to see each of her privy councillors in turn personally to persuade them of the necessity for England to go to war. She even threatened 'some with death, some with the loss of their goods and estates, if they did not consent to the will of her husband'. Then, in late May, to her terrible distress, the Queen learned that the Pope had excommunicated Philip and deprived Pole of his legatine status. In her anguish, she realised that she would have to choose between the obedience she owed her husband and that which she must render to Christ's Vicar on Earth. It was a heart-breaking decision, but Philip won. In the Queen's mind there could now be no question of England remaining neutral, and she harangued her councillors accordingly. At the same time, both she and Philip wrote to the Pope, protesting at his treatment of Pole, reminding him of all the good work the Cardinal had carried out in the cause of the Counter Reformation, and warning Paul that without him the welfare of the Catholic Church in England would be severly endangered. The Council wrote in similar vein, as did Pole, though his letter read more like a lecture on the duties of a pope than a plea for reinstatement.

For a time, everyone thought that Paul would give in to pressure and restore Pole as legate. They could not know that on 31 May Cardinal Giovanni Morone, a close associate of Pole's, had been arrested in Rome by the Inquisition on a charge of suspected heresy, nor that the Pope had confided to the Venetian ambassador that he believed Pole to be guilty also. He knew he had no good reason for recalling the

Cardinal, yet a charge of heresy would be regarded as sufficient cause for bringing him back.

Back in England, the Queen was still trying to bully her councillors into supporting Philip, assuring them that the King would finance the war out of his own funds, but what really convinced them of the necessity for war was a minor French-backed invasion of Yorkshire by one Thomas Stafford, in whose veins ran some Plantagenet blood. This was easily dealt with, but it left the government feeling nervous and angry, and provoked a declaration of war on France on 7 June. On that same day, Norroy Herald was sent to the French court to throw down the gauntlet to Henry II.

A jubilant Philip at once threw himself into preparations for an offensive, enthusiastically supported by young English noblemen eager for military glory and – in the case of pardoned offenders such as the Dudley brothers, Sir Peter Carew and Sir James Crofts – the chance of rehabilitation. The fleet was made ready, having been augmented on Philip's orders with two new ships, the 'Philip and Mary' and the 'Mary Rose', the latter being named after Henry VIII's famous warship which had sunk off Southampton in 1545. Finally, the King dispatched Ruy Gomez to Spain to bring to England a fleet of ships and £48,000 in gold to defray the government's expenses. For Mary, it was as if Philip was already gone from her, for she knew that when Gomez returned, her husband would sail away to war.

In June, the Pope, ignoring Mary's pleas, sent a nuncio to England with the brief recalling Pole, and appointed Friar William Peto legate in the Cardinal's place. Mary knew Peto well: he had been her mother's confessor, as well as her own in childhood, and he had chosen exile after openly preaching against Henry VIII's nullity suit. He had returned to England after Mary's accession, and was now living in quiet retirement in the restored convent of the Observant Friars at Greenwich. He was, however, patently unsuited to becoming legate, being 'over eighty and of no ability whatever, but a good man and a Christian, who recognises his own shortcomings'. He was also a victim of senile dementia.

Mary was furious at his appointment, and refused to allow the papal nuncio to enter England. To her mind, the Supreme Pontiff was showing himself to be motivated entirely by vindictiveness and envy, qualities that rode ill with his role as Christ's earthly representative. Nor would she allow Pole to leave England. He had not received his papers of recall, so could not be accused of disobedience to the Holy See.

In Rome, however, the Pope had instructed the Inquisition to proceed against Pole on the grounds of heresy. This was preposterous, for while it was true that the Cardinal had openly supported reform within the Catholic Church, his orthodoxy had never yet been called into question, nor had he ever given any cause for it to be. But Paul believed Pole to be a secret agent working on Philip's behalf, and meant to destroy him. Sir Edward Carne, England's ambassador at the Vatican, warned Pole early in July that, if he once set foot in Rome, he would be arrested. The Cardinal responded by sending a representative, Dr Ormanetto, to plead his case with the Pope. At the same time, news came that Paul had appointed Peto a cardinal, but Peto, who was no keener to be legate than Mary was to have him, refused this honour, and returned his red hat to the Pope.

On 20 June, the returning Spanish fleet was sighted in the Channel, and preparations for Philip's departure began in earnest. The royal couple left Whitehall on 3 July, staying overnight at Sittingbourne and then Canterbury before arriving in Dover on the 5th. On each night they shared a bed, the Queen never having given up hope of conceiving another child.

Before he left, the King instructed his confessor, Francisco Bernarda de Fresneda, 'a man very dear to the Queen', to remain in England and do his utmost to persuade Mary that it was vital that Elizabeth be married without delay to Savoy. He was to warn her of what might happen if Elizabeth took a husband of her own choosing, 'who might convulse the whole kingdom into confusion', and to impress upon her the need for haste. If necessary, the match might take place in the King's absence. Fresneda was above all to convince the Queen of the desirability of naming Elizabeth her heir.

At three o'clock in the morning on 6 July, Mary said an emotional farewell to Philip on the quayside at Dover, then stood watching as his ship sailed into the distance. It may have occurred to her that she would never see him again.

The King was in Calais by noon that day, and reached Brussels on 9 July. Two days later he summoned his Spanish household to join him. This time, there was no pretence that his absence would be a short one.

Fresneda was already doing his best to persuade the Queen to carry out her husband's wishes, but according to a secret Venetian report, 'For many days he found [her] utterly averse to giving the Lady Elizabeth any hope of the succession, obstinately maintaining that she was neither her sister nor the daughter of King Henry. Nor would she hear of favouring her, as she was born of an infamous woman who had so greatly outraged the Queen her mother, and herself.'

Distressed that she could not please him in this respect, Mary wrote to Philip, explaining that although he had told her to 'examine her conscience' on the matter, and although she had listened to all the arguments 'with a true and sincere heart', she knew she was in the right, 'for that which my conscience holds it has held this four and twenty years', as long as Elizabeth had been in the world.

Fresneda did not desist. He was a fine orator and frequently got the better of Mary in arguments, but he could not make her change her mind. Philip, learning of her continuing obstinacy, made it clear that he was extremely displeased, but even this did not move his wife. It was fortunate for her, therefore, that his attention was soon diverted away from English affairs to the war with France.

Late in July, Mary, hearing of the Pope's heresy proceedings against Pole, wrote again to the Pontiff, expressing her indignation that he had taken such unprecedented action against the Cardinal. Pole, she said, had given no cause for offence, and had indeed had a record of outstanding and distinguished service to the English Church. He did not therefore deserve to be recalled in such a manner.

In militant mood, Mary sent Pembroke with a force of 7000 men over to Philip, who had laid siege to the town of St Quentin. Robert Dudley also raised a company of soldiers at his own expense, and accompanied them. Although his brother Henry was killed during the siege, he himself displayed notable bravery and skill, and was mentioned in despatches home. On 10 July, the French King sent an army under Anne de Montmorency, Constable of France, to relieve the besieged town, but it was successfully routed by the Anglo-Spanish forces. On 27 August, Philip's men stormed into the town and occupied it, and afterwards the King praised Pembroke's soldiers for their valour. In England, Mary gave heartfelt thanks to God for her husband's miraculous victory, and prayed that this would increase his popularity with her subjects. There seemed little sign of this however, even after news of his capture of other towns and fortresses filtered across the Channel.

When the Pope learned of the fall of St Quentin, he again denounced Philip, provoking the King to order Alba to march on Rome and force the Holy Father to make peace. Acting on Philip's instructions, the Duke knelt at Paul's feet and begged his pardon for having invaded his territories, but it was clear all the same who held the upper hand. The Pope therefore had no choice but to accept Philip's terms, and an uneasy peace was negotiated on 12 September, which was celebrated with *Te Deums* being sung in London. By October, the

English troops were on their way home, and Philip's army was seeking out winter quarters.

Although the Pope eventually agreed to restore legatine status to the See of Canterbury, he would not consent to dropping the charges against Pole, despite receiving further anguished letters from Queen Mary, and when Dr Ormanetto was granted an audience with the Pontiff in September, his arguments fell on deaf ears. In fact, by the end of 1557, Paul had persuaded himself that Pole was a secret Lutheran and had for years been involved in a treacherous conspiracy against the Church, supported by Morone and others. Yet for reasons of his own the Holy Father stayed his hand and never pressed the charges against Pole, probably realising that Mary would never allow the Cardinal to go to Rome to answer them. For the rest of his life, though, the threat of heresy proceedings would hang over Reginald Pole like a dark shadow.

Six months after Philip's departure, the Queen announced that she was expecting another child. As she explained in a letter to her husband, she had delayed making the announcement until she was absolutely certain of her condition, although the Venetian ambassador thought she had really done so 'lest the like should happen as last time'. But Mary insisted that she had 'very sure signs' of pregnancy, and that the child would be due in March.

Few people believed her. Some thought it was a ruse to make Philip return to her. Most thought she was deluding herself. The King expressed his satisfaction at the news, but entertained private doubts, as did most of the English courtiers. This time, the Queen did not even look pregnant when she was supposed to be in her sixth month. Yet there is no doubt that she herself was genuinely convinced that she was carrying a child, for she was hardly likely to have risked a second humiliation by staging an elaborate charade. What may have convinced her could have been the cessation of menstruation – her periods were notoriously erratic and it seems likely that she had entered the menopause by then in any case – and the slight swelling of her stomach, as yet imperceptible under the stiff court gowns of the period with their flattening stomachers. Once again, though, she was most probably deluding herself.

Winter had brought a natural lull in the fighting in France, and therefore the Queen and her people were surprised and shocked to learn that on 7 January 1558 the French had mounted a surprise attack on Calais and taken it. The news was 'the heaviest tidings to England that ever was heard of'. Calais had been the last remaining bastion of the Plantagenet Empire in France, and had been in English hands for over two hundred years. Now it had fallen, to England's utter humiliation and the Queen's abject distress. For the rest of her life she would look upon the loss of Calais as the worst failure of her reign. It was she who bore the blame, for people said that, had she not agreed to involving England in her husband's war in the first place, this would never have happened. What made matters worse was that it quickly became apparent, not only at home but also abroad, that the kingdom did not have the resources to attempt to recapture Calais. England's weakness was therefore exposed for all Europe to see, and the morale of her people plummeted.

The loss of Calais, catastrophic as it was, was not the only evil to afflict the country that winter. Despite the first good harvest for years and an end to famine, the kingdom was in a desperate state. In 1560, Sir Thomas Smith, Secretary of State under Edward VI, recalled,

> I never saw England weaker in strength, money, men and riches. As much affectionate as you know me to be to my country and countrymen, I assure you I was ashamed of them both. Here was nothing but fining, heading, hanging, quartering and burning, taxing, levying and beggaring, and losing our strongholds abroad. A few priests ruled all, who, with setting up of six foot roods, thought to make all cocksure.

And in 1558 Armagil Waad, another of Edward VI's councillors, reported,

> The Queen is poor, the realm exhausted, the nobility poor and decayed. The people are out of order. Justice is not executed. All things are dear. There are divisions amongst ourselves, wars with France and Scotland. The French King is bestriding this realm. There is steadfast enmity but no steady friendship abroad.

The Queen was vilified in seditious pamphlets as 'an utter destroyer of her own subjects, a lover of strangers, and an unnatural stepdame both to these and to thy mother England'. It was said that she was a traitor to God and her country, a promoter of idolatry and a persecutor of saints.

To make matters worse, a great epidemic of influenza had broken out the previous autumn, and would rage for the best part of a year, killing a great number of people and giving the Protestants cause to say that this was a plague sent by God to punish the Queen for her sins.

★

It was believed in England that Philip had not lifted a finger to save Calais, but in fact he had done what he could to avert disaster in the limited time available. Pole wrote and told the King that Mary had taken the bitter blow in a spirit of patient acceptance; he also told him that she was still certain she was with child. Philip thanked the Cardinal for the comforting news 'of the pregnancy of the Queen my beloved wife, which has given me greater joy than I can express to you, as it is the one thing in the world I have most desired, and which is of the greatest importance for the cause of religion and the welfare of the realm. I therefore render thanks to Our Lord for this mercy He has shown me, and I am obliged to you for the news you have given me of it, which has gone so far to lighten the sorrow I have felt for the loss of Calais.'

In order to reassure himself about his wife's condition, Philip sent the Count of Feria to England, ostensibly to convey the King's congratulations, but in reality to look for signs of pregnancy. He was also to ask for more men to be sent to France.

Having seen Mary, the Count reported back to his master, 'The one thing that matters to her is that Your Majesty come hither, and it seems to me she is making herself believe that she is with child, though she does not own up to it.' In fact, although she now had a distended belly, Mary looked ill rather than pregnant, and seemed overwhelmed by the strain of her royal duties. The court was rife with squabbles, the demoralised councillors divided by dissensions, and the only person with the power to control them was Mary, who was in no fit state to do so. 'It would be well if those who govern this kingdom shared the Queen's spirit,' commented Feria.

At the end of February 1558, Elizabeth visited the court 'with a great company of lords and noblemen and noblewomen'. Mary received her graciously enough, but Feria decided not to see the princess for fear of offending the Queen. Elizabeth brought with her a layette of baby clothes that she had herself made; these still exist, and can be seen today at Hever Castle in Kent.

Shortly after Elizabeth's arrival, the Queen 'took to her chamber' to await the birth of her child. In France, the Cardinal of Lorraine, hearing of this, remarked, 'We shall not have so long to wait this time, since it is eight months since the King left England.' Few people were optimistic about a happy outcome.

In March, Friar Peto died. The Pope did not replace him, and Pole tried to carry on as before, but his health was failing and he was no longer able to assist Mary in the onerous task of governing England. 'The Cardinal is a dead man,' wrote Feria. The Queen seemed to be overwhelmed by her problems. Her councillors were demoralised and squabbling, and her court was seething with discontent. The treasury was empty, and even the food served to Mary was of inferior quality. Yet no one seemed to be doing anything about any of these problems.

'I am at my wits' end with these people,' raged Feria. 'It is impossible to make them realise what a state they are in, although it is the worst any country has ever fallen into.'

That spring, a flood of vituperative Protestant propaganda poured into England, in which the Queen was pilloried as 'a raging madwoman' or 'mischievous Mary' and insulting remarks were made about King Philip's attitude towards her. One writer even asked, 'what shall the King do with such an old bitch?' It was at this time that the Scots reformer John Knox issued his scathing attack on petticoat government, *First Blast of the Trumpet against the Monstrous Regiment of Women*, which was targeted at Mary Tudor and Mary of Guise, the Regent of Scotland.

In March, Philip received a report from Renard, who had continued to take an interest in English affairs, summarising the problems of the succession, and urging that Mary be made to acknowledge Elizabeth as her successor. No mention was made of the possibility of the Queen producing an heir, and it appears that neither the King nor Renard believed it would happen. Fearful lest Mary would die without making her intentions clear, Philip urged her to make her will, which she did on 30 March.

'I Mary, Queen of England,' it began, 'thinking myself to be with child in lawful marriage between my dearly beloved husband and lord and I, being at this present (thanks be unto Almighty God) otherwise in good health, yet, foreseeing the great danger which, by God's ordinance, remains to all women in their travail of children, have thought good both for discharge of my conscience and continuance of good order within my realm, to declare my last will and testament.'

Her kingdom she bequeathed to 'the heirs, issue and fruit of my body', designating Philip as regent if she died before their child came of age. To her husband she left 'her chiefest jewel', the love of her subjects, along with the more substantial jewels he had given her at the time of their marriage. He would be her chief executor, assisted by Cardinal Pole. The will concluded with a long list of generous bequests, in which the London poor, destitute scholars and prisoners were remembered.

As the wording of the will shows, Mary still believed herself to be pregnant at the end of March; this was confirmed in a codicil added on 18 October, in which she stated that in the spring she had 'thought

myself to be with child'. Yet when April came the infant had not
arrived.

That month, Gustav Vasa, the Protestant King of Sweden, sent an
envoy to England offering his son, Eric, Duke of Finland, as a husband
for Elizabeth. The envoy, disregarding royal protocol, approached the
princess before consulting the Queen, but she dismissed him without
giving him an answer and informed Mary at once what had happened.
Mary was agitated in case Philip should think that she herself had
instigated the Swedish proposal when she was supposed to be urging
Elizabeth to accept Savoy, and make this an occasion to demand that
she renew the pressure on her sister. In fact, Gustav's suggestion quite
appealed to the Queen, and she sent Sir Thomas Pope, Elizabeth's
good friend, to discover what the princess thought of it. On 26 April,
Pope informed Mary that her sister had no wish to marry anyone at all,
but had said that she wished 'to remain in that estate that I was, which of
all others best liked me. I so well like this estate as I persuade myself
there is not any kind of life comparable to it.'

Pope commented, 'The Queen's Majesty may conceive this rather
to proceed out of a maidenly shamefastness than upon any such certain
determination. Few or none would believe but that Her Grace could
be right well contented to marry, so that there were some honourable
marriage offered her by the Queen's Highness.'

When the King heard of the affair he reminded Mary that she was
supposed to be promoting the match with Savoy; it was time, he said,
that she reconsidered her objections to it. All she would agree to,
however, was laying the matter before Parliament, knowing that the
Lords and Commons would not sanction a forced marriage. The cool
tone of her husband's letters had distressed her greatly, however, and
she felt that now was not the time to be bothering her with this quarrel.
She wrote to Philip, 'I beseech you in all humility to put off the business
until your return. For otherwise Your Highness will be angry against
me, and that will be worse than death for me, for I have already begun
to taste your anger all too often, to my great sorrow.'

The King, however, thought she was dissembling, because on 1 May
Feria informed him that the Queen was still taking a passionate interest
in the Swedish proposal, which was the last alliance Philip wanted for
Elizabeth. As for Elizabeth, she felt as if she was being 'buried alive'
with the pressure on her to take a husband.

Early in May, Mary gradually faced up to the fact that she was not
pregnant. On the 19th Pole, who was himself ill with a tertian fever,
wrote to inform Philip of her 'Christian resignation' to what must have

been the most bitter disappointment. Philip responded with a loving letter to his wife, apologising for not having been able to come and see her as he had hoped, and saying how impressed he was by her bravery. He also wrote to Pole, thanking him for 'cheering her loneliness'.

In fact, Mary soon became ill with a depression so terrible that she refused to leave her apartments and lay unmoving and withdrawn in her bed. According to Foxe, she was also afflicted with a painful 'dropsy'. Early in May Feria noted that she was weak and melancholy and could not sleep – natural enough in one whose hopes of a child had just been dashed for ever. On 18 May, he referred obscurely to her 'usual ailments', but at the beginning of June he described Mary's condition as 'worse than usual'. In her misery she imagined that everyone was against her, and even wore armour when she was well enough to leave her bed, which was by the end of June, at which time the King was expressing concern because he had not heard from her for several days. 'I cannot help being anxious,' he had written.

There was certainly enough in Mary's life to make her unhappy. She could not forget the loss of Calais, nor her failure to carry out her husband's wishes. Her greatest fear was of losing him, and it grieved her that he was so far away. She had expected to see him in May, but, as he informed Feria, affairs of state had kept him away. 'I had greatly desired to go, and it would have given the Queen and myself much happiness had I been able to do so. I thank you for keeping the Queen company and the devotion you show in her service, and affectionately beg you to continue to cheer her loneliness, for thus you are doing us the greatest pleasure.'

Mary, however, remained hopeful that Philip would come to her, and gave orders that a fleet be kept waiting in readiness to escort him across the Channel and that lodgings on the road between Dover and London be prepared for him.

There was now no doubt in Philip's mind that Elizabeth would succeed Mary, probably quite soon, and he instructed Feria to pay the princess a visit on his behalf to present his compliments and express his goodwill. The ambassador was also to cultivate those who were friendly with Elizabeth and might be influential when she came to power. What Philip did not tell Feria was that, if he could not force Mary to marry Elizabeth to Savoy, he was considering marrying the princess himself if he could persuade cantankerous old Pope Paul to grant the necessary dispensation. In fact, in Brussels it was expected that Philip would marry his sister-in-law.

In June, Feria went to Hatfield and was warmly received by the princess, who was 'very much pleased by his visit'. She was gratified by the King's kindness and favour to her and expressed herself ready and willing to do his pleasure if it were in her power. When the Queen learned of the ambassador's visit, and several subsequent ones, she was most displeased, but she dared not risk alienating Philip by complaining. Even Feria was not entirely at ease about the situation, for he did not relish the prospect of England being governed by a Protestant queen – like many others, he did not believe in the sincerity of the princess's conversion. When he conveyed this concern to his master, Philip wrote to Mary suggesting that she make Elizabeth give an undertaking to uphold the Catholic faith when she became queen, but Mary still could not bring herself to accept her sister as her heir.

In August, the Queen left Richmond, where she had been staying since her illness, and moved to Whitehall. Here, she began 'suffering from intermittent fever', which may have been influenza; the epidemic had lasted all through the cold, wet summer. Mary was also bringing up a lot of 'black bile'.

The burnings were still taking place in London and elsewhere – in June, seven were burned in one fire at Smithfield – and in August the Queen wrote personally to the Sheriff of Hampshire to reprimand him for reprieving a heretic who had recanted as the fire was lit. Other sheriffs received similar rebukes from the Council. Bishop Bonner of London, notorious for his cruelty to heretics, was now so terrified of 'tumults' at executions, that he begged the Queen to order that they take place early in the mornings, but Mary would not allow it. By now, nearly 300 people had been burned in four years, a vast number compared to the numbers burned under other Tudor monarchs: Henry VII had burned ten in 24 years, Henry VIII 81 in 38 years, and Elizabeth I would burn only five in 45 years. The persecution had become irrevocably associated with the papacy and the Spaniards in people's minds, causing a national hatred of the Roman Catholic religion that would endure for centuries, and robbing Mary of her popularity. She was now hated and feared by the subjects who had welcomed her to the throne with such enthusiasm.

Englishmen longed for stable government, economic recovery, and an end to the persecution and foreign interference in English affairs. According to John Hayward's *Annals*, they longed for 'their Elizabeth'.

Philip was keeping a close eye on bulletins concerning his wife's health, and was relieved to hear from Pole, himself suffering from a 'double quartan ague', that she was taking good care of herself. The Cardinal asked Philip to come to England, but the King did not do so because early in September, he heard that his wife had recovered and moved to Hampton Court. She had not been there long, though, before the fever recurred, worse than before. Her doctors assured everyone that there was no cause for alarm, and the Queen insisted on returning to London and taking up residence in St James's Palace, but once there, her condition became so grave that the physicians began to despair. However, they continued to issue reassuring bulletins, stating that 'Through this malady, she will obtain relief from her habitual indisposition' – the old, ill-defined autumn sickness that had troubled her all her life. Again, Mary 'took the greatest care of herself', and there were periods when she rallied, but then the fever would take hold again and she would suffer violent convulsions, which weakened her resistance, and a black pall of depression, which impaired her will to recover. 'The truth is', wrote one ambassador, 'that her malady is evidently incurable and will end her life sooner than later, according to the increase or decrease of her mental anxieties, which harass her more than the disease, however dangerous it may be.'

On 21 September, Charles V died at Yuste. The news took six weeks to reach Philip, and longer to reach England, and it may be that Mary never learned of the passing of the man whom she had looked upon as a second father.

By the end of September her condition had worsened, and again Philip was sent for, but he still declined to come, pleading the pressure of official business. There is no doubt that he felt some concern for Mary, but matters of state had to take precedence.

The Council had constantly pressed Mary to name her successor, but she was still refusing to do so. On 18 October she did agree to make a codicil to her will, because 'God hath hitherto sent me no fruit nor heir of my body, and it is only in His most divine providence whether I shall have any or no,' and also because she was 'feeling myself presently sick and weak in body, and yet of whole and perfect remembrance, Our Lord be thanked'. Whilst not naming her successor, she ordered that 'my most Dear Lord and Husband shall, for default of an heir of my body, have no further government, order and rule within this realm', yet requested him to be as a father, brother and friend to the next sovereign.

By the middle of October the Queen's life was perceived to be in danger, and in London it was rumoured that she was already dead. Feria was back in Brussels, but when, on the 22nd, Philip realised how serious Mary's illness was, he ordered the Count to prepare to return to England. The Venetian ambassador heard that 'The matter to be treated by him is the marriage of my Lady Elizabeth, to keep that kingdom in any event in the hands of a person in His Majesty's confidence, and that the Count's instructions purport that he is to try and dispose the Queen to consent to Lady Elizabeth being married as her sister, and with the hope of succeeding to the crown.' Feria was also, as Philip's representative, 'to serve the Queen during her illness'.

Feria was by no means unhappy to be returning to England because during his earlier visit he had fallen in love with Jane Dormer, who had accepted his proposal of marriage. Jane had recently been ill with influenza, but her loving mistress had displayed great 'care and regard' for her, commanding that she be attended by one of the royal physicians. Jane had quickly recovered, and when she learned that Feria was coming to England, she asked for the Queen's blessing on their union. Mary had for a long time been averse to losing Jane, but she now told her that she 'deserved a very good husband', and that the Count was 'a most perfect gentleman' whom she held in 'great favour'. The prospect of their wedding cheered Mary considerably, although she asked Jane to delay it until the King's return.

All the signs were that Elizabeth's accession was imminent, but because the Queen had not named a successor, those close to the princess anticipated that she might have to fight for her throne. Cecil and Parry therefore contacted Sir Thomas Markham, commander of the garrison at Berwick against the Scots, who diligently canvassed the northern magnates for their support, securing a potential force of 10,000 men 'to serve for the maintenance of her royal state, title and dignity'. Already, a number of supporters, among them substantial gentry like John Thynne of Wiltshire, were making contact with the princess. A letter from Elizabeth to an unnamed adherent, dated 28 October 1558 at Brocket Hall in Hertfordshire, survives, thanking the recipient for his readiness to provide soldiers and 'to do unto us all the pleasure you can'. The letter ends with an assurance that she will not forget such kindness 'whensoever time and power may serve'.

The Council were praying daily for the Queen's recovery, but because her condition was so grave, Parliament was recalled on 5 November. Mary had just rewarded one of her physicians, Dr Cesar, with £100 for using his skills to bring her back from the brink of death, and was quite capable of discussing Parliament's agenda with her councillors on the 4th, although she was 'both sick and very weak' and could not talk for long. It was obvious to all that she was dying, and on 6 November the councillors all trooped into her bedchamber 'with a view to persuading her to make certain declarations in favour of the Lady Elizabeth concerning the succession'. Sick and worn down by arguments, the dying Queen at last gave in, asking only that Elizabeth 'would maintain the old religion and pay her debts'. Two days later, the Master of the Rolls and John Boxall, Controller of the Royal Household, were dispatched on the Queen's orders to Hatfield to convey the news to Elizabeth, and Jane Dormer was also sent, to ensure that Elizabeth swore to uphold the ancient faith, take care of her sister's servants, and see that the provisions in her will were faithfully carried out. Mary, meanwhile, had lapsed into a stupor from which she would now only occasionally awaken.

The King, who was keeping a close eye on events in England, had received the sad news, not only of the death of his father, but also that of his aunt, Mary of Hungary. In his grief, he wrote to his sister Juana:

> You may imagine what a state I am in. It seems to me that everything is being taken from me at once. The Queen my wife has been ill, and although she has recovered somewhat, her infirmities are such that grave fears must be entertained on her score.

He had felt it right to retire to a monastery to observe a period of mourning, and could not go to visit Mary until a memorial service for his father had taken place. Instead, he was sending with Feria, who was just about to depart, his own physician, a Portuguese called Lodovicus Nonnius, to attend her. It is likely that news of the Emperor's death was withheld from Mary in case the shock of it hastened her end.

On 9 November, Feria arrived in London to find that the Queen was too ill to receive him. The ambassador therefore decided that he could most usefully deploy his time by supporting the Lady Elizabeth's claim to the succession. But when he informed the Council that he had come to serve her 'on all occasions and employ every effort to enable her to ascend the throne', he was astonished to find himself received 'like a man accredited with bulls from a dead pope'. It was then explained to him that the Queen had already acknowledged Elizabeth as her heir, and he was invited, as the King's representative, to preside over the Council meeting convened that day to confirm the princess's right to the succession.

Feria suspected that Mary could not live long, and perceiving that his presence at St James's Palace was not needed for the moment, rode off to Hatfield, where the princess was in residence. There, he found her already assembling a court, in which 'young folk, heretics and traitors' seemed to be predominant. This, Feria felt, did not augur well for the future of Catholicism in England.

Nevertheless, although Elizabeth – who now had 'a certain air of authority about her' – did not receive him 'as joyfully as she did last time', they shared a pleasant dinner, during which 'we laughed and enjoyed ourselves a great deal'. Afterwards, the ambassador and the princess had a serious private talk, in which she expressed her appreciation of all that King Philip had done for her and showed herself eager to be his friend in the future. She declared that, while the French held Calais, they should never have her friendship. This was just what Philip had wanted to hear, but Feria was uneasy, thinking he detected a note of insincerity in Elizabeth's voice. He also found her too independent, and lacking in the modesty considered becoming in a woman. When he suggested that it was Philip whom she had to thank for making Mary acknowledge her as heir to the throne, Elizabeth shook her head, saying 'she owed her crown not to Philip but the attachment of the people of England, to whom she seemed much devoted'. Providence, she concluded, had brought her where she was.

Feria asked her about marriage, to which she replied with a smile that she knew the King wanted her to marry the Duke of Savoy, but had seen how her sister had lost the affection of her people as a result of her marrying a foreigner, and she did not wish to make the same mistake. She might, she said laughing, marry Arundel. Then she became serious, making it clear that she was 'highly indignant about what has been done to her during the Queen's lifetime'. It was small wonder, thought the Count, that some members of the Council were anxious about the future. Already it was clear that Elizabeth had her own ideas as to who should serve her; she had, Feria reported, already appointed William Cecil her secretary, and other courtiers, hopeful of preferment, were already arriving at Hatfield to declare their loyalty. Similarly, the princess was receiving a growing pile of letters from supporters. 'There is not a traitor or heretic in the country who has not risen to welcome her accession,' he wrote sourly.

On 14 November, the Count reported his visit to Philip, concluding, 'She is a very vain, clever woman, who has been thoroughly schooled in the manner in which her father conducted his affairs.'

On 10 November, five heretics went to the stake at Canterbury, the last to suffer under the Marian persecution. On that day, Feria returned to court, where he was informed that the Queen had recovered consciousness and would see him. Her physicians, who could do nothing more for her, had been dismissed, and she was attended only by her ladies. Feria delivered a loving message from Philip, but Mary was too weak to read the letters her husband had sent her.

She did, however, call Dormer to her, and apologised to the young couple for having delayed their marriage. She knew now that she would not live to see it, and gave them her blessing. She also, with 'much sighing', gave Feria a ring to take to Philip as a sign of her undying love. Her ladies told Feria afterwards that their mistress was dying of 'thought and sorrow' rather than of any bodily illness.

On 12 November, it was reported in Brussels that the Queen was on the point of death, but on the next day she was able to sign a warrant for the burning of two London heretics; it was never issued, though, and the fortunate wretches were spared the flames. The persecution was, in effect, over.

After 14 November, Mary declined rapidly, drifting in and out of consciousness. Jane Dormer remembered one occasion when, waking to see her ladies weeping, the Queen 'comforted those that grieved', saying 'what good dreams she had, seeing many little children, like angels, play before her, singing pleasing notes, giving her more than earthly comfort'.

Mass was celebrated daily in her bedchamber, and she derived her greatest comfort from it during these final days of her life. A mile or so away, at Lambeth Palace, Cardinal Pole was also dying, and he and Mary consoled each other with loving messages.

Even so, the Queen spent many of her waking hours in tears, impervious to the attempts of her ladies to comfort her. Some visiting councillors asked the Queen why she was so sad, thinking 'that she took some thought for the King's Majesty, her husband, which was gone from her'.

'Indeed, that may be one cause,' she answered, 'but that is not the greatest wound that pierceth mine oppressed mind.' Despite their entreaties, she would not tell them what so grieved her, but later, when just Clarencieux and an attendant called Mrs Rise were with her, she returned to the subject.

'Is it for King Philip's departing from you?' asked Mrs Rise.

'Not only that,' said the Queen, sighing, 'but when I am dead, you will find Calais lying in my heart.' Years later, Mrs Rise reported the Queen's words to the chronicler Raphael Holinshed, who recorded them for posterity.

One of the Queen's last conscious acts was to send a message to Elizabeth, exhorting her to preserve the Roman Catholic faith. Pole sent a similar message, and his secretary expressed himself satisfied with Elizabeth's answer. The princess had secretly arranged with Sir Nicholas Throckmorton that he would inform her immediately of the Queen's death, bringing with him as proof Mary's betrothal ring that never left her finger. Cecil, meanwhile, was drafting proclamations announcing Elizabeth's accession. By now, the road from London to Hatfield was busy with courtiers hastening to transfer their allegiance to their future queen. Although she was gratified, the princess was also shocked at the alacrity with which they had deserted their lawful sovereign, and when, forty-five years later, her own turn came to die, she took care not to name her successor until the last possible moment.

On 16 November, the Lord Chancellor and privy councillors presented themselves in the Queen's bedchamber to read out her will, as was customary. But Mary did not hear them, being too far lapsed into unconsciousness.

Before dawn on the following morning, the Queen woke and, realising that her end was near, summoned her ladies.

'Always remain steadfast to the true faith,' she told them. She then asked that her priests celebrate mass, and, according to Dormer, made the responses clearly, 'with so good attention and devotion', praying 'that the weakness of my flesh be not overcome by the fear of death. Grant me, merciful Father, that when death has shut up the eyes of my body, yet that the eyes of my soul may still behold and look upon Thee.' At the moment when the Host was elevated, she shuddered with emotion and bent her head forward.

When her ladies looked at her again, they thought she had fallen asleep, but Jane Dormer alone realised that the Queen had 'made her passage'. The last thing she had seen had been the image of 'her Saviour and Redeemer, no doubt to behold Him presently hereafter in His glorious body, in Heaven'.

Epilogue: Elizabeth

.·..

Q ueen Mary's death was announced by the Lord Chancellor in the House of Lords on the morning of 17 November 1558.

'As it is most heavy and grievous to us,' he said, 'so have we no less cause another way to rejoice with praise to Almighty God for that He hath left unto us a true, lawful and right inheritrice to the crown of this realm, which is the Lady Elizabeth, of whose lawful right and title we need not to doubt. Wherefore the Lords of this House have determined, with your assents and consents, to pass from hence into the palace, and there to proclaim the said Lady Elizabeth Queen of this realm.'

Nicholas Throckmorton had not waited to hear the new Queen proclaimed, but, bearing Mary Tudor's ring, had set out early that morning for Hatfield. The road was familiar to him, for he had travelled along it several times during the past weeks, but he was at some point overtaken by the Earls of Arundel and Pembroke, come officially on behalf of the Council to deliver news of her accession to Queen Elizabeth and kiss her hand.

It was they who arrived first at Hatfield, a little before noon, and as they traversed the park they came across their new sovereign, impervious to the cold, seated under an oak tree (the remains of which are still preserved today at Hatfield House) reading the New Testament in Greek. As she saw the lords approaching, she stood up, realising that they brought her news of great import. Then they knelt before her and saluted her as queen of England.

Elizabeth was overcome with emotion and for some moments was unable to speak. At last, 'after a good time of respiration', she fell to her knees on the grass and quoted the Latin version of the 118th Psalm: '*A Domine factum est illud et est mirabile in oculis nostris!* – This is the Lord's doing; it is marvellous in our eyes!'

Afterwards

By the middle of that afternoon, all the church bells in London were ringing for joy at Elizabeth's accession, and that night, wrote Machyn, the people made 'bonfires and set tables in the street, and made merry for the new Queen'. Already, it was being said that her accession day should ever afterwards be a public holiday, and it was indeed celebrated as such for more than a century.

Lying in his sick-bed at Lambeth Palace, Cardinal Pole heard the bells pealing and asked his attendants what they signified, but they were reluctant to break the news of Mary's death to him in case he suffered a relapse. He could, however, tell by their mournful faces that something was wrong, and insisted that they tell him. As they had feared, he took this 'final catastrophe' badly and died at seven o'clock that evening, exactly twelve hours after Mary. His death left the See of Canterbury vacant and the way clear for a new Anglican religious settlement.

When the Pope was informed of the deaths of Queen Mary and Cardinal Pole, he expressed conventional regrets, but was inwardly relieved, and did not try to hide the fact that he preferred the Protestant Elizabeth to the devoutly Catholic but obstinate Queen Mary.

King Philip was informed of his wife's death by Viscount Montague, who had ridden post haste to Brussels as soon as the news was made public. To his sister Juana, his chief confidante at this time, the King wrote, 'The Queen my wife is dead. May God have received her in His glory. I felt a reasonable regret for her death. I shall miss her.' We have no means of knowing how deeply these feelings were felt by Philip, for they were the standard sentiments of grief used on several occasions by a devout man who believed that it was wrong to display an excess of grief for one who had, after all, achieved eternal bliss.

*

The dead Queen's body was embalmed and then left at St James's Palace for a month before being buried in one of the side chapels of the Henry VII Chapel in Westminster Abbey with full Roman Catholic ceremonial on 14 December. The chief mourner was Margaret, Countess of Lennox. John White, Bishop of Winchester, preached the funeral sermon, saying, 'She was a king's daughter, she was a king's sister, she was a king's wife; she was a queen, and by the same title a king also. What she suffered in each of these degrees I will not chronicle. Only this I say: howsoever it pleased God to will her patience to be exercised in the world, she had in all estates the fear of God in her heart.' The requiem masses said for Mary and, a few days later, Charles V, were the last ever to be sung in the Abbey.

The lavish ceremonies, which took place over two days, cost the Exchequer £7763, and Queen Elizabeth must have felt that this was quite sufficient, for she did not go to the expense of raising a tomb over the unmarked vault where her sister lay. In fact, during her reign, stones from broken-up altars were heaped on top of it. All that remained as a memorial was the wax effigy that had been carried at the Queen's funeral, of which only the head, much altered, survives today. It was only when James I built a magnificent tomb for Elizabeth I in the same chapel that Mary, whose coffin rests below that of her sister within it, was remembered in an epitaph:

> Consorts both in throne and grave, here rest we two sisters,
> Elizabeth and Mary, in the hope of one resurrection.

Queen Elizabeth ignored the provisions of Mary's will. She did not, as Mary had requested, bring the body of Katherine of Aragon from Peterborough to rest beside her daughter in Westminster Abbey, nor did she return Philip's jewels to him, nor honour any of the other bequests.

Within days of her death, according to Feria, the late Queen's policies were being scathingly criticised, and there was little pretence of mourning. Most of her former subjects were profoundly relieved to hear of her death, and to learn that, on the day of her accession, Elizabeth had ordered the persecution of heretics to cease. In fact, for generations to come, thanks to her own reputation and to anti-Catholic propaganda disseminated in the reigns of her successors, Mary's name would be remembered with horror and revulsion. After Elizabeth had re-established the Church of England, those who had suffered persecution under Mary were revered as martyrs, and John Foxe's book, *Acts and Monuments of the Church*, which recounted their deaths and became popularly known as 'Foxe's Book of Martyrs', was by order of the Queen placed in every church in the land alongside Thomas Cranmer's revived Book of Common Prayer. Foxe spoke for multitudes when he wrote, 'We shall never find any reign of any prince in this land or any other which did ever show in it so many great arguments of God's wrath and displeasure as were to be seen in the reign of this Queen Mary, whether we behold the shortness of her time or the unfortunate event of all her purposes.'

Time had not been on Mary's side, and the misfortunes she suffered were not all of her own making. It was not her fault that her reign had seen a succession of bad harvests, nor that she had failed to produce an heir. Yet these calamities were seen by her contemporaries as a judgement of God upon a ruler who had forced her own faith upon an unwilling people, given the realm over into the hands of foreigners, and unleashed the worst religious persecution ever seen in England. Her reign was remembered as a dark, tumultuous period in English history, and Raphael Holinshed, writing in the 1570s, picturesquely evoked the feelings of his countrymen at the time of her death when he wrote, 'After all the stormy, tempestuous and blustery windy weather of Queen Mary was overblown, the darksome clouds of discomfort dispersed, the palpable fogs and mists of most intolerable misery consumed, and the dashing showers of persecution overpast, it pleased God to send England a calm and quiet season, a clear and lovely sunshine, a quietus from former broils, and a world of blessings by good Queen Elizabeth.'

Bibliography

Primary Sources

Acts of the Privy Council (ed. John Roche Dasent, Rolls Series, 1890–1918)

Ambassades des Messieurs de Noailles en Angleterre (ed. René A. de Vertot, 1681–1714, published Leyden, 1763)

The Antiquarian Repertory: A Miscellany Intended to Preserve and Illustrate Several Valuable Remains of Old Times (ed. F. Grose, T. Astle, 1808, and Stephen Perlin, Francis Blyth, 1775–84)

Archaeologia, or Miscellaneous Tracts Relating to Antiquity (Society of Antiquaries, 1773–1969)

Archives of the English Tournament (ed. S. Anglo, *Journal of the Society of Archivists*, 2, 1960)

Ascham, Roger: *The Whole Works of Roger Ascham* (ed., with a Life of the Author, by Rev. Dr J.A. Giles, 1865)

The Bedingfield Papers: State Papers Relating to the Custody of the Princess Elizabeth at Woodstock in 1554 (ed. C.R. Manning, Norfolk and Norwich Archaeological Society, Vol. IV, Norwich, 1855)

Bradford, John: *The Copy of a Letter sent by John Bradford to the Right Honourable Lords, the Earls of Arundel, Derby, Shrewsbury and Pembroke* (London?, 1556)

Brice, Thomas: *Register of the Martyrs* (Tudor Tracts, 1903)

Calendar of Letters, Despatches and State Papers relating to Negotiations between England and Spain, preserved in the Archives at Simancas and Elsewhere (ed. G.A. Bergenroth, P. de Goyangos, G. Mattingly, R. Tyler and others, HMSO, 1862–1965)

Calendar of the Patent Rolls, Edward VI – Philip and Mary (Rolls Series, 1924–39)

Calendar of State Papers, Domestic Series, of the Reigns of Edward VI, Mary, Elizabeth, 1547–80 (ed. Robert Lemon and M.A.E. Green, Longman, Brown, Longman & Roberts, *1856–72*)

Calendar of State Papers, Foreign Series, of the Reign of Edward VI, 1547–1553. Preserved in the State Papers Department of Her Majesty's Public Record Office (ed. William B. Turnbull, Longman, Green, Longman & Roberts, 1861)

Calendar of State Papers, Foreign Series, of the Reign of Elizabeth I (ed. J. Stevenson and others, Longman, Green, Longman & Roberts, 1863)

Calendar of State Papers, Foreign Series, of the Reign of Mary, 1553–1558, Preserved in the State Papers Department of Her Majesty's Public Record Office (ed. William. B. Turnbull, Longman, Green, Longman & Roberts, 1861)

Calendar of State Papers and Manuscripts Existing in the Archives and Collections of Milan (ed. A.B. Hinds, 1912)

Calendar of State Papers and Manuscripts relating to English Affairs Preserved in the Archives of Venice and in the Other Libraries of Northern Italy (ed. L. Rawdon Brown and others, HMSO 1864–1937)

Calendar of State Papers relating to English Affairs, Preserved Principally at Rome in the Vatican Archives and Library (ed. J.M. Rigg, 1916–26)

Calendar of State Papers Relating to Scotland and Mary, Queen of Scots, 1547–1603

Camden, William: *Annales rerum Anglicarum et Hibernicarum, regnanto Elizabetha, ad annum salutis MDLXXXIX* (London, 1615)

Camden, William: *The History of the Most Renowned and Victorious Princess Elizabeth* (1675)

The Cecil Papers: A Collection of State Papers Relating to Affairs from the Year 1552 to 1570, left by William Cecil, Lord Burghley, at Hatfield House (ed. Samuel Haynes, 1740)

A Chronicle of London (ed. N.H. Nicolas, 1827)

The Chronicle of Queen Jane and of the First Two Years of Queen Mary, especially of the Rebellion of Sir Thomas Wyatt (ed. J.G. Nichols. Camden Miscellany, Camden Society, XLVIII, 1850)

The Chronicle and Political Papers of Edward VI (ed. W.K. Jordan, London, 1966)

Clifford, Henry: *The Life of Jane Dormer, Duchess of Feria* (trans. Canon E.E. Estcourt and ed. Rev. Joseph Stevenson, Burns & Oates, 1887)

A Complete Collection of State Trials (ed. D. Thomas, William Cobbett and T.B. Rowell, 1809; Routledge & Kegan Paul, 1972)

Coryat, Thomas; *Thomas Coryat's Crudities* (Glasgow, 1905)

Cotton MSS. (British Library)

The Count of Feria's Despatch to Philip II of 14th November 1558 (ed. M.J. Rodriguez Salgado and S. Adams. *Camden Miscellany*, Camden Society, XXVIII, 1984)

Documents from Simancas relating to the Reign of Queen Elizabeth (ed. Tomas Gonzalez, trans. and ed. Spencer Hall, 1865)

Documents relating to the Office of the Revels in the Time of King Edward VI and Queen Mary (ed. Albert Feuillerat, Louvain and London, 1908–14)

Elder, John: *The Copy of a Letter sent into Scotland* (London?, 1555) *An Epitaph upon the Death of the Most Excellent and Our Late Virtuous Queen Mary* (Anon., London, 1558)

Florio, M.: *Historia della Vita Giovanna Graia*

Foxe, John: *Acts and Monuments of the Church* (known as 'Foxe's Book of Martyrs'; ed. G. Townshend and S.R. Cattley, Seeley and Burnside, 1837–41 and ed. Rev. Josiah Pratt, Religious Tracts Society, 1877)

Fuller, Thomas: *The Church History of Britain* (1655)

Gardiner, Stephen: *The Letters of Stephen Gardiner* (ed. J.A. Muller, Cambridge, 1933)

Greyfriars Chronicle (ed. J.G. Nichols. *Camden Miscellany*, Camden Society, LIII, 1852)

Guaras, Antonio de: *The Accession of Queen Mary, Being the Contemporary Narrative of Antonio de Guaras, a Spanish Merchant Resident in London* (ed. and trans. Richard Garnett, Lawrence & Bullen, 1892)

Harington, John: *Nugae Antiquae: Being a Miscellaneous Collection of Original Papers in Prose and Verse, Written in the Reigns of Henry VIII, Queen Mary, Elizabeth, King James, etc.* (ed. Rev. Henry Harington, J. Dodsley, 1779)

Harington, John: *A Tract on the Succession to the Crown* (Roxburghe Club, 1880)

Harleian MSS. (British Library)

Hayward, Sir John: *Annals of the First Four Years of the Reign of Queen Elizabeth* (ed. John Bruce. *Camden Miscellany*, Camden Society, 1840)

Hayward, Sir John: *The Life and Reign of King Edward VI* (1636; in White Kennett's *Complete History of England*; Vol. II, 1706)

Hearne, Thomas: *Sylloge Epistolarum* (in Titus Livius' *Vita Henrici Quinti*, ed. T. Hearne, 1716)

Heywood, Thomas: *England's Elizabeth* (*Harleian Miscellany*, 1813)

Holinshed, Raphael: *Chronicles of England, Scotland and Ireland* (1577; ed. H. Ellis, G. Woodfall, Printer, 1807–8)

Household Expenses of the Princess Elizabeth During her Residence at

Hatfield (ed. P.C.S. Smythe, Viscount Strangeford. *Camden Miscellany* 2, Camden Society, LV, 1853)

Household Ordinances: A Collection of Ordinances and Regulations for the Government of the Royal Household (Society of Antiquaries, 1790)

Intimate Letters of England's Queens (ed. Margaret Sanders, 1957)

Knox, John: *First Blast of the Trumpet Against the Monstrous Regiment of Women* (ed. E. Arber, The English Scholar's Library of Old and Modern Works, 1878)

Leti, Gregorio: *Historia o vero vita di Elizabetta, regina d'Inghilterra* (survives only in a French translation published as *La Vie d'Elisabeth, Reine d'Angleterre*, Amsterdam 1692)

Letters of Queen Elizabeth (ed. G.B. Harrison, 1935)

Letters of Royal and Illustrious Ladies (ed. M.A.E. Green, 1846)

The Literary Remains of King Edward VI (ed. J.G. Nichols, Roxburghe Club, 1857)

Machyn, Henry: *The Diary of Henry Machyn, Citizen and Merchant Tailor of London, from A.D. 1550 to A.D. 1563* (ed. J.G. Nichols. *Camden Miscellany*, Camden Society, XLII, 1848)

Malfatti, C.V.: *Two Italian Accounts of Tudor England* (Barcelona, 1953)

Memorials and Literary Remains of Lady Jane Grey (ed. N.H. Nicolas)

Monarchs and the Muse: Poems by Monarchs and Princes of England, Scotland and Wales (ed. Sally Purcell, Carcanet Press, 1972)

Mumby, Frank: *The Girlhood of Queen Elizabeth* (1909)

Narratives of the Days of the Reformation, Chiefly from the Manuscripts of John Foxe, the Martyrologist (ed. J.G. Nichols. *Camden Miscellany*, Camden Society, 1859)

Naunton, Sir Robert: *Fragment Regalia* (ed. Edward Arber, 1895)

Original Letters Illustrative of English History, Including Numerous Royal Letters (ed. Henry Ellis, Richard Bentley, 1824–46)

Original Letters Relative to the English Reformation (ed. H. Robinson, Parker Society, 1846–7)

Papiers d'Etat du Cardinal de Granvelle, 1500–1565 (ed. C. Weiss, in *Collection de Documents Inedits sur l'Histoire de France*, Paris, 1841–52)

Parsons, Robert: *A Temperate Ward-Word* (1599)

Pole, Reginald: *Pro Ecclesiasticae Unitatis Defensione* (1536; Rome, 1698)

Pollino, Girolamo: *Istoria dell' Ecclesiastica della Rivoluzion d'Inghilterra* (Rome, 1594)

Privy Purse Expenses of the Princess Mary, Daughter of King Henry the Eighth, Afterwards Queen Mary: with a Memoir of the Princess and Notes (ed. F. Madden, William Pickering, 1831)

Proceedings and Ordinances of the Privy Council of England (ed. N.H. Nicolas, Records Commissioners, 1834–7)

Proctor, John: *The History of Wyatt's Rebellion* (London?, 1554)

Rotuli Parliamentorum (The Rolls of Parliament) (ed. J. Strachey and others, Records Commissioners, 1767–1832)

Rymer, Thomas: *Foedera* (ed. T. Hardy, Records Commissioners, 1816–69)

The Statutes, A.D. 1235–1770 (HMSO, 1950)

Statutes of the Realm (ed. A. Luders and others, Records Commissioners, 1810–28)

Stow, John: *The Annals of England* (1592; ed. E. Howes, London, 1631)

Strype, John: *Ecclesiastical Memorials (1721–33)* (Clarendon Press, 1822)

Strype, John: *Life of John Aylmer* (1821)

A Supplication to the Queen's Majesty (Anon., London, 1555)

Thou, J. de: *History of His Own Time*

Throckmorton, Nicholas: *The Legend of Sir Nicholas Throckmorton* (ed. J.G. Nichols)

Tres cartas de lo sucedido en al viaje de Su Alteza a Inglaterra (Sociedad de los Bibliofilos Espanoles, Madrid, 1877)

Tudor Royal Proclamations (ed. P.L. Hughes and J.F. Larkin, New Haven, Connecticut, 1964, 1969)

Tytler, P.F.: *England under the Reigns of Edward VI and Mary, with the Contemporary History of Europe, Illustrated in a Series of Original Letters Never Before Printed* (Richard Bentley, 1839)

Underhill, Edward: *The Narrative of Edward Underhill* (in E. Arber, *An English Garner* IV, London, 1879–82)

Vives, Juan Luis: *De Institutione Foeminae Christianae* (Basle, 1538; trans. R. Hyrd, and printed by Thomas Berthelet in London, 1540)

Weever, John: *Ancient Funeral Monuments within the United Monarchy of Great Britain* (Thomas Harper, 1631)

Wingfield, Robert: *Vitae Maria Reginae* (ed. D. MacCulloch, Camden Miscellany, Camden Society, XXVIII, 1984)

Wriothesley, Charles: *A Chronicle of England during the Reigns of the Tudors from 1485 to 1559* (ed. William Douglas Hamilton. *Camden Miscellany*, Camden Society, 1875, 1877)

Wyatt, George: *The Papers of George Wyatt* (ed. D.M. Loades. *Camden Miscellany*, Camden Society, 4th Series, V, 1968)

Secondary Sources

Abbott, D.: *Tortures of the Tower of London* (David and Charles, 1986)

Anglo, S.: *Spectacle, Pageantry and Early Tudor Policy* (Oxford University Press, 1969)

Ashdown, Dulcie M.: *Ladies in Waiting* (Arthur Barker, 1976)

Bassnett, Susan: *Elizabeth I: A Feminist Perspective* (Berg, 1988)

Bayley, J.: *History and Antiquities of the Tower of London* (Jennings & Chaplin, 1830)

Beckinsale, B.W.: *Elizabeth I* (Batsford, 1963)

Beer, Barrett L.: *Northumberland: the Political Career of John Dudley* (Kent State University Press, 1973)

Bell, D.C.: *Notices of Historic Persons Buried in the Tower* (1877)

Bindoff, S.T.: *Tudor England* (1950)

Black, J.B.: *The Reign of Elizabeth, 1558–1603* (Oxford University Press, 1959)

Braddock, R.C.: *The Character and Composition of the Duke of Northumberland's Army in 1553 (Albion, 8, 1976)*

Carpenter, Edward: *Cantuar: The Archbishops in their Office* (Baker, 1971)

Carter, Alison: *Mary Tudor's Wardrobe (Costume: The Journal of the Costume Society, XVIII, 1984)*

Chamberlin, Frederick: *The Private Character of Queen Elizabeth* (1921)

Chapman, Hester W.: *Lady Jane Grey* (Jonathan Cape, 1962)

Chapman, Hester W.: *The Last Tudor King* (Jonathan Cape, 1958)

Chapman, Hester W.: *Two Tudor Portraits* (Jonathan Cape, 1960)

Charlton, John: *The Tower of London: Its Buildings and Institutions* (HMSO, 1978)

The Complete Peerage (ed. G.H. White and others, St Catherine's Press, 1910–59)

Davies, C.S.L: *Peace, Print and Protestantism, 1450–1558* (Hart-Davis & MacGibbon, 1976)

Dewhurst, Jack: *Royal Confinements* (Weidenfeld & Nicolson, 1980)

Dictionary of National Biography (ed. L. Stephen and S. Lee, Oxford University Press, 1885–1900)

Dowsing, James: *Forgotten Tudor Palaces in the London Area* (Sunrise Press, no date)

Dunlop, Ian: *Palaces and Progresses of Queen Elizabeth I* (Jonathan Cape, 1962)

Durant, Horatia: *Sorrowful Captives: The Tudor Earls of Devon* (Griffin Press, 1960)

Dutton, Ralph: *English Court Life from Henry VII to George II* (Batsford, 1963)

Elton, G.R.: *England under the Tudors* (Methuen, 1955)

Erickson, Carolly: *Bloody Mary* (Dent, 1978)

Fenlon, D.B.: *Heresy and Obedience in Tridentine Italy* (Cambridge University Press, 1972)

Garrett, C.H.: *The Marian Exiles, 1553–59* (Cambridge University Press, 1938; reprinted 1966)

Graeme, Bruce: *The Story of St James's Palace* (Hutchinson, 1929)

Grattan Flood, W.H.: *Queen Mary's Chapel Royal* (*English Historical Review*, 33, 1918)

Handbook of British Chronology (ed. F. Maurice Powicke and E.B. Fryde, Royal Historical Society, 1961)

Harbison, E. Harris: *French Intrigues at the Court of Queen Mary* (*American Historical Review*, XLV, 3, April 1940)

Harbison, E. Harris: *Rival Ambassadors at the Court of Queen Mary* (Princeton University Press, 1940)

Harrison, David: *Tudor England* (1955)

Hearsey, John E.N.: *The Tower* (John Murray, 1960)

Hibbert, Christopher: *The Court at Windsor* (Longman, Green & Co., 1964)

Hibbert, Christopher: *The Virgin Queen: the Personal History of Elizabeth I* (Penguin Books, 1992)

Howard, George: *Lady Jane Grey and her Times* (1822)

Howard, Maurice: *The Early Tudor Country House: Architecture and Politics, 1490–1550* (George Philip, 1987)

Howard, Philip: *The Royal Palaces* (Hamish Hamilton, 1960)

Hume, M.A.S.: *The Visit of Philip II* (*English Historical Review*, VII, 26, 1892)

Jenkins, Elizabeth: *Elizabeth the Great* (Victor Gollancz, 1958)

Johnson, Paul: *Elizabeth I: a Study in Power and Intellect* (Weidenfeld & Nicolson, 1974)

Jordan, W.K.: *Edward VI: The Threshold of Power* (Allen & Unwin)

Jordan, W.K.: *Edward VI: The Young King* (Allen & Unwin, 1968)

Loades, David M.: *Mary Tudor: A Life* (Basil Blackwell, 1989)

Loades, David M.: *The Reign of Mary Tudor: Politics, Government and Religion in England, 1553–1558* (Ernest Benn, 1979)

Loades, David M.: *The Tudor Court* (Batsford, 1986)

Loades, David M.: *Two Tudor Conspiracies* (Cambridge University Press, 1965)

Longman, William: *A History of the Three Cathedrals Dedicated to St Paul in London* (Longman, Green & Co., 1973)

Luke, Mary M.: *A Crown for Elizabeth* (Muller, 1971)

McCoy, R.C.: *From the Tower to the Tiltyard: Robert Dudley's Return to Glory* (*Historical Journal*, 27, 1984)

Mackie, J.D.: *The Earlier Tudors, 1485–1558* (Oxford University Press, 1952)

Marshall, Rosalind K.: *Elizabeth I* (HMSO, 1991)

374 Bibliography

Marshall, Rosalind K.: *Mary I* (HMSO, 1991)

Martienssen, Anthony: *Queen Katherine Parr* (Secker & Warburg, 1973)

Minney, R.J.: *The Tower of London* (Cassell, 1970)

Morris, Christopher: *The Tudors* (Batsford, 1965)

Neale, J.E.: 'The Accession of Elizabeth I' (in *Essays in Elizabethan History*, Jonathan Cape, 1958)

Neale, J.E.: *Elizabeth I* (Jonathan Cape, 1934)

The Oxford Book of Royal Anecdotes (ed. Elizabeth Longford, Oxford University Press, 1989)

Plowden, Alison: *Elizabethan England* (Readers Digest Association, 1982)

Plowden, Alison: *Lady Jane Grey and the House of Suffolk* (Sidgwick & Jackson, 1985)

Plowden, Alison: *Marriage with my Kingdom: the Courtships of Queen Elizabeth I* (Macmillan, 1977)

Plowden, Alison: *Tudor Women: Queens and Commoners* (Weidenfeld & Nicolson, 1979)

Plowden, Alison: *The Young Elizabeth* (Macmillan, 1971)

Prescott, H.F.M.: *Mary Tudor* (Eyre & Spottiswoode, revised edition, 1952)

Prescott, William H.: *History of the Reign of Philip II, King of Spain*, (ed. John Foster Kirk, Lippincott, 1883)

Ridley, Jasper: *Elizabeth I* (Constable, 1987)

Ridley, Jasper: *The Life and Times of Mary Tudor* (Weidenfeld & Nicolson, 1973)

Roulstone, M.: *The Royal House of Tudor* (Balfour, 1974)

Routh, C.R.N.: *They Saw it Happen, 1485–1688* (Blackwell, 1956)

Routh, C.R.N.: *Who's Who in History, 1485–1603* (Blackwell, 1964)

Rowse, A.L.: *The Tower of London in the History of the Nation* (Weidenfeld & Nicolson, 1972)

Rowse, A.L.: *Windsor Castle in the History of the Nation* (Weidenfeld & Nicolson, 1974)

Ryan, Lawrence V.: *Roger Ascham* (Stanford, California, 1963)

Schenk, W.: *Reginald Pole, Cardinal of England* (Longman, Green & Co., 1950)

Seymour, William: *Ordeal by Ambition: An English Family in the Shadow of the Tudors* (Sidgwick & Jackson, 1972)

Simpson, Helen: *The Spanish Marriage* (Peter Davies, 1933)

Simpson, W.S.: *St Paul's Cathedral and Old City Life* (Elliot Stock, 1894)

Sitwell, Edith: *Fanfare for Elizabeth* (Macmillan, 1963)

Sitwell, Edith: *The Queens and the Hive* (1963)

Smith, Lacey Baldwin: *Elizabeth Tudor: Portrait of a Queen* (Hutchinson/Cape, 1976)

Somerset, Anne: *Elizabeth I* (Weidenfeld & Nicolson, 1991)

Stanley, Arthur Penrhyn: *Historical Memorials of Westminster Abbey* (1886)

Stone, J.: *The History of Mary I, Queen of England* (Sands, 1901)

Strickland, Agnes: *Life of Queen Elizabeth* (Everyman, 1906)

Strickland, Agnes: *Lives of the Queens of England* (Henry Colburn, 1851; Portway Reprint by Cedric Chivers of Bath, 1972)

Strony, Roy: *The English Icon: Elizabethan and Jacobean Portraiture* (Routledge & Kegan Paul, 1969)

Strong, Roy: *Tudor and Jacobean Portraits* (HMSO, 1969)

Thurley, Simon: *The Royal Palaces of Tudor England* (Yale University Press, 1993)

Tittler, Robert: *The Reign of Mary I* (Longman, 1983)

Treasures of Britain (Drive Publications, 1968, 1972)

Turton, Godfrey: *The Dragon's Breed: The Story of the Tudors, from Earliest Times to 1603* (Peter Davies, 1969)

Waldman, Milton: *The Lady Mary* (Collins, 1972)

Weir, Alison: *Britain's Royal Families* (The Bodley Head, 1989)

Weir, Alison: *The Six Wives of Henry VIII* (The Bodley Head, 1991)

Westminster Abbey: *Official Guide* (various editions)

White, Beatrice: *Mary Tudor* (Macmillan, 1935)

Wiesener, Louis: *The Youth of Queen Elizabeth I* (trans. C.M. Yonge, 1879)

Williams, Neville: *Elizabeth, Queen of England* (Weidenfeld & Nicolson, 1967)

Williams, Neville: *The Life and Times of Elizabeth I* (Weidenfeld & Nicolson, 1972)

Woodward, G.W.O.: *Reformation and Resurgence, 1485–1603* (Blandford, 1963)

Youngs, F.A.: *The Proclamations of the Tudor Queens* (Cambridge University Press, 1976)

The Heirs of Henry VIII, 1547-1558

m. = married
☓ = killed in battle
ex. = executed

Henry VII m. Elizabeth of York
1457-1509   1466-1503

Arthur,
Prince of
Wales
1486-1502

Margaret
1489-1541
m.1. James IV,
King of Scots
1473-1513 ☓
2. Archibald
Douglas,
Earl of Angus
1490?-1557

James V,
King of Scots
1512-1542

Mary,
Queen of Scots
1542-1587 ex.
m. François,
Dauphin of France,
later François II
1544-1560

Margaret Douglas
1515-1578
m.
Matthew Stewart,
Earl of Lennox
1516-1571
↓

Henry VIII m.1. Katherine of Aragon
1491-1547   1485-1536
2. Anne Boleyn
1501?-1536 ex.
3. Jane Seymour
1508?-1537
4. Anne of Cleves
1515-1557
5. Katherine Howard
1525?-1542 ex.
6. Katherine Parr
1512?-1548

Mary I
1516-1558
m.
Philip II,
King of
Spain
1527-1598

Elizabeth I
1533-1603

Edward VI
1537-1553

Mary
1495-1533
m.1. Louis XII,
King of
France
1462-1515
2. Charles
Brandon,
Duke of
Suffolk
1484-1545

Frances
Brandon
1517-1559
m.
Henry Grey,
Duke of Suffolk
1517-1554 ex.

Jane,
Queen of England
1537-1554 ex.
m.
Lord Guilford Dudley
1536-1554 ex.

Katherine
1540-1568

Mary
1545-1578

Index

Alba, Duchess of 274, 284
Alba, Duke of 260, 281 306, 335, 348
d'Aler, Madame 321
Allington Castle, Maidstone, Kent 234–5
Aluksne, Latvia 272
Anne of Cleves, Queen of England 3, 9,
    14, 36, 190, 216–17, 263, 338
Anne, Queen of Great Britain 264
Antwerp, Flanders 108, 249
Arundel, Earl of (*see* FitzAlan, Henry)
Ashby-de-la-Zouche, Leics. 235
Ascham, Roger 9–10, 11, 44–5, 51–2,
    54, 56, 66, 90, 99–100, 102–3, 106,
    319, 322, 332
Ashley, John 7, 42–3, 54, 60–1
Ashley, Katherine 7, 10, 34, 36, 38,
    42–4, 50, 53, 56–7, 60–1, 63–4,
    66–75, 77–8, 90, 131, 265, 322, 331,
    336
Ashridge House, Herts. 8, 25, 62, 89,
    102, 228–9, 231, 233, 235–6, 247–8,
    259
Astley, Co. Warwick 243
Aubrey, John 136
Audley, Lord 234
Augsburg, Germany 124
Aylmer, John 45–7, 52, 75, 99–100, 116,
    132, 319

Baden, Margrave of 288
Badoer, Federico 321, 325, 337
Bale, John 33, 48
Banister, Dr John 145
Barclay, Alexander 112–15

Basingstoke, Hants. 280
Baynard's Castle, London 145, 178, 180
Beaufort, Lady Margaret 147
Beaulieu, Essex (*see* Newhall)
Bedford, Earl of (*see* Russell, John)
Bedingfield, Sir Edmund 162, 262
Bedingfield, Sir Henry 162, 262–6,
    269–70, 279, 299, 302–3, 332
Bedwyn Brail, Somerset 35
Belmayne, John 14
Benett, Mr, of Ware 123
Berwick, Northld. 357
Bill, Dr Thomas 89–90
Bishop's Waltham, Hants. 271
Blackheath, Kent 136, 237
Black Prince, The 265
Blenheim Palace, Oxon. 264–5
Blount, Gertrude, Marchioness of Exeter
    190–1, 199, 208, 220–1, 248, 299
Boacher, Joan 33, 115
Bohemia, King and Queen of 329
Boisdaulphin, French envoy 306–7
Boleyn, Anne, Queen of England 2, 4, 7,
    9, 12, 13, 79, 200, 203, 206, 208, 215,
    223, 227, 246, 258, 263, 278, 343
Boleyn, Mary 206
Bonner, Edmund, Bishop of London 34,
    49, 98, 294, 327, 355
Boulogne, France 91, 324
Bourchier, John, Earl of Bath 162
Bourne, Sir John 252
Boxall, John 358
Bradgate Manor, Leics. 46, 75, 99
Brandenburg, Margrave of 104

Brandon, Charles, Duke of Suffolk 45
Brandon, Frances, Marchioness of
    Dorset, Duchess of Suffolk 45–8, 56,
    58, 75, 99–100, 114, 131–3, 140,
    144–7, 151, 158, 163, 165–7, 169,
    181, 185–6, 224, 251
Brandon, Henry, Duke of Suffolk 14–15
Bray, John 328
Bridges, Sir John 166, 230, 243–4,
    256–60
Brocket Hall, Herts. 357
Browne, Sir Anthony, later Viscount
    Montague 25, 29, 120, 190, 272, 364
Brussels, Flanders 105, 108, 211, 238,
    269, 277, 287, 289–90, 298–9, 308,
    313, 319, 324–5, 329, 334, 340, 344,
    347, 356, 360, 364
Bryan, Lady Margaret 7, 162
Bull Inn, Woodstock 265
Burgh, Lady 160
Bury St Edmunds, Suffolk 160, 172, 177,
    182, 196

Calagila, Dr 307
Calais, France 150, 178, 186, 289, 341,
    347, 349–51, 354, 359–60
Calvin, John 10–11
Cambridge, City and University of 51,
    56, 66, 99, 177–8, 180, 182, 184
Camden, William 11, 80, 170
Campeggio, Cardinal Lorenzo 289
Canterbury, Kent 317, 333, 347, 359
Cardano, Dr Girolamo 137
Carew, Sir Peter 173, 227–8, 231,
    233–6, 249, 346
Carey, Katherine, Lady Knollys 206
Carlos of Spain, Don 211–12, 228, 288,
    330
Carne, Sir Edward 347
Carranza, Fr Bartolomeo 294
Castelnau, French ambassador 259
Castiglione, Battista 10, 11, 331
Castro, Alfonso de, Bishop of Cuenca
    294, 297, 325
Catherine de' Medici, Queen of France
    199
Cecil, Robert 8
Cecil, Thomas 304
Cecil, William 64, 87, 90, 93, 102,
    113–14, 126, 131, 142, 148, 152, 157,
    171, 176, 184, 282, 304, 322, 357,
    359, 361
Cesar, Dr 357
Champernowne, Joan, Lady Denny
    53–5

Champernowne, Katherine (*see* Ashley,
    Katherine)
Chapuys, Eustache 3
Charles V, Holy Roman Emperor, King
    of Spain 2, 3, 28, 30, 31, 42, 62, 81–4,
    88, 91, 95, 97–101, 103–8, 110,
    112–13, 118, 122, 124, 127, 129, 133,
    138, 142, 148–50, 152, 158, 162, 168,
    173, 178, 183–9, 195, 197, 200–2,
    205, 209–12, 215–16, 218, 220–3,
    228–30, 232–4, 237, 241, 249–51,
    260–1, 269, 272, 275, 277, 279–82,
    284, 287, 290, 295, 298–9, 301,
    304–6, 308, 315–16, 319–21, 326,
    329–30, 332, 336, 356, 358, 365
Cheapside, London 166, 179, 262
Cheke, John 9, 10, 14, 15, 48–51, 99,
    106, 117, 139, 170, 178, 185
Cheke, Mrs 64
Chelsea Palace, London 33–4, 37, 39, 41,
    43–5, 47–8, 54, 59, 145, 151, 163
Cheshunt, Herts. 53–4, 56, 59, 67
Chester, City of 162
Cholmley, Mr 248
Christina of Denmark, Duchess of
    Lorraine 341–2, 345
Christmas, Muriel 186
Christ's Hospital School, Newgate 135
Clarencieux, Susan 5, 42, 110, 208, 222,
    308–9, 330. 360
Cleobury, schoolmaster 333–4
Clifford, Rosamund 265
Clinton, Sir Humphrey 240
Clinton, Lord 159, 171
Colchester, Essex 185, 296
Copt Hall, Essex 125–6
Cornwallis, Sir Thomas 247
Courtenay, Edward, Earl of Devon 159,
    183, 190–1, 204–6, 208–10, 215–16,
    218–23, 227–9, 231–2, 234–6, 240,
    247–8, 252, 257, 259–61, 267, 295,
    297–300, 324, 326, 328, 333, 334–5
Courtenay, Henry, Marquess of Exeter
    204, 218
Coventry, City of 235
Coxe, Richard, Bishop of Ely 9, 14, 15
Cranmer, Thomas, Archbishop of
    Canterbury 2, 24, 25, 27, 28, 31, 35,
    61–2, 81, 93, 96, 115, 122, 148, 171,
    178, 195, 202, 206, 224, 262, 290,
    320–1, 325, 327, 329–30, 366
Crofts, Sir James 227, 231–2, 234–5, 243,
    249, 252, 260, 346
Cromwell, Thomas 7, 13, 92
Croydon Palace, Surrey 199, 336

Dacre, Lady Magdalen 279
Dartford, Kent 317
Dee, Dr John 93, 310
Delft, Francis van der 28, 31, 34, 42, 62,
    82–4, 87–8, 95, 97–101, 103–8, 120,
    126
Denmark, King of 124
Denny, Sir Anthony 53–5, 69–70
Denny, Lady (*see* Champernowne, Joan)
Derby, Earl of 119, 173, 217, 275
Dod, Randall 42
Donnington Castle, Newbury, Berks.
    235–6, 260
Dormer, Jane, later Duchess of Feria 5,
    12, 17, 42, 79, 103, 122, 199, 215,
    219, 357–8, 360–1
Dormer, Sir William 264
Dorset House, Westminster 46
Dorset, Marquess of (*see* Grey, Henry)
Dover, Kent 289, 317, 341, 347, 354
Douglas, Margaret, Countess of Lennox
    224, 249, 251, 275, 365
Dubois, Jean 62, 106, 108–12
Dudley, Lord Ambrose 92
Dudley Castle, West Midlands 92
Dudley, Edmund 91–2
Dudley, Lord Guilford 92, 140, 143–5,
    150, 163, 165–9, 173–4, 181, 185,
    195, 200–1, 208, 224, 230, 236, 241,
    243–4, 253
Dudley, Lord Henry 92, 346, 348
Dudley, Sir Henry 178, 187, 324–5, 328,
    330–2
Dudley, John, Earl of Warwick 92, 185
Dudley, John, Viscount Lisle, later Earl
    of Warwick and Duke of
    Northumberland 15, 27, 29, 30, 33,
    76, 78–9, 82–3, 86, 91–9, 101, 103–7,
    112–17, 119, 121, 129–52, 157–78,
    180, 182–6, 195, 200, 207–8, 219,
    246, 324
Dudley, Lord Robert, later Earl of
    Leicester 9, 15, 92, 158, 160, 171–4,
    182, 185, 259, 346, 348
Dudley, Lady Temperance 93
Durham House, Strand, London 62, 70,
    144, 151, 173–4, 232
Dussindale, Norfolk 87
Dymoke, Sir Edward 217

Edward IV, King of England 203–4
Edward VI, King of England xiii, xiv, 3,
    7, 8, 9, 13–18, 25–36, 38–40, 42, 45,
    47–51, 58–9, 61–73, 75–8, 82–5,
    87–99, 101–4, 106–7, 109–26, 129,

153, 157–61, 163–5, 168–70, 175,
    179, 183–5, 187–9, 195, 200, 202,
    207, 217, 227, 297, 310, 350
Egmont, Count 232, 237–8, 251
Elisabeth of France 124, 142
Elizabeth, the Lady, later Elizabeth I,
    Queen of England xiii, 2, 6–13,
    16–18, 25–6, 33–4, 36, 38–9, 41,
    42–5, 47, 50–7, 59–64, 66–7, 68–75,
    77–80, 89–92, 95, 98–9, 102–3,
    116–17, 119, 124, 130–3, 135,
    138–41, 146, 151–2, 162, 164, 170,
    186, 189–90, 199–200, 206–8,
    213–19, 221, 223–4, 227–33, 235–6,
    247–9, 251–67, 269–70, 279–80, 285,
    288–9, 295, 297–9, 302–4, 309–10,
    316–17, 319–24, 326, 328, 330–9,
    341–5, 347–8, 351–66
Ellen, Mrs 47, 132, 167, 185, 244–5
Elsynge Place, Enfield, Herts. 8–9
Ely, Bishop of 171
Ely Place, Holborn, London 92, 94, 147
Emmanuel Philibert, Duke of Savoy
    288–9, 299, 337–8, 341–2, 344–5,
    347, 353–4, 359
Enfield Palace, Herts. 8, 25, 26, 102
Englefield, Sir Francis 42, 85, 87–8,
    125–6, 129, 215, 221, 328, 331
Erasmus, Desiderius 4, 10
Eric, Duke of Finland 353
Eton College, Berks. 264
Euston Hall, Thetford, Suffolk 160
Eworth, Hans 199
Exeter, Devon 86, 233–4
Exeter, Marchioness of (*see* Blount,
    Gertrude)

Farmor, Mr 131
Farnham, Surrey 269–70
Feckenham, Richard, Abbot of
    Westminster 241–2, 244–5
Ferdinand of Austria, Holy Roman
    Emperor 320, 326
Feria, Count (later Duke) of 12, 351,
    354–60
Ferrara, Duke of 124
Ferrers, Mr 133
Figueroa, Don Juan de 272
Fillol, Katherine 29
Fisher, John, Bishop of Rochester 257
FitzAlan, Henry, Earl of Arundel 93, 96,
    133, 162, 168–9, 171, 174, 176, 178,
    180–5, 190, 216–17, 221, 225, 228,
    260, 268, 271, 303, 359, 362
FitzPatrick, Barnaby 15, 16

Fleet Prison, London 120, 331, 336
Florence, Duke of 124
Florio, John 163
Forty Hall, Enfield 9
Fotheringhay Castle, Northants. 267, 297, 299
Fowler, John 36, 39–40, 48, 65, 67–8, 76
Foxe, John 89, 239, 266, 294, 309, 354, 365–6
Framlingham Castle, Suffolk 31, 172, 175, 180–2, 184
François, Dauphin of France 124
Fresneda, Francisco Bernardo de 347–8

Gage, Sir John 240, 258
Gardiner, Stephen, Bishop of Winchester 29, 34, 35, 49, 57, 98, 159, 191, 196, 200–2, 204–5, 207–10, 214–17, 220–2, 224–5, 228, 232, 234–7, 239, 248, 251–3, 259, 261–2, 272–3, 275–6, 280–1, 288, 291–8, 303, 317, 322–3
Gates, Sir John 112, 183, 185, 207
George Inn, Colnbrook 303
Gillam, John 306
Gloucester, City of 296
Goldsmith, Master 51
Gomez, Ruy 274, 277–9, 281–92, 307, 309, 312, 315, 326, 339, 346
Granvelle, Cardinal du 197
Gravesend, Kent 237, 289, 317, 341
Greenwich Palace, Kent 2, 33, 116, 136, 140, 144–6, 150–3, 157, 159, 316–18, 325, 330, 338, 341
Greenwich Park, Kent 159
Grey, Henry, Marquess of Dorset, Duke of Suffolk 45–8, 55–9, 66, 68, 75, 86, 96, 99–100, 114, 131–3, 141, 143–5, 158, 163, 165–6, 169, 171, 173–8, 180–1, 186, 195, 201, 230–1, 234–6, 241, 243, 250–1, 253, 280
Grey, Lady Jane, Queen of England xiii, 15, 34, 45–9, 55–9, 65, 69, 75, 99–100, 114, 132, 134, 140–1, 143–8, 150–2, 158–9, 163–9, 171, 173–9, 181–2, 185–6, 195, 200–1, 208, 224, 230–1, 235–6, 241–8, 253, 263, 280
Grey, Lady Katherine 46, 144–5, 166, 169, 180, 217, 242, 250–1
Grey, Lady Mary 46, 251
Greyfriars Monastery, Newgate 135
Grindal, William 9, 10, 14, 34, 44–5, 50–1
Guildford, Surrey 269
Guildhall, London 179, 224, 238

Guilford, Jane, Countess of Warwick, Duchess of Northumberland 92, 143, 145, 151, 163, 167–9, 181, 185
Guilford, Sir Richard 92
Guise, Duke of 124
Guisnes, France 178
Gustav Vasa, King of Sweden 353

Hampton Court Palace, Surrey 13, 33, 50, 68, 94, 125, 137, 301–3, 305–6, 313, 315–16, 345, 355
Hanseatic League 263
Hanworth, Middx. 33, 41, 44, 50, 58, 251
Harding, Dr 46
Harington, John 48, 58, 68
Harwich, Suffolk 108
Hastings, Sir Edward 237, 247, 288, 331
Hastings, Henry, Lord 15
Hatfield Palace, Herts. 8, 59, 63, 64, 66, 68, 69, 73–4, 77, 89–90, 102, 133, 152, 170, 322, 331–2, 336, 338, 342, 345, 354, 358–9, 361–2
Havering-atte-Bower, Essex 31, 188
Hayward, Sir John 29, 31, 355
Heath, Nicholas, Lord Chancellor 323
Henry I, King of England 264
Henry II, King of England 264
Henry IV, King of England 293
Henry V, King of England 23, 293
Henry VII, King of England 91–2, 147, 265, 355
Henry VIII, King of England xiii, 1–11, 13–29, 31–7, 39, 42, 45, 49, 60–2, 82, 91–2, 102, 120–1, 123–4, 128, 130, 133, 140–1, 145, 153, 160–1, 164, 171, 179, 184–5, 187, 190–1, 195–6, 198, 201, 203–4, 208–9, 215, 217–18, 249, 272, 281, 289, 291, 328, 342, 346, 347, 355
Henry II, King of France 18, 91, 113, 124, 178, 188, 200, 205, 208–9, 225, 229–30, 255, 298, 306, 308, 324–5, 328, 330, 334–9, 346
Herbert, William, Lord, later Earl of Pembroke 86, 131, 144–5, 162–3, 168–9, 171, 174, 176–8, 180, 195, 220, 240, 250, 275, 310, 348, 362
Herbert, William, Lord 144–5, 166, 169, 180, 251
Hertford, Castle, Herts. 25
Hertford, Earl of (*see* Seymour, Edward)
Hever Castle, Kent 351
Heywood, John 131
Highgate, London 248

High Wycombe, Bucks. 264
Hoddesdon, Herts. 157
Holbein, Hans 14
Holinshed, Raphael 266, 360, 366
Hooper, John, Bishop of Gloucester 96, 98, 123, 134, 175, 206, 296
Hopton, Dr John 85, 87
Howard family 157, 172
Howard, Katherine, Queen of England 3, 9, 14, 79, 208, 246
Howard, Thomas, 3rd Duke of Norfolk 29, 159–60, 172, 175, 191, 195, 207, 216–17, 236
Howard, Lord William 5–6, 138, 247, 262, 268–9, 271, 274
Huddlestone, John 159–60
Hughes, Dr Thomas 160
Huicke, Dr Robert 269
Hungate, Thomas 160, 167
Hundson House, Herts. 18–19, 128, 151
Huntingdon, Earl of 162–3, 169, 171, 185, 235, 243
Hyde Park, London 133

Ingatestone, Essex 188
Ipswich, Suffolk 184–5
Isabella of Portugal, Empress, Queen of Spain 211
Isabella, Queen of Castile 311
Isle of Wight, The 271

Jack, Mother 14
James I, King of Great Britain 365
Jane, Queen of England (*see* Grey, Lady Jane)
Jerningham, Henry 42, 172, 174, 328
Juana of Austria 364
Juana, Queen of Castile 269, 308
Julius III, Pope 184, 202, 209, 285, 298

Katherine of Aragon, Queen of England 1–2, 3, 29, 162, 186, 203, 218, 223, 262, 289, 302, 365
Kempe, Eleanor 42
Kenninghall, Norfolk 81, 84, 86, 88, 157, 160, 162, 168, 170, 172
Ket, Robert 86–7, 94
Killigrew, Sir Peter 328
Kimbolton Castle, Hunts. 262
King's Lynn, Norfolk 172–3
Kingston, Surrey 240
Knightsbridge, Middx. 240
Knollys, Sir Francis 206
Knox, John 32, 96, 181, 352

La Coruña, Spain 250, 269, 271
Lambeth Palace, London 290, 360, 364
Latimer, Hugh, Bishop of Worcester 78, 96, 125, 162, 206, 262, 320–1
Laycock Abbey, Wilts. 65
Leicester, City of 235
Leigh Priory, Essex 115
Lennox, Countess of (*see* Douglas, Margaret)
Leti, Gregorio 36, 78
Linacre, Thomas 3
Lisle, Viscount (*see* Dudley, John)
Lorraine, Cardinal of 351
Ludlow Castle, Salop. 4
Luis of Portugal, Dom 97, 103

Machyn, Henry 138, 172, 179, 284, 305–6, 341, 364
Macaulay, Lord 246
Madrid, Spain 269
Maidstone, Kent 235
Maldon, Essex 105–9, 111–12
Mallet, Francis 112–15, 123
Malt, Isabel 312
Manners, Henry, Earl of Rutland 59
Marcellus II, Pope 298
Margaret, Duchess of Parma 341–2, 345
Maria of Portugal, wife of Philip of Spain 211
Maria of Portugal 212
Marienbourg, Germany 272
Markham, Sir Thomas 357
Marlborough, Duke of 264
Mary of Guise, Queen of Scotland 132–3, 352
Mary of Hungary, Regent of the Netherlands 106, 110, 112–13, 118, 124, 197, 217, 225, 269, 358
Mary, The Lady, later Mary I, Queen of England xiii, 2–7, 9, 12–13, 16–19, 29–31, 36–9, 41–2, 49, 61, 62, 66, 68, 71, 78–9, 82–9, 93, 95, 97–130, 132–42, 146, 148–53, 157–68, 170–91, 195–210, 212–45, 247–62, 264–339, 341–62, 364–6
Mary, Queen of Scots, Dauphine of France 18, 48, 124, 200, 251, 298–9
Mason, Sir John 153, 180, 290, 306, 311, 313, 328–9
Massey, Perotine, of Guernsey 296
Matilda, The Empress 197
Mechelin, Flanders 329
Meeckeren, Vice-Admiral Van 108, 112
Melanchthon, Philip 52
Merchant, Peter 108

Michieli, Giovanni 11, 197, 274, 284, 303–4, 306–8, 310–11, 313, 315–16, 319–20, 322–3, 326, 330–1, 333, 335, 337, 342–3

Monmouth, Duke of 257

Montague, Sir Edward, Lord Chief Justice 147–8, 185

Montague, Viscount (*see* Sir Anthony Browne)

Montmorency, Anne de, Constable of France 326, 348

More, Mr 131

More, Sir Thomas 3, 257, 332

Morgan, Chief Justice 224

Morone, Cardinal Giovanni 345, 349

Moryson, Sir Richard 46, 92, 99

Morton, John, Cardinal, Archbishop of Canterbury 8

Mousehold Heath, Norwich 86

National Portrait Gallery, London 32

Navas, Marquess de Las 268–9, 271

Neville, Frances 5–6

Newhall, Essex 18–19, 31, 62, 98, 111–15, 122, 124, 185–6, 188

Newmarket, Suffolk 173

Noailles, Antoine de 143, 149, 168, 178, 191, 199–200, 204–6, 208–10, 214–15, 217, 220–1, 224–5, 227–34, 236, 245, 247–8, 252, 263, 267–9, 297, 304, 307–8, 314, 320, 324, 326–7, 332–3

Noailles, François de, Bishop of Acqs 297, 332–3, 335, 337–9, 342

Nonnius, Lodovicus 358

Norfolk, Duchess of (*see* Stafford, Elizabeth)

Norfolk, Duke of (*see* Howard, Thomas)

North, Lord 312

Northampton, Marquess of (*see* Parr, William)

Northumberland, Duchess of (*see* Guilford, Jane)

Northumberland, Duke of (*see* Dudley, John)

Norwich, Norfolk 86–7, 160, 172

Oatlands, Surrey 313

Observant Friars, Convent of the, Greenwich 346

Ormanetto, Dr 347, 349

Ormond, Earl of 15

Osario, Doña Isabel de 211–12, 269

Owen, Dr George 153, 247, 269

Oxburgh Hall, Norfolk 162, 262, 303

Oxford, City of 114, 253, 262, 269, 321, 329

Oxford, Earl of 114, 177

Padus, Italy 306, 334–5

Paget, Sir William 25, 28, 29, 30, 34, 88, 91, 174, 180–1, 183, 218, 220–1, 228, 237, 253, 260–1, 282, 288, 297, 323, 329

Palmer, Sir Thomas 183, 185, 207

Paris, France 324

Parr, Katherine, Queen of England 3, 4, 9, 10, 12, 14, 16, 24, 29–30, 33–4, 37–44, 47–8, 50–1, 53–5, 57–60, 64, 67, 76, 145

Parr, William, Marquess of Northampton 30, 59, 66, 86, 96, 112, 158, 162, 171, 184–5, 195

Parry, Blanche 10

Parry, Thomas 43, 53, 58, 62–4, 66–74, 77–8, 80, 90, 99, 114, 265, 322, 357

Partridge, Master 185, 208, 230, 242

Paul IV, Pope 298, 319–20, 325, 335, 338, 342–9, 351, 354, 364

Paulet, William, Lord St John, Marquess of Winchester 69, 88, 93, 131, 138, 166–7, 169, 176–7, 185, 195, 216, 254, 256–8, 275

Peckham, Sir Edmund 173

Pembroke, Earl of (*see* Herbert, William)

Perrot, Sir John 328

Perwick, Alice 297

Peterborough Cathedral 365

Peto, Fr William 250, 346–7, 351

Petre, Sir William 29, 84, 112, 115, 122, 126, 174, 188, 221, 303

Philip of Spain, Prince, later Philip II, King of Spain and England 112, 188–9, 202–3, 205, 209–12, 216, 218–28, 230–1, 233–4, 241, 250–1, 260–2, 267–95, 297–9, 301–4, 306, 308–13, 315–49, 351–60, 364–5

Pickering, Sir William 227, 231

Pole, Margaret, Countess of Salisbury 203

Pole, Reginald, Cardinal, Archbishop of Canterbury 16, 202–4, 209, 217, 250, 278, 285, 287–94, 297–8, 303, 316, 318–20, 323, 325, 328, 330, 333, 335–6, 338–9, 344–9, 351–5, 360, 364

Poley, Thomas 86

Pollini, Girolamo 163

Ponet, John, Bishop of Rochester 122

Pontefract Castle, Yorks. 262

Pope, Sir Thomas 331–3, 336, 353

Portsmouth, Hants. 136
Potter, Gilbert 166
Prado, Madrid 225

Randolph, Master 14
Ratcliffe, Henry, Earl of Sussex 162,
    177, 254, 256, 258, 260
Raynes, Robert 157, 160
Reading, Berks. 280
Renard, Simon 149, 153, 157, 168, 174,
    180, 183, 185–90, 195–202, 204–5,
    207–10, 212–26, 229–34, 236–7, 239,
    241, 247–8, 250, 252–3, 260–2,
    266–8, 270, 278, 280–1, 286–7, 289,
    295, 297–9, 301, 304, 308, 312, 319,
    322–3, 352
Rich, Sir Richard, later Lord 30, 76, 84,
    112, 114–15, 126–8
Richard II, King of England 262, 293
Richard III, King of England 75, 203
Richmond Palace, Surrey 33, 206, 213,
    263, 280, 341, 355
Ridley, Nicholas, Bishop of London
    122, 128–9, 134, 162, 175, 183, 185,
    206, 262, 320–1
Rise, Mrs 360
Robsart, Amy, Lady Dudley 259
Rochester, Kent 235–6
Rochester, Sir Robert 42, 85, 87–8,
    108–12, 123, 125–6, 129, 172, 215,
    328
Rogers, John, Prebendary of St Paul's
    206, 296
Rome, Italy 184, 298, 338, 345, 348–9
Russell, John, Lord, later Earl of Bedford
    61, 86, 131, 171, 174, 252, 275
Rutland, Earl of (*see* Manners, Henry)
Rycote, Oxon. 264

St Bartholomew's Hospital, London 89
St Botolph's Church, Aldgate, London
    250
St Cross, Hospital of, Winchester 273
St George's Chapel, Windsor 29
St James's Palace, London 50, 135, 338,
    356, 358, 365
St James's Park, London 38, 135, 240
St John, Lord (*see* Paulet, William)
St John's College, Cambridge 10, 14
St John's Hospital, Clerkenwell, London
    119, 121–2, 138
St Mary Overy, Priory of, Southwark,
    London 239
St Paul's Cathedral, London 31, 56,
    165–6, 178, 202, 290, 292

St Paul's School, London 345
St Peter ad Vincula, Chapel of, Tower of
    London 207, 244, 246, 250
St Quentin, Siege of 348
St Thomas's Hospital, Southwark 135
Saintlow, Sir William 235, 252
Salisbury, Wilts. 136
Salmon, Christopher 153
Sands, Elizabeth 266
Sandys, Dr 177, 182, 185
Savoy, Duke of (*see* Emmanuel Philibert)
Sawston Hall, Cambs. 159
Scepperus, Admiral Cornille 108, 110
Scheyfve, Jehan 107–8, 113, 116,
    118–22, 124, 126, 129, 132–3, 138,
    140–2, 147–53, 157–8, 160, 168, 172,
    174, 177, 180, 183, 186, 209, 216
Schurts, Mr 109, 111–12
Scory, John, Bishop of Chichester 202
Segovia, Duke of 288
Segovia, Spain 269
Seymour, Edward, Earl of Hertford,
    Duke of Somerset 24–30, 34–40,
    47–50, 57–61, 64–79, 81–4, 86–9, 91,
    93–8, 101, 104, 113, 119–20, 126–7,
    130–4, 143, 169, 208, 246, 255
Seymour, Edward, Lord Hertford 47,
    58, 143–4, 251
Seymour, Elizabeth, Marchioness of
    Winchester 275
Seymour, Jane, Queen of England 3, 9,
    24, 29, 31
Seymour, John 59
Seymour, Margaret, Lady 58
Seymour, Mary 57, 79
Seymour, Place, London 41, 44, 62, 68
Seymour, Thomas, Lord Sudeley 29,
    35–44, 47–51, 52–79, 89, 230, 255
Sharington, Sir William 65, 67–8
Sheen, Surrey 145, 180–1, 186, 234–5
Shelley, Mr 173
Shrewsbury, Earl of 119, 123, 171, 174,
    303
Sidney, Henry 147, 153
Sidney, Lady Mary 163
Sittingbourne, Kent 347
Smeaton, Mark 13, 215, 343
Smith, Sir Thomas 87, 350
Smithfield, London 296, 310, 337, 355
Solway Moss, Battle of 18
Somerset, Duke of (*see* Seymour,
    Edward)
Somerset House, London 35, 186, 289,
    330, 337
Somers, Will 133

Soranzo, Francesco 6, 198–9
Southampton, Earl of (*see* Wriothesley, Thomas)
Southampton, Hants. 268–73, 345
Southwark, London 239–40, 249, 252, 280
Southwell, Sir Richard 162
Southwell, Sir Robert 248
Spinola, Battista 143
Stafford, Elizabeth, Duchess of Norfolk 190
Stafford, Thomas 346
Stanhope, Anne, Countess of Hertford, Duchess of Somerset 29, 40, 63, 64, 66, 132, 191, 251, 267
Stansgate, Essex 111
Steelyard, The, London 263
Stephen, King of England 197
Stokes, Adrian 251
Stokes, Elizabeth 251
Stow, John 137
Strelley, Frideswide 42, 313
Sturm, Johann 102–3, 319
Sudeley Castle, Gloucs. 54–8, 75, 77
Suffolk, Duchesses of (*see* Brandon, Frances; Willoughby, Katherine)
Suffolk, Dukes of (*see* Brandon, Charles; Brandon, Henry; Grey, Henry)
Suffolk Place, London 143–5, 280
Sussex, Countess of 337–8
Sussex, Earl of (*see* Ratcliffe, Henry)
Syon House, Isleworth, Middx. 35, 163, 168

Tallis, Thomas 295
Thirlby, Thomas, Bishop 327
Thomas, William 11, 14, 227
Throckmorton, Lady 181, 185
Throckmorton, Sir Nicholas 36, 157, 160, 171, 179, 227, 360, 362
Thynne, John 357
Tilney, Mrs 167, 185, 244–5
Tilty, Essex 114, 133
Titian 212, 225
Toledo, Spain 269
Tordesillas, Spain 269
Tothill Fields, Westminster 172
Tower Hill, London 78, 134, 181, 207, 224, 230, 244, 250, 261
Tower of London, The 28–9, 34, 57, 67–9, 71–2, 76, 78–9, 95, 97–8, 101, 121, 123, 126, 129, 132–3, 151, 158–9, 165–9, 171, 173–81, 183, 185–6, 190–1, 200–2, 204–8, 210, 213, 216, 221, 224, 230, 232, 235,
237, 240, 242–4, 248–50, 253–60, 262–4, 267, 284, 301, 317, 323, 331, 334, 338
Tresham, Sir Thomas 267
Trinity College, Oxford 332
Tudor, Arthur, Prince of Wales 1, 3
Tudor, Edward (*see* Edward VI)
Tudor, Elizabeth (*see* Elizabeth I)
Tudor, Margaret, Queen of Scotland 17, 249
Tudor, Mary (*see* Mary I)
Tudor, Mary, Duchess of Suffolk xiii, 17, 45, 140
Tyburn, London 240
Tyrwhit, Lady 64, 74–5, 79–80
Tyrwhit, Sir Robert 69–75, 77

Ubaldini, Petruccio 50
Udall, Nicholas, Provost of Eton 4, 32, 136, 283
Underhill, Edward 179
Underhill, Guilford 179, 181
Underhill, Mrs 179
Uniformity, Act of 62, 81, 84, 86, 98, 105, 217

Valladolid, Spain 211, 283
Vannes, Peter 334–5
Varegas, Luis 288
Vatican, The 347
Venice, Italy 334
Verney, Francis 331
Vives, Juan Luis 3, 4

Waad, Armagil 350
Waldegrave, Edward 42, 125–6, 129, 172, 215, 221
Wanstead, Essex 31, 189
Ware, Herts. 176
Warren, Mr 130–1
Warsaw, Poland 312
Warwick, Earl of (*see* Dudley, John)
Wendy, Dr Thomas 247, 269
Wentworth, Thomas, Lord 177
Westminster Abbey, London 31–2, 35, 136, 159, 166, 173, 202, 216, 232, 251, 365
Westminster Hall, London 133, 207, 217
White, John, Bishop of Winchester 365
White, Thomas 328
Whitehall Palace, London 23, 25, 26, 31, 33, 119, 131, 135, 138, 214, 216, 218, 229, 237, 239–40, 249, 251, 254, 269, 281, 284–6, 289, 291, 322, 341–2, 345, 347, 355

Wight, Isle of 328
Wilbraham, Richard 42
Wilder, Philip von 14
Williams, Lord, of Thame 263–4
Willoughby family 114
Willoughby, Katherine, Duchess of
  Suffolk 79
Willoughby, Lord 133
Wiltshire, Earl of 271
Wimbledon, Surrey 33
Winchester, Hants. 269, 273, 275–6,
  280
Winchester House, Southwark, London
  234, 239, 280, 322
Winchester, Marchioness of (*see*
  Seymour, Elizabeth)
Winchester, Marquess of (*see* Paulet,
  William)
Windsor Castle, Berks. 33, 94–5, 137,
  158, 237, 264, 280, 301, 315
Wingfield, Sir Anthony 119, 126
Wingfield House, Ipswich, Suffolk 184
Wingfield, Robert 172, 175
Wolfhall, Somerset 35

Wolsey, Cardinal Thomas 92
Wolvesey Palace, Winchester 273,
  275–7
Woodham Walter, Essex 105–6, 108,
  110, 112
Woodstock Palace, Oxon. 262–5, 270,
  279, 285, 289, 302
Wotton, Sir Nicholas 122, 124
Wriothesley, Sir Thomas, later Earl of
  Southampton 7, 29–30, 35, 66, 93, 96
Wroth, Dr 153
Wyatt, James 8
Wyatt, Jane 249
Wyatt, Sir Thomas, the elder 227
Wyatt, Sir Thomas, the younger 227,
  230–7, 239–41, 247–50, 252–5, 261,
  267, 293, 303

Yarmouth, Norfolk 173–5, 177, 326
Yaxley, Francis 282
Yaxley, Hunts. 333
Yuste, Spain 336, 356

Zwingli, Ulrich 134